P9-DOG-849

Collecting *and* Interpreting Qualitative Materials

Norman K. Denzin
Yvonna S. Lincoln
Editors

SAGE Publications
International Educational and Professional Publisher
Thousand Oaks   London   New Delhi

Copyright © 1998 by Sage Publications, Inc.

All rights reserved. No part of this book may be reproduced or utilized in any form or by any means, electronic or mechanical, including photocopying, recording, or by any information storage and retrieval system, without permission in writing from the publisher.

For information:

SAGE Publications, Inc.
2455 Teller Road
Thousand Oaks, California 91320
E-mail@sagepub.com

SAGE Publications Ltd.
6 Bonhill Street
London EC2A 4PU
United Kingdom

SAGE Publications India Pvt. Ltd.
M-32 Market
Greater Kailash I
New Delhi 110048 India

Printed in the United States of America

Library of Congress Cataloging-in-Publication Data

Main entry under title:

Collecting and interpreting qualitative materials / edited by Norman
    K. Denzin and Yvonna S. Lincoln.
        p. cm.
    Includes bibliographical references and index.
    ISBN 0-7619-1434-X (pbk. : acid-free paper)
    1. Social sciences—Research—Methodology. 2. Qualitative
reasoning. I. Denzin, Norman K. II. Lincoln, Yvonna S.
H62.C566 1998
300'.7'23—dc21   98-8868

98 99 00 01 02 03 04 8 7 6 5 4 3 2

Acquiring Editor:	Peter Labella
Production Editor:	Astrid Virding
Production Assistant:	Karen Wiley
Typesetter/Designer:	Danielle Dillahunt
Indexer:	Juniee Oneida
Cover Designer:	Ravi Balasuriya
Print Buyer:	Anna Chin

Collecting
and
Interpreting
Qualitative
Materials

INTERNATIONAL ADVISORY BOARD

James A. Anderson
Communication, University of Utah

Robert Burgess
Sociology, University of Warwick

Arlene Kaplan Daniels
Sociology, Northwestern University

Michelle Fine
Social Psychology, CUNY-Graduate Center

Anton Kuzel
Family Medicine, Medical College of Virginia

Kenneth J. Gergen
Psychology, Swarthmore College

Henry Giroux
Education, Pennsylvania State University

Jaber F. Gubrium
Sociology, University of Florida

Meaghan Morris
Cultural Studies, Independent Scholar

David Silverman
Sociology, Goldsmith College, University of London

Robert E. Stake
Education, University of Illinois, Urbana-Champaign

John Van Maanen
Sloan School, Massachusetts Institute of Technology

William Foote Whyte
Sociology, Cornell University

Harry Wolcott
Education and Anthropology, University of Oregon

Contents

Part II. The Art of Interpretation, Evaluation, and Presentation   **275**

Preface

◆ For more than two decades, a quiet methodological revolution has been taking place in the social sciences. A blurring of disciplinary boundaries has occurred. The social sciences and humanities have drawn closer together in a mutual focus on an interpretive, qualitative approach to research and theory. Although these trends are not new, the extent to which the "qualitative revolution" has overtaken the social sciences and related professional fields has been nothing short of amazing.

Reflecting this revolution, a host of textbooks, journals, research monographs, and readers have been published in recent years. In 1994, we published the *Handbook of Qualitative Research* in an attempt to represent the field in its entirety, to take stock of how far it had come and how far it might yet go. Although it became abundantly clear that the "field" of qualitative research is defined primarily by tensions, contradictions, and hesitations—and that they exist in a less-than-unified arena—we believed that the handbook could be valuable for solidifying, interpreting, and organizing the field in spite of the essential differences that characterize it.

Putting together the *Handbook* was a massive undertaking that was carried out over several years, the full story of which can be found in the preface to the *Handbook* (which can also be found on the Web site for the *Handbook*: http://www.sagepub.com/sagepage/denzin_lincoln.htm).

We have been enormously gratified and heartened by the response to the *Handbook* since its publication. Especially gratifying has been that it has been used and adapted by such a wide variety of scholars and graduate students in precisely the way we had hoped: as a starting point, a spring-board for new thought and new work.

◆ The Paperback Project

There was one constituency we did not focus on centrally as we developed the plan for the *Handbook*: students in the classroom. The sheer size of the *Handbook,* with its corresponding expense, seemed to make the book a difficult one to assign in courses. Yet within a year of publication, it became clear that the material contained in the *Handbook* was deemed sufficiently valuable to override some considerations of size and expense.

Despite the reception the *Handbook* received in the classroom, students and teachers alike have urged us to publish the book in a less expensive, paperback iteration. We and our publisher, Sage Publications, decided to figure out a plan to do this.

Peter Labella, our editor at Sage, canvassed more than 50 scholars and students about the way the *Handbook* works in the classroom setting. Through a series of phone interviews and e-mail surveys—which themselves led to an ongoing conversation—a plan to do the book as a series of paperbacks began to emerge. The three-volume plan was codified at a series of meetings in the spring of 1997.

It was decided that the part structure of the *Handbook* could serve as a useful point of departure for the organization of the paperbacks. Thus Volume 1, titled *The Landscape of Qualitative Research: Theories and Issues,* takes a look at the field from a broadly theoretical perspective, and is composed of the *Handbook*'s Parts I ("Locating the Field"), II ("Major Paradigms and Perspectives"), and VI ("The Future of Qualitative Research." Volume 2, titled *Strategies of Qualitative Inquiry,* focuses on just that, and consists of Part III of the *Handbook*. Volume 3, titled *Collecting and Interpreting Qualitative Materials,* considers the tasks of collecting, analyzing, and interpreting empirical materials, and comprises the *Handbook*'s Parts IV ("Methods of Collecting and Analyzing Empirical Materials") and V ("The Art of Interpretation, Evaluation, and Presentation").

We decided that nothing should be cut from the original *Handbook*. Nearly everyone we spoke to who used the *Handbook* had his or her own way of using it, leaning heavily on certain chapters and skipping others altogether. But there was great consensus that this reorganization made a great deal of sense both pedagogically and economically. We and Sage are committed to making this iteration of the *Handbook* accessible for classroom use. This commitment is reflected in the size, organization, and price of the paperbacks, as well as in the addition of end-of-book bibliographies.

It also became clear in our conversations with colleagues who used the *Handbook* that the single-volume, hard-cover version has a distinct place and value, and Sage will keep the original version available until a revised edition is published.

◆ Organization of This Volume

Collecting and Interpreting Qualitative Materials introduces the researcher to basic methods of gathering, analyzing, and interpreting qualitative data. Part I moves from interviewing to observation; to the use of artifacts, documents, and records from the past; to visual, personal experience; to data management and computerized, narrative, content, and semiotic methods of analysis. Part II focuses on interpretation, evaluation, and presentation. It begins with a discussion of criteria for judging the adequacy of qualitative materials, then turns to the interpretive process, the written text, and qualitative program evaluation before concluding with a look at the ways in which qualitative research can influence the policy process.

◆ Acknowledgments

Of course, this book would not exist without its authors or the editorial board members for the *Handbook* on which it is based. These individuals were able to offer both long-term, sustained commitments to the project and short-term, emergency assistance.

In addition, we would like to thank the following individuals and institutions for their assistance, support, insights, and patience: our respective universities and departments, as well as Jack Bratich and Rob Leffel, our respective graduate students. Without them, we could never have kept this project on course. There are also several people to thank at Sage Publications. We thank Peter Labella, our new editor; this three-volume version of the *Handbook* would not have been possible without Peter's wisdom, support, humor, and grasp of the field in all its current diversity. Peter had the vision to understand how a three-volume set could be better suited to the classroom and to the needs of students than the original format of the *Handbook.*

As always, we appreciate the efforts of Lenny Friedman, the director of marketing at Sage, along with his staff, for their indefatigable efforts in getting the word out about the *Handbook* to teachers, researchers, and methodologists around the world. Astrid Virding was essential in moving this project through production; we are also grateful to the copy editor, Judy Selhorst, and to those whose proofreading and indexing skills were so central to the publication of the *Handbook* on which these volumes are based. Finally, as ever, we thank our spouses, Katherine Ryan and Egon Guba, for their forbearance and constant support.

The idea for this three-volume paperback version of the *Handbook* did not arise in a vacuum, and we are grateful for the feedback we received from countless teachers and students, both informally and in response to our formal survey. We wish especially to thank the following individuals: Jim Barott, University of Utah; Joanne Cooper, University of Hawaii; Fran Crawford, Curtin University; Morten Ender, University of North Dakota; Rich Hoffman, Miami University of Ohio; Patti Lather, Ohio State University; Michael Lissack, Henley-on-Thames; Martha MacLeod, University of Northern British Columbia; Suzanne Miller, University of Buffalo; Peggy Rios, University of Miami; Cynthia Russell, University of Tennessee, Memphis; Diane Schnelker, University of Northern Colorado; Coleen Shannon, University of Texas at Arlington; Barry Shealy, University of Buffalo; Ewart Skinner, Bowling Green State University; Jack Spencer, Purdue University; and Carol Tishelman, Karolinska Institute.

NORMAN K. DENZIN
University of Illinois at Urbana-Champaign

YVONNA S. LINCOLN
Texas A&M University

1

Introduction

Entering the Field of
Qualitative Research

Norman K. Denzin & Yvonna S. Lincoln

Qualitative research has a long and distinguished history in the human disciplines. In sociology the work of the "Chicago school" in the 1920s and 1930s established the importance of qualitative research for the study of human group life. In anthropology, during the same period, the pathbreaking studies of Boas, Mead, Benedict, Bateson, Evans-Pritchard, Radcliffe-Brown, and Malinowski charted the outlines of the fieldwork method, wherein the observer went to a foreign setting to study the customs and habits of another society and culture (for a critique of this tradition, see Rosaldo, 1989, pp. 25-45). Soon qualitative research would be employed in other social science disciplines, including education, social work, and communications. The opening chapter in Part I, Volume 1, by Vidich and Lyman, charts key features of this history.

In this introductory chapter we will briefly define the field of qualitative research, then review the history of qualitative research in the human disciplines, so that this volume and its contents may be located in their proper historical moment. A conceptual framework for reading the qualitative

AUTHORS' NOTE: We are grateful to the many people who have helped with this chapter, including Mitch Allen, Katherine E. Ryan, and Harry Wolcott.

1

research act as a multicultural, gendered process will be presented. We will then provide a brief introduction to the chapters that follow.

◆ Definitional Issues

Qualitative research is a field of inquiry in its own right. It crosscuts disciplines, fields, and subject matter.[1] A complex, interconnected family of terms, concepts, and assumptions surround the term *qualitative research*. These include the traditions associated with positivism, poststructuralism, and the many qualitative research perspectives, or methods, connected to cultural and interpretive studies (the chapters in Part II of Volume 1 take up these paradigms). There are separate and detailed literatures on the many methods and approaches that fall under the category of qualitative research, such as interviewing, participant observation, and visual methods.

Qualitative research operates in a complex historical field that crosscuts five historical moments (we discuss these in detail below). These five moments simultaneously operate in the present. We describe them as the traditional (1900-1950), the modernist or golden age (1950-1970), blurred genres (1970-1986), the crisis of representation (1986-1990), and postmodern or present moments (1990-present). The present moment is defined, Laurel Richardson (1991) argues, by a new sensibility, the core of which "is doubt that any discourse has a privileged place, any method or theory a universal and general claim to authoritative knowledge" (p. 173).

Successive waves of epistemological theorizing move across these five moments. The traditional period is associated with the positivist paradigm. The modernist or golden age and blurred genres moments are connected to the appearance of postpositivist arguments. At the same time, a variety of new interpretive, qualitative perspectives made their presence felt, including hermeneutics, structuralism, semiotics, phenomenology, cultural studies, and feminism.[2] In the blurred genres phase the humanities became central resources for critical, interpretive theory, and the qualitative research project was broadly conceived. The blurred genres phase produced the next stage, the crisis of representation, where researchers struggled with how to locate themselves and their subjects in reflexive texts. The postmodern moment is characterized by a new sensibility that doubts all previous paradigms.

Any description of what constitutes qualitative research must work within this complex historical field. *Qualitative research* means different things in each of these moments. Nonetheless, an initial, generic definition can be offered: Qualitative research is multimethod in focus, involving an interpretive, naturalistic approach to its subject matter. This means that qualitative researchers study things in their natural settings, attempting to make sense of, or interpret, phenomena in terms of the meanings people bring to them. Qualitative research involves the studied use and collection of a variety of empirical materials—case study, personal experience, introspective, life story, interview, observational, historical, interactional, and visual texts—that describe routine and problematic moments and meanings in individuals' lives. Accordingly, qualitative researchers deploy a wide range of interconnected methods, hoping always to get a better fix on the subject matter at hand.

The Qualitative Researcher as *Bricoleur*

The multiple methodologies of qualitative research may be viewed as a *bricolage,* and the researcher as *bricoleur.* Nelson, Treichler, and Grossberg (1992, p. 2), Lévi-Strauss (1966, p. 17), and Weinstein and Weinstein (1991, p. 161) clarify the meaning of these two terms.[3] A *bricoleur* is a "Jack of all trades or a kind of professional do-it-yourself person" (Lévi-Strauss, 1966, p. 17). The *bricoleur* produces a *bricolage,* that is, a pieced-together, close-knit set of practices that provide solutions to a problem in a concrete situation. "The solution (bricolage) which is the result of the *bricoleur's* method is an [emergent] construction" (Weinstein & Weinstein, 1991, p. 161) that changes and takes new forms as different tools, methods, and techniques are added to the puzzle. Nelson et al. (1992) describe the methodology of cultural studies "as a bricolage. Its choice of practice, that is, is pragmatic, strategic and self-reflexive" (p. 2). This understanding can be applied equally to qualitative research.

The qualitative researcher-as-*bricoleur* uses the tools of his or her methodological trade, deploying whatever strategies, methods, or empirical materials as are at hand (Becker, 1989). If new tools have to be invented, or pieced together, then the researcher will do this. The choice of which tools to use, which research practices to employ, is not set in advance. The "choice of research practices depends upon the questions that are asked, and the questions depend on their context" (Nelson et al., 1992, p. 2), what is available in the context, and what the researcher can do in that setting.

Qualitative research is inherently multimethod in focus (Brewer & Hunter, 1989). However, the use of multiple methods, or triangulation, reflects an attempt to secure an in-depth understanding of the phenomenon in question. Objective reality can never be captured. Triangulation is not a tool or a strategy of validation, but an alternative to validation (Denzin, 1989a, 1989b, p. 244; Fielding & Fielding, 1986, p. 33; Flick, 1992, p. 194). The combination of multiple methods, empirical materials, perspectives and observers in a single study is best understood, then, as a strategy that adds rigor, breadth, and depth to any investigation (see Flick, 1992, p. 194).

The *bricoleur* is adept at performing a large number of diverse tasks, ranging from interviewing to observing, to interpreting personal and historical documents, to intensive self-reflection and introspection. The *bricoleur* reads widely and is knowledgeable about the many interpretive paradigms (feminism, Marxism, cultural studies, constructivism) that can be brought to any particular problem. He or she may not, however, feel that paradigms can be mingled, or synthesized. That is, paradigms as overarching philosophical systems denoting particular ontologies, epistemologies, and methodologies cannot be easily moved between. They represent belief systems that attach the user to a particular worldview. Perspectives, in contrast, are less well developed systems, and can be more easily moved between. The researcher-as-*bricoleur*-theorist works between and within competing and overlapping perspectives and paradigms.

The *bricoleur* understands that research is an interactive process shaped by his or her personal history, biography, gender, social class, race, and ethnicity, and those of the people in the setting. The *bricoleur* knows that science is power, for all research findings have political implications. There is no value-free science. The *bricoleur* also knows that researchers all tell stories about the worlds they have studied. Thus the narratives, or stories, scientists tell are accounts couched and framed within specific storytelling traditions, often defined as paradigms (e.g., positivism, postpositivism, constructivism).

The product of the *bricoleur*'s labor is a *bricolage,* a complex, dense, reflexive, collagelike creation that represents the researcher's images, understandings, and interpretations of the world or phenomenon under analysis. This *bricolage* will, as in the case of a social theorist such as Simmel, connect the parts to the whole, stressing the meaningful relationships that operate in the situations and social worlds studied (Weinstein & Weinstein, 1991, p. 164).

Qualitative Research as a Site of
Multiple Methodologies and Research Practices

Qualitative research, as a set of interpretive practices, privileges no single methodology over any other. As a site of discussion, or discourse, qualitative research is difficult to define clearly. It has no theory, or paradigm, that is distinctly its own. As Part II of this volume reveals, multiple theoretical paradigms claim use of qualitative research methods and strategies, from constructivism to cultural studies, feminism, Marxism, and ethnic models of study. Qualitative research is used in many separate disciplines, as we will discuss below. It does not belong to a single discipline.

Nor does qualitative research have a distinct set of methods that are entirely its own. Qualitative researchers use semiotics, narrative, content, discourse, archival, and phonemic analysis, even statistics. They also draw upon and utilize the approaches, methods, and techniques of ethnomethodology, phenomenology, hermeneutics, feminism, rhizomatics, deconstructionism, ethnographies, interviews, psychoanalysis, cultural studies, survey research, and participant observation, among others (see Nelson et al., 1992, p. 2).[4] All of these research practices "can provide important insights and knowledge" (Nelson et al., 1992, p. 2). No specific method or practice can be privileged over any other, and none can be "eliminated out of hand" (p. 2).

Many of these methods, or research practices, are also used in other contexts in the human disciplines. Each bears the traces of its own disciplinary history. Thus there is an extensive history of the uses and meanings of ethnography and ethnology in education (Hymes, 1980; LeCompte & Preissle, 1992); participant observation and ethnography in anthropology (Marcus, Volume 1, Chapter 12), sociology (Atkinson & Hammersley, Volume 2, Chapter 5), and cultural studies (Fiske, Volume 1, Chapter 11); textual, hermeneutic, feminist, psychoanalytic, semiotic, and narrative analysis in cinema and literary studies (Lentricchia & McLaughlin, 1990; Nichols, 1985; see also Manning & Cullum-Swan, Volume 3, Chapter 9); archival, material culture, historical, and document analysis in history, biography, and archaeology (Hodder, Volume 3, Chapter 4; Smith, Volume 2, Chapter 8; Tuchman, Volume 2, Chapter 9); and discourse and conversational analysis in communications and education (Holstein & Gubrium, Volume 2, Chapter 6).

The many histories that surround each method or research strategy reveal how multiple uses and meanings are brought to each practice. Textual analysis in literary studies, for example, often treat texts as self-contained systems. On the other hand, a researcher employing a cultural studies or feminist perspective would read a text in terms of its location within a historical moment marked by a particular gender, race, or class ideology. A cultural studies use of ethnography would bring a set of understandings from postmodernism and poststructuralism to the project. These understandings would likely not be shared by mainstream postpositivist sociologists (see Atkinson & Hammersley, Volume 2, Chapter 5; Altheide & Johnson, Volume 3, Chapter 10). Similarly, postpositivist and poststructural historians bring different understandings and uses to the methods and findings of historical research (see Tuchman, Volume 2, Chapter 9). These tensions and contradictions are all evident in the chapters presented here.

These separate and multiple uses and meanings of the methods of qualitative research make it difficult for researchers to agree on any essential definition of the field, for it is never just one thing.[5] Still, a definition must be established for use here. We borrow from, and paraphrase, Nelson et al.'s (1992, p. 4) attempt to define cultural studies:

> Qualitative research is an interdisciplinary, transdisciplinary, and sometimes counterdisciplinary field. It crosscuts the humanities and the social and physical sciences. Qualitative research is many things at the same time. It is multiparadigmatic in focus. Its practitioners are sensitive to the value of the multimethod approach. They are committed to the naturalistic perspective, and to the interpretive understanding of human experience. At the same time, the field is inherently political and shaped by multiple ethical and political positions.
>
> Qualitative research embraces two tensions at the same time. On the one hand, it is drawn to a broad, interpretive, postmodern, feminist, and critical sensibility. On the other hand, it is drawn to more narrowly defined positivist, postpositivist, humanistic, and naturalistic conceptions of human experience and its analysis.

This rather awkward statement means that qualitative research, as a set of practices, embraces within its own multiple disciplinary histories constant tensions and contradictions over the project itself, including its methods and the forms its findings and interpretations take. The field sprawls between and crosscuts all of the human disciplines, even including, in some cases, the physical sciences. Its practitioners are variously committed to modern and postmodern sensibilities and the approaches to social research that these sensibilities imply.

Resistances to Qualitative Studies

The academic and disciplinary resistances to qualitative research illustrate the politics embedded in this field of discourse. The challenges to qualitative research are many. Qualitative researchers are called journalists, or soft scientists. Their work is termed unscientific, or only exploratory, or entirely personal and full of bias. It is called criticism and not theory, or it is interpreted politically, as a disguised version of Marxism, or humanism.

These resistances reflect an uneasy awareness that the traditions of qualitative research commit the researcher to a critique of the positivist project. But the positivist resistance to qualitative research goes beyond the "ever-present desire to maintain a distinction between hard science and soft scholarship" (Carey, 1989, p. 99). The positive sciences (physics, chemistry, economics, and psychology, for example) are often seen as the crowning achievements of Western civilization, and in their practices it is assumed that "truth" can transcend opinion and personal bias (Carey, 1989, p. 99). Qualitative research is seen as an assault on this tradition, whose adherents often retreat into a "value-free objectivist science" (Carey, 1989, p. 104) model to defend their position. They seldom attempt to make explicit, or to critique, the "moral and political commitments in their own contingent work" (Carey, 1989, p. 104). The opposition to positive science by the postpositivists (see below) and the poststructuralists is seen, then, as an attack on reason and truth. At the same time, the positive science attack on qualitative research is regarded as an attempt to legislate one version of truth over another.

This political terrain defines the many traditions and strands of qualitative research: the British tradition and its presence in other national contexts; the American pragmatic, naturalistic, and interpretive traditions in sociology, anthropology, communications, and education; the German and French phenomenological, hermeneutic, semiotic, Marxist, structural, and poststructural perspectives; feminist, African American studies, Latino studies, gay and lesbian studies, and studies of indigenous and aboriginal cultures (Nelson et al., 1992, p. 15). The politics of qualitative research creates a tension that informs each of the above traditions. This tension itself is constantly being reexamined and interrogated, as qualitative research confronts a changing historical world, new intellectual positions, and its own institutional and academic conditions.

To summarize: Qualitative research is many things to many people. Its essence is twofold: a commitment to some version of the naturalistic, interpretive approach to its subject matter, and an ongoing critique of the politics and methods of positivism. We turn now to a brief discussion of the major differences between qualitative and quantitative approaches to research.

Qualitative Versus Quantitative Research

The word *qualitative* implies an emphasis on processes and meanings that are not rigorously examined, or measured (if measured at all), in terms of quantity, amount, intensity, or frequency. Qualitative researchers stress the socially constructed nature of reality, the intimate relationship between the researcher and what is studied, and the situational constraints that shape inquiry. Such researchers emphasize the value-laden nature of inquiry. They seek answers to questions that stress how social experience is created and given meaning. In contrast, quantitative studies emphasize the measurement and analysis of causal relationships between variables, not processes. Inquiry is purported to be within a value-free framework.

Research Styles: Doing the Same Things Differently?

Of course, both qualitative and quantitative researchers "think they know something about society worth telling to others, and they use a variety of forms, media and means to communicate their ideas and findings" (Becker, 1986, p. 122). Qualitative research differs from quantitative research in five significant ways (Becker, 1993). These points of difference turn on different ways of addressing the same set of issues. They return always to the politics of research, and who has the power to legislate correct solutions to these problems.

Uses of positivism. First, both perspectives are shaped by the positivist and postpositivist traditions in the physical and social sciences (see the discussion below). These two positive science traditions hold to naive and critical realist positions concerning reality and its perception. In the positivist version it is contended that there is a reality out there to be studied,

8

captured, and understood, whereas postpositivists argue that reality can never be fully apprehended, only approximated (Guba, 1990, p. 22). Postpositivism relies on multiple methods as a way of capturing as much of reality as possible. At the same time, emphasis is placed on the discovery and verification of theories. Traditional evaluation criteria, such as internal and external validity, are stressed, as is the use of qualitative procedures that lend themselves to structured (sometimes statistical) analysis. Computer-assisted methods of analysis that permit frequency counts, tabulations, and low-level statistical analyses may also be employed.

The positivist and postpositivist traditions linger like long shadows over the qualitative research project. Historically, qualitative research was defined within the positivist paradigm, where qualitative researchers attempted to do good positivist research with less rigorous methods and procedures. Some mid-century qualitative researchers (e.g., Becker, Geer, Hughes, & Strauss, 1961) reported participant observation findings in terms of quasi-statistics. As recently as 1990, two leaders of the grounded theory approach to qualitative research attempted to modify the usual canons of good (positivistic) science to fit their own postpositivist conception of rigorous research (Strauss & Corbin, 1990; see also Strauss & Corbin, Volume 2, Chapter 7; but also see Glaser, 1992). Some applied researchers, while claiming to be atheoretical, fit within the positivist or postpositivist framework by default. Spindler and Spindler (1992) summarize their qualitative approach to quantitative materials: "Instrumentation and quantification are simply procedures employed to extend and reinforce certain kinds of data, interpretations and test hypotheses across samples. Both must be kept in their place. One must avoid their premature or overly extensive use as a security mechanism" (p. 69).

Although many qualitative researchers in the postpositivist tradition use statistical measures, methods, and documents as a way of locating a group of subjects within a larger population, they seldom report their findings in terms of the kinds of complex statistical measures or methods to which quantitative researchers are drawn (e.g., path, regression, or log-linear analyses). Much of applied research is also atheoretical.

Acceptance of postmodern sensibilities. The use of quantitative, positivist methods and assumptions has been rejected by a new generation of qualitative researchers who are attached to poststructural, postmodern sensibilities (see below; see also Vidich & Lyman, Volume 1, Chapter 2, and Richardson, Volume 3, Chapter 12). These researchers argue that positivist methods are but one way of telling a story about society or the social world. They may be no better or no worse than any other method; they just tell a different kind of story.

This tolerant view is not shared by everyone. Many members of the critical theory, constructivist, poststructural, and postmodern schools of thought reject positivist and postpositivist criteria when evaluating their own work. They see these criteria as irrelevant to their work, and contend that these criteria reproduce only a certain kind of science, a science that silences too many voices. These researchers seek alternative methods for evaluating their work, including verisimilitude, emotionality, personal responsibility, an ethic of caring, political praxis, multivoiced texts, and dialogues with subjects. In response, positivists and postpositivists argue that what they do is good science, free of individual bias and subjectivity; as noted above, they see postmodernism as an attack on reason and truth.

Capturing the individual's point of view. Both qualitative and quantitative researchers are concerned about the individual's point of view. However, qualitative investigators think they can get closer to the actor's perspective through detailed interviewing and observation. They argue that quantitative researchers seldom are able to capture the subject's perspective because they have to rely on more remote, inferential empirical materials. The empirical materials produced by the softer, interpretive methods are regarded by many quantitative researchers as unreliable, impressionistic, and not objective.

Examining the constraints of everyday life. Qualitative researchers are more likely than quantitative researchers to confront the constraints of the everyday social world. They see this world in action and embed their findings in it. Quantitative researchers abstract from this world and seldom study it directly. They seek a nomothetic, or etic, science based on probabilities derived from the study of large numbers of randomly selected cases. These kinds of statements stand above and outside the constraints of everyday life. Qualitative researchers are committed to an emic, idiographic, case-based position, which directs their attention to the specifics of particular cases.

Securing rich descriptions. Qualitative researchers believe that rich descriptions of the social world are valuable, whereas quantitative researchers, with their etic, nomothetic commitments, are less concerned with such detail.

The five points of difference described above (uses of positivism, acceptance of postmodern sensibilities, capturing the individual's point of view, examining the constraints of everyday life, and securing rich descriptions) reflect commitments to different styles of research, different epistemologies, and different forms of representation. Each work tradition is governed by a different set of genres; each has its own classics, its own preferred forms of representation, interpretation, and textual evaluation (see Becker, 1986, pp. 134-135). Qualitative researchers use ethnographic prose, historical narratives, first-person accounts, still photographs, life histories, fictionalized facts, and biographical and autobiographical materials, among others. Quantitative researchers use mathematical models, statistical tables, and graphs, and often write about their research in impersonal, third-person prose.

With the differences between these two traditions understood, we will now offer a brief discussion of the history of qualitative research. We can break this into four historical moments, mindful that any history is always somewhat arbitrary.

◆ The History of Qualitative Research

The history of qualitative research reveals, as Vidich and Lyman remind us in Chapter 2 of Volume 1, that the modern social science disciplines have taken as their mission "the analysis and understanding of the patterned conduct and social processes of society." The notion that this task could be carried out presupposed that social scientists had the ability to observe this world objectively. Qualitative methods were a major tool of such observations.[6]

Throughout the history of qualitative research, investigators have always defined their work in terms of hopes and values, "religious faiths, occupational and professional ideologies" (Vidich & Lyman, Volume 1, Chapter 2). Qualitative research (like all research) has always been judged on the "standard of whether the work communicates or 'says' something to us" (Vidich & Lyman, Volume 1, Chapter 2), based on how we conceptualize our reality and our images of the world. *Epistemology* is the word that has historically defined these standards of evaluation. In the contemporary period, as argued above, many received discourses on epistemology have been "disprivileged," or cast into doubt.

The history presented by Vidich and Lyman covers the following (somewhat) overlapping stages: early ethnography (to the seventeenth century); colonial ethnography (seventeenth-, eighteenth-, and nineteenth-century explorers); the ethnography of the American Indian as "other" (late nineteenth- and early twentieth-century anthropology); the ethnography of the "civic other," or community studies, and ethnographies of American immigrants (early twentieth century through the 1960s); studies of ethnicity and assimilation (mid-century through the 1980s); and the present, which we call the *fifth moment*.

In each of these eras researchers were and have been influenced by their political hopes and ideologies, discovering findings in their research that confirmed prior theories or beliefs. Early ethnographers confirmed the racial and cultural diversity of peoples throughout the globe and attempted to fit this diversity into a theory about the origin of history, the races, and civilizations. Colonial ethnographers, before the professionalization of ethnography in the twentieth century, fostered a colonial pluralism that left natives on their own as long as their leaders could be co-opted by the colonial administration.

European ethnographers studied Africans and other Third World peoples of color. Early American ethnographers studied the American Indian from the perspective of the conqueror, who saw the life world of the primitive as a window to the prehistoric past. The Calvinist mission to save the Indian was soon transferred to the mission of saving the "hordes" of immigrants who entered the United States with the beginnings of industrialization. Qualitative community studies of the ethnic other proliferated from the early 1900s to the 1960s, and included the work of E. Franklin Frazier, Robert Park, and Robert Redfield and their students, as well as William Foote Whyte, the Lynds, August Hollingshead, Herbert Gans, Stanford Lyman, Arthur Vidich, and Joseph Bensman. The post-1960s' ethnicity studies challenged the "melting pot" hypothesis of Park and his followers and corresponded to the emergence of ethnic studies programs that saw Native Americans, Latinos, Asian Americans, and African Americans attempting to take control over the study of their own peoples.

The postmodern challenge emerged in the mid-1980s. It questioned the assumptions that had organized this earlier history, in each of its colonializing moments. Qualitative research that crosses the "postmodern divide" requires one, Vidich and Lyman argue, to "abandon all established and preconceived values, theories, perspectives, . . . and prejudices as resources for ethnographic study." In this new era the qualitative researcher does more than observe history; he or she plays a part in it. New tales of the field will now be written, and they will reflect the researcher's direct and personal engagement with this historical period.

Vidich and Lyman's analysis covers the full sweep of ethnographic history. Ours, presented below, is confined to the twentieth century and complements many of their divisions. We begin with the early foundational work of the British and French, as well the Chicago, Columbia, Harvard, and Berkeley schools of sociology and anthropology. This early foundational period established the norms of classical qualitative and ethnographic research.

◆ The Five Moments of Qualitative Research

As noted above, we divide our history of qualitative research in this century into five phases, each of which is described in turn below.

The Traditional Period

We call the first moment the traditional period (this covers Vidich and Lyman's second and third phases). It begins in the early 1900s and continues until World War II. In this period, qualitative researchers wrote "objective," colonializing accounts of field experiences that were reflective of the positivist scientist paradigm. They were concerned with offering valid, reliable, and objective interpretations in their writings. The "other" who was studied was alien, foreign, and strange.

Here is Malinowski (1967) discussing his field experiences in New Guinea and the Trobriand Islands in the years 1914-1915 and 1917-1918:

> Nothing whatever draws me to ethnographic studies. . . . On the whole the village struck me rather unfavorably. There is a certain disorganization . . . the rowdiness and persistence of the people who laugh and stare and lie discouraged me somewhat. . . . Went to the village hoping to photograph a few stages of the *bara* dance. I handed out half-sticks of tobacco, then watched a few dances; then took pictures—but results were poor. . . . they

would not pose long enough for time exposures. At moments I was furious at them, particularly because after I gave them their portions of tobacco they all went away. (quoted in Geertz, 1988, pp. 73-74)

In another work, this lonely, frustrated, isolated field-worker describes his methods in the following words:

> In the field one has to face a chaos of facts. . . . in this crude form they are not scientific facts at all; they are absolutely elusive, and can only be fixed by interpretation. . . . Only laws and generalizations are scientific facts, and field work consists only and exclusively in the interpretation of the chaotic social reality, in subordinating it to general rules. (Malinowski, 1916/1948, p. 328; quoted in Geertz, 1988, p. 81)

Malinowski's remarks are provocative. On the one hand they disparage fieldwork, but on the other they speak of it within the glorified language of science, with laws and generalizations fashioned out of this selfsame experience.

The field-worker, during this period, was lionized, made into a larger-than-life figure who went into and then returned from the field with stories about strange people. Rosaldo (1989) describes this as the period of the Lone Ethnographer, the story of the man-scientist who went off in search of his native in a distant land. There this figure "encountered the object of his quest . . . [and] underwent his rite of passage by enduring the ultimate ordeal of 'fieldwork' " (p. 30). Returning home with his data, the Lone Ethnographer wrote up an objective account of the culture he studied. These accounts were structured by the norms of classical ethnography. This sacred bundle of terms (Rosaldo, 1989, p. 31) organized ethnographic texts in terms of four beliefs and commitments: a commitment to objectivism, a complicity with imperialism, a belief in monumentalism (the ethnography would create a museumlike picture of the culture studied), and a belief in timelessness (what was studied never changed). This model of the researcher, who could also write complex, dense theories about what was studied, holds to the present day.

The myth of the Lone Ethnographer depicts the birth of classic ethnography. The texts of Malinowski, Radcliffe-Brown, Margaret Mead, and Gregory Bateson are still carefully studied for what they can tell the novice about fieldwork, taking field notes, and writing theory (see the discussion of Bateson and Mead in Harper, Volume 3, Chapter 5). Today this image has been shattered. The works of the classic ethnographers are seen by many as relics of the colonial past (Rosaldo, 1989, p. 44). Although many feel nostalgic about this image, others celebrate its passing. Rosaldo (1989) quotes Cora Du Bois, a retired Harvard anthropology professor, who lamented this passing at a conference in 1980, reflecting on the crisis in anthropology: "[I feel a distance] from the complexity and disarray of what I once found a justifiable and challenging discipline. . . . It has been like moving from a distinguished art museum into a garage sale" (p. 44).

Du Bois regards the classic ethnographies as pieces of timeless artwork, such as those contained in a museum. She detests the chaos of the garage sale, which Rosaldo values: "It [the garage sale] provides a precise image of the postcolonial situation where cultural artifacts flow between unlikely places, and nothing is sacred, permanent, or sealed off. The image of anthropology as a garage sale depicts our present global situation" (p. 44). Old standards no longer hold. Ethnographies do not produce timeless truths. The commitment to objectivism is now in doubt. The complicity with imperialism is openly challenged today, and the belief in monumentalism is a thing of the past.

The legacies of this first period begin at the end of the nineteenth century, when the novel and the social sciences had become distinguished as separate systems of discourse (Clough, 1992, pp. 21-22). However, the Chicago school, with its emphasis on the life story and the "slice-of-life" approach to ethnographic materials, sought to develop an interpretive methodology that maintained the centrality of the narrated life history approach. This led to the production of the texts that gave the researcher-as-author the power to represent the subject's story. Written under the mantle of straightforward, sentiment-free social realism, these texts used the language of ordinary people. They articulated a social science version of literary naturalism, which often produced the sympathetic illusion that a solution to a social problem had been found. Like films about the Depression-era juvenile delinquent and other social problems (Roffman & Purdy, 1981), these accounts romanticized the subject. They turned the deviant into a sociological version of a screen hero. These sociological stories, like their film counterparts, usually had happy endings, as they followed individuals through the three stages of the classic morality tale: existence in a state of grace, seduction by evil and the fall, and finally redemption through suffering.

The Modernist Phase

The modernist phase, or second moment, builds on the canonical works of the traditional period. Social realism, naturalism, and slice-of-life ethnographies are still valued. This phase extended through the postwar years to the 1970s; it is still present in the work of many (see Wolcott, 1992, for a review). In this period many texts attempted to formalize qualitative methods (see, for example, Bogdan & Taylor, 1975; Cicourel, 1964; Filstead, 1970; Glaser & Strauss, 1967; J. Lofland, 1971; Lofland & Lofland, 1984).[7] The modernist ethnographer and sociological participant observer attempted rigorous, qualitative studies of important social processes, including deviance and social control in the classroom and society. This was a moment of creative ferment.

A new generation of graduate students, across the human disciplines, encountered new interpretive theories (ethnomethodology, phenomenology, critical theory, feminism). They were drawn to qualitative research practices that would let them give a voice to society's underclass. Postpositivism functioned as a powerful epistemological paradigm in this moment. Researchers attempted to fit the arguments of Campbell and Stanley (1963) about internal and external validity to constructionist and interactionist models of the research act. They returned to the texts of the Chicago school as sources of inspiration (see Denzin, 1970, 1978).

A canonical text from this moment remains *Boys in White* (Becker et al., 1961). Firmly entrenched in mid-century methodological discourse, this work attempted to make qualitative research as rigorous as its quantitative counterpart. Causal narratives were central to this project. This multimethod work combined open-ended and quasi-structured interviewing with participant observation and the careful analysis of such materials in standardized, statistical form. In a classic article, "Problems of Inference and Proof in Participant Observation," Howard S. Becker (1958/1970) describes the use of quasi-statistics:

> Participant observations have occasionally been gathered in standardized form capable of being transformed into legitimate statistical data. But the exigencies of the field usually prevent the collection of data in such a form to meet the assumptions of statistical tests, so that the observer deals in what have been called "quasi-statistics." His conclusions, while implicitly numerical, do not require precise quantification. (p. 31)

In the analysis of data, Becker notes, the qualitative researcher takes a cue from statistical colleagues. The researcher looks for probabilities or support for arguments concerning the likelihood that, or frequency with which, a conclusion in fact applies in a specific situation. Thus did work in the modernist period clothe itself in the language and rhetoric of positivist and postpositivist discourse.

This was the golden age of rigorous qualitative analysis, bracketed in sociology by *Boys in White* (Becker et al., 1961) at one end and *The Discovery of Grounded Theory* (Glaser & Strauss, 1967) at the other. In education, qualitative research in this period was defined by George and Louise Spindler, Jules Henry, Harry Wolcott, and John Singleton. This form of qualitative research is still present in the work of such persons as Strauss and Corbin (1990) and Miles and Huberman (1993), and is represented in their chapters in this three-volume set.

The "golden age" reinforced a picture of qualitative researchers as cultural romantics. Imbued with Promethean human powers, they valorized villains and outsiders as heroes to mainstream society. They embodied a belief in the contingency of self and society, and held to emancipatory ideals for which "one lives and dies." They put in place a tragic and often ironic view of society and self, and joined a long line of leftist cultural romantics that included Emerson, Marx, James, Dewey, Gramsci, and Martin Luther King, Jr. (West, 1989, chap. 6).

As this moment came to an end, the Vietnam War was everywhere present in American society. In 1969, alongside these political currents, Herbert Blumer and Everett Hughes met with a group of young sociologists called the "Chicago Irregulars" at the American Sociological Association meetings held in San Francisco and shared their memories of the "Chicago years." Lyn Lofland (1980) describes the 1969 meetings as a

> moment of creative ferment—scholarly and political. The San Francisco meetings witnessed not simply the Blumer-Hughes event but a "counter-revolution." . . . a group first came to . . . talk about the problems of being a sociologist and a female. . . . the discipline seemed literally to be bursting with new . . . ideas: labelling theory, ethnomethodology, conflict theory, phenomenology, dramaturgical analysis. (p. 253)

Thus did the modernist phase come to an end.

Blurred Genres

By the beginning of the third stage (1970-1986), which we call the moment of blurred genres, qualitative researchers had a full complement of paradigms, methods, and strategies to employ in their research. Theories ranged from symbolic interactionism to constructivism, naturalistic inquiry, positivism and postpositivism, phenomenology, ethnomethodology, critical (Marxist), semiotics, structuralism, feminism, and various ethnic paradigms. Applied qualitative research was gaining in stature, and the politics and ethics of qualitative research were topics of considerable concern. Research strategies ranged from grounded theory to the case study, to methods of historical, biographical, ethnographic action and clinical research. Diverse ways of collecting and analyzing empirical materials were also available, including qualitative interviewing (open-ended and quasi-structured) and observational, visual, personal experience, and documentary methods. Computers were entering the situation, to be fully developed in the next decade, along with narrative, content, and semiotic methods of reading interviews and cultural texts.

Two books by Geertz, *The Interpretation of Cultures* (1973) and *Local Knowledge* (1983), defined the beginning and end of this moment. In these two works, Geertz argued that the old functional, positivist, behavioral, totalizing approaches to the human disciplines were giving way to a more pluralistic, interpretive, open-ended perspective. This new perspective took cultural representations and their meanings as its point of departure. Calling for "thick description" of particular events, rituals, and customs, Geertz suggested that all anthropological writings were interpretations of interpretations. The observer had no privileged voice in the interpretations that were written. The central task of theory was to make sense out of a local situation.

Geertz went on to propose that the boundaries between the social sciences and the humanities had become blurred. Social scientists were now turning to the humanities for models, theories, and methods of analysis (semiotics, hermeneutics). A form of genre dispersion was occurring: documentaries that read like fiction (Mailer), parables posing as ethnographies (Castañeda), theoretical treatises that look like travelogues (Lévi-Strauss). At the same time, many new approaches were emerging: post-structuralism (Barthes), neopositivism (Philips), neo-Marxism (Althusser), micro-macro descriptivism (Geertz), ritual theories of drama and culture

(V. Turner), deconstructionism (Derrida), ethnomethodology (Garfinkel). The golden age of the social sciences was over, and a new age of blurred, interpretive genres was upon us. The essay as an art form was replacing the scientific article. At issue now is the author's presence in the interpretive text, or how the researcher can speak with authority in an age when there are no longer any firm rules concerning the text, its standards of evaluation, and its subject matter (Geertz, 1988).

The naturalistic, postpositivist, and constructionist paradigms gained power in this period, especially in education in the works of Harry Wolcott, Egon Guba, Yvonna Lincoln, Robert Stake, and Elliot Eisner. By the end of the 1970s several qualitative journals were in place, from *Urban Life* (now *Journal of Contemporary Ethnography*) to *Qualitative Sociology, Symbolic Interaction,* and *Studies in Symbolic Interaction.*

Crisis of Representation

A profound rupture occurred in the mid-1980s. What we call the fourth moment, or the crisis of representation, appeared with *Anthropology as Cultural Critique* (Marcus & Fischer, 1986), *The Anthropology of Experience* (Turner & Bruner, 1986), *Writing Culture* (Clifford & Marcus, 1986), *Works and Lives* (Geertz, 1988), and *The Predicament of Culture* (Clifford, 1988). These works made research and writing more reflexive, and called into question the issues of gender, class, and race. They articulated the consequences of Geertz's "blurred genres" interpretation of the field in the early 1980s.

New models of truth and method were sought (Rosaldo, 1989). The erosion of classic norms in anthropology (objectivism, complicity with colonialism, social life structured by fixed rituals and customs, ethnographies as monuments to a culture) was complete (Rosaldo, 1989, pp. 44-45). Critical and feminist epistemologies and epistemologies of color now compete for attention in this arena. Issues such as validity, reliability, and objectivity, which had been settled in earlier phases, are once more problematic. Interpretive theories, as opposed to grounded theories, are now more common, as writers continue to challenge older models of truth and meaning (Rosaldo, 1989).

Stoller and Olkes (1987) describe how the crisis of representation was felt in their fieldwork among the Songhay of Niger. Stoller observes: "When I began to write anthropological texts, I followed the conventions of my training. I 'gathered data,' and once the 'data' were arranged in neat piles, I 'wrote them up.' In one case I reduced Songhay insults to a series of neat logical formulas" (p. 227). Stoller became dissatisfied with this form of writing, in part because he learned "everyone had lied to me and . . . the data I had so painstakingly collected were worthless. I learned a lesson: Informants routinely lie to their anthropologists" (Stoller & Olkes, 1987, p. 229). This discovery led to a second, that he had, in following the conventions of ethnographic realism, edited himself out of his text. This led Stoller to produce a different type of text, a memoir, in which he became a central character in the story he told. This story, an account of his experiences in the Songhay world, became an analysis of the clash between his world and the world of Songhay sorcery. Thus did Stoller's journey represent an attempt to confront the crisis of representation in the fourth moment.

Clough (1992) elaborates this crisis and criticizes those who would argue that new forms of writing represent a way out of it:

> While many sociologists now commenting on the criticism of ethnography view writing as "downright central to the ethnographic enterprise" [Van Maanen, 1988, p. xi], the problems of writing are still viewed as different from the problems of method or fieldwork itself. Thus the solution usually offered is experiments in writing, that is a self-consciousness about writing. (p. 136)

However, it is this insistence on the difference between writing and fieldwork that must be analyzed.

In writing, the field-worker makes a claim to moral and scientific authority. These claims allow the realist and the experimental ethnographic text to function as sources of validation for an empirical science. They show, that is, that the world of real lived experience can still be captured, if only in the writer's memoirs, fictional experimentations, or dramatic readings. These works have the danger of directing attention away from the ways in which the text constructs sexually situated individuals in a field of social difference. They also perpetuate "empirical science's hegemony" (Clough, 1992, p. 8), for these new writing technologies of the subject become the site "for the production of knowledge/power . . . [aligned] with . . . the capital/state axis" (Aronowitz, 1988, p. 300, quoted in Clough, 1992, p. 8). Such experiments come up against, and then back away from, the difference between empirical science and social criticism. Too often they fail to engage fully a new politics of textuality that would "refuse the identity of empirical science" (Clough, 1992, p. 135). This new social criticism "would intervene in the relationship of information economics, nation-state politics, and technologies of mass communication, especially in terms of the empirical sciences" (Clough, 1992, p. 16). This, of course, is the terrain occupied by cultural studies.

Richardson, in Volume 3, Chapter 12, and Clandinin and Connelly, Volume 3, Chapter 6, develop the above arguments, viewing writing as a method of inquiry that moves through successive stages of self-reflection. As a series of writings, the field-worker's texts flow from the field experience, through intermediate works, to later work, and finally to the research text that is the public presentation of the ethnographic and narrative experience. Thus do fieldwork and writing blur into one another. There is, in the final analysis, no difference between writing and fieldwork. These two perspectives inform each other throughout every chapter in this volume. In these ways the crisis of representation moves qualitative research in new, critical directions.

A Double Crisis

The ethnographer's authority remains under assault today. A double crisis of representation and legitimation confronts qualitative researchers in the social sciences. Embedded in the discourses of poststructuralism and postmodernism (Vidich & Lyman, Volume 1, Chapter 2; Richardson, Volume 3, Chapter 12), these two crises are coded in multiple terms, variously called and associated with the *interpretive, linguistic,* and *rhetorical* turns in social theory. This linguistic turn makes problematic two key assumptions of qualitative research. The first is that qualitative researchers can directly capture lived experience. Such experience, it is now argued, is created in the social text written by the researcher. This is the representational crisis. It confronts the inescapable problem of representation, but does so within a framework that makes the direct link between experience and text problematic.

The second assumption makes the traditional criteria for evaluating and interpreting qualitative research problematic. This is the legitimation crisis. It involves a serious rethinking of such terms as *validity, generalizability,* and *reliability,* terms already retheorized in postpositivist, constructionist-naturalistic (Lincoln & Guba, 1985, p. 36), feminist (Fonow & Cook, 1991, pp. 1-13; Smith, 1992), and interpretive (Atkinson, 1990; Hammersley, 1992; Lather, 1993) discourses. This crisis asks, How are qualitative studies to be evaluated in the poststructural moment? Clearly these two crises blur together, for any representation must now legitimate itself in terms of some set of criteria that allows the author (and the reader) to make connections between the text and the world written about.

The Fifth Moment

The fifth moment is the present, defined and shaped by the dual crises described above. Theories are now read in narrative terms, as "tales of the field" (Van Maanen, 1988). Preoccupations with the representation of the "other" remain. New epistemologies from previously silenced groups emerge to offer solutions to this problem. The concept of the aloof researcher has been abandoned. More action-, activist-oriented research is on the horizon, as are more social criticism and social critique. The search for grand narratives will be replaced by more local, small-scale theories fitted to specific problems and specific situations (Lincoln, 1993).

Reading History

We draw four conclusions from this brief history, noting that it is, like all histories, somewhat arbitrary. First, each of the earlier historical moments is still operating in the present, either as legacy or as a set of practices that researchers still follow or argue against. The multiple, and fractured, histories of qualitative research now make it possible for any given researcher to attach a project to a canonical text from any of the above-described historical moments. Multiple criteria of evaluation now compete for attention in this field. Second, an embarrassment of choices now characterizes the field of qualitative research. There have never been so many paradigms, strategies of inquiry, or methods of analysis to draw upon and utilize. Third, we are in a moment of discovery and rediscovery, as new ways of looking, interpreting, arguing, and writing are debated and discussed. Fourth, the qualitative research act can no longer be viewed from within a neutral, or objective, positivist perspective. Class, race, gender, and ethnicity shape the process of inquiry, making research a multicultural process. It is to this topic that we next turn.

◆ Qualitative Research as Process

Three interconnected, generic activities define the qualitative research process. They go by a variety of different labels, including *theory, method* and *analysis,* and *ontology, epistemology,* and *methodology.* Behind these terms stands the personal biography of the gendered researcher, who speaks from a particular class, racial, cultural, and ethnic community perspective. The gendered, multiculturally-situated researcher approaches the world with a set of ideas, a framework (theory, ontology) that specifies a set of questions (epistemology) that are then examined (methodology, analysis) in specific ways. That is, empirical materials bearing on the question are collected and then analyzed and written about. Every researcher speaks from within a distinct interpretive community, which configures, in its special way, the multicultural, gendered components of the research act.

Behind all of these phases of interpretive work stands the biographically-situated researcher. This individual enters the research process from inside an interpretive community that incorporates its own historical research traditions into a distinct point of view. This perspective leads the researcher to adopt particular views of the "other" who is studied. At the same time, the politics and the ethics of research must also be considered, for these concerns permeate every phase of the research process.

◆ The Other as Research Subject

From its turn-of-the-century birth in modern, interpretive form, qualitative research has been haunted by a double-faced ghost. On the one hand, qualitative researchers have assumed that qualified, competent observers can with objectivity, clarity, and precision report on their own observations of the social world, including the experiences of others. Second, researchers have held to a belief in a real subject, or real individual, who is present in the world and able, in some form, to report on his or her experiences. So armed, researchers could blend their observations with the observations provided by subjects through interviews and life story, personal experience, case study, and other documents.

These two beliefs have led qualitative researchers across disciplines to seek a method that would allow them to record their own observations accurately while still uncovering the meanings their subjects bring to their life experiences. This method would rely upon the subjective verbal and written expressions of meaning given by the individuals studied, these expressions being windows into the inner life of the person. Since Dilthey (1900/1976), this search for a method has led to a perennial focus in the human disciplines on qualitative, interpretive methods.

Recently, this position and its beliefs have come under attack. Poststructuralists and postmodernists have contributed to the understanding that there is no clear window into the inner life of an individual. Any gaze is always filtered through the lenses of language, gender, social class, race, and ethnicity. There are no objective observations, only observations socially situated in the worlds of the observer and the observed. Subjects, or individuals, are seldom able to give full explanations of their actions or intentions; all they can offer are accounts, or stories, about what they did and why. No single method can grasp the subtle variations in ongoing human experience. As a consequence, as argued above, qualitative researchers deploy a wide range of interconnected interpretive methods, always seeking better ways to make more understandable the worlds of experience that have been studied.

Table 1.1 depicts the relationships we see among the five phases that define the research process. Behind all but one of these phases stands the biographically situated researcher. These five levels of activity, or practice, work their way through the biography of the researcher.

Phase 1: The Researcher

Our remarks above indicate the depth and complexity of the traditional and applied qualitative research perspectives into which a socially situated researcher enters. These traditions locate the researcher in history, both guiding and constraining work that will be done in any specific study. This field has been characterized constantly by diversity and conflict, and these, David Hamilton argues in Volume 1, Chapter 3, are its most enduring traditions. As a carrier of this complex and contradictory history, the researcher must also confront the ethics and politics of research. The age of value-free inquiry for the human disciplines is over, and researchers now struggle to develop situational and transsituational ethics that apply to any given research act.

TABLE 1.1 The Research Process

Phase 1: The Researcher as a Multicultural Subject
        history and research traditions
        conceptions of self and the other
        ethics and politics of research
Phase 2: Theoretical Paradigms and Perspectives
        positivism, postpositivism
        constructivism
        feminism(s)
        ethnic models
        Marxist models
        cultural studies models
Phase 3: Research Strategies
        study design
        case study
        ethnography, participant observation
        phenomenology, ethnomethodology
        grounded theory
        biographical method
        historical method
        action and applied research
        clinical research
Phase 4: Methods of Collection and Analysis
        interviewing
        observing
        artifacts, documents, and records
        visual methods
        personal experience methods
        data management methods
        computer-assisted analysis
        textual analysis
Phase 5: The Art of Interpretation and Presentation
        criteria for judging adequacy
        the art and politics of interpretation
        writing as interpretation
        policy analysis
        evaluation traditions
        applied research

Phase 2: Interpretive Paradigms

All qualitative researchers are philosophers in that "universal sense in which all human beings . . . are guided by highly abstract principles" (Bateson, 1972, p. 320). These principles combine beliefs about ontology (What kind of being is the human being? What is the nature of reality?), epistemology (What is the relationship between the inquirer and the known?), and methodology (How do we know the world, or gain knowledge of it?) (see Guba, 1990, p. 18; Lincoln & Guba, 1985, pp. 14-15; see also Guba & Lincoln, Volume 1, Chapter 6). These beliefs shape how the qualitative researcher sees the world and acts in it. The researcher is "bound within a net of epistemological and ontological premises which—regardless of ultimate truth or falsity—become partially self-validating" (Bateson, 1972, p. 314).

This net that contains the researcher's epistemological, ontological, and methodological premises may be termed a *paradigm* (Guba, 1990, p. 17), or interpretive framework, a "basic set of beliefs that guides action" (Guba, 1990, p. 17). All research is interpretive, guided by a set of beliefs and feelings about the world and how it should be understood and studied. Some of these beliefs may be taken for granted, only assumed; others are highly problematic and controversial. However, each interpretive paradigm makes particular demands on the researcher, including the questions that are asked and the interpretations that are brought to them.

At the most general level, four major interpretive paradigms structure qualitative research: positivist and postpositivist, constructivist-interpretive, critical (Marxist, emancipatory), and feminist-poststructural. These four abstract paradigms become more complicated at the level of concrete specific interpretive communities. At this level it is possible to identify not only the constructivist, but also multiple versions of feminist (Afrocentric and poststructural)[8] as well as specific ethnic, Marxist, and cultural studies paradigms. These perspectives, or paradigms, are examined in Part II of Volume 1.

The paradigms examined in Volume 1, Part II, work against and alongside (and some within) the positivist and postpositivist models. They all work within relativist ontologies (multiple constructed realities), interpretive epistemologies (the knower and known interact and shape one another), and interpretive, naturalistic methods.

Table 1.2 presents these paradigms and their assumptions, including their criteria for evaluating research, and the typical form that an interpre-

26

TABLE 1.2 Interpretive Paradigms

Paradigm/Theory	Criteria	Form of Theory	Type of Narration
Positivist/ postpositivist	internal, external validity	logical-deductive, scientific, grounded	scientific report
Constructivist	trustworthiness, credibility, transferability, confirmability	substantive-formal	interpretive case studies, ethnographic fiction
Feminist	Afrocentric, lived experience, dialogue, caring, accountability, race, class, gender, reflexivity, praxis, emotion, concrete grounding	critical, standpoint	essays, stories, experimental writing
Ethnic	Afrocentric, lived experience, dialogue, caring, accountability, race, class, gender	standpoint, critical, historical	essays, fables, dramas
Marxist	emancipatory theory, falsifiable, dialogical, race, class, gender	critical, historical, economic	historical, economic, sociocultural analysis
Cultural studies	cultural practices, praxis, social texts, subjectivities	social criticism	cultural theory as criticism

tive or theoretical statement assumes in the paradigm.[9] Each paradigm is explored in considerable detail in Volume 1, Part II, by Guba and Lincoln (Chapter 6), Schwandt (Chapter 7), Kincheloe and McLaren (Chapter 8), Olesen (Chapter 9), Stanfield (Chapter 10), and Fiske (Chapter 11). The positivist and postpositivist paradigms have been discussed above. They work from within a realist and critical realist ontology and objective epistemologies, and rely upon experimental, quasi-experimental, survey, and rigorously defined qualitative methodologies. In Volume 3, Chapter 7, Huberman and Miles develop elements of this paradigm.

The constructivist paradigm assumes a relativist ontology (there are multiple realities), a subjectivist epistemology (knower and subject create understandings), and a naturalistic (in the natural world) set of methodo-logical procedures. Findings are usually presented in terms of the criteria of grounded theory (see Strauss & Corbin, Volume 2, Chapter 7). Terms such as *credibility, transferability, dependability,* and *confirmability* replace the usual positivist criteria of *internal* and *external validity, reliability,* and *objectivity.*

Feminist, ethnic, Marxist, and cultural studies models privilege a mate-rialist-realist ontology; that is, the real world makes a material difference in terms of race, class, and gender. Subjectivist epistemologies and naturalistic methodologies (usually ethnographies) are also employed. Empirical materials and theoretical arguments are evaluated in terms of their emancipatory implications. Criteria from gender and racial communities (e.g., African American) may be applied (emotionality and feeling, caring, personal accountability, dialogue).

Poststructural feminist theories emphasize problems with the social text, its logic, and its inability ever to represent fully the world of lived experience. Positivist and postpositivist criteria of evaluation are replaced by others, including the reflexive, multivoiced text that is grounded in the experiences of oppressed peoples.

The cultural studies paradigm is multifocused, with many different strands drawing from Marxism, feminism, and the postmodern sensibility. There is a tension between humanistic cultural studies stressing lived experiences and more structural cultural studies projects stressing the structural and material determinants (race, class, gender) of experience. The cultural studies paradigm uses methods strategically, that is, as resources for understanding and for producing resistances to local structures of domination. Cultural studies scholars may do close textual readings and discourse analysis of cultural texts as well as local ethnographies, open-ended interviewing, and participant observation. The focus is on how race, class, and gender are produced and enacted in historically specific situations.

Paradigm and history in hand, focused on a concrete empirical problem to examine, the researcher now moves to the next stage of the research process, namely, working with a specific strategy of inquiry.

Phase 3: Strategies of Inquiry and Interpretive Paradigms

Table 1.1 presents some of the major strategies of inquiry a researcher may use. Phase 3 begins with research design, which, broadly conceived, involves a clear focus on the research question, the purposes of the study, "what information most appropriately will answer specific research questions, and which strategies are most effective for obtaining it" (LeCompte & Preissle, 1993, p. 30). A research design describes a flexible set of guidelines that connects theoretical paradigms to strategies of inquiry and methods for collecting empirical material. A research design situates researchers in the empirical world and connects them to specific sites, persons, groups, institutions, and bodies of relevant interpretive material, including documents and archives. A research design also specifies how the investigator will address the two critical issues of representation and legitimation.

A strategy of inquiry comprises a bundle of skills, assumptions, and practices that researchers employ as they move from their paradigm to the empirical world. Strategies of inquiry put paradigms of interpretation into motion. At the same time, strategies of inquiry connect the researcher to specific methods of collecting and analyzing empirical materials. For example, the case study method relies on interviewing, observing, and document analysis. Research strategies implement and anchor paradigms in specific empirical sites, or in specific methodological practices, such as making a case an object of study. These strategies include the case study, phenomenological and ethnomethodological techniques, as well as the use of grounded theory, the biographical, historical, action, and clinical methods. Each of these strategies is connected to a complex literature; each has a separate history, exemplary works, and preferred ways for putting the strategy into motion.

Phase 4: Methods of Collecting and Analyzing Empirical Materials

The researcher has several methods for collecting empirical materials,[10] ranging from the interview to direct observation, to the analysis of artifacts, documents, and cultural records, to the use of visual materials or personal experience. The researcher may also use a variety of different methods of reading and analyzing interviews or cultural texts, including content, narrative, and semiotic strategies. Faced with large amounts of qualitative materials, the investigator seeks ways of managing and interpreting these documents, and here data management methods and computer-assisted models of analysis may be of use.

Phase 5: The Art of Interpretation

Qualitative research is endlessly creative and interpretive. The researcher does not just leave the field with mountains of empirical materials and then easily write up his or her findings. Qualitative interpretations are constructed. The researcher first creates a field text consisting of field notes and documents from the field, what Roger Sanjek (1990, p. 386) calls "indexing" and David Plath (1990, p. 374) calls "filework." The writer-as-interpreter moves from this text to a research text: notes and interpretations based on the field text. This text is then re-created as a working interpretive document that contains the writer's initial attempts to make sense out of what he or she has learned. Finally, the writer produces the public text that comes to the reader. This final tale of the field may assume several forms: confessional, realist, impressionistic, critical, formal, literary, analytic, grounded theory, and so on (see Van Maanen, 1988).

The interpretive practice of making sense of one's findings is both artful and political. Multiple criteria for evaluating qualitative research now exist, and those we emphasize stress the situated, relational, and textual structures of the ethnographic experience. There is no single interpretive truth. As we argued earlier, there are multiple interpretive communities, each having its own criteria for evaluating an interpretation.

Program evaluation is a major site of qualitative research, and qualitative researchers can influence social policy in important ways. David Hamilton, in Volume 1, Chapter 3, traces the rich history of applied qualitative research in the social sciences. This is the critical site where theory, method, praxis, or action, and policy all come together. Qualitative researchers can isolate target populations, show the immediate effects of certain programs on such groups, and isolate the constraints that operate against policy changes in such settings. Action-oriented and clinically-oriented qualitative researchers can also create spaces for those who are studied (the other) to speak. The evaluator becomes the conduit for making such voices heard. Greene, in Volume 3, Chapter 13, and Rist, in Volume 3, Chapter 14, develop these topics.

◆ The Fifth Moment: What Comes Next?

Marcus, in Volume 1, Chapter 12, argues that we are already in the post "post" period—post-poststructuralism, post-postmodernism. What this means for interpretive, ethnographic practices is still not clear, but it is certain that things will never be the same. We are in a new age where messy, uncertain, multivoiced texts, cultural criticism, and new experimental works will become more common, as will more reflexive forms of fieldwork, analysis, and intertextual representation. The subject of our final essay in this volume is this "fifth moment." It is true that, as the poet said, the center cannot hold. We can reflect on what should be at a new center.

Thus we come full circle. The chapters in these volumes take the researcher through every phase of the research act. The contributors examine the relevant histories, controversies, and current practices associated with each paradigm, strategy, and method. They also offer projections for the future—where specific paradigms, strategies, or methods will be 10 years from now.

In reading the chapters that follow, it is important to remember that the field of qualitative research is defined by a series of tensions, contradictions, and hesitations. This tension works back and forth between the broad, doubting postmodern sensibility and the more certain, more traditional positivist, postpositivist, and naturalistic conceptions of this project. All of the chapters that follow are caught in and articulate this tension.

◆ Notes

1. Qualitative research has separate and distinguished histories in education, social work, communications, psychology, history, organizational studies, medical science, anthropology, and sociology.

2. Definitions of some of these terms are in order here. *Positivism* asserts that objective accounts of the world can be given. *Postpositivism* holds that only partially objective accounts of the world can be produced, because all methods are flawed. *Structuralism* asserts that any system is made up of a set of oppositional categories embedded in language. *Semiotics* is the science of signs or sign systems—a structuralist project. According to *poststructuralism,* language is an unstable system of referents, thus it is impossible ever to capture completely the meaning of an action, text, or intention. *Postmodernism* is a contemporary sensibility, developing since World War II, that privileges no single authority, method, or paradigm. *Hermeneutics* is an approach to the analysis of texts that stresses how prior understandings and prejudices shape the interpretive process. *Phenomenology* is a complex system of ideas associated with the works of Husserl, Heidegger, Sartre, Merleau-Ponty, and Alfred Schutz. *Cultural studies* is a complex, interdisciplinary field that merges critical theory, feminism, and poststructuralism.

3. According to Weinstein and Weinstein (1991), "The meaning of *bricoleur* in French popular speech is 'someone who works with his (or her) hands and uses devious means compared to those of the craftsman.' . . . the *bricoleur* is practical and gets the job done" (p. 161). These authors provide a history of this term, connecting it to the works of the German sociologist and social theorist Georg Simmel and, by implication, Baudelaire.

4. Here it is relevant to make a distinction between techniques that are used across disciplines and methods that are used within disciplines. Ethnomethodologists, for example, employ their approach as a method, whereas others selectively borrow that method as a technique for their own applications. Harry Wolcott (personal communication, 1993) suggests this distinction. It is also relevant to make distinctions among topic, method, and

resource. Methods can be studied as topics of inquiry—for instance, how a case study gets done. In this ironic, ethnomethodological sense, method is both a resource and a topic of inquiry.

5. Indeed, any attempt to give an essential definition of qualitative research requires a qualitative analysis of the circumstances that produce such a definition.

6. In this sense all research is qualitative, because "the observer is at the center of the research process" (Vidich & Lyman, Volume 1, Chapter 2).

7. See Lincoln and Guba (1985) for an extension and elaboration of this tradition in the mid-1980s.

8. Olesen (Volume 1, Chapter 9) identifies three strands of feminist research: mainstream empirical, standpoint and cultural studies, and poststructural, postmodern, placing Afrocentric and other models of color under the cultural studies and postmodern categories.

9. These, of course, are our interpretations of these paradigms and interpretive styles.

10. *Empirical materials* is the preferred term for what are traditionally described as data.

◆ References

Aronowitz, S. (1988). *Science as power: Discourse and ideology in modern society.* Minneapolis: University of Minnesota Press.

Atkinson, P. A. (1990). *The ethnographic imagination: Textual constructions of reality.* London: Routledge.

Bateson, G. (1972). *Steps to an ecology of mind.* New York: Ballantine.

Becker, H. S. (1970). Problems of inference and proof in participant observation. In H. S. Becker, *Sociological work.* Chicago: Aldine. (Reprinted from *American Sociological Review,* 1958, *23,* 652-660)

Becker, H. S. (1986). *Doing things together.* Evanston, IL: Northwestern University Press.

Becker, H. S. (1989). Tricks of the trade. *Studies in Symbolic Interaction, 10,* 481-490.

Becker, H. S. (1993, June 9). *The epistemology of qualitative research.* Paper presented at the MacArthur Foundation Conference on Ethnographic Approaches to the Study of Human Behavior, Oakland, CA.

Becker, H. S., Geer, B., Hughes, E. C., & Strauss, A. L. (1961). *Boys in white: Student culture in medical school.* Chicago: University of Chicago Press.

Bogdan, R., & Taylor, S. J. (1975). *Introduction to qualitative research methods: A phenomenological approach to the social sciences.* New York: John Wiley.

Brewer, J., & Hunter, A. (1989). *Multimethod research: A synthesis of styles.* Newbury Park, CA: Sage.

Campbell, D. T., & Stanley, J. C. (1963). *Experimental and quasi-experimental designs for research.* Chicago: Rand McNally.

Carey, J. W. (1989). *Communication as culture: Essays on media and society.* Boston: Unwin Hyman.

Cicourel, A. V. (1964). *Method and measurement in sociology.* New York: Free Press.

Clifford, J. (1988). *The predicament of culture: Twentieth-century ethnography, literature, and art.* Cambridge, MA: Harvard University Press.

Clifford, J., & Marcus, G. E. (Eds.). (1986). *Writing culture: The poetics and politics of ethnography.* Berkeley: University of California Press.

Clough, P. T. (1992). *The end(s) of ethnography: From realism to social criticism.* Newbury Park, CA: Sage.

Denzin, N. K. (1970). *The research act.* Chicago: Aldine.

Denzin, N. K. (1978). *The research act* (2nd ed.). New York: McGraw-Hill.

Denzin, N. K. (1989a). *Interpretive interactionism.* Newbury Park, CA: Sage.

Denzin, N. K. (1989b). *The research act* (3rd ed.). Englewood Cliffs, NJ: Prentice Hall.

Dilthey, W. L. (1976). *Selected writings.* Cambridge: Cambridge University Press. (Original work published 1900)

Fielding, N. G., & Fielding, J. L. (1986). *Linking data.* Beverly Hills, CA: Sage.

Filstead, W. J. (Ed.). (1970). *Qualitative methodology.* Chicago: Markham.

Flick, U. (1992). Triangulation revisited: Strategy of validation or alternative? *Journal for the Theory of Social Behaviour, 22,* 175-198.

Fonow, M. M., & Cook, J. A. (1991). Back to the future: A look at the second wave of feminist epistemology and methodology. In M. M. Fonow & J. A. Cook (Eds.), *Beyond methodology: Feminist scholarship as lived research* (pp. 1-15). Bloomington: Indiana University Press.

Geertz, C. (1973). *The interpretation of cultures: Selected essays.* New York: Basic Books.

Geertz, C. (1983). *Local knowledge: Further essays in interpretive anthropology.* New York: Basic Books.

Geertz, C. (1988). *Works and lives: The anthropologist as author.* Stanford, CA: Stanford University Press.

Glaser, B. G. (1992). *Emergence vs. forcing: Basics of grounded theory.* Mill Valley, CA: Sociology Press.

Glaser, B. G., & Strauss, A. L. (1967). *The discovery of grounded theory: Strategies for qualitative research.* Chicago: Aldine.

Guba, E. G. (1990). The alternative paradigm dialog. In E. G. Guba (Ed.), *The paradigm dialog* (pp. 17-30). Newbury Park, CA: Sage.

Hammersley, M. (1992). *What's wrong with ethnography? Methodological explorations.* London: Routledge.

Hymes, D. (1980). Educational ethnology. *Anthropology and Education Quarterly, 11,* 3-8.

Lather, P. (1993). Fertile obsession: Validity after poststructuralism. *Sociological Quarterly, 34,* 673-693.

LeCompte, M. D., & Preissle, J. (1992). Toward an ethnology of student life in schools and classrooms: Synthesizing the qualitative research tradition. In M. D. LeCompte, W. L. Millroy, & J. Preissle (Eds.), *The handbook of qualitative research in education* (pp. 815-859). New York: Academic Press.

LeCompte, M. D., & Preissle, J., with Tesch, R. (1993). *Ethnography and qualitative design in educational research* (2nd ed.). New York: Academic Press.

Lentricchia, F., & McLaughlin, T. (Eds.). (1990). *Critical terms for literary study.* Chicago: University of Chicago Press.

Lévi-Strauss, C. (1966). *The savage mind* (2nd ed.). Chicago: University of Chicago Press.

Lincoln, Y. S. (1993, January 27-28). *Notes toward a fifth generation of evaluation: Lessons from the voiceless, or, Toward a postmodern politics of evaluation.* Paper presented at the Fifth Annual Meeting of the Southeast Evaluation Association, Tallahassee, FL.

33

Lincoln, Y. S., & Guba, E. G. (1985). *Naturalistic inquiry*. Beverly Hills, CA: Sage.

Lofland, J. (1971). *Analyzing social settings: A guide to qualitative observation and analysis*. Belmont, CA: Wadsworth.

Lofland, J., & Lofland, L. H. (1984). *Analyzing social settings: A guide to qualitative observation and analysis* (2nd ed.). Belmont, CA: Wadsworth.

Lofland, L. (1980). The 1969 Blumer-Hughes talk. *Urban Life, 8,* 248-260.

Malinowski, B. (1948). *Magic, science and religion, and other essays*. New York: Natural History Press. (Original work published 1916)

Malinowski, B. (1967). *A diary in the strict sense of the term*. New York: Harcourt Brace.

Marcus, G., & Fischer, M. (1986). *Anthropology as cultural critique: An experimental moment in the human sciences*. Chicago: University of Chicago Press.

Miles, M. B., & Huberman, A. M. (1993). *Qualitative data analysis: A sourcebook of new methods* (2nd ed.). Newbury Park, CA: Sage.

Nelson, C., Treichler, P. A., & Grossberg, L. (1992). Cultural studies. In L. Grossberg, C. Nelson, & P. A. Treichler (Eds.), *Cultural studies* (pp. 1-16). New York: Routledge.

Nichols, B. (Ed.). (1985). *Movies and methods* (Vol. 2). Berkeley: University of California Press.

Plath, D. (1990). Fieldnotes, filed notes, and the conferring of note. In R. Sanjek (Ed.), *Fieldnotes: The makings of anthropology* (pp. 371-384). Albany: State University of New York Press.

Richardson, L. (1991). Postmodern social theory. *Sociological Theory, 9,* 173-179.

Roffman, P., & Purdy, J. (1981). *The Hollywood social problem film*. Bloomington: Indiana University Press.

Rosaldo, R. (1989). *Culture and truth: The remaking of social analysis*. Boston: Beacon.

Sanjek, R. (Ed.). (1990). *Fieldnotes: The makings of anthropology*. Albany: State University of New York Press.

Smith, D. (1992). Sociology from women's perspective: A reaffirmation. *Sociological Theory, 10,* 88-97.

Spindler, G., & Spindler, L. (1992). Cultural process and ethnography: An anthropological perspective. In M. D. LeCompte, W. L. Millroy, & J. Preissle (Eds.), *The handbook of qualitative research in education* (pp. 53-92). New York: Academic Press.

Stoller, P., & Olkes, C. (1987). *In sorcery's shadow: A memoir of apprenticeship among the Songhay of Niger*. Chicago: University of Chicago Press.

Strauss, A. L., & Corbin, J. (1990). *Basics of qualitative research: Grounded theory procedures and techniques*. Newbury Park, CA: Sage.

Turner, V., & Bruner, E. (Eds.). (1986). *The anthropology of experience*. Urbana: University of Illinois Press.

Van Maanen, J. (1988). *Tales of the field: On writing ethnography*. Chicago: University of Chicago Press.

West, C. (1989). *The American evasion of philosophy*. Madison: University of Wisconsin Press.

Weinstein, D., & Weinstein, M. A. (1991). Georg Simmel: Sociological flaneur bricoleur. *Theory, Culture & Society, 8,* 151-168.

Wolcott, H. F. (1992). Posturing in qualitative research. In M. D. LeCompte, W. L. Millroy, & J. Preissle (Eds.), *The handbook of qualitative research in education* (pp. 3-52). New York: Academic Press.

PART I

◆ Methods of Collecting and Analyzing Empirical Materials

The constructionist (and constructivist) position tells us that the socially situated researcher creates, through interaction, the realities that constitute the places where empirical materials are collected and analyzed. In such sites, the interpretive practices of qualitative research are implemented. These practices are methods and techniques for producing empirical materials as well as theoretical interpretations of the world. These chapters examine the multiple practices and methods of analysis qualitative researchers-as-*bricoleurs* now employ.

◆ The Interview

The interview is the favorite methodological tool of the qualitative researcher. Andrea Fontana and James Frey review the history of the interview in the social sciences, noting its three major forms—structured, unstructured, and open-ended—while showing how the tool is modified and changed during use.

The interview is a conversation, the art of asking questions and listening. It is not a neutral tool, for the interviewer creates the reality of the interview situation. In this situation answers are given. Thus the interview produces situated understandings grounded in specific interactional episodes. This method is influenced by the personal characteristics of the interviewer, including race, class, ethnicity, and gender.

Fontana and Frey review the important work of feminist scholars on the interview, especially the arguments of British sociologist Ann Oakley (1981), who has identified a major contradiction between scientific, positivistic research, which requires objectivity and detachment, and feminist-based interviewing, which requires openness, emotional engagement, and the development of a potentially long-term, trusting relationship between the interviewer and the subject. Guiding Oakley's highly influential model is a proposed "feminist ethic of commitment and equalitarianism in contrast with the scientific ethic of detachment and role differentiation between researcher and subject" (Reinharz, 1992, p. 27).

A feminist interviewing ethic, as Fontana and Frey suggest, redefines the interview situation. It directs attention to the fact that research is activity "fundamentally grounded in talk . . . and that language itself reflects male experiences, and that its categories are often incongruent with women's lives" (DeVault, 1990, pp. 96-97). This ethic transforms interviewers and respondents into coequals who are carrying on a conversation about mutually relevant, often biographically critical, issues. This personalization of the interview method makes it a potential agent of social change, where new identities and new definitions of problematic situations are created, discussed, and experimented with. This ethic changes the interview into an important tool for the types of clinical and applied action research discussed by Reason and by Miller and Crabtree.

◆ Observational Methods

Naturalistic observation, going to a social situation and looking, is another favorite way of gathering material about the social world. Noting that observation methods remain a stepchild to their more widely recognized offshoot, participant observation, Patricia and Peter Adler take up the history, forms, stages and some of the ethical problems involved with this technique.[1]

From the postpositivist perspective as developed by the Adlers, the problems of observation are legion, involving questions of validity and reliability, observer and setting bias, observer effects, and the absence of member checks. Adler and Adler discuss traditional, multimethod strategies for addressing these issues, and also show how the method has been put to excellent use by formal sociologists of the "new" Iowa school, as well as scholars working in the traditions of dramaturgical and introspective sociology and ethnomethodology.

Adler and Adler outline the ethical problems involved with this method, especially those involving invasions of privacy and disguised research. They note that the hidden or disguised voyeur has been one of the many identities social science observers have utilized. Their chapter can be read as suggesting that it is time to rethink the warrant and high value the social sciences have given to voyeurism and the voyeuristic activities of the detached, watchful observer who invades the personal, sacred spaces of others. Indeed, although they do not develop this point, a feminist ethic of caring and commitment seems to undercut the pure observational project, for it requires the formation of a long-term trusting relationship between the observer and those studied.

Finally, the Adlers confront an obdurate fact of contemporary academic life, the institutional review board (IRB). They challenge the right of IRBs to limit, or prohibit, disguised observation. Yet, as many have argued, these boards are not likely to go away. The issue, in our view, is learning how to live with them. This may well involve the institutional development of the implications of a consequentialist-feminist ethics committed to caring, trust, and long-term relationships. Under such an ethical model the surveillance ethics of review boards become muted, if not moot.

◆ Reading Material Culture and Its Records

Mute evidence—that is, written texts and cultural artifacts—endures physically and leaves its traces on the past. It is impossible to talk to these materials. They must be interpreted, for in them are found important meanings about the past and the human shape of lived cultures. Archaeologists study these materials. In a chapter that moves with ease across and within the postpositivist and postmodern sensibilities, Ian Hodder shows how this is done. Central to his position is the constructionist (and constructivist) argument that researchers create, through a set of interpretive practices, the materials and evidence they then theoretically analyze. Material culture is a social and political construction, and how the past is reconstructed very much determines how it will be constituted in the present.

◆ Visual Methods

Visual sociologists and anthropologists use film, video, and photography as means of recording and documenting social life. Often called the mirror with a memory, photography takes the researcher into the subject's world, where the issues of observer identity, the subject's point of view, and what to photograph become problematic. Douglas Harper presents a history of this method and brings it up against postmodern developments in ethnography.

Historically, visual sociology began within the postpositivist tradition, providing visual information for the realist tales of traditional ethnography. However, like ethnography, visual sociology is in a period of deep questioning and great change. Visual sociology, Harper contends, must find a place in this new ethnography. He engages this new turn, discussing the ideological aspects of representation, the social construction of images, the authority of visual knowledge, and the ethics of a new visual sociology. He articulates his new perspective by showing how visual sociologists resolve particular problems in their research, including using the mechanical capabilities of the camera, framing (point of view), printing techniques, image sequencing, and the influences of the photographer on the lives of the people studied.

It is clear that visual methods will soon have a place of increased importance and centrality in the qualitative research project. Visual ethnographies, documentaries, and the reading of film as social texts are important strategies and resources for this project. Visual literacy, which is replacing print literacy, and visual texts, which are replacing print texts, define this historical moment. The new visual sociology will lead the way in reading, constructing, and interpreting these texts. These are further reasons for qualitative researchers to pay more attention to these alternative forms of representing and collecting empirical materials.

◆ Personal Experience Methods

Personal experience reflects the flow of thoughts and meanings persons bring to their immediate situations. These experiences can be routine or problematic. They occur within the life of a person. When they are related, they assume the shape of a story, or a narrative. It is very difficult to study direct, lived experience, because language, speech, and thought mediate and define the very experience one attempts to describe. Accordingly, researchers study the stories people tell one another about the experiences they have had. These stories may be personal experience narratives or self-stories, accounts made up as the person goes along. Jean Clandinin and Michael Connelly review these methods of studying personal experience, anchoring their use in the discourses of poststructuralism and postmodernism.

Clandinin and Connelly outline three methodological questions, or issues, that confront the researcher who uses personal experience methods; these begin with the field experience, then involve the texts written about the experience, and conclude with the research accounts of the experience. These three issues lead to a consideration of field notes, photographs, field texts, oral histories, research interviews, and autobiographical writing. The research texts that are produced out of such material implicate the investigator in a feminist, caring, committed ethic with those who have been studied. These texts are also shaped by the use of voice, signature, and the imagined presence of a reading audience. Thus do Clandinin and

Connelly show how personal experience becomes part of the post-modern project.

◆ Data Management and Analysis Methods

The management, analysis, and interpretation of qualitative empirical materials is a complex process. Michael Huberman and Matthew Miles advance a sophisticated and comprehensive model of this process. Their framework model distinguishes within- from between-case analysis while emphasizing the necessary connection between a theory and its concepts and the empirical indicators that reflect back through the concepts to the theory. Drawing on the grounded theory approach, they show how codes, memos, and diagrams can help a researcher work from field notes to some conceptual understanding of the processes being studied. This model stresses variables and causal links between variables while focusing on an iterative approach that is fully open to discovery and the treatment of negative cases. This framework is very compatible with computer-assisted methods of analysis.

This is an elegant and systematic postpositivist approach to the problem. Huberman and Miles are transcendental realists (i.e., they believe that social phenomena exist in the objective world and there are lawful relationships among them), and their model argues for rigor in the collection, production, analysis, and presentation of qualitative empirical materials. They use analytic induction and grounded theory, and they believe in studies that can be replicated and judged against the canons of good science. The reflexive turn organizing their concluding arguments is a reflexivity contained within the postpositivist paradigm.

As deployed by Huberman and Miles, this model satisfies the positivist critics of qualitative research, hence its enormous appeal and widespread use. Yet we believe the framework remains basically unresponsive to the more poststructural, constructionist, cultural studies, feminist, and critical theory perspectives. These models argue against a transcendental realism. They see the world of data (empirical materials) as one that is created in and through the interactions that occur between the observer and the observed. Still, many of the guidelines Huberman and Miles set forth in their chapter would be useful to, and could easily be used by, these other approaches, especially those versions still attached to the postpositivist paradigm. They are, after all, tools for building qualitative interpretations. Thus the tools are not at issue, only what is done with them.

◆ Computer-Assisted Qualitative Analysis

Many qualitative researchers now work with computers. In the past decade, multiple software programs have appeared that assist in the analysis of qualitative materials. Field research, as Clandinin and Connelly note, leads to the production of large amounts of textual material, notes, journal entries, recorded conversations, descriptions of the field setting, memos, thoughts on coding schemes, emotional experiences, and so on. These materials all take the form of texts, the analysis of which can be very time-consuming.

Thomas Richards and Lyn Richards analyze the most influential programs in this field. These programs have multiple text management uses, including coding, locating, and retrieving key materials, phrases, and words; building conceptual models; sorting categories; attaching key words and codes to text segments; isolating negative or deviant cases; and creating indices. Team research is also facilitated through the use of computers: Files can be shared, mailed back and forth, or transmitted electronically. Computer programs can also be used for theory construction. Some implement the logic and structure of the grounded theory model of Glaser, Strauss, and Corbin.[2] Richards and Richards review all of these uses.

In using any of these models, Richards and Richards note, it is important not to let the computer (or the software package) determine the form and content of interpretive activity. The emphasis on codes and categories can produce endless variable analyses that fail to take account of important situational and contextual factors.[3] There is a frequent tendency to reduce field materials to only codable data. There is also the danger that the transcription of field notes may be turned over to persons who lack intimate familiarity with the field setting and the processes being studied (Lee & Fielding, 1991, p. 12).

Seidel (1991) speaks of a form of analytic madness that can accompany the use of these methods. This madness can create several problems. It can lead to an infatuation with the large volume of data one can deal with. In addition, researchers may develop understandings based on misunderstandings; that is, patterns identified in the data may be "artifacts of a relationship we have with the data" (p. 114). Further, the researcher may focus only on those aspects of the research that can be helped by computer methods (Agar, 1991, p. 193). The researcher selects software and readies it for use on the study materials. A problem arises when the researcher limits him- or herself to conducting only research that fits available software.

Finally, there are possible ethical problems. Akeroyd (1991) isolates the crux of the matter: the potential loss of personal privacy that can occur when a personal, confidential database is developed on an individual or group. When such materials are entered into a computer database, the problem of security is immediately created. In multiuser systems, privacy cannot be guaranteed (Akeroyd, 1991, p. 100): Nothing is any longer completely private and completely secure.

This cautionary discussion needs to be balanced with a treatment of the positive features and uses of these methods, which are thoroughly developed by Richards and Richards.[4] Their text sketches the history of software programs in this field, stressing those that are most user friendly. They emphasize the need for interactional programs that allow the researcher to learn from and build on the analysis as it is occurring.

◆ Narrative, Content, and Semiotic Analysis

Qualitative researchers study spoken and written records of human experience, including transcribed talk, films, novels, and photographs. Historically, these have been the three major social science approaches to textual-discourse analysis. Each is associated with a long theoretical and research tradition: content analysis with the quantitative approach to media studies, semiotics with the structural tradition in literary criticism, and narrative or discourse analysis with the recent poststructural development in interpretive theory.

Documents of experience can be content analyzed; that is, themes, issues, and recurring motifs within them can be isolated, counted, and interpreted. Alternatively, such documents can be read as narratives, or stories, wherein the researcher analyzes the narrative, temporal, and dramatic structures of a text, forsaking the rigor of counting, for a close, interpretive reading of the subject matter at hand. This reading can be supplemented by the semiotic method, which searches for oppositions, categories, and linguistic structures in the text. Peter Manning and Betsy Cullum-Swan examine these three strategies of interpretation in their chapter.

Traditional, classic content analysis is marked by Bernard Berelson's classic *Content Analysis in Communication Research* (1952). This text and its influences are still felt today. In it, Berelson offered a rigorous quantitative approach to the content analysis of media messages. This work was immediately challenged by Siegfried Kracauer (1953), a German critical theorist, who called for qualitative content analysis techniques drawing on hermeneutical, textual procedures. Kracauer argued that the "inadequacy of quantitative analyses stems from the methods themselves: when trying to establish the meaning of texts by breaking them down into quantifiable units (words, expressions), analysts in fact destroy the very object they are supposed to be studying" (quoted in Larsen, 1991, p. 123). Kracauer advocated an approach that examined the content of a text as a totality. The task of the analyst is to bring out the hidden meanings in the text.

The structuralist project elaborated Kracauer's arguments by developing a more consistent theory of the text and its constituent elements. The science of signs, called semiotics, was the key to this project. From it emerged the more contemporary poststructural methods, discussed in a previous volume of this series by Fiske and addressed here by Clandinin and Connelly. Manning and Cullum-Swan extend and expose the limits of each of these perspectives. Their powerful reading of the menus at McDonald's reveals how semiotics and fieldwork can be combined in a semiotic discourse analysis. The postmodern world can be read as a giant text. An understanding of this world requires the use of the narrative methods discussed by Manning and Cullum-Swan.

43

◆ Conclusion

The researcher-as-*bricoleur* should have a working familiarity with all of the methods of collecting and analyzing empirical materials presented in this section. This familiarity should include an understanding of the history of each method and technique as well as hands-on experience with it. Only in this way can a researcher fully appreciate the limitations and strengths of each. At the same time, he or she will more clearly see how each, as a set of practices, creates its own subject matter.

In addition, it must be understood that each paradigm and perspective has a distinct history with these methods of research. Although the methods-as-tools are somewhat universal in application, they are not uniformly used by researchers from all paradigms, or, if they are used, they are fitted to the particularities of the paradigm in question.

Of the five specific methods presented in this section (interviews, observation, cultural artifacts, visual methods, and personal experience methods), positivists and postpositivists are most likely to make use of structured interviews and those cultural artifacts that lend themselves to formal analysis. Constructionists and critical theorists also have histories of using all of the five methods, as do feminists, ethnic researchers, and cultural studies investigators. Similarly, researchers from all paradigms and perspectives can profitably make use of the data management and analysis methods and the computer-assisted models discussed by Huberman and Miles and Richards and Richards.

◆ Notes

1. Of course, psychologists and educators in the ecological tradition (such as Barker and Wright) have long used observational methods, yet these rigorous methods have seldom been employed by sociologists.

2. Tesch (1991, pp. 18-20) has enumerated a variety of interpretive traditions and text-based forms of analysis that now use computer-assisted methods: classic and ethnographic content analysis, discourse and ethnographic analyses of conversations, document analysis of historical materials, event structure analysis, and grounded theory construction.

3. The potential shift to variable analysis moves computer-assisted methods firmly in the direction of positivist and postpositivist models of interpretation.

4. In this regard, Tesch's (1993) discussion of personal computers in qualitative research should be examined.

◆ References

Agar, M. (1991). The right brain strikes back. In N. G. Fielding & R. M. Lee (Eds.), *Using computers in qualitative research* (pp. 181-194). Newbury Park, CA: Sage.

Akeroyd, A. V. (1991). Personal information and qualitative research data: Some practical and ethical problems arising from data protection legislation. In N. G. Fielding & R. M. Lee (Eds.), *Using computers in qualitative research* (pp. 89-106). Newbury Park, CA: Sage.

Berelson, B. (1952). *Content analysis in communication research.* Glencoe, IL: Free Press.

DeVault, M. L. (1990). Talking and listening from women's standpoint: Feminist strategies for interviewing and analysis. *Social Problems, 37,* 96-116.

Kracauer, S. (1953). The challenge to qualitative content analysis. *Public Opinion Quarterly, 16,* 631-642.

Larsen, P. (1991). Textual analysis of fictional media content. In K. B. Jensen & N. W. Janowski (Eds.), *A handbook of qualitative methodologies for mass communication research* (pp. 121-134). New York: Routledge.

Lee, R. M., & Fielding, N. G. (1991). Computing for qualitative research: Options, problems, and potential. In N. G. Fielding & R. M. Lee (Eds.), *Using computers in qualitative research* (pp. 1-13). Newbury Park, CA: Sage.

Oakley, A. (1981). Interviewing women: A contradiction in terms. In H. Roberts (Ed.), *Doing feminist research* (pp. 30-61). London: Routledge.

Reinharz, S. (1992). *Feminist methods in social research.* New York: Oxford University Press.

Seidel, J. (1991). Method and madness in the application of computer technology to qualitative data analysis. In N. G. Fielding & R. M. Lee (Eds.), *Using computers in qualitative research* (pp. 107-116). Newbury Park, CA: Sage.

Tesch, R. (1991). Software for qualitative researchers: Analysis needs and program capabilities. In N. G. Fielding & R. M. Lee (Eds.), *Using computers in qualitative research* (pp. 16-37). Newbury Park, CA: Sage.

Tesch, R. (1993). Personal computers in qualitative research. In M. D. LeCompte & J. Preissle, with R. Tesch (Eds.), *Ethnography and qualitative design in educational research* (2nd ed., pp. 279-314). New York: Academic Press.

2

Interviewing

The Art of Science

Andrea Fontana & James H. Frey

> If all the problems of question wording could be traced to a
> single source, their common origin would probably prove
> to be in taking too much for granted.
>
> —S. Payne, *The Art of Asking Questions,* 1951

◆ Asking questions and getting answers is a much harder task than it may seem at first. The spoken or written word has always a residue of ambiguity, no matter how carefully we word the questions and report or code the answers. Yet, interviewing is one of the most common and most powerful ways we use to try to understand our fellow human beings. Interviewing is a paramount part of sociology, because interviewing is interaction and sociology is the study of interaction (see Benney & Hughes, 1956). Thus the interview becomes both the tool and the object, the art of sociological sociability, an encounter in which "both parties behave as though they are of equal status for its duration, whether or not this is actually so" (Benney & Hughes, 1956, p. 142).

AUTHORS' NOTE: We wish to thank, for insightful comments and wonderfully encouraging suggestions, Norman Denzin, Yvonna Lincoln, Arlene Daniels, and David Silverman. We followed their suggestions and their ideas.

Interviewing has a wide variety of forms and a multiplicity of uses. The most common type of interviewing is individual, face-to-face verbal interchange, but it can also take the form of face-to-face group interviewing, mailed or self-administered questionnaires, and telephone surveys. Interviewing can be structured, semistructured, or unstructured. It can be used for marketing purposes, to gather political opinions, for therapeutic reasons, or to produce data for academic analysis. It can be used for the purpose of measurement or its scope can be the understanding of an individual or a group perspective. An interview can be a one-time, brief exchange, say five minutes over the telephone, or it can take place over multiple, lengthy sessions, sometimes spanning days, as in life-history interviewing.

In this chapter we briefly outline the history of interviewing before turning to a discussion of the academic uses of interviewing. Although the focus of this volume is qualitative methodology, in order to illustrate the full import of interviewing we need to discuss the major types of interviewing—structured, group, and unstructured—as well as other ways to conduct interviews. Next, we address in detail the various elements of qualitative interviewing. We then discuss some problems of gender as it relates to interviewing, as well as issues of interpretation and reporting. Finally, we broach some considerations related to ethical issues.

◆ The History of Interviewing

Some form or another of interviewing has been with us for a very long time, as even ancient Egyptians conducted censuses of their population (Babbie, 1992). In recent times, the tradition of interviewing has been twofold. Interviewing found great popularity and widespread use in clinical diagnosis and counseling, where the concern was on the quality of the response, and later, during World War I, interviewing came to be widely employed in psychological testing, with an emphasis on measurement (Maccoby & Maccoby, 1954).

The individual generally credited with being the first to develop a social survey relying on interviewing was Charles Booth (see Converse, 1987). In 1886, Booth embarked on a comprehensive survey of the economic and social conditions of the people of London; this survey was later published as *Life and Labour of the People in London* (1902-1903). In this early study, Booth embodied what were to become separate interviewing methods; he not only implemented survey research but triangulated his work by relying on unstructured interviews and ethnographic observations

> The data were checked and supplemented by visits to many neighborhoods, streets and homes, and by conferences with various welfare and community leaders. From time to time Booth lived as a lodger in districts where he was not known, so that he could become more intimately acquainted with the lives and habits of the poorer classes. (Parten, 1950, pp. 6-7)

Many other surveys of London and other English cities followed, patterned after Booth's example. In the United States similar work ensued. Among others, an 1885 study attempted to do in Chicago what Booth had done in London (see Converse, 1987) and, in 1896, admittedly following Booth's lead, the American sociologist W. E. B. Du Bois studied the black population of Philadelphia (see Du Bois, 1899). Surveys of cities and small towns followed; most notable among them were R. S. Lynd and H. M. Lynd's *Middletown* (1929) and *Middletown in Transition* (1937).

Opinion polling was another early form of interviewing. Some took place well before the turn of the century, but this form really came into its own in 1935 with the founding of the American Institute of Public Opinion by George Gallup. Preceding Gallup, both in psychology and in sociology, in the 1920s there was a movement toward the study (and usually measurement) of attitudes. W. I. Thomas and Florian Znaniecki used the documentary method to introduce the study of attitudes in social psychology. Thomas's influence, along with that of Robert Park, sparked a number of community studies at the University of Chicago that came to be known collectively as the works of the Chicago school. Although researchers from the Chicago school are reputed to have used the ethnographic method in their inquiries, some scholars disagree and have noted that many of the Chicago school studies lacked the analytic component of modern-day ethnography and thus are, at best, "first hand descriptive studies" (Harvey, 1987, p. 50). Regardless of the correct label for the Chicagoans' fieldwork, they clearly relied on a combination of observation, personal documents, and informal interviews in their studies. Interviews were especially in evidence in the work of Thrasher (1927), who, in his study of gang members, relied primarily on about 130 qualitative interviews, and in that of Nels Anderson (1923), whose classic study of hoboes relied on informal, in-depth conversations.

While it was left to Howard Becker and Everett Hughes to formalize and give impetus to sociological ethnography in the 1950s and 1960s, interviewing began to lose both the eclectic flavor given to it by Charles Booth and the qualitative accent of the Chicagoans. Understanding gang members or hoboes through interviews lost importance; what became relevant was the use of interviewing in survey research as a tool to quantify data. This was not new; opinion polls and market research had been doing it for years. But during World War II there was a tremendous increase in survey research, as the U.S. armed forces hired great numbers of sociologists as survey researchers. More than half a million American soldiers were interviewed in one manner or another (Young, 1966), and their mental and emotional lives were reported in a four-volume survey, *Studies in Social Psychology in World War II.* The research for the first two volumes of this study, titled *The American Soldier,* was directed by Samuel Stouffer. This work had tremendous impact and led the way to a widespread use of systematic survey research.

What was new, however, was that quantitative survey research was to move into academia and come to dominate sociology for the next three decades. An Austrian immigrant, Paul Lazarsfeld, spearheaded this move. He welcomed *The American Soldier* with great enthusiasm. In fact, Robert Merton and Lazarsfeld (1950) edited a book of reflections on *The American Soldier.* Lazarsfeld moved to Columbia in 1940, taking with him his market research and other applied grants, and became instrumental in the directing of the Bureau of Applied Social Research. Two other "survey organizations" were also formed: In 1941, Harry Field began the National Opinion Research Center, first at Denver and then at Chicago; and in 1946, Likert and his group founded the Survey Research Center at Michigan.

Academia at the time was dominated by theoretical concerns, and there was some resistance to this applied, numerically based, kind of sociology. Sociologists and other humanists were critical of Lazarsfeld and the other survey researchers. Herbert Blumer, C. Wright Mills, Arthur Schlesinger, Jr., and Pitirin Sorokin, among others, voiced their displeasure, as reported by Converse (1987):

- Sorokin: "The new emphasis on quantitative work was obsessive, and he called the new practitioners 'quantophrenics'—with special reference to Stouffer and Lazarsfeld" (p. 253).
- Mills: "Those in the grip of the methodological inhibition often refuse to say anything about modern society unless it has been through the fine little mill of the Statistical Ritual" (p. 252).
- Schlesinger: "[They are] social relations huck- sters" (p. 253).

But the survey researchers had powerful allies also, such as Merton, who joined the Survey Center at Columbia in 1943, and government monies were becoming increasing available for survey research. The 1950s saw the growth of survey research in the universities and a proliferation of survey research texts. Gradually, survey research increased its domain over sociology, culminating in 1960 with the election of Lazarsfeld to the presidency of the American Sociological Association. The methodological dominance of survey research continued unabated through the 1970s and 1980s and into the 1990s, although other methods began to erode the prominence of survey research.

Qualitative interviewing continued to be practiced, hand in hand with participant observation methods, but it too assumed some of the quantifiable scientific rigor that so preoccupied survey research. This was especially visible in grounded theory (Glaser & Strauss, 1967), with its painstaking emphasis on coding data, and in ethnomethodology, with its quest for invariant properties of social action (Cicourel, 1970), albeit ethnomethodology was critical of interviewing and its assumptions, especially the fact that interactants act "as if" they understand each other, while instead relying on glosses to "fill gaps" in understanding (Cicourel, 1964; Garfinkel, 1967). Other qualitative researchers suggested variations. John Lofland (1971) criticized grounded theory for paying little attention to data gathering techniques; Jack Douglas (1985) suggested lengthy, existential one-on-one interviews lasting one or more days; and James Spradley (1980) stressed the importance of sequencing in both ethnographic observation and ethnographic interviewing.

Recently, postmodernist ethnographers have concerned themselves with some of the assumptions and moral problems present in interviewing and with the controlling role of the interviewer. These concerns have led to new directions in qualitative interviewing, focusing on increased attention to the voices and feelings of the respondents (Marcus & Fischer, 1986) and the interviewer-respondent relation (Crapanzano, 1980). The importance of the researcher's gender in interviewing (Gluck & Patai, 1991) has also come to the fore in feminist/postmodernist studies, as has the issue of race (Stanfield, 1985). Both have further problematized concerns about membership and understanding in interviewing. On a less positive note, it must be mentioned that the interview has become a commodity in popular culture (and sports). Thus celebrities such as Bob Dylan and John Lennon (Wenner, 1992) or Charles Barkley (Montville, 1993) become objectified, living (or dead but nostalgic) commodities in a media market.

51

◆ Structured Interviewing

Structured interviewing refers to a situation in which an interviewer asks each respondent a series of preestablished questions with a limited set of response categories. There is generally little room for variation in response except where an infrequent open-ended question may be used. The responses are also recorded by the interviewer according to a coding scheme that has already been established by the project director or research supervisor. The interviewer controls the pace of the interview by treating the questionnaire as if it were a theatrical script to be followed in a standardized and straightforward manner. Thus all respondents receive the same set of questions, asked in the same order or sequence, by an interviewer who has been trained to treat every interview situation in a like manner. There is very little flexibility in the way questions are asked or answered in the structured interview setting. Instructions to interviewers often include some of the following guidelines:

- Never get involved in long explanations of the study; use standard explanation provided by supervisor.
- Never deviate from the study introduction, sequence of questions, or question wording.
- Never let another person interrupt the interview; do not let another person answer for the respondent or offer his or her opinions on the question.
- Never suggest an answer or agree or disagree with an answer. Do not give the respondent any idea of your personal views on the topic of the question or survey.
- Never interpret the meaning of a question; just repeat the question and give instructions or clarifications that are provided in training or by supervisors.
- Never improvise, such as by adding answer categories, or make wording changes.

Interviews by telephone, face-to-face interviews in households, intercept interviews in shopping malls and parks, or the interviews generally associated with survey research are most likely to be included in this category.

This interview context calls for the interviewer to play a neutral role, never interjecting his or her opinions of the respondent's answers. The interviewer is to establish what has been called "balanced rapport"; he or she must be, on the one hand, casual and friendly but, on the other hand, directive and impersonal. The interviewer must perfect a style of "interested listening" that rewards the respondent's participation but does not evaluate the responses (Converse & Schuman, 1974).

The guidelines set forth above are intended to produce an ideal interview, but in practice this does not happen. Errors occur, and they commonly evolve from three sources: (a) respondent behavior, as when the respondent gives a "socially desirable" response to please the interviewer or omits relevant information to hide something from the interviewer (Bradburn, 1983); (b) the type of questionnaire (face-to-face or telephone) or the wording of the questions; and (c) an interviewer with flawed questioning techniques, or who changes the wording of the interview (Bradburn, Sudman, & Associates, 1979; Frey, 1989; Peneff, 1988).

The predetermined nature of structured interviewing is aimed at minimizing errors. However, structured interviewers are aware that interviews take place in a social interaction context, and they are influenced by that context. As Converse and Schuman (1974) observe, "There is no single interview style that fits every occasion or all respondents" (p. 53). This means that interviewers must be aware of respondent differences and must be flexible enough to make proper adjustments for unanticipated developments.

It is not enough to understand the mechanics of interviewing; it is also important to understand the respondent's world and forces that might stimulate or retard response (Kahn & Cannell, 1957). Still, the structured interview proceeds under a stimulus-response format, assuming that if questions (previously determined to elicit adequate indicators of the variable under examination) are phrased correctly, the respondent will answer them truthfully. Such an interviewing style often elicits rational responses, but it overlooks or inadequately assesses the emotional dimension.

◆ Group Interviews

There is a developing form of interviewing that can be implemented in structured, semistructured, or unstructured format and that is gaining some popularity among social scientists. It is the group interview, or the systematic questioning of several individuals simultaneously in formal or informal settings (Frey & Fontana, in press). The use of the group interview is not meant to replace individual interviewing, but it is an option that deserves consideration because it can provide another level of data gathering or a perspective on the research problem not available through individual interviews.

Group interviewing has ordinarily been associated with marketing research, where the "focus group" has been used for some time to gather consumer opinions on product characteristics, advertising themes, and service delivery. This format has also been used to a considerable extent by political parties and candidates who are interested in voter reactions to issues and policies. The group interview has also been used in sociological research. Bogardus (1926) used groups to test his social distance scale, Zuckerman (1972) interviewed Nobel laureates, Thompson and Demerath (1952) looked at management problems in the military, Morgan and Spanish (1984) studied health issues, and Merton and his associates studied the impact of propaganda using group interviews. In fact, Merton, Fiske, and Kendall (1956) coined the term "focus group" to apply to a situation in which the interviewer asks group members very specific questions about a topic after considerable research has already been completed. There is some evidence that established anthropologists such as Malinowski used this technique, even though it was not reported (Frey & Fontana, 1991). Blumer (1969) also notes the importance of interviewing a select group; he mentions "seeking participants . . . who are acute observers and who are well informed. . . . A small number of such individuals brought together as a discussion and resource group, is more valuable many times over than any representative sample" (p. 41). Blumer (1967) used this method in the Oakland drug study. Today, group interviews in general are generically designated "focus group" interviews, even though there is considerable variation in the natures and types of group interviews.

The group interview is essentially a qualitative data gathering technique that finds the interviewer/moderator directing the interaction and inquiry in a very structured or very unstructured manner, depending on the interview's purpose. For instance, the purpose may be exploratory; the researcher may bring several persons together to test a methodological technique, to try out a definition of a research problem, or to identify key informants. An extension of the exploratory intent is the use of the group interview for the purpose of pretesting questionnaire wording, measurement scales, or other elements of a survey design. This is now quite common in survey research (Desvousges & Frey, 1989). Group interviews can also be used for triangulation (Denzin, 1989b) purposes or employed in conjunction with other data gathering techniques. Finally, phenomenological purposes are served where group interviews are conducted in an

TABLE 2.1 Type of Group Interviews and Dimensions

Type	Setting	Role of Interviewer	Question Format	Purpose
Focus group	formal-preset	directive	unstructured	exploratory pretest
Brainstorming	formal or informal	nondirective	very unstructured	exploratory
Nominal/Delphi	formal	directive	structured	pretest exploratory
Field, natural	informal spontaneous	moderately nondirective	very unstructured	exploratory phenomenological
Field, formal	preset, but in field	somewhat directive	semistructured	phenomenological

SOURCE: Frey and Fontana (in press).

unstructured way in the field. Table 2.1 compares the types of group interviews on various dimensions.

The skills required of a group interviewer are not significantly different from those needed by an interviewer of individuals. The interviewer must be flexible, objective, empathic, persuasive, a good listener, and so on. But the group does present some unusual problems. Merton et al. (1956) note three specific skills needed by the group interviewer: First, the interviewer must keep one person or a small coalition of persons from dominating the group; second, he or she must encourage recalcitrant respondents to participate; and third, he or she must obtain responses from the entire group to ensure the fullest possible coverage of the topic. In addition, the interviewer must balance the directive interviewer role with the role of moderator, which calls for the management of the dynamics of the group being interviewed: "The group interviewer must simultaneously worry about the script of questions and be sensitive to the evolving patterns of group interaction" (Frey & Fontana, in press).

The group interview has the advantages of being inexpensive, data rich, flexible, stimulating to respondents, recall aiding, and cumulative and elaborative, over and above individual responses. This type of interview is not, however, without problems. The emerging group culture may interfere with individual expression, the group may be dominated by one person, the group format makes it difficult to research sensitive topics, "group-think" is a possible outcome, and the requirements for interviewer skills are greater because of group dynamics. Nevertheless, the group interview is a viable option for both qualitative and quantitative research.

◆ Unstructured Interviewing

Unstructured interviewing provides a greater breadth than the other types, given its qualitative nature. In this section we will discuss the traditional type of unstructured interview: the open-ended ethnographic (in-depth) interview. Many qualitative researchers differentiate between in-depth (or ethnographic) interviewing and participant observation. Yet, as Lofland (1971) points out, the two go hand in hand, and many of the data gathered in participant observation come from informal interviewing in the field. Consider the following report, from Malinowski's (1989) diary:

> Saturday 8 [December 1917]. Got up late, felt rotten, took enema. At about 1 I went out; I heard cries; [people from] Kapwapu were bringing *uri* to Teyava. I sat with the natives, talked, took pictures. Went back. Billy corrected and supplemented my notes about *wasi*. At Teyava, an old man talked a great deal about fishes, but I did not understand him too well. Then we moved to his *bwayama*. Talked about *lili'u*. They kept questioning me about the war—In the evening I talked to the policeman about *bwaga'u*, *lili'u* and *yoyova*. I was irritated by their laughing. Billy again told me a number of interesting things. Took quinine and calomel. (p. 145)

Malinowski's "day in the field" shows how very important unstructured interviewing is in conducting fieldwork and clearly illustrates the difference between structured and unstructured interviewing. Malinowski has some general topics he wishes to know about, but he does not use closed-ended questions or a formal approach to interviewing. What's more, he commits (as most field-workers do) what structured interviewers would see as two "capital offenses": (a) He answers questions asked by the respondents, and (b) he lets his personal feelings influence him (as all field-workers do), and thus deviates from the "ideal" of a cool, distant, and rational interviewer.

Malinowski's example captures the differences between structured and unstructured interviewing. The former aims at capturing precise data of a codable nature in order to explain behavior within preestablished categories, whereas the latter is used in an attempt to understand the complex behavior of members of society without imposing any a priori categorization that may limit the field of inquiry. Indeed, Malinowski goes beyond any form of interviewing; he "immerses" himself in the native culture, letting it soak in by his mere interacting with the natives and "being there."

Spradley (1979) describes the following interviewer-respondent interaction, which would be unthinkable in traditional sociological circles yet is the very essence of unstructured interviewing—the establishment of a human-to-human relation with the respondent and the desire to *understand* rather than to *explain*:

> Presently she smiled, pressed her hand to her chest, and said: "Tsetchwe." It was her name. "Elizabeth," I said, pointing to myself. "Nisabe," she answered. . . . Then, having surely suspected that I was a woman, she put her hand on my breast gravely, and, finding out that I was, she touched her own breast. Many Bushmen do this; to them all Europeans look alike. "Tasu si" (women), she said. Then after a moment's pause Tsetchwe began to teach me. (pp. 3-4)

Spradley goes on to discuss all the things an interviewer learns from the natives about them, their culture, their language, their ways of life. Although each and every study is different, these are some of the basic elements of unstructured interviewing. These elements have been discussed in detail elsewhere, and we need not elaborate upon them too much (for detailed accounts of unstructured interviewing, see, among others, Adams & Preiss, 1960; Denzin, 1989b; Lofland, 1971; Spradley, 1979). Here we provide brief synopses; please remember that they are presented as heuristic devices, as every study uses slightly different elements and often in different combinations.

Accessing the Setting

How do we "get in"? This of course varies with the group one is attempting to study. One may have to disrobe and casually stroll in the nude if doing a study of nude beaches (Douglas & Rasmussen, 1977), or one may have to buy a huge motorcycle and frequent seedy bars in certain locations if attempting to befriend and study the Hell's Angels (Thompson, 1985). The different ways and attempts to "get in" vary tremendously, but they all share the common goal of gaining access to the setting. Sometimes there is no setting per se, as when one of the authors (Fontana, 1977) attempted to study poor elderly on the streets and had to gain access anew with each interviewee.

Understanding the Language
and Culture of the Respondents

Irwin Deutscher (1968) wrote a seminal article on problems of language (lexicon, syntax, and phoneme) and meaning. To emphasize and clarify some of the problematics of language, Deutscher addressed the difficult task of asking questions cross-culturally.

Rosalie Wax (1960) gives perhaps the most poignant description available of learning the language and culture of the respondents in her study of "disloyal" Japanese in concentration camps in the United States between 1943 and 1945. She had to overcome a number of language and cultural problems in her study. Respondents may be fluent in the language of the interviewer, but there are different ways of saying things, and, indeed, certain things should not be said at all, linking language and cultural manifestations. Wax (1960) makes this point:

> I remarked that I would like to see the letter. The silence that fell on the chatting group was almost palpable, and the embarrassment of the hosts was painful to see. The *faux pas* was not asking to see a letter, for letters were passed about rather freely. It rested on the fact that one did not give a Caucasian a letter in which the "disloyal" statement of a friend might be expressed. (p. 172)

Some researchers, especially in anthropological interviews, tend to rely on interpreters, and thus become vulnerable to an added layer of meanings, biases, and interpretations that may lead to disastrous misunderstanding (Freeman, 1983). At times, a specific jargon, such as the medical metalanguage of physicians, may be a code that is hard for nonmembers to understand.

Deciding on How to Present Oneself

Do we present ourselves as representatives from academia studying medical students (Becker, 1956)? Do we approach an interview as a woman-to-woman discussion (Spradley, 1979)? Do we "dress down" to look like the respondents (Fontana, 1977; Thompson, 1985)? Do we represent the colonial culture (Malinowski, 1922) or do we humbly present ourselves as "learners" (Wax, 1960)? The decision of how to present oneself is very important, because after one's presentational self is "cast" it leaves a profound impression on the respondents and has great influence on the success (or failure) of the study. Sometimes, inadvertently, the researcher's presentational self may be misrepresented, as John Johnson (1976) discovered in studying a welfare office, when some of the employees assumed he was a "spy" for management despite his best efforts to convince them of the contrary.

Locating an Informant

The researcher must find an insider, a member of the group studied, willing to be an informant and to act as a guide to and translator of cultural mores and, at times, jargon or language. Although interviews can be conducted without an informant, a researcher can save much time and avoid many mistakes if a good informant becomes available. The "classic" sociological informant is Doc in William Foote Whyte's *Street Corner Society* (1943). Without Doc's help and guidance, it is doubtful that Whyte would have been able to learn about his subjects to the level he did. Very instructive is Paul Rabinow's (1977) discussion of his relation with his main informant, Abd al-Malik ben Lahcen. Malik acted as a translator but also provided Rabinow with access to the cultural ways of the subjects, and by his actions provided insights for Rabinow to the vast differences between a University of Chicago researcher and a native Moroccan.

Gaining Trust

Survey researchers asking respondents whether or not they would favor the establishment of a nuclear dump in their state (Frey, 1993) do not have too much work to do in the way of gaining trust; respondents have opinions about nuclear dumps and are very willing to express them, sometimes forcefully. But what about asking respondents about their frequency of sexual intercourse or their preferred birth-control practices? That is clearly a different story, and one needs to establish some trust with such respondents (Cicourel, 1974). Paul Rasmussen (1989) had to spend months as a "wallflower" in the waiting room of a massage parlor before any of the masseuses gained enough trust in him to divulge to him, in unstructured interviews, the nature of their "massage" relations with clients. Gaining trust is essential to an interviewer's success, and even once it is gained trust

59

can be very fragile indeed; any *faux pas* by the researcher may destroy days, weeks, or months of painstakingly gained trust.

Establishing Rapport

Because the goal of unstructured interviewing is *understanding,* it becomes paramount for the researcher to establish rapport. He or she must be able to put him- or herself in the role of the respondents and attempt to see the situation from their perspective, rather than impose the world of academia and preconceptions upon them. Close rapport with respondents opens doors to more informed research, but it may also create problems, as the researcher may become a spokesperson for the group studied, losing his or her distance and objectivity, or may "go native" and become a member of the group and forgo the academic role. At times, what the researcher may feel is good rapport turns out not to be, as Thompson (1985) found out in a nightmarish way when he was subjected to a brutal beating by the Hell's Angels just as his study of them was coming to a close. At the other end of the spectrum, some researchers may never feel they have good rapport with subjects; for example, Malinowski (1989) always mistrusted the motives of the natives and at times was troubled by what he saw as their brutish sensuality or angered by their outright lying or deception: "After lunch I [carried] yellow calico and spoke about the *baloma.* I made a small *sagali,* Navavile. I was *fed up* with the *niggers*" (p. 154).

Collecting Empirical Materials

Being out in the field does not afford one the luxury of videotapes, soundproof rooms, and high-quality recording equipment. Lofland (1971) provides detailed information on doing and writing up interviews and on the types of field notes one ought to take and how to organize them. Yet often one must make do; the "tales" of field-workers' attempts to make field notes range from holding a miniature tape recorder as inconspicuously as possible to taking mental notes and then rushing to the privacy of a bathroom to jot them down, on toilet paper at times. We agree with Lofland (1971) that regardless of the circumstances one ought to (a) take notes regularly and promptly; (b) write everything down, no matter how unimportant it may seem at the time; (c) try to be as inconspicuous as possible in note taking; and (d) analyze one's notes frequently.

◆ Other Types of Unstructured Interviewing

We will consider the issue of interpreting and reporting empirical materials later in this chapter. Now we will briefly outline some different types of unstructured interviews.

Oral History

The oral history does not differ from the unstructured interview methodologically, but in purpose. Oral collection of historical material goes back to ancient days, although its modern formal organization can be traced to 1948, when Allan Nevins began the Oral History Project at Columbia University (Starr, 1984, p. 4). Oral history captures a variety of people's lives, from common folks talking about their jobs, as in Studs Terkel's *Working* (1975), to historical recollections of famous people, such as President Harry Truman in Merle Miller's *Plain Speaking* (see Starr, 1984). Often, oral history transcripts are not published but may be found in libraries, silent memoirs awaiting someone to rummage through them and bring their testimony to life.

Often oral history is a way to reach groups and individuals who have been ignored, oppressed, and/or forgotten. A classic example is the work of Lomax and Lomax (1934/1966), who used ballads and folk songs as verbal expressions and cultural commentaries on "the cowboy, the miner, the tramp, the lumberjack, the Forty-niner, the soldier, the sailor, the Plantation Negro" (p. xxvii). Also, the forgotten people involved in the Vietnam War—blacks (Terry, 1984) and women (Fontana & Collins, 1993; Marshall, 1987)—have been brought to the fore through their personal accounts.

Recently, oral history has found popularity among feminists (Gluck & Patai, 1991) as a way to understand and bring forth the history of women in a culture that has traditionally relied on a masculine interpretation: "Refusing to be rendered historically voiceless any longer, women are creating a new history—using our own voices and experiences" (Gluck, 1984, p. 222). The attempt continues, through the use of oral history to reconnect to the women missing in history and the women who are missing in their own histories, to capture the work of women, the lives and experiences of women, and the social and personal meanings of women (Gluck & Patai, 1991; Reinharz, 1992).

Creative Interviewing

Close to oral history but used more conventionally as a sociological tool is Jack Douglas's (1985) "creative interviewing." Douglas argues against the "how-to" ways to conduct interviews because unstructured interviews take place in the largely situational everyday world of members of society. Thus interviewing and interviewers must necessarily be creative, forget "how-to" rules, and adapt themselves to the ever-changing situations they face. Like oral historians, Douglas sees interviewing as collecting oral reports from the members of society. These reports go well beyond the length of conventional unstructured interviews and may become "life histories," taking multiple sessions over many days with the subject(s). "Forgetting the rules" in creative interviewing allows research subjects to express themselves more freely, and thus to have a greater voice both in the research process and in the research report.

Postmodern Interviewing

Douglas's concern with the important role played by the interviewer *qua* human being, which is also shared by the feminist oral historians, became a paramount element of postmodern anthropologists and sociologists in the mid-1980s. Marcus and Fischer (1986) address ethnography at large, but their discussion is very germane to unstructured interviewing because, as we have seen, it constitutes the major way of collecting data in fieldwork. Marcus and Fischer voice reflexive concerns about the ways in which the researcher influences the study, in both the methods of data collection and the techniques of reporting findings; this concern leads to new ways to conduct interviews in the hope of minimizing the interviewer's influence. This influence, of course, cannot be eliminated, but it can be neutralized if its assumptions and premises are made as clear as possible.

One way to do this is through *polyphonic* interviewing, in which the voices of the subjects are recorded with minimal influence from the researcher and are not collapsed together and reported as one, through the interpretation of the researcher. Instead, the multiple perspectives of the various subjects are reported and differences and problems encountered are discussed, rather than glossed over (see Krieger, 1983). *Interpretive* interactionism follows in the footsteps of creative and polyphonic interviewing, but, borrowing from James Joyce, adds a new element, that of epiphanies, described as "those interactional moments that leave marks on people's lives [and] have the potential for creating transformational experiences for the person" (Denzin, 1989a, p. 15). Thus the topic of inquiry becomes dramatized by the focus on existential moments in people's lives, producing richer and more meaningful data. *Critical ethnography* (and interviewing) (Giroux, 1992; Lincoln & Guba, 1985) relies on critical theory; it is ethnography that accounts for the historical, social, and economical situations. Critical ethnographers realize the strictures caused by these situations and their value-laden agendas. Critical ethnographers see themselves as blue-collar "cultural workers" (Giroux, 1992) attempting to broaden the political dimensions of cultural work while undermining existing oppressive systems. Finally, as postmodernists seek new ways of understanding and reporting data, some are combining visual and written modes of communication. Ulmer (1989) introduces the concept of *oralysis*, "referring to the ways in which oral forms, derived from everyday life, are, with the recording powers of video, applied to the analytical tasks associated with literate forms" (p. xi). In oralysis, the traditional product of interviewing, talk, is coupled with the visual, providing, according to Ulmer, a product more consonant with a society that is dominated by the medium of television. Becker (1981) also engages in visual/written sociological commentaries, as does Douglas Harper (1982). The journal *Visual Sociology* is devoted to such commentaries.

◆ Gendered Interviews

> The housewife goes into a well-stocked store to look for a frying pan. Her thinking probably does not proceed exactly this way, but it is helpful to think of the many possible two-way choices she might make: Cast iron or aluminum? Thick or thin? Metal or wooden handle? Covered or not? Deep or shallow? Large or small? This brand or that? Reasonable or too high in price? To buy or not? Cash or charge? Have it delivered or carry it. . . . The two-way question is simplicity itself when it comes to recording answers and tabulating them. (Payne, 1951, pp. 55-56)

This quote represents the prevalent paternalistic attitude toward women in interviewing (see Oakley, 1981, p. 39) as well as the paradigmatic concern with coding answers and therefore presenting limited, dichotomous choices. Apart from a tendency to be condescending toward women, the traditional interview paradigm does not account for gendered differences. In fact, Babbie's classic text *The Practice of Social Research* (1992) briefly references gender only three times and says nothing about the influence of gender on interviews. As Ann Oakley (1981) cogently points out, both the interviewers and the respondents are considered faceless and invisible, and they must be if the paradigmatic assumption of gathering value-free data is to be maintained. Yet, as Denzin (1989a, p. 116) tells us, "gender filters knowledge"; that is, the sex of the interviewer and of the respondent does make a difference, as the interview takes place within the cultural boundaries of a paternalistic social system in which masculine identities are differentiated from feminine ones.

In typical interviews there exists a hierarchical relation, with the respondent being in the subordinate position. The interviewer is instructed to be courteous, friendly, and pleasant:

> The interviewer's manner should be friendly, courteous, conversational and unbiased. He should be neither too grim nor too effusive; neither too talkative nor too timid. The idea should be to put the respondent at ease, *so that he will talk freely and fully.* (Selltiz, Jahoda, Deutsch, & Cook, 1965, p. 576; emphasis added)

Yet, as the last above-quoted line shows, this demeanor is a ruse to gain the trust and confidence of the respondent without reciprocating in any way. Interviewers are not to give their own opinions and are to evade direct questions. What seems to be a conversation is really a one-way pseudoconversation, raising the ethical dilemma (Fine, 1983-1984) of studying people for opportunistic reasons. When the respondent is female the interview presents added problems, because the preestablished format directed at information relevant for the study tends both to ignore the respondent's own concerns and to curtail any attempts to digress and elaborate. This format also stymies any revelation of personal feelings and emotions.

Warren (1988) discusses problems of gender in both anthropological and sociological fieldwork, and many of them apply to the ethnographic interview. Some of these problems are the traditional ones of entrée and trust, which may be heightened by the sex of the interviewer, especially in highly sex-segregated societies: "I never witnessed any ceremonies that were barred to women. Whenever I visited compounds I sat with the women while the men gathered in the parlors or in front of the compound. . . . I never entered any of the places where men sat around to drink beer or palm wine and to chat" (Sudarkasa, 1986; quoted in Warren, 1988, p. 16).

Solutions to the problem have been to view the female anthropologist as androgyne or to grant her honorary male status for the duration of her research. Warren (1988) points to some advantages of being female and therefore seen as harmless or invisible; Hanna Papanek (1964) addresses the greater role flexibility of women interviewers in countries where women are secluded. Other problems concern the researcher's status or race and the context of the interview; again, these problems are magnified for female researchers in a paternalistic world. Female interviewers at times face the added burden of sexual overtures or covert sexual hassle (Warren, 1988, p. 33), or are considered low-status strangers (Daniels, 1967).

Feminist researchers have suggested ways to circumvent the traditional interviewing paradigm. It has been suggested that interviewing is a masculine paradigm (Oakley, 1981), embedded in a masculine culture and stressing masculine traits while at the same time excluding from interviewing traits such as sensitivity, emotionality, and others that are culturally viewed as feminine.

There is a growing reluctance, especially among female researchers (Oakley, 1981; Reinharz, 1992; Smith, 1987), to continue interviewing women as "objects," with little or no regard for them as individuals. Whereas this reluctance stems from moral and ethical issues, it is also very relevant methodologically. As Oakley (1981) points out, in interviewing there is "no intimacy without reciprocity" (p. 49). Thus the emphasis is shifting to allow the development of a closer relation between interviewer and respondent, attempting to minimize status differences and doing away with the traditional hierarchical situation in interviewing. Interviewers can show their human side and answer questions and express feelings. Methodologically, this new approach provides a greater spectrum of responses and a greater insight into respondents—or "participants," to avoid the hierarchical pitfall (Reinharz, 1992, p. 22)—because it encourages them to control the sequencing and the language of the interview and also allows them the freedom of open-ended responses (Oakley, 1981; Reinharz, 1992; Smith, 1987). Thus: "Women were always . . . encouraged to 'digress' into details of their personal histories and to recount anecdotes of their working lives. Much important information was gathered in this way" (Yeandle, 1984; quoted in Rienharz, 1992, p. 25).

This commitment to maintaining the integrity of the phenomena and preserving the viewpoint of the subjects as expressed in their everyday language is akin to phenomenological and existential sociologies (Douglas & Johnson, 1977; Kotarba & Fontana, 1984) and also reflects the concern of postmodern ethnographers (Marcus & Fischer, 1986). The differences are (a) the heightened moral concern for subjects/participants; (b) the attempt to redress the male-female hierarchy and existing paternalistic power structure; (c) the paramount importance placed upon membership, as the effectiveness of male researchers in interviewing female subjects has been largely discredited; and (d) the realization that the old "distanced" style of interviewing cuts the subjects' involvement drastically and, thus, rather than giving us an "objective" interview, gives us a one-sided and therefore inaccurate picture.

Some feminist sociologists have gone beyond the concern with interviewing or fieldwork in itself. Laurel Richardson (1992) is striving for new forms of expression to report findings and has presented some of her fieldwork in the form of poetry. Patricia Clough (1992) questions the whole enterprise of fieldwork under the current paradigm and calls for a reassessment of the whole sociological enterprise and for a rereading of existing sociological texts in a light that is not marred by paternalistic bias. These researchers' voices echo the concern of Dorothy Smith (1987), who eloquently states:

> The problem [of a research project] and its particular solution are analogous to those by which fresco painters solved the problems of representing the different temporal moments of a story in the singular space of the wall. The problem is to produce in a two-dimensional space framed as a wall a world of action and movement in time. (p. 281)

◆ Framing and Interpreting Interviews

Besides the problem of framing real-life events in a two-dimensional space, we face the added problems of how the framing is being done and who is doing the framing. In sociological terms this means that the type of interviewing selected, the techniques used, the ways of recording information, all come to bear on the results of the study. Additionally, data must be interpreted and the researcher has a great deal of influence on what part of the data will be reported and how it will be reported.

Framing Interviews

There have been numerous volumes published on the techniques of structured interviewing (see, among others, Babbie, 1992; Bradburn et al., 1979; Gorden, 1980; Kahn & Cannell, 1957). There is also a voluminous literature on group interviewing, especially in marketing and survey research (for an up-to-date review of literature in this area, see Stewart & Shamdasani, 1990). Recently, the uses of group interviewing have been linked to qualitative sociology also (Frey & Fontana, in press; Morgan, 1988). Unstructured interviewing techniques have been covered abundantly (Denzin, 1989b; Lofland, 1971; Lofland & Lofland, 1984; Spradley, 1979). Also noteworthy is Kuhn's article "The Interview and the Professional Relationship" (1962), in which he considers interview as a "performance" and warns against "mystification," or loss of sincerity in the interview by attempting to overmanage it.

As we have noted, unstructured interviews vary widely, given their informal nature and the nature of the setting, and some eschew any preestablished set of techniques (Douglas, 1985). Yet, there are techniques involved in interviewing, whether one is just being "a nice person" or is following a format. Techniques can be varied to meet various situations, and varying one's techniques is known as employing tactics. Traditional techniques tell us that the researcher is involved in an informal conversation with the respondent, thus he or she must maintain a tone of "friendly" chat while trying to remain close to the guidelines of the topics of inquiry he or she has in mind. The researcher begins by "breaking the ice" with general questions and gradually moves on to more specific ones, while also, as inconspicuously as possible, asking questions intended to check the veracity of statements made by the respondent. The researcher, again according to traditional techniques, should avoid getting involved in a "real" conversation in which he or she answers questions asked by the respondent or provides personal opinions on the matters discussed. One avoids "getting trapped" by shrugging off the relevance of one's opinions (e.g., "It doesn't matter how I feel, it's your opinion that's important") or by feigning ignorance (e.g., "I really don't know enough about this to say anything—you're the expert"). Of course, as noted in the above discussion on gendered interviewing, the researcher may reject these outdated techniques and "come down" to the level of the respondent and engage in a "real" conversation with "give and take" and empathic understanding (see Daniels, 1983). This makes the interview more honest, morally sound, and reliable, because it treats the respondent as an equal, allows him or her to express personal feelings, and therefore presents a more "realistic" picture than can be uncovered using traditional interview methods.

The use of language and specific terms is very important for creating a "sharedness of meanings" in which both interviewer and respondent understand the contextual nature of the interview. For instance, in studying nude beaches, Douglas and Rasmussen (1977) discovered that the term "nude beach virgin" had nothing to do with chastity, but referred to the fact that a person's buttocks were white, thus indicating to others that he or she was a newcomer to the nude beach. Language is also important in delineating the type of question (broad, narrow, leading, instructive, and so on). Unstructured conversation, mere chitchat, listening to others without taking notes or trying to direct the conversation is also important to establish rapport and immerse oneself in the situation, while gathering a store of "tacit knowledge" about the people and the culture being studied (see our discussion of Malinowski above).

Nonverbal elements are also important in interviewing. There are basically four kinds of nonverbal technique:

> *Proxemic* communication is the use of interpersonal space to communicate attitudes, *chronemics* communication is the use of pacing of speech and length of silence in conversation, *kinesic* communication includes any body movements or postures, and *paralinguistic* communication includes all the variations in volume, pitch and quality of voice. (Gorden, 1980, p. 335)

All of these are very important for the researcher and the researched alike, because nonverbal communication both informs and sets the tone for the interview. Looks, body postures, long silences, the way one dresses—all are significant in the interactional interview situation. Goffman (1959, 1971) has explored in detail the importance of nonverbal features in interaction as well as the consonance between verbal and nonverbal features. An amusing example of the wrong use of nonverbal communication is provided by Thompson (1985). Because he was attempting to be allowed to study the Hell's Angels as a participant observer, he began to frequent their hangouts, dress the part, and speak the proper jargon. He even bought a motorcycle—however, he got into trouble by buying a British model; he had failed to realize that for true-blue Angels, only a Harley-Davidson will do.

Finally, techniques vary with the group being interviewed. One will need a different approach for interviewing children (Fine & Sandstrom, 1988) from that required for interviewing widows (Lopata, 1980); drug dealers will not wish to be interviewed at all (Adler, 1985). The researcher must adapt to the world of the individuals studied and try to share their concerns and outlooks. Only by doing so can he or she learn anything at all. As Patricia Adler (1985) slowly and painfully discovered, it is not easy to gain the trust of drug dealers so that they will allow you to interview them.

Interpreting Interviews

Many studies using unstructured interviews are not reflexive enough about the interpreting process; common platitudes proclaim that data speak for themselves, that the researcher is neutral, unbiased, and "invisible." Data reported tend to flow nicely, there are no contradictory data and no mention of what data were excluded and/or why. Improprieties never happen and the main concern seems to be the proper, if unreflexive, filing, analyzing, and reporting of events. But anyone who has engaged in fieldwork knows better; no matter how organized the researcher may be, he or she slowly becomes buried under a growing mountain of field notes, transcripts, newspaper clippings, and tape recordings. Traditionally, readers were presented with the researcher's interpretation of the data, cleaned and streamlined and collapsed in rational, noncontradictory accounts. More recently, sociologists have come to grips with the reflexive, problematic, and, at times, contradictory nature of data and with the tremendous, if unspoken, influence of the researcher as an author (see Dickens & Fontana, 1994; Geertz, 1988). What Van Maanen (1988) calls "confessional style" began in earnest in the 1970s (see Johnson, 1976) and has continued unabated to the present day, in a soul cleansing by researchers of problematic feelings and sticky situations in the field. Although perhaps somewhat overdone at times, these "confessions" are very valuable, as they make readers aware of the complex and cumbersome nature of interviewing people in their natural settings and lend a tone of realism and veracity to studies: "Yesterday I slept very late. Got up around 10. The day before I had engaged Omaga, Koupa, and a few others. They didn't come. Again I fell into a rage" (Malinowski, 1967/1989, p. 67).

Showing the human side of the researcher and the problems of unstructured interviewing has taken new forms in deconstructionism (Derrida, 1976), where the influence of the author is brought under scrutiny. The text created by the rendition of events by the researcher is "deconstructed," as his or her biases and taken-for-granted notions are exposed and, at times, alternative ways to look at the data are introduced (Clough, 1992).

Postmodern social researchers, as we have seen, attempt to expose and openly acknowledge the role of the researcher *qua* field-worker and *qua* author. Thus, for instance, Crapanzano (1980) reports Tuhami's accounts, whether they be sociohistorical renditions, dreams, or outright lies, because they all constitute parts of his Morrocan Arab subject's sense of self and personal history. In interviewing Tuhami, Crapanzano learns not only about his subject but about himself:

> As Tuhami's interlocutor, I became an active participant in his life history, even though I rarely appear directly in his recitations. Not only did my presence, and my questions, prepare him for the text he was to produce, but they produced what I read as a change of consciousness in him. They produced a change of consciousness in me too. We were both jostled from our assumptions about the nature of the everyday world and ourselves and groped for common reference points within this limbo of interchange. (p. 11)

No longer pretending to be faceless subject and invisible researcher, Tuhami and Crapanzano are portrayed as individual human beings with their own personal histories and idiosyncrasies, and we, the readers, learn about two people and two cultures.

◆ Ethical Considerations

Because the objects of inquiry in interviewing are human beings, extreme care must be taken to avoid any harm to them. Traditional ethical concerns have revolved around the topics of *informed consent* (consent received from the subject after he or she has been carefully and truthfully informed about the research), *right to privacy* (protecting the identity of the subject) and *protection from harm* (physical, emotional, or any other kind). Whereas no sociologist or other social scientist would dismiss these three concerns as trivial, there are other ethical concerns that are less unanimously upheld. The controversy over overt/covert fieldwork is more germane to participant observation, but could include the surreptitious use of tape-recording devices. Warwick and Douglas, for instance, argue for the use of covert methods because they mirror the deceitfulness of everyday-life reality, whereas others, such as Kai Erikson, are vehemently opposed to the study of uninformed subjects (see Punch, 1986).

Another problematic issue stems from the degree of involvement on the part of the researcher with the group under study. Whyte was asked to vote illegally (to vote more than once) during local elections by the members of the group he had gained access to and befriended, gaining their trust. He used "situational ethics," and judged the legal infraction to be minor in comparison to the loss of his fieldwork if he refused to vote as he was asked. Thompson was faced with a more serious possible legal breach. He was terrified of having to witness one of the alleged rapes for which the Hell's Angels have become notorious, but, as he reports, none took place during his research. The most famous, and probably most widely discussed, case of questionable ethics in qualitative sociology is Laud Humphreys's research for *Tearoom Trade* (1970). Humphreys studied homosexual encounters in public restrooms in parks ("tearooms") by acting as a lookout ("watchqueen"). This fact in itself may be seen as ethically incorrect, but it is the following one that has raised many academic eyebrows. Unable to interview the men in the "tearooms," Humphreys recorded their car license plate numbers, which he used to trace the men to their residences. He then changed his appearance and interviewed many of the men in their homes, without being recognized.

Another ethical problem is raised by those who question the veracity of reports made by researchers. For example, Whyte's (1943) famous study of Italian men in Boston has recently come under severe scrutiny (Boelen, 1992), as some have alleged that he portrayed the "Corner Boys" in demeaning ways that did not reflect their visions of themselves. Whyte's case is still unresolved, but it does illustrate the delicate issue of ethical decisions in the field and in reporting field notes, even some 50-odd years later!

A growing number of scholars, as we have seen (Oakley, 1981), feel that most of traditional in-depth interviewing is unethical, whether wittingly or unwittingly, and we agree wholeheartedly. The techniques and tactics of interviewing are really ways of manipulating respondents while treating them as objects or numbers rather than individual human beings. Should the quest for objectivity supersede the human side of those whom we study? Consider the following experience that one of us had:

> One day while doing research at the convalescent center, I was talking to one of the aides while she was beginning to change the bedding of one of

the patients who had urinated and soaked the bed. He was the old, blind, ex-wrestler confined in the emergency room. Suddenly, the wrestler decided he was not going to cooperate with the aide and began striking violently at the air about him, fortunately missing the aide. Since nobody else was around, I had no choice but to hold the patient pinned down to the bed while the aide proceeded to change the bedding. It was not pleasant: The patient was squirming and yelling horrible threats at the top of his voice; the acid smell of urine was nauseating; I was slowly losing my grip on the much stronger patient, while all along feeling horribly like Chief Bromden when he suffocates the lobotomized Mac Murphy in Ken Kesey's novel. *But there was no choice, one just could not sit back and take notes while the patient tore apart the aide.* (Fontana, 1977, p. 187; emphasis added)

Clearly, as we move forward with sociology, we cannot, to paraphrase what Herbert Blumer said so many years ago, let the methods dictate our images of human beings. As Punch (1986) suggests, as field-workers we need to exercise common sense and moral responsibility, and, we would like to add, to our subjects first, to the study next, and to ourselves last.

◆ Conclusion

In this chapter we have outlined the history of interviewing, with its qualitative and quantitative origins. We have looked at structured, group, and various types of unstructured interviewing. We have examined the importance of gender in interviewing and the ways in which framing and interpreting affect interviews. Finally, we have examined the importance of ethics in interviewing.

Clearly, different types of interviewing are suited to different situations. If we wish to find out how many people oppose a nuclear repository, survey research is our best tool, and we can quantify and code the responses and use mathematical models to explain our findings (Frey, 1993). If we are interested in opinions about a given product, a focus group interview will provide us with the most efficient results; if we wish to know and understand about the lives of Palestinian women in the resistance (Gluck, 1991), we need to interview them at length and in depth in an unstructured way.

Many scholars are now realizing that to pit one type of interviewing against another is a futile effort, a leftover from the paradigmatic quantitative/qualitative hostility of past generations. Thus an increasing number of researchers are using multimethod approaches to achieve broader and often better results. This is referred to as *triangulation* (Denzin, 1989b). In triangulating, a researcher may use several methods in different combinations. For instance, group interviewing has long been used to complement survey research and is now being used to complement participant observation (Morgan, 1988).

Interviewing is currently undergoing not only a methodological change but a much deeper one, related to self and other (see Fine, Chapter 4, Volume 1, this series). The "other" is no longer a distant, aseptic, quantified, sterilized, measured, categorized, and cataloged faceless respondent, but has become a living human being, usually a forgotten or an oppressed one—a black combatant in a Vietnam camp or myriad women, up to now sociologically invisible, finally blossoming to full living color and coming into focus as real persons, as the interviewer recognizes them as such. Also, in learning about the other we learn about the self (Crapanzano, 1980). That is, as we treat the other as a human being, we can no longer remain objective, faceless interviewers, but become human beings and must disclose ourselves, learning about ourselves as we try to learn about the other.

The brief journey we have taken through the world of interviewing should allow us to be better informed and perhaps more sensitized to the problematics of asking questions for sociological reasons. We must remember that each individual has his or her own social history and an individual perspective on the world. Thus we cannot take our task for granted. As Oakley (1981) notes, "Interviewing is rather like a marriage: everybody knows what it is, an awful lot of people do it, and yet behind each closed front door there is a world of secrets" (p. 41). She is quite correct—we all think we know how to ask questions and talk to people, from common, everyday folks to highly qualified quantophrenic experts. Yet, to learn about people we must remember to treat them as people, and they will uncover their lives to us. As long as many researchers continue to treat respondents as unimportant, faceless individuals whose only contribution is to fill one more boxed response, the answers we, as researchers, will get will be commensurable with the questions we ask and with the way we ask them. We are no different from Gertrude Stein, who, on her deathbed, asked her lifelong companion, Alice B. Toklas, "What is the answer?" And when Alice could not bring herself to speak, Gertrude asked, "Then what is the question?" The question must be asked person-to-person if we want it to be answered fully.

◆ References

Adams, R. N., & Preiss, J. J. (1960). *Human organizational research: Field relations and techniques*. Homewood, IL: Dorsey.

Adler, P. (1985). *Wheeling and dealing*. New York: Columbia University Press.

Anderson, N. (1923). *The hobo: The sociology of the homeless man*. Chicago: University of Chicago Press.

Babbie, E. (1992). *The practice of social research* (6th ed.). Belmont, CA: Wadsworth.

Becker, H. S. (1956). Interviewing medical students. *American Journal of Sociology, 62*, 199-201.

Becker, H. S. (1981). *Exploring society photographically*. Evanston, IL: Northwestern University, Mary and Leigh Block Gallery.

Benney, M., & Hughes, E. (1956). Of sociology and the interview: Editorial preface. *American Journal of Sociology, 62*, 137-142.

Blumer, H. (1969). *Symbolic interactionism: Perspective and method*. Englewood Cliffs, NJ: Prentice Hall.

Blumer, H., with Sutter, A., Smith, R., & Ahmed, S. (1967). *The world of youthful drug use*. Berkeley: University of California Press.

Boelen, W. A. M. (1992). *Street corner society*: Cornerville revisited. *Journal of Contemporary Ethnography, 21*, 11-51.

Bogardus, E. S. (1926). The group interview. *Journal of Applied Sociology, 10*, 372-382.

Booth, C. (1902-1903). *Life and labour of the people in London*. London: Macmillan.

Bradburn, N. M. (1983). Response effects. In P. H. Rossi, J. D. Wright, & A. B. Anderson (Eds.), *Handbook of survey research* (pp. 289-328). New York: Academic Press.

Bradburn, N. M., Sudman, S., & Associates. (1979). *Improving interview method and questionnaire design*. San Francisco: Jossey-Bass.

Cicourel, A. (1964). *Method and measurement in sociology*. New York: Free Press.

Cicourel, A. (1970). The acquisition of social structure: Toward a developmental sociology of language and meaning. In J. D. Douglas (Ed.), *Understanding everyday life: Toward a reconstruction of social knowledge* (pp. 136-168). Chicago: Aldine.

Cicourel, A. (1974). *Theory and method in a study of Argentine fertility*. New York: John Wiley.

Clough, P. T. (1992). *The end(s) of ethnography: From realism to social criticism*. Newbury Park, CA: Sage.

Converse, J. M. (1987). *Survey research in the United States: Roots and emergence 1890-1960*. Berkeley: University of California Press.

Converse, J. M., & Schuman, H. (1974). *Conversations at random: Survey research as interviewers see it*. New York: John Wiley.

Crapanzano, V. (1980). *Tuhami: Portrait of a Moroccan*. Chicago: University of Chicago Press.

Daniels, A. K. (1967). The low-caste stranger in social research. In G. Sjoberg (Ed.), *Ethics, politics, and social research* (pp. 267-296). Cambridge, MA: Schenkman.

Daniels, A. K. (1983). Self-deception and self-discovery in field work. *Qualitative Sociology, 6*, 195-214.

Denzin, N. K. (1989a). *Interpretive interactionism*. Newbury Park, CA: Sage.

Denzin, N. K. (1989b). *The research act* (3rd ed.). Englewood Cliffs, NJ: Prentice Hall.

Desvousges, W. H., & Frey, J. H. (1989). Integrating focus groups and surveys: Examples from environmental risk surveys. *Journal of Official Statistics, 5,* 349-363.

Deutscher, I. (1968). Asking questions cross-culturally: Some problems of linguistic comparability. In H. S. Becker, B. Geer, D. Riesman, & R. Weiss (Eds.), *Institutions and the person* (pp. 318-341). Chicago: Aldine.

Derrida, J. (1976). *Of grammatology* (G. C. Spivak, Trans.). Baltimore: Johns Hopkins University Press.

Dickens, D., & Fontana, A. (Eds.). (1994). *Postmodernism and social inquiry.* New York: Guilford.

Douglas, J. D. (1985). *Creative interviewing.* Beverly Hills, CA: Sage.

Douglas, J. D., & Johnson, J. M. (1977). *Existential sociology.* Cambridge: Cambridge University Press.

Douglas, J. D., & Rasmussen, P., with Flanagan, C. A. (1977). *The nude beach.* Beverly Hills, CA: Sage.

Du Bois, W. E. B. 1899). *The Philadelphia Negro: A social study.* Philadelphia: Ginn.

Fine, G. A., & Sandstrom, K. (1988). *Knowing children: Participant observation with minors.* Newbury Park, CA: Sage.

Fine, M. (1983-1984). Coping with rape: Critical perspectives on consciousness. *Imagination, Cognition and Personality, 3,* 249-267.

Fontana, A. (1977). *The last frontier: The social meaning of growing old.* Beverly Hills, CA: Sage.

Fontana, A., & Collins, C. (1993). *The forgotten self: Women in Vietnam.* Paper presented at the annual meeting of the Society for the Study of Symbolic Interaction, Miami, FL.

Freeman, D. (1983). *Margaret Mead and Samoa: The making and unmaking of an anthropological myth.* Cambridge, MA: Harvard University Press.

Frey, J. H. (1989). *Survey research by telephone* (2nd ed.). Newbury Park, CA: Sage.

Frey, J. H. (1993). Risk perception associated with a high-level nuclear waste repository. *Sociological Spectrum.*

Frey, J. H., & Fontana, A. (1991). The group interview in social research. *Social Science Journal, 28,* 175-187.

Frey, J. H., & Fontana, A. (in press). *The group interview.* Newbury Park, CA: Sage.

Garfinkel, H. (1967). *Studies in ethnomethodology.* Englewood Cliffs, NJ: Prentice Hall.

Geertz, C. (1988). *Works and lives: The anthropologist as author.* Stanford, CA: Stanford University Press.

Giroux, H. (1992). *Border crossings: Cultural workers and the politics of education.* New York: Routledge.

Glaser, B. G., & Strauss, A. L. (1967). *The discovery of grounded theory: Strategies for qualitative research.* Chicago: Aldine.

Gluck, S. B. (1984). What's so special about women: Women's oral history. In D. Dunaway & W. K. Baum (Eds.), *Oral history: An interdisciplinary anthology* (pp. 221-237). Nashville, TN: American Association for State and Local History.

Gluck, S. B. (1991). Advocacy oral history: Palestinian women in resistance. In S. B. Gluck & D. Patai (Eds.), *Women's words: The feminist practice of oral history* (pp. 205-220). London: Routledge.

Gluck, S. B., & Patai, D. (Eds.). (1991). *Women's words: The feminist practice of oral history*. London: Routledge.

Goffman, E. (1959). *The presentation of self in everyday life*. Garden City, NY: Anchor.

Goffman, E. (1971). *Relations in public*. New York: Harper & Row.

Gorden, R. L. (1980). *Interviewing: Strategy, techniques, and tactics*. Homewood, IL: Dorsey.

Harper, D. (1982). *Good company*. Chicago: University of Chicago Press.

Harvey, L. (1987). *Myths of the Chicago school of sociology*. Aldershot, England: Avebury.

Humphreys, L. (1970). *Tearoom trade: Impersonal sex in public places*. Chicago: Aldine.

Johnson, J. (1976). *Doing field research*. New York: Free Press.

Kahn, R., & Cannell, C. F. (1957). *The dynamics of interviewing*. New York: John Wiley.

Kotarba, J. A., & Fontana, A. (Eds.). (1984). *The existential self in society*. Chicago: University of Chicago Press.

Krieger, S. (1983). *The mirror dance: Identity in a women's community*. Philadelphia: Temple University Press.

Kuhn, M. (1962). The interview and the professional relationship. In A. Rose (Ed.), *Human behavior and social processes: An interactionist approach* (pp. 193-206). Boston: Houghton Mifflin.

Lincoln, Y. S., & Guba, E. G. (1985). *Naturalistic inquiry*. Beverly Hills, CA: Sage.

Lofland, J. (1971). *Analyzing social settings*. Belmont, CA: Wadsworth.

Lofland, J., & Lofland, L. (1984). *Analyzing social settings: A guide to qualitative observation and analysis* (2nd ed.). Belmont, CA: Wadsworth.

Lomax, J., & Lomax, A. (1966). *American ballads and folk songs*. New York: Macmillan. (Original work published 1934)

Lopata, H. Z. (1980). Interviewing American widows. In W. Shaffir, R. Stebbins, & A. Turowetz (Eds.), *Fieldwork experience: Qualitative approaches to social research* (pp. 68-81). New York: St. Martin's.

Lynd, R. S., & Lynd, H. M. (1929). *Middletown: A study in American culture*. New York: Harcourt, Brace.

Lynd, R. S., & Lynd, H. M. (1937). *Middletown in transition: A study in cultural conflicts*. New York: Harcourt, Brace.

Maccoby, E. E., & Maccoby, N. (1954). The interview: A tool of social science. In G. Lindzey (Ed.), *Handbook of social psychology: Vol. 1. Theory and method* (pp. 449-487). Reading, MA: Addison-Wesley.

Malinowski, B. (1922). *Argonauts of the western Pacific*. London: Routledge & Kegan Paul.

Malinowski, B. (1989). *A diary in the strict sense of the term*. Stanford, CA: Stanford University Press. (Original work published 1967)

Marcus, G. E., & Fischer, M. (1986). *Anthropology as cultural critique: An experimental moment in the human sciences*. Chicago: University of Chicago Press.

Marshall, K. (1987). *In the combat zone*. New York: Penguin.

Merton, R. K., Fiske, M., & Kendall, P. L. (1956). *The focused interview*. Glencoe, IL: Free Press.

Merton, R. K., & Lazarsfeld, P. F. (Eds.). (1950). *Continuities in social research: Studies in the scope and method of "The American soldier."* Glencoe, IL: Free Press.

Montville, L. (1993). He's everywhere. *Sports Illustrated, 78*(17), 78-90.

Morgan, D. (1988). *Focus groups as qualitative research*. Newbury Park, CA: Sage.

Morgan, D., & Spanish, M. T. (1984). Focus groups: A new tool for qualtiative research. *Qualitative Sociology, 7,* 253-270.

Oakley, A. (1981). Interviewing women: A contradiction in terms. In H. Roberts (Ed.), *Doing feminist research* (pp. 30-61). London: Routledge & Kegan Paul.

Papanek, H. (1964). The woman field worker in a purdah society. *Human Organization, 22,* 160-163.

Parten, M. (1950). *Surveys, polls, and samples.* New York: Harper.

Payne, S. L. (1951). *The art of asking questions.* Princeton, NJ: Princeton University Press.

Peneff, J. (1988). The observers observed: French survey researchers at work. *Social Problems, 35,* 520-535.

Punch, M. (1986). *The politics and ethics of fieldwork.* Newbury Park, CA: Sage.

Rabinow, P. (1977). *Reflections on fieldwork in Morocco.* Berkeley: University of California Press.

Rasmussen, P. (1989). *Massage parlor prostitution.* New York: Irvington.

Reinharz, S. (1992). *Feminist methods in social research.* New York: Oxford University Press.

Richardson, L. (1992). The poetic representation of lives: Writing a postmodern sociology. In N. K. Denzin (Ed.), *Studies in symbolic interaction* (Vol. 13, pp. 19-28). Greenwich, CT: JAI.

Selltiz, C., Jahoda, M., Deutsch, M., & Cook, S. W. (1965). *Research methods in social relations.* London: Methuen.

Smith, D. E. (1987). *The everyday world as problematic: A feminist sociology.* Boston: Northeastern University Press.

Spradley, J. P. (1979). *The ethnographic interview.* New York: Holt, Rinehart & Winston.

Spradley, J. P. (1980). *Participant observation.* New York: Holt, Rinehart & Winston.

Starr, L. (1984). Oral history. In D. Dunaway & W. K. Baum (Eds.), *Oral history: An interdisciplinary anthology* (pp. 3-26). Nashville, TN: American Association for State and Local History.

Stanfield, J. (1985). *Philanthropy and Jim Crow in American social sciences.* Westport, CT: Greenwood.

Stewart, D., & Shamdasani, P. (1990). *Focus groups: Theory and practice.* Newbury Park, CA: Sage.

Sudarkasa, N. (1986). In a world of women: Field work in a Yoruba community. In P. Golde (Ed.), *Women in the field: Anthropological experiences* (pp. 167-191). Berkeley: University of California Press.

Terkel, S. (1975). *Working.* New York: Avon.

Terry, W. (1984). *Bloods: An oral history of the Vietnam War by black veterans.* New York: Random House.

Thompson, H. (1985). *Hell's Angels.* New York: Ballantine.

Thompson, J., & Demerath, M. J. (1952). Some experiences with the group interview. *Social Forces, 31,* 148-154.

Thrasher, F. M. (1927). *The gang: A study of 1,313 gangs in Chicago.* Chicago: University of Chicago Press.

Ulmer, G. (1989). *Teletheory: Grammatology in an age of video.* New York: Routledge.

Van Maanen, J. (1988). *Tales of the field: On writing ethnography.* Chicago: University of Chicago Press.

Warren, C. A. B. (1988). *Gender issues in field research*. Newbury Park, CA: Sage.

Wax, R. (1960). Twelve years later: An analysis of field experiences. In R. N. Adams & J. J. Preiss (Eds.), *Human organization research* (pp. 166-178). Homewood, IL: Dorsey.

Wenner, J. (1992, October 15). A letter from the editor. *Rolling Stone*.

Whyte, W. F. (1943). *Street corner society: The social structure of an Italian slum*. Chicago: University of Chicago Press.

Yeandle, S. (1984). *Women's working lives: Patterns and strategies*. New York: Tavistock.

Young, P. (1966). *Scientific social surveys and research* (4th ed.). Englewood Cliffs, NJ: Prentice Hall.

Zuckerman, H. (1972). Interviewing an ultra-elite. *Public Opinion, 36*, 159-175.

3

Observational Techniques

Patricia A. Adler & Peter Adler

◆ This chapter builds upon the previous abstract and theoretical discussions of qualitative methods to focus on one specific mode of
qualitative data gathering: naturalistic observation. In the following pages
we examine some of the essential features of naturalistic observation,
discussing methodological issues, strengths, and weaknesses in its practice.
We then consider several theoretical traditions underlying observation,
showing how exemplary individuals and their works in these paradigms
enact the conceptual and epistemological themes. We then bring select
themes into sharper focus in a discussion of ethical issues related to
observational research and the influence of scholarly and political forces
in shaping these. We conclude by extrapolating from the present into the
future, speculating on how these forces will play out against the tide of
shifting epistemological currents.

For as long as people have been interested in studying the social and
natural world around them, observation has served as the bedrock source

AUTHORS' NOTE: We would like to acknowledge gratefully the assistance of Spencer Cahill, Carol
Brooks Gardner, Lyn Lofland, Jeff Nash, and Carol Warren, who shared ideas with us and permitted
us a glimpse into their methodological worlds.

of human knowledge. Early classicists rooted their understandings of the world, from Aristotle's botanical observations on the island of Lesbos to Herodotus's chronicled observations of the Greco-Persian wars, in their own visions, travels, and direct experiences. Comte, the founder of sociology, elucidated observation as one of the four core research methods (along with comparison, historical analysis, and experimentation) appropriate to his fledgling science of society. Not only is observation one of the earliest and most basic forms of research, but it is the most likely to be used in conjunction with others, such as participant observation, experimental design, and interviewing.

As members of society, we also make observations of the everyday world. These guide us in forging paths of action and interpreting the actions and reactions of others. They also generate the kind of "common sense" or "cultural knowledge" that Johnson (1975, p. 21) has argued lies at the base of all knowledge and theory, from that amassed by the layperson to that conducted by the survey, experimental, participant, or simple observational methodologist. What differentiates the observations of social scientists from those of everyday-life actors is the former's systematic and purposive nature. Social science researchers study their surroundings regularly and repeatedly, with a curiosity spurred by theoretical questions about the nature of human action, interaction, and society.

Morris (1973) offers a broad explanation of observation that defines it as "the act of noting a phenomenon, often with instruments, and recording it for scientific or other purposes" (p. 906). Although we sometimes think of observation as involving only visual data gathering, this is far from true; all of the senses can also be fully engaged in this endeavor, from smell to hearing, touch, and taste. Observation thus consists of gathering impressions of the surrounding world through all relevant human faculties. This generally necessitates direct contact with the subject(s) of observation, although remote observation can be carried out by recording the data with photography, audiotape, or videotape and studying it either concurrently or later.[1] In either case, researchers must actively witness the phenomena they are studying in action.

One of the hallmarks of observation has traditionally been its noninterventionism. Observers neither manipulate nor stimulate their subjects. They do not ask the subjects research questions, pose tasks for them, or deliberately create new provocations. This stands in marked contrast to researchers using interview questionnaires, who direct the interaction and introduce potentially new ideas into the arena, and to experimental researchers, who often set up structured situations where they can alter certain conditions to measure the covariance of others. Simple observers follow the flow of events. Behavior and interaction continue as they would without the presence of a researcher, uninterrupted by intrusion.

Yet often when we think of the social scientist as observer, we conjure up an image of a laboratory scientist in a white coat, jotting notes on a clipboard while observing people from behind a one-way mirror. This detached and sterile view of observation is rooted in the quantitative observational paradigm, one enhanced by the prestige accorded science since the birth of the Enlightenment. Quantitative observational research has forged a stronghold in experimental psychology and sociological small group research through careful attention to the precise operationalization and measurement of dependent variables.

Quantitative observations, conducted in situations deliberately designed to ensure standardization and control, differ markedly from observations framed by the qualitative paradigm. Qualitative observation is fundamentally naturalistic in essence; it occurs in the natural context of occurrence, among the actors who would naturally be participating in the interaction, and follows the natural stream of everyday life. As such, it enjoys the advantage of drawing the observer into the phenomenological complexity of the world, where connections, correlations, and causes can be witnessed as and how they unfold. Qualitative observers are not bound, thus, by predetermined categories of measurement or response, but are free to search for concepts or categories that appear meaningful to subjects. As Carol Brooks Gardner (personal communication, 1993) told us in describing her recognition of significant findings: "I look for the 'Click!' experience— something of a sudden, though minor, epiphany as to the emotional depth or importance of an event or a phenomenon." Naturalistic observers thus often differ from quantitative observers in the scope of their observations: Whereas the latter focus on minute particles of the world that can be agglomerated into a variable, the former look for much larger trends, patterns, and styles of behavior. These differences are rooted not only in variations between the ways the two groups observe, but in the types of questions they pose.

Qualitative observation has remained underaddressed in the methodological literature. It has been elaborated for the student audience in some general methods texts that treat observation as one research strategy in a broad consideration of all data gathering techniques (e.g., Kidder, 1981; Phillips, 1985). Other exemplary works that have more specifically addressed qualitative observational methods include Webb, Campbell, Schwartz, and Sechrest's (1966) early work on unobtrusive measures; Gold's (1958) classic typology of observational roles; Schatzman and Strauss's (1973) interpretive guide to naturalistic research; Spradley's (1980) more formal handbook, which focuses on the stages of observation; and Denzin's (1989) comprehensive description of research methods for studying social interaction.

Yet observation by itself has remained a stepchild to its more widely recognized offshoot: participant observation. Most of the major research treatments of qualitative methods (Berg, 1989; Douglas, 1976; Glesne & Peshkin, 1992; Hammersley & Atkinson, 1983; Jorgensen, 1989; Lofland & Lofland, 1984) focus on participant observation to the virtual exclusion of observation as a method in its own right. This may be traced to the strong theoretical roots of participant observation in the symbolic interaction perspective; interactionist researchers usually want to gather data from their subjects while interacting with them. Although pure observation is somewhat propelled by the symbolic interactionist perspective, the questions it answers make it more compatible with the scope of the dramaturgical perspective and, to a secondary extent, ethnomethodology. Yet dramaturgy has failed to inspire methodological discussions and expositions comparable to those of symbolic interactionism. In fact, few of the dramaturgical perspective's major exponents, Goffman included, have discussed their methodology explicitly. This may be because it is seen as subjective and, hence, difficult to legitimate. Ethnomethodology, and especially its late twentieth-century incarnation, conversation analysis, suffers from no such reticence, however, and is well explicated methodologically in such works as Handel (1982), Heritage (1984), and Jefferson (1989).

Yet what is missing in all of these treatments is a comprehensive elaboration of the theory, methods, and epistemology grounding naturalistic observation. Our aim, in this chapter, is to provide such a comprehensive treatment by integrating more general comments about observational methods with a discussion of its theoretical roots and current major practitioners. We discuss these features of naturalistic observation and describe and analyze its role as both an independent and an integrated research technique.

◆ Methodological Issues

Observational research can vary considerably in its character among different practitioners, through the stages of a research project, in various settings, and depending on the relationship of researchers to their subjects.

Researchers may choose to focus on a group where they intentionally place themselves in a particular location to observe subjects' behavior, or they may observe the behavior of those falling naturally around them. For example, Carpenter, Glassner, Johnson, and Loughlin (1988) observed adolescents in junior and senior high schools during their lunch and recess periods to learn about how these young people structured their leisure time. In addition to observing them at school before, after, and during lunch break from classes, they followed their subjects into recreational activities around town, to parks, skating rinks, video arcades, bars, movie theaters, people's homes, and various other places. These observations involved subjects with whom the researchers were not previously familiar and foreign locations. Others who study more generic populations, behavior, or spaces may not have to travel to make their observations. In describing her research on public space, Lyn Lofland (personal communication, 1993) has noted:

> For the past twenty years the "vantage point" when I'm doing direct observation has continued to be [constant]. Since I'm "passing" as someone who is simply hanging about in public, I get engaged by others in interaction, though I have rarely initiated it myself. . . . A lot of my data have come from situations in which I was out in public for nonresearch purposes. That is, I watch myself acting in public and note what I do and what others do vis-à-vis me, just as if I were someone else. So, I guess you could say that I move from being the largely uninvolved observer to the fully involved participant observer. . . . Obviously I don't take myself as a stand-in for "everywoman," but neither do I think my reactions are likely to be that peculiar.

In contrast, Lofland's studies of public space show the observer in a familiar location, observing people like herself, and drawing on her own background familiarity with the setting and behavior. These projects show some of the differences observers encounter between subjects who are demographically different from themselves, in having to travel intentionally to research settings, and in the types of research relationships that may occur. Yet they also show some of the constancy: Observers are likely to employ all their faculties in data gathering and are also likely to draw on their broad cultural or commonsense knowledge, what Douglas (1976) has called "general cultural understanding."

Research Roles

As Lofland has also noted, the role of the researcher in the setting may vary in involvement. In Gold's (1958) classic typology of naturalistic research roles, he outlined four modes through which observers may gather data: the complete participant, the participant-as-observer, the observer-as-participant, and the complete observer. The midpoint of these roles sought to balance involvement with detachment, familiarity with strangeness, closeness with distance, based on the classical Chicago school conceptualization of research (see Adler & Adler, 1987). New conceptions of qualitative research have evolved since these were first proposed, with practitioners' attitudes shifting toward greater involvement, even membership roles, as we have previously outlined, in their settings (Adler & Adler, 1987). Three membership roles appear to predominate: the complete-member-researcher, the active-member-researcher, and the peripheral-member-researcher. The current span of observational research roles includes some combination of these two groups of typologies.

Gold's complete observer role describes researchers who are fundamentally removed from their settings. Their observations may occur from the outside, with observers being neither seen nor noticed. Contemporary varieties of this role might include the videotaping, audiotaping, or photographing noninteractive observer. This role most closely approximates the traditional ideal of the "objective" observer. The observer-as-participant role describes researchers primarily observing their subjects for extremely brief periods as they attempt to conduct structured interviews. In Gold's conceptualization, this role did not have much use for the naturalistic observer. It has assumed a more useful meaning for contemporary researchers, however, depicting those who enter settings for the purpose of data gathering, yet who interact only casually and nondirectively with subjects while engaged in their observational pursuits (e.g., the Carpenter et al. study mentioned above). This is clearly an overt role, as the observer's identity remains strongly research oriented and does not cross into the friendship domain. Neither of these roles is currently as popular with qualitative researchers as it was at mid-century.

Instead, naturalistic social scientists have moved into a variety of membership roles in their settings. Researchers in peripheral membership roles feel that an insider's perspective is vital to forming an accurate appraisal of human group life, so they observe and interact closely enough with members to establish an insider's identity without participating in those activities constituting the core of group membership. Both covert and overt stances are possible here, sometimes in concert. For example, we took peripheral membership roles in our research on upper-level drug dealers and smugglers (reported in P. A. Adler, 1985), where we established ourselves as members of the social crowd, accepted as "wise" and trustworthy individuals who refrained from participating in the actual trafficking. We also took peripheral membership roles in our observations of the peer culture of elementary school children (Adler, Kless, & Adler, 1992), studying them while we circulated as adult parents, coaches, car pool drivers, and so on in their lives.

The active membership role describes researchers who become more involved in the setting's central activities, assuming responsibilities that advance the group, but without fully committing themselves to members' values and goals. Peter Adler assumed such a posture in our research on college athletes (Adler & Adler, 1991a) by becoming an assistant coach on the basketball team, supervising the academic progress of team members and counseling them informally on career options. Observers in this role often take an overt stance as they forge close and meaningful bonds with setting members.

Finally, researchers in the complete membership role are those who study scenes where they are already members or those who become converted to genuine membership during the course of their research. This stance draws either on the burgeoning tradition of opportunistic research (Riemer, 1977) and "auto-ethnography" (Hayano, 1979), including Hayano's (1982) observations of fellow denizens of California's all-night card rooms, or on the early ethnomethodological stricture to "become the phenomenon" (Mehan & Wood, 1975) in order to immerse oneself and grasp the complete depth of the subjectively lived experience.

Observers can thus take roles that range anywhere from the hidden or disguised voyeur, who watches from outside or with a passive (even electronic) presence, to the active participant, involved in the setting, who acts as a member and not as a researcher so as not to alter the flow of the interaction unnaturally.

Stages of Observation

The observational research process evolves through a series of different activities as it progresses from start to finish. The observer's first task is to select a setting. This can be done for one of several reasons: The observer may have a theoretical interest in a particular type of scene or behavior, or may have potential access to a particular setting; the observer may be already ensconced in a setting and may "opportunistically" decide to study it (Riemer, 1977), or he or she may be commissioned to study it. For an observer not already in the setting, the next task is to gain entrée. Depending on the setting, its accessibility to outsiders, and its degree of organization (see Adler & Adler, 1991b), the observer may be able to pass freely through the setting at will, may be able to scope out the people and customs informally prior to committing him- or herself to a research role or identity, or may have to apply to official gatekeepers for formal entrée. The unobtrusiveness of observational research, compared with other means of data gathering, makes the first two possibilities more likely.

If the researcher is working alone, he or she may begin observing immediately. Researchers working in teams may have to train members on how and what to observe. In Nash's work with student observers, for example, he has often used students from his course on dramaturgical sociology, who are knowledgeable about the conceptual issues driving their observational frame (personal communication, 1993). The concrete products of observations may vary; some observers record written text that follows a free-association form, whereas others incorporate more structure. In his "tearoom" observations, Humphreys (1975) used sheets that he designed specifically for the project, featuring divided pages: On one part of the page the layout of the tearoom was depicted, and he used that to draw simple diagrams of the interaction; the rest of the page was devoted to explicit descriptions of participants' appearance, clothing, modes of transportation, roles, interactions, and exits. Denzin (1989) has suggested that all observation notational records should contain explicit reference to participants, interactions, routines, rituals, temporal elements, interpretations, and social organization. Most observational notes incorporate some combination of these features.

The nature of researchers' observations inevitably shifts in range and character from the early to later stages of an observational project. Spradley

(1980), and Jorgensen (1989) following him, has discussed initial observations as primarily "descriptive" in nature. Unfocused and general in scope,
they are usually based on broad questions, providing a base for the
researcher to branch out in myriad future directions. After observers
become more familiar with their settings and grasp the key social groups
and processes in operation, they may distinguish features of the scenes that
most interest them. At this point they are likely to shift to more "focused
observations," directing their attention to a deeper and narrower portion
of the people, behaviors, times, spaces, feelings, structures, and/or processes. Research questions or problems may emerge that shape future
observations and begin the formation of typologies. This stage of observation generates clearer research questions and concepts that then require
"selected observations." At this point, researchers focus on establishing and
refining the characteristics of and relations among the elements they have
previously selected as objects of study. Specific questions arise that must be
answered in constructing models about the categories within and among
things in the setting. Overall, as Spradley has noted, the stages of observation form a funnel, progressively narrowing and directing researchers'
attention deeper into the elements of the setting that have emerged as
theoretically and/or empirically essential.

Observational data gathering continues until researchers achieve theoretical saturation (Glaser & Strauss, 1967)—that is, when the generic
features of their new findings consistently replicate earlier ones. Researchers' analysis of the data, begun from earliest conceptualization, is
related to existing models in relevant literature. Depending on the observers' styles of data analysis, they may engage in more casual theorization
or more formal theory building. In pursuing this deepening and restriction
of concentration, observers may move through the stages of research from
open-ended search, to hypothesis formation, to theory conceptualization.
Although greater emphasis has traditionally been placed on the context
of discovery, observation can yield findings consonant with the context of
verification as well, through systematic attention to regular patterns of
occurrences and their conditions.

Problems of Observation

One of the chief criticisms leveled against observational research lies in
the area of *validity*. Without the benefit of members' analyses, observers
are forced to rely more exclusively on their own perceptions. They are

therefore more susceptible to bias from their subjective interpretations of situations (Denzin, 1989; Schatzman & Strauss, 1973; Webb et al., 1966). Without subjects' quotes to enrich and confirm researchers' analyses, or interobserver cross-checking to lend greater credence to their representations, some observers have had difficulty legitimating their work to a scholarly audience. This may explain why so few articles based *solely* on observational research are published, even in qualitative journals.

Yet there are measures observers can take to overcome this problem and enhance the validity of their research. First, using multiple observers or teams, especially if they are diverse in age and gender, can enhance the validity of observations, as researchers can cross-check each others' findings and eliminate inaccurate interpretations (Adler & Adler, 1987; Denzin, 1989; Phillips, 1985). Second, following an analytic inductive methodology by testing emergent propositions in the search for negative cases generates assertions that are more likely to be perceived as grounded and universal (Schatzman & Strauss, 1973). Third, in presenting their data, observers can use *verisimilitude,* or *vraisemblance,* a style of writing that draws the reader so closely into subjects' worlds that these can be palpably felt. When such written accounts contain a high degree of internal coherence, plausibility, and correspondence to what readers recognize from their own experiences and from other realistic and factual texts, they accord the work (and the research on which it is based) a sense of "authenticity" (Atkinson, 1990). Thus observational research derives validity from the *vraisemblance* of its textual renderings.

A second main criticism of observational research suggests that it lacks *reliability;* without statistical analysis to confirm the significance of observed patterns or trends, researchers cannot ensure that their findings are real and not merely the effects of chance (Denzin, 1989; Kidder, 1981). Like many qualitative methods, naturalistic observation yields insights that are more likely to be accurate for the group under study and unverified for extension to a larger population. Yet there are measures observers can follow that will enhance the generalizability of their findings. Observations conducted systematically and repeatedly over varying conditions that yield the same findings are more credible than those gathered according to personal patterns (Denzin, 1989). The two variables that particularly warrant varying are time (for what Kidder, 1981, calls test-retest comparisons) and place (Lofland, 1994), in order to ensure the widest range of observational consistency. Lofland (1994) has particularly noted variations and contradictions that have arisen in observations of the public realm at different times (day, night), under different climates (winter, summer), and by researchers of different gender. These concerns over validity and reliability derive from a postpositivist paradigm (see Richardson, Chapter 12, this volume) and lose salience as issues in the postmodern framework.

Rigors of Observation

One great strength of the observational method lies in the ease through which researchers can gain *entrée* to settings. Because it is unobtrusive and does not require direct interaction with participants, observation can be conducted inconspicuously (Webb et al., 1966). In fact, there are entire settings and types of behavior, as Humphreys (1975) has shown, that could not be studied through other, more blatant, methods.

Relatedly, observational methods embody the least potential for generating *observer effects*. There are many ways researchers can affect their subjects, from the self-fulfilling to the self-negating prophesy (Kidder, 1981). Many people believe that entirely avoiding researcher influence on subjects is an idealistic improbability (Adler & Adler, 1987; Jarvie, 1969; Johnson, 1975), yet there are ways that such effects can be diminished. The naturalness of the observer role, coupled with its nondirection, makes it the least noticeably intrusive of all research techniques (Phillips, 1985).

Another of the strengths associated with observational research lies in its *emergence*. Although not the only such method, observation, like participant observation and unstructured depth interviewing, draws both strength and weakness from its potential for creativity. Instead of working with predetermined categories, observers construct theories that generate categories and posit the linkages among them. At any point in the process, observers are free to alter the problems and questions they are pursuing as they gain greater knowledge of their subjects. Compared with more structured methods, then, observation has the flexibility to yield insight into new realities or new ways of looking at old realities (Kidder, 1981). This is particularly exemplified in Goffman's work (e.g., Goffman, 1961, 1963).

Finally, observation produces especially great rigor *when combined with other methods*. In contrast to experiments conducted in the laboratory that lack a natural setting and context of occurrence, and interviews with subjects that are constructions of subjects' recollection and (sometimes self-serving) perceptions, researchers' observations of their settings and subjects can be considered hard evidence. These are especially valuable as an alternate source of data for enhancing cross-checking (Douglas, 1976) or triangulation (Denzin, 1989) against information gathered through other means. Although direct observation may be marred by researcher biases, at least these are consistent and known. Direct observation, when added onto other research yielding depth and/or breadth, enhances consistency and validity.

◆ Observational Paradigms

A number of theoretical and/or research traditions are closely associated with observational methods. Looking back from the classical period of sociology into more contemporary movements, in this section we discuss some of the concerns, beliefs, and research questions that have driven observational research. For each field we present some of the core concerns and the work of exemplary researchers to show not only the common base of observational research, but its flexibility in service to diverse purposes.

Formal Sociology

The formal approach to sociology was advocated by Georg Simmel, one of the classical progenitors of the discipline. Rather than focusing exclusively on the content of social interactions and relations, Simmel argued that we should study the forms, or structures, according to which these are patterned. What especially fascinated Simmel, and what he saw as the base of social order, was "sociation," the crystallized interactions among people. This intricate web of multiple relations between individuals in constant interaction with one another constituted society. Some of the major forms of sociation Simmel analyzed include superordination and subordination, marital and martial conflict, and dyads and triads. Such relationships, whether fleeting and ephemeral or institutionalized, formed his unit of analysis.

Simmel also directed his attention to relationships in his study of social types. These types generally had two features in common: (a) They were defined by their relationship to others, such as "the stranger," who was among the people but not one of them, and "the poor," whose definition resided in their being regarded as deserving assistance; and (b) they were marginal. Whereas the relational feature is central to Simmel's theoretical perspective, the marginality is tied to his method.

90

Like many other theorists, Simmel based his ideas about society on his own direct observations. Simmel's position in society placed him in an excellent vantage point from which to observe; throughout his life he himself was a marginal man. Although a brilliant scholar, he was held back from the kind of academic appointment he deserved by anti-Semitism and his wide-ranging, interdisciplinary interests. Simmel's marginality highlights a common feature of the observer role: It may integrate participation with nonparticipation in such a way that both total detachment and full membership are precluded. Observers need close access to their settings and subjects to enhance direct insight and understanding, but their failure to be admitted to the center of action gives them a role that fosters scrutiny of those in the center as well as those on the outside. Frisby (1981) has suggested that Simmel represents a sort of "sociological *flaneur*," a stroller through life who makes observations in a detached manner, usually from a safe distance (Smith, 1992). As we will see, the marginal vantage emerges as one that often calls forth observation as a methodology.

Contemporary practitioners of formal sociology include members of the "new" Iowa school (see Buban, 1986; Couch, Saxton, & Katovich, 1986). Following the original direction of Manford Kuhn and the more recent inspiration of Carl Couch, these symbolic interactionists focus on the structuredness of human interaction. They see social reality and social process as jointly constructed by self and other through the forms of sociation residing in the interconnections developed among people. The dyad, not the individual, is their unit of analysis.

Methodologically, they follow Kuhn's propensity toward data gathered in a controlled, systematic fashion. Eschewing the limiting Twenty Statements Test, they prefer to videotape interactions, thereby creating complete records of social events (Saxton & Couch, 1975). Videotaping the data offers the advantages of being able to freeze interactions to reexamine them repeatedly, to subject them to rescrutiny by multiple observers, and to capture behavioral nuances precisely (Couch, 1984; Katovich, Weiland, & Couch, 1978). To ensure a greater degree of control over behavior, and hence over concepts and hypotheses to be developed and later tested as well, new Iowa school proponents prefer to bring their data to their videotape equipment, rather than to carry their equipment into the field. They thus situate their subjects in laboratories. Although aware of the possible drawbacks inherent in this unnatural environment and the necessary simplification of the social acts performed there, they see a greater payoff in the control gained. Research from this perspective has focused on how people develop solidary relationships (Miller, Hintz, & Couch, 1975), how they operate giant bureaucracies (Katovich, Weiland, & Couch, 1981), and how they turn others into stutterers.

Dramaturgical Sociology

Often regarded as the intellectual successor to Simmel, Erving Goffman focused his gaze on the interaction order. By studying how people act, interact, and form relationships, he sought to understand how they accomplish meaning in their lives. He was particularly interested in how people construct their self-presentations and carry them off in front of others. His dramaturgy suggested that there was an intentionality behind the planning and execution of these performances, that they were accomplished with an eye toward people's achieving the best impression of themselves in the view of others. In so doing, they go beyond the simple role making envisioned by Mead (1934) to more manipulative role playing. Goffman's view of the self was based on its empirical manifestations. His writings were conceptually oriented but empirically grounded, more persuasive in their appeal to the commonalities of people's joint experiences than empirically rigorous. Yet he was fundamentally an observer of social life. As Brissett and Edgley (1990) have described his perspective: "The theater of performances is not in people's heads, it is in their public acts. People encounter each other's minds only by interacting, and the quality and character of these interactions come to constitute the consequential reality of everyday life" (p. 37). To grasp that reality, Goffman studied the interaction rituals of public behavior.

Goffman's vantage on the field came from a position of self-imposed marginality. Unlike Simmel, who could not find acceptance, Goffman would not seek it. He preferred social distance, from which he could observe the actions of those around him, even those closest to himself, with cynical detachment. He also took an aloof stance toward the academy, eschewing the normative forums of presenting scholarly ideas, preferring instead to write essays (Brissett & Edgley, 1990). Like Simmel, he took the role of the *flaneur* (Smith, 1992).

Goffman seldom remarked on his own methodology. Generally, he preferred to let his conceptualizations validate his methods if they proved to be insightful. In a rare comment, however, he characterized his methodological approach: "The method that is often resorted to here—unsystematic, naturalistic observation—has very serious limitations. I claim as a defense that the traditional research designs thus far employed have considerable limitations of their own" (Goffman, 1971, p. xv).

Observation is well suited to the dramaturgical perspective because it enables researchers to capture the range of acts, from the minimovements to the grand gestures, of people in all ranks of life. Although Goffman established a precedent for being inattentive to methodology, this tradition has been carried on by others following his interests in the dramaturgical construction of the interaction order. Notable among these successors is the work of Spencer Cahill and Carol Brooks Gardner. Cahill is best known for his studies of children in the public order, especially their role in public life. He suggests that, contrary to others' assertions, the boundaries between children and adults are strong, and can be recognized in the way children are treated in public (Cahill, 1990). In a study of children's socialization into the "religion of civility" forming contemporary American culture, he describes the means by which adults treat instances of children's public deviant behavior, using these as means to teach their offspring appropriate behavioral comportment (Cahill, 1987).

In these and other studies, Cahill employed teams of student observers who went to public arenas such as city streets, shopping malls, parks, restaurants, and laundromats to make observations. Commenting on his methodology, he noted:

> We visited these settings at different times of the day and week for the explicit purpose of observing children's behavior and treatment in public places. We recorded observed episodes of interaction in field notes either while the interactions were occurring or immediately thereafter. In addition, we also occasionally recorded episodes of interaction in field notes that we observed in the course of our daily rounds. Although we typically wrote our field notes in full view of those whom we were observing, they were apparently unaware that we were recording their behavior. (Cahill, 1987, p. 314)

Gardner's work has focused on gender and stigma in public space. Her studies of the disabled examine how they deal with stigma and the reactions of others who both assist and ignore them when they attempt to navigate the physical difficulties of the outside world. In some of her work on gender she has examined the differences between men's and women's openness to others in public. Drawing on observations conducted in public and semi-public places such as bars, restaurants, stores, streets, rodeos, operas, and movie theaters, she noticed that women employ several strategies to restrict their "access information," maintaining closure and withholding knowledge of their names and addresses as well as being guarded about whom they allow themselves to trust for public conversation, in order to protect themselves from becoming crime victims (Gardner, 1988). Like her subjects, Gardner (personal communication, 1993) noted an awareness about her own safety in public while conducting observations that influenced where she went and how she positioned herself in relation to her subjects. Yet in discussing the traditional marginal role of the observer, Gardner (personal communication, 1993) notes a certain feeling of marginality herself: "I often think of myself as something of a marginal person in every milieu I find myself in: a Jew among Christians; a converted Jew among born Jews; an observational sociologist among number-worshipers; a hyper-aware person in a land of mellowed-out satisfaction."

Gardner's and Cahill's research highlights several dimensions of the observational method through both differences and similarities. Whereas Gardner worked alone, Cahill used an observational team. Both used unstructured recording techniques, jotting immediate notes about what they saw, to be analyzed later. Both went to public and semipublic locations for research and nonresearch purposes, blending the observer-as-participant with the participant-as-observer roles. They also discovered that taking notes about others' behavior in public aroused little notice, and found it unnecessary and unproblematic to disclose their research intentions.

Studies of the Public Realm

Building off the dramaturgical tradition are a range of observational studies focusing on behavior in public space. This was Goffman's preferred location of study, and through his inspiration it has blossomed into a research arena in its own right. Studies of the public realm address issues of moral order, interpersonal relations, forms of functioning, and norms of relating to strange individuals and different categories of individuals. The public realm represents an arena particularly characteristic of modern, urban society, with its density, heterogeneity, and danger. Observational techniques are particularly suited to studying this phenomenon because they enable researchers to gather data on large groups of people at a time, and to isolate patterns of group behavior.

Two major progenitors of this field are Lyn Lofland and Jeff Nash. Lofland's (1973) early work on cities examined the nature of existence in an arena filled with strangers. She suggests that people work to reduce the anonymity and alienation of an urban living situation by creating enclaves of private and semiprivate space around themselves. When they venture out from beyond these, they must be sufficiently knowledgeable about the potential range of social types they might encounter to know how to interpret people's actions.

Lofland employed a mixture of intentional and serendipitous research strategies, going into the field to make observations and remaining four and five hours at a time as well as being attentive to public behavior while she was engaged in her regular everyday pursuits. She made immediate notations of her impressions, often writing voluminously for hours. At all times she assumed the role of the covert observer, which was particularly natural as there were no gatekeepers in the public and semipublic settings she frequented (bus depots, airports, restaurants, theaters, libraries, university residence halls, and parks). In reflecting on her methodology, one thing Lofland (personal communication, 1993) highlights is the safety issue:

> I have put limits on myself. I never tried to test boundaries—that is, I was never interested in going to places where I was pretty sure I'd be unwelcome or in danger. That is, I generally played it safe in terms of possible psychic and physical threats. But just being out in public a lot means that one is going to be exposed to at least mild threat at least occasionally, and my researcher self, at least, welcomed these occasions. I might add that I've always paid pretty close attention to those situations in which I felt uncomfortable or frightened—that is, I have always made extensive notes (or in some instances photographs) of the social and/or physical character of the setting in which such feelings emerged.

Some of Nash's research on public order includes studies of bus ridership (1975), outdoor behavior in frozen places (1981), and indoor behavior in public skyways (Nash & Nash, 1994). In these works, respectively, he draws on observations made during three years of his own bus riding to describe a mobile urban community, he describes the breakdown of public norms that occurs under conditions of unusual thermal hardship, and he analyzes a series of skyways designed to replace the frigid outdoor space of the Minneapolis-St. Paul area. In the last of these studies, Jeff Nash and Anedith Nash assembled a research team of students to make observations in these connected plazas, buildings, and passageways. Their joint analysis looks at the influence of structural conditions on the relative vitality and population diversity of these locales, as well as the techniques by which people develop environmental mastery of the system.

Although Nash's transit observations were collected routinely (with the exception that he made no field notes while riding), his discussion of leading observational teams offers insight. Students were gathered from intersession courses on public life and later from courses on data analysis, where they read Goffman's *Relations in Public* (1971) and discussed conceptual analysis. Although the students' observations reflected inexperience, their field notes could be distilled at the end of the observational sessions to identify overlaps, similarities, and correlations. This resembles Cahill's (1987) role with his team, where he "continually reorganized and reviewed [their] field notes in order to discover common patterns, uncover general themes, and evaluate emerging hypotheses" (p. 314).

Another notable observational work falling within the public realm is Laud Humphreys's *Tearoom Trade* (1975). Like the others previously discussed, Humphreys assumed a covert observer-as-participant role in his setting (the "watchqueen"), observing men engage in impersonal homosexual activities at a bathroom in a public park. His observations were rigorous, as after each encounter he meticulously filled out a "systematic observation sheet" on which he recorded the date, place, description of the activity and its participants, license plate numbers of the participants' automobiles, and a sketch of the participants' placements. Although public and private restrooms have elsewhere been studied by observational teams as backstage regions (Cahill, 1985), this research focused on a highly deviant and hitherto unresearched behavior. Humphreys described the various roles in the setting (waiter, voyeur, masturbator, insertor, insertee) as well as the means by which potential members nonverbally conducted the negotiations for the deviant transaction. He described the characteristics of participants and their relations both among themselves and vis-à-vis potentially dangerous outsiders.

Although the book received widespread scholarly acclaim, it also set off waves of concern, as Humphreys tracked down his subjects through their license plate numbers and interviewed them anonymously one year later, looking totally different, as part of a large public health survey. This enabled him to gather demographic information about the characteristics of his population he would not otherwise have been able to obtain. The stigma associated with his topic and the unorthodox nature of his mixed methodology resulted in scrutiny of his observational methods they might not otherwise have encountered. We discuss these issues below.

What we see in these observational studies are variations in researcher involvement, researcher openness, use of teams, and gender issues. Observers have successfully taken roles ranging from total participation to studied detachment and have been both open and secretive about their research intent. Teams have been used as successfully as lone observation, and have yielded the benefit of greater diversity, energy, and scope. One aspect of observational research raised by both female but none of the male researchers we have examined is the safety issue. Women in the public domain find themselves sensitive to concerns men might not ever consider. This highlights the gendered nature of fieldwork and suggests that more mixed-gender observational teamwork might be fruitful.

Auto-Observation

Thus far we have discussed observations that focus on the group level, studying strangers and friends, often in public or semipublic places. But observation is also a powerful research tool when focused on more intimate levels of analysis. Social scientists have applied observational techniques with great success to studying themselves and their companions. The use of the self as a research tool for understanding society is rooted in the early origins of sociology. It was Dilthey (1961) who first proposed that we seek *Verstehen* (understanding) of human beings by empathizing with them. Incorporated by Weber into his methodological stance, *Verstehen* became a cornerstone of neoidealist and, subsequently, contemporary interpretive epistemology. Its strongest embodiment has been realized within existential sociology (see Douglas & Johnson, 1977), the proponents of which argue that "one must immerse oneself in everyday reality—feel it, touch it, hear it, and see it—in order to understand it" (Kotarba & Fontana, 1984, p. 6). This approach draws somewhat upon Schutz's (1971) notion of "reciprocity of perspective," that people can see the world from the eyes of others, in assuming that people experience similar feelings and emotions in reacting to the world around them. Observers who place themselves in the same situations as their subjects will thereby gain a deeper existential understanding of the world as the members see and feel it. This notion fosters a research role that is very close to the members, and augments researchers' observations of these others with observations of their own thoughts and feelings.

One such auto-observational study was conducted by Kretzmann (1992) in a blood plasma center. Assuming an active membership role, he took a covert stance and observed, eavesdropped on, and casually interacted with participants. From his vantage point he was able to experience the disdain and distrust staff members directed toward donors, and to describe and analyze the negative identity work they visited upon their clientele.

In contrast to Kretzmann's study, where he entered a setting and assumed the behavior of participants in order to acquire these self-observations, others opportunistically turn settings in which they are members or experiences they are having into topics of auto-observation. Ellis's (1993) recent book documents her relationship with her partner and his subsequent demise to emphysema over a grueling eight-year period. In the book, Ellis relies on systematic sociological introspection (Ellis, 1991) to plumb and record the depths of the emotional feelings she experienced throughout this time. Her text chronicles in narrative, often diarylike, form the events of those years and her emotional reactions to them. She then analyzes how this emotional journey took her through a renegotiation of meaning and identity common to many who suffer such loss or significant change in their life circumstances.

Ellis's auto-observation, like that of others, led her to become both subject and object of inquiry. She notes, "Taking the observer role gives me distance from the experience" (1993, pp. 1-2). This is a vital component of naturalistic observation via membership roles and shows once again the marginal role of observers, even in settings where they naturally belong. The detachment formerly lodged in researchers' objectivity and uninvolvement with their subjects is relocated in the withdrawal from what Schutz (1967) has called the "natural stance" of the everyday-life member to what Douglas (1976) has called the "theoretic stance" of the social scientific analyst. It is here that the conceptual optic scans and interprets the reams of raw, unprocessed data.

This observational approach offers the advantage of great depth, yielding insights about core meanings and experiences. It complements the more formal observational concerns that emphasize structure over content. Other notable works in which researchers have openly acknowledged using self-observation as a legitimate and insightful source of data include Johnson's (1975) study of social workers, Krieger's (1985) study of a lesbian community, Crapanzano's (1970) study of Morocco, Hayano's (1982) study of card rooms, and our study of a college basketball team (see particularly P. Adler, 1984).

Ethnomethodology

Whereas auto-observers and existential sociologists focus on the depth of meaningful experience, ethnomethodologists are concerned with how people accomplish their everyday lives (for a fuller discussion, see Holstein & Gubrium, Chapter 6, Volume 2, this series). They take as their goal the elucidation of how everyday life is forged, hence socially constructed, by members. Much of their interest lies with processes that are below the surface of conscious awareness, at the taken-for-granted level. Such researchers thus eschew interview data, even from depth interviews, as mere "accounts," valueless for their purpose because of the problems of subject bias, self-deception, lack of insight, and dishonesty. Instead, they prefer to use observational techniques that focus on very micro exchanges, from the "adjacency pairs" that occur during the first seven seconds of a telephone call (Schegloff, 1968) to the means through which people yield and seize the floor during turn taking in conversations (McHoul, 1978). Ethnomethodologists gather data that can be analyzed later in minute detail, such as through audio- and videotaping. These tapes are often transcribed and analyzed via an intricate notational system that allows readers to view the conversational overlaps, pauses, and intonations to within one-tenth of a second. Researchers are less concerned with the vicissitudes of their role in the setting than they are with making (or obtaining) recordings of mundane, everyday life that illustrate people operating naturally, in their native contexts of occurrence.

Contemporary ethnomethodologists have directed a particular emphasis toward conversation analysis (Heritage, 1984). They regard language as the fundamental base of communication, the base of social order. Yet Sacks (1963) asserts that language should not be part of an analytic apparatus until it is described. Conversation analysts have thus aimed to describe and analyze language use. Their end goal has been to build upward from a base of language and communication to understand the nature of roles, relationships, and social norms in settings and thereby discern the underlying structure of social reality.

A major study of the language of courtroom negotiation was conducted by Douglas Maynard (1984), in which he observed the negotiations occurring in a single courtroom and judges' chambers among participants in 54 misdemeanor cases. He audiotaped as many situations as he could and supplemented these with handwritten notes on conversations and situations he could not record. His role, he notes, was somewhere between the known and unknown observer: He had been granted entrée by the presiding judge and formally introduced to the most regular courtroom members, but there were many others (defendants, members of the public, attorneys who visited the courtroom less frequently) who were unaware of his research role. His analysis of his recordings offered him several benefits: He could reproduce as much detail from the conversations as possible; he could use this detail to build rigor and enhance the replicability of the research for others examining the same data; and he could obtain a record that did not rely on what the researcher thought was interesting or important before analyzing the data.

This research shows the differences that can be obtained through observational research conducted under different theoretical auspices. Compared with observations made from within the interpretive perspective, ethnomethodological observation yields a product that is more structural and objective, less mediated by the subjective perspective of the researcher. The detailed transcriptions produced of the speech, pauses, overlaps, and intonations of everyday conversations can also be reexamined repeatedly by multiple observers. This approach also entails a different role for the researcher, who is less likely to interact with setting participants than to operate recording equipment.

Maynard took notes and ran his tape recorder as he was present in the setting, but others may be either more or less intrusive. In studying the Watergate tapes, for example, Molotch and Boden (1985) analyzed the videotapes of the Watergate hearings. More common is the use of videotape recording to capture such things as the hesitations, restarts, pauses, and gaze behavior of participants (e.g., Goodwin, 1981). With their intrusive camera lenses, videotaping observers are more likely to produce unnatural influences on their subjects. These types of observations are also more focused than those made by interactionist researchers, as they are fixed in their location and restricted to the immediate communicative features of situations.

◆ Ethical Issues

Several features of observational research make it vulnerable to questions of ethical malpractice. Of all social science data gathering techniques, it is the least obtrusive. Although this is one of its great strengths, it also renders it liable to abuse in the invasion of privacy. Invasion of privacy can take two forms: venturing into private places, and misrepresenting oneself as a member. In this section we draw on the example of Humphreys's (1975) tearoom research to facilitate our discussion of these two issues.

By the nature of their inconspicuousness, observers can venture into places to gather data that are inaccessible to the general public. Deviant behavior often takes place in such private locales, away from the prying eyes of moral entrepreneurs. Some sociologists, in discussing ethical guidelines, have suggested that private locales ought to remain protected from the prying eyes of sociologists as well (Erikson, 1967). Summarizing the comments of others, Humphreys (1975) noted:

Are there, perhaps, some areas of human behavior that are not fit for social scientific study at all? Should sex, religion, suicide or other socially sensitive concerns be omitted from the catalogue of possible fields of sociological research? At first glance, few would answer yes to this question. Nevertheless, several have suggested to me that I should have avoided this research subject altogether. Their contention has been that in an area of such sensitivity it would be best to "let sleeping dogs lie." (pp. 167-168)

Responding to this ethical contention, Humphreys laid out his rationale for such research:

You do walk a really perilous tightrope in regard to ethical matters in studies like this, but unless someone will walk it, the only source of information will be the police department, and that's dangerous for a society. The methods I used were the least obtrusive possible. Oh, I could have hidden in the ceiling as the police do, but then I would have been an accomplice in what they were doing. (pp. 179-180)

The debate following publication of Humphreys's work drew enough attention to be noticed outside of academic circles. Reacting for the press, columnist Nicholas von Hoffman (1975) of the *Washington Post* presented another view:

This newspaper could probably learn a lot of things that the public has a right and need to know if its reporters were to use disguises and the gimmickry of modern, transistorized, domestic espionage, but there is a policy against it. No information is valuable enough to obtain by nipping away at personal liberty, and that is true no matter who's doing the gnawing, John Mitchell and the conservatives over at the Justice Department or Laud Humphreys and the liberals over at the Sociology Department. (p. 181)

Yet even if observers forgo observation in private places, they cannot easily escape this dilemma. Much observational research, as we have seen from the examples discussed, takes place in public or semipublic settings; the theoretical traditions guiding them foster an interest in social order and the forms of social structure. However, as Lofland (1973) noted in her study of urban living, even public spaces can be transformed, through their use, into private enclaves. Carol Warren (personal communication, 1993) describes such an invasion of her privacy while out in public:

I was sitting with a friend in a coffee shop chatting. A man wandered in, scoped the place out, and sat down at a table in front of ours. He did not go buy any food or drink at the counter. After a short while he moved from the table to a bench directly next to our table. I observed all this peripherally, and did not think much about it. After a while, he got out a pen and started writing on this pad he was carrying. It occurred to me then that he was an ethnographer taking notes on this public setting. As soon as I had this thought I became furiously indignant, and felt invaded. I was very surprised at my own reactions, since the arguments about not observing in public space had made no sense to me. Later I thought that although this was a public space it was also a privatized one, in which each separate unit in that space had their own focus of attention and interaction.

What we learn from these potentially similar reactions to observational research is that the definitions of public and private may be inadequate for describing the public realm. Lofland (1989) has suggested a third form of social territory in the public realm, the parochial, which is characterized by a sense of commonality among acquaintances and neighbors who are involved in interpersonal networks that are located within "communities." Humphreys's tearooms could fall either into this parochial category or could be viewed as a private realm "bubble" within the public realm (Lofland, 1994). Second, situational factors affect nearly all absolute issues; an unobtrusive observer in a more private setting offended no members, whereas an obtrusive observer in a public setting offended his subjects. In choosing between these two polar positions, researchers might temper their decisions by considering the relative harm and benefits to both private persons in society and the advancement of scientific knowledge. Their own needs must then be fettered by a sensitivity to the rights of unknowing others.

The related ethical issue concerns disguised research. Humphreys purposely disguised himself as the "watchqueen," or lookout, in his tearooms, after unsuccessfully trying out the roles of straight person and waiter. The former had met with a disruption of activity followed by the general exodus of participants from the scene, and the latter, which he tried next, with invitations to join the action. A cooperating respondent suggested the watchqueen role to Humphreys as a membership role that was not overtly sexual. By serving as the voyeur-lookout he was able to move around the room freely, observe all the action, and avoid pressures into more active participation.

Disguised or covert research has come under significant moral attack from social scientists. These calls have echoed forcefully in the hallways of the federal government, with momentous effects subsequently ensuing in the funding, sponsoring, and outlawing of research. Erikson (1967) has proposed two rules regarding misrepresentation in research:

> It is unethical for a sociologist to deliberately misrepresent his identity for the purpose of entering a private domain to which he is not otherwise eligible.
>
> It is unethical for a sociologist to deliberately misrepresent the character of the research in which he is engaged. (p. 373)

Several of the reactions to Humphreys's work suggested that he had no right to misrepresent himself deliberately as a member to gain access to the scene (von Hoffman, 1975), that he was overly concerned with the needs of the researcher and not enough with the freedom of the subjects (Warwick, 1973), that he inadequately considered the potential costs to his subjects should their activity be exposed (Warwick, 1973), and that he underestimated the power of the government to compel him to surrender evidence about his subjects should it become interested in this illegal activity (Glazer, 1975).

Others reacted in defense of Humphreys's work, arguing that the crucial issue is the need for research to cast light on social science areas otherwise blanketed by "ignorance and darkness." They praised the scrupulous attention Humphreys gave to protecting the identities of his subjects and argued that the goal of social scientists, unlike those of journalists and police, who sensationalize and expose, is to generalize from their subjects' actions to generic understandings of human behavior (Horowitz & Rainwater,

1975). *Tearoom Trade* was praised for its meticulous and sophisticated attention to social science research procedure (Glazer, 1975) and was granted the prestigious C. Wright Mills Award from the Society for the Study of Social Problems for its contribution to the study of critical social issues.

The Humphreys research offers a vivid illustration of disguised research, but the overt versus covert nature of most observers' roles is often more ambiguous. Maynard reflected on how he and his research were unknown to many in the courtroom, and Lofland noted that she generally passed as a member while doing her observation. Observers of public space usually find themselves in the same situation, as do many who make social science observations while engaged in their normal public or private activities. In guiding researchers to think about this issue, there are those who feel that we have enough legal and moral strictures guiding us to provide us with sensible and sensitive frameworks (Douglas, 1979), whereas others believe that people should be bound by firmer policies and restrictions rather than left to their own judgment (Reiman, 1979). At the present time, the policies and restrictions established by institutional review boards guiding research on human subjects, which exist at every university receiving government funding, have outlawed disguised research. It is up to each university to interpret how broadly it wants to apply this mandate to nonfunded research. Once again, researchers are reminded that they must take into account subjects' rights to freedom from manipulation when weighing the potential benefits of the research role against the harms that could accrue.

◆ The Future of Observation

Forecasting the wax and wane of social science research methods is always uncertain, but it is possible to extrapolate on existing trends. Editors of scholarly journals have found it difficult to accept the legitimacy of solely observational research, and they probably will continue to do so. Problems of subjectivity and excessive reliance on observer articulation still hamper this technique, and the theoretical traditions driving it are not that actively populated. Thus observation is unlikely to disappear, but it is also unlikely to ascend swiftly in acclaim.

The recent vast incursion of institutional review boards, importing with them government regulation of research, may alter the data gathering landscape, however. According to these standards, all observation (including observation by participants) of public behavior must be submitted for committee approval. Any such research where (a) human subjects could potentially be identified (either directly or through identifiers linked to the subjects), (b) the recorded observations could reasonably place the subjects at risk of criminal or civil liability or be damaging to the subjects' financial standing or employability, or (c) the research deals with sensitive aspects of the subjects' own behavior, such as illegal conduct, drug use, sexual behavior, or use of alcohol, is subject to potential censure (University of Colorado, Informed Consent Packet, Human Research Committee).

According to these guidelines, Humphreys never could have researched or written *Tearoom Trade*. In fact, these criteria fundamentally outlaw data gathered through direct experience or observation on nearly all aspects of deviant behavior. The implications for the future of this field of sociology are large. And as long as universities remain in dire financial straits and continue to be propelled by a fear of lawsuits from disgruntled subjects, administrators of higher education will never stand up for the needs or rights of scholarship against the flow of government grant funding.

Where the future of observation shines more brightly is in the use of this technique as an integrated rather than a primary method. When employed as part of a methodological spectrum that includes member-articulated data gathering strategies such as depth interviewing or participant observation, it is the most powerful source of validation. Freed from subjects' whimsical shifts in opinion, self-evaluation, self-deception, manipulation of self-presentation, embarrassment, and outright dishonesty, observation rests on something researchers can find constant: their own direct knowledge and their own judgment. It thus stands as the fundamental base of all research methods. With the dwindling of federal money for large survey research and the rise of public health problems lodged among hidden populations, researcher-gathered data has received an increase of support. This has already begun and will continue to generate more grant money, more research interest, and more scholarly legitimation of integrated field research techniques resting on a base of direct observation.

◆ Note

1. Some exceedingly interesting work is being done in the realm of visual sociology via photography. For more detailed information than is possible to include in this treatment, see Becker (1981, 1986), the journal *Visual Sociology* (sponsored by the International Visual Sociology Association), and Douglas Harper's contribution to this volume (Chapter 5).

◆ References

Adler, P. (1984). The sociologist as celebrity: The role of the media in field research. *Qualitative Sociology, 7,* 319-326.

Adler, P. A. (1985). *Wheeling and dealing.* New York: Columbia University Press.

Adler, P. A., & Adler, P. (1987). *Membership roles in field research.* Newbury Park, CA: Sage.

Adler, P. A., & Adler, P. (1991a). *Backboards and blackboards.* New York: Columbia University Press.

Adler, P. A., & Adler, P. (1991b). Stability and flexibility: Maintaining relations within organized and unorganized groups. In W. Shaffir & R. Stebbins (Eds.), *Experiencing fieldwork* (pp. 173-183). Newbury Park, CA: Sage.

Adler, P. A., Kless, S. J., & Adler, P. (1992). Socialization to gender roles: Images of popularity among elementary school boys and girls. *Sociology of Education, 65,* 169-187.

Atkinson, P. A. (1990). *The ethnographic imagination: Textual constructions of reality.* London: Routledge.

Becker, H. S. (1981). *Exploring society photographically.* Evanston, IL: Northwestern University, Mary and Leigh Block Gallery.

Becker, H. S. (1986). *Doing things together: Selected papers.* Evanston, IL: Northwestern University Press.

Berg, B. (1989). *Qualitative research methods for the social sciences.* Boston: Allyn & Bacon.

Brissett, D., & Edgley, C. (1990). *Life as theater* (2nd ed.). New York: Aldine de Gruyter.

Buban, S. L. (1986). Studying social process: The Chicago and Iowa schools revisited. In C. J. Couch, S. Saxton, & M. A. Katovich (Eds.), *Studies in symbolic interaction: Supplement 2. The Iowa school* (Part A) (pp. 25-38). Greenwich, CT: JAI.

Cahill, S. (1987). Children and civility: Ceremonial deviance and the acquisition of ritual competence. *Social Psychology Quarterly, 50,* 312-321.

Cahill, S. (1990). Childhood and public life: Reaffirming biographical divisions. *Social Problems, 37,* 390-402.

Cahill, S., with Distler, W., Lachowetz, C., Meaney, A., Tarallo, R., & Willard, T. (1985). Meanwhile backstage: Public bathrooms and the interaction order. *Urban Life, 14,* 33-58.

Carpenter, C., Glassner, B., Johnson, B., & Loughlin, J. (1988). *Kids, drugs, and crime.* Lexington, MA: Lexington.

Couch, C. J. (1984). *Constructing civilizations.* Greenwich, CT: JAI.

Couch, C. J., Saxton, S., & Katovich, M. A. (Eds.). (1986). *Studies in symbolic interaction: Supplement 2. The Iowa school* (Part A). Greenwich, CT: JAI.

Crapanzano, V. (1970). The writing of ethnography. *Dialectical Anthropology, 2,* 69-73.

Denzin, N. K. (1989). *The research act* (3rd ed.). Englewood Cliffs, NJ: Prentice Hall.

Dilthey, W. (1961). *Patterns and meanings in history* (H. P. Rickman, Trans.). New York: Harper & Row.

Douglas, J. D. (1976). *Investigative social research.* Beverly Hills, CA: Sage.

Douglas, J. D. (1979). Living morality versus bureaucratic fiat. In C. Klockars & F. O'Connor (Eds.), *Deviance and decency: The ethics of research with human subjects* (pp. 13-34). Beverly Hills, CA: Sage.

Douglas, J. D., & Johnson, J. (1977). *Existential sociology.* Cambridge: Cambridge University Press.

Ellis, C. (1991). Sociological introspection and emotional experience. *Symbolic Interaction, 14,* 23-50.

Ellis, C. (1993). *Final negotiations.* Manuscript submitted for publication.

Erikson, K. T. (1967). A comment on disguised observation in sociology. *Social Problems, 14,* 366-373.

Frisby, D. (1981). *Sociological impressionism: A reassessment of the social theory of Georg Simmel.* London: Heinemann.

Gardner, C. B. (1988). Access information: Public lies and private peril. *Social Problems, 35,* 384-397.

Glaser, B. G., & Strauss, A. L. (1967). *The discovery of grounded theory: Strategies for qualitative research.* Chicago: Aldine.

Glazer, M. (1975). Impersonal sex. In L. Humphreys, *Tearoom trade: Impersonal sex in public places* (enlarged ed., pp. 213-222). New York: Aldine.

Glesne, C., & Peshkin, A. (1992). *Becoming qualitative researchers.* White Plains, NY: Longman.

Goffman, E. (1961). *Asylums.* Garden City, NY: Doubleday.

Goffman, E. (1963). *Stigma: Notes on the management of spoiled identity.* Englewood Cliffs, NJ: Prentice Hall.

Goffman, E. (1971). *Relations in public.* New York: Basic Books.

Gold, R. L. (1958). Roles in sociological field observations. *Social Forces, 36,* 217-223.

Goodwin, C. (1981). *Conversational organization: Interaction between speakers and hearers.* New York: Academic Press.

Hammersley, M., & Atkinson, P. (1983). *Ethnography: Principles in practice.* London: Tavistock.

Handel, W. (1982). *Ethnomethodology.* Englewood Cliffs, NJ: Prentice Hall.

Hayano, D. (1979). Auto-ethnography: Paradigms, problems, and prospects. *Human Organization, 38,* 99-104.

Hayano, D. (1982). *Poker faces.* Berkeley: University of California Press.

Heritage, J. (1984). *Garfinkel and ethnomethodology.* Cambridge: Polity.

Horowitz, I. L., & Rainwater, L. (1975). On journalistic moralizers. In L. Humphreys, *Tearoom trade: Impersonal sex in public places* (enlarged ed., pp. 181-190). New York: Aldine.

Humphreys, L. (1975). *Tearoom trade: Impersonal sex in public places* (enlarged edition). New York: Aldine.

Jarvie, I. C. (1969). The problem of ethical integrity in participant-observation. *Current Anthropology, 10,* 505-508.

Jefferson, G. (Ed.). (1989). *Harvey Sacks lectures 1964-65.* Dordrecht, Netherlands: Kluwer Academic Publishers.

Johnson, J. (1975). *Doing field research.* New York: Free Press.

Jorgensen, D. L. (1989). *Participant observation.* Newbury Park, CA: Sage.

Katovich, M. A., Weiland, M. W., & Couch, C. J. (1978). *The impact of news on representative-constituent relationships: Toward a theory of representative democracy.* Unpublished manuscript.

Katovich, M. A., Weiland, M. W., & Couch, C. J. (1981). Access to information and internal structures of partisan groups: Some notes on the iron law of oligarchy. *Sociological Quarterly, 22,* 431-446.

Kidder, L. H. (1981). *Selltiz, Wrightsman and Cook's research methods in social relations* (4th ed.). New York: Holt, Rinehart & Winston.

Kotarba, J. A., & Fontana, A. (Eds.). (1984). *The existential self in society.* Chicago: University of Chicago Press.

Kretzmann, M. J. (1992). Bad blood: The moral stigmatization of paid plasma donors. *Journal of Contemporary Ethnography, 20,* 416-441.

Krieger, S. (1985). Beyond subjectivity: The use of the self in social science. *Qualitative Sociology, 8,* 309-324.

Lofland, J., & Lofland, L. (1984). *Analyzing social settings: A guide to qualitative observation and analysis* (2nd ed.). Belmont, CA: Wadsworth.

Lofland, L. (1973). *A world of strangers.* New York: Basic Books.

Lofland, L. (1989). Social life in the public realm: A review. *Journal of Contemporary Ethnography, 17,* 453-482.

Lofland, L. (1994). Observations and observers in conflict: Field research in the public realm. In S. Cahill & L. Lofland (Eds.), *The community of the streets.* Greenwich, CT: JAI.

Maynard, D. W. (1984). *Inside plea bargaining: The language of negotiation.* New York: Plenum.

McHoul, A. (1978). The organization of turns at formal talk in the classroom. *Language in Society, 7,* 183-213.

Mead, G. H. (1934). *Mind, self and society: From the standpoint of a social behaviorist.* Chicago: University of Chicago Press.

Mehan, H., & Wood, H. (1975). *The reality of ethnomethodology.* New York: John Wiley.

Miller, D. E., Hintz, R. A., Jr., & Couch, C. J. (1975). The elements and structure of openings. In C. J. Couch & R. A. Hintz, Jr. (Eds.), *Constructing social life* (pp. 1-24). Champaign, IL: Stipes.

Molotch, H. L., & Boden, D. (1985). Talking social structure. *American Sociological Review, 50,* 273-287.

Morris, W. (Ed.). (1973). *The American Heritage dictionary of the English language.* Boston: Houghton Mifflin.

Nash, J. (1975). Bus riding: Community on wheels. *Urban Life, 4,* 99-124.

Nash, J. (1981). Relations in frozen places: Observations on winter public order. *Qualitative Sociology, 4,* 229-243.

Nash, J., & Nash, A. (1994). The skyway system and urban space: Vitality in enclosed public places. In S. Cahill & L. Lofland (Eds.), *The community of the streets.* Greenwich, CT: JAI.

Phillips, B. (1985). *Sociological research methods.* Homewood, IL: Dorsey.

Reiman, J. (1979). Research subjects, human subjects, and political subjects. In C. Klockars & F. O'Connor (Eds.), *Deviance and decency: The ethics of research with human subjects* (pp. 35-57). Beverly Hills, CA: Sage.

Riemer, J. (1977). Varieties of opportunistic research. *Urban Life, 5,* 467-477.

Sacks, H. (1963). On sociological description. *Berkeley Journal of Sociology, 8,* 1-16.

Saxton, S. L., & Couch, C. J. (1975). Recording social interaction. In C. J. Couch & R. A. Hintz, Jr. (Eds.), *Constructing social life* (pp. 255-262). Champaign, IL: Stipes.

Schatzman, L., & Strauss, A. L. (1973). *Field research: Strategies for a natural sociology.* Englewood Cliffs, NJ: Prentice Hall.

Schegloff, E. A. (1968). Sequencing in conversational openings. *American Anthropologist, 70,* 1075-1095.

Schutz, A. (1967). *The phenomenology of the social world* (G. Walsh & F. Lehnert, Trans.). Evanston, IL: Northwestern University Press.

Schutz, A. (1971). *Collected papers* (Vol. 1) (M. Natanson, Ed.). The Hague: Martinus Nijhoff.

Smith, G. (1992, October 13). *A Simmelian reading of Goffman's rhetoric.* Guest lecture presented at the University of Colorado.

Spradley, J. P. (1980). *Participant observation.* New York: Holt, Rinehart & Winston.

von Hoffman, N. (1975). Sociological snoopers. In L. Humphreys, *Tearoom trade: Impersonal sex in public places* (enlarged ed., pp. 177-181). New York: Aldine.

Warwick, D. P. (1973). Tearoom trade: Means and ends in social research. *Hastings Center Studies, 1,* 27-38.

Webb, E. J., Campbell, D. T., Schwartz, R. C., & Sechrest, L. (1966). *Unobtrusive measures: Nonreactive research in the social sciences.* Chicago: University of Chicago Press.

4

The Interpretation of Documents and Material Culture

Ian Hodder

◆ This chapter is concerned with the interpretation of mute evidence—
that is, with written texts and artifacts. Such evidence, unlike the
spoken word, endures physically and thus can be separated across space
and time from its author, producer, or user. Material traces thus often have
to be interpreted without the benefit of indigenous commentary. There is
often no possibility of interaction with spoken emic "insider" as opposed
to etic "outsider" perspectives. Even when such interaction is possible,
actors often seem curiously inarticulate about the reasons they dress in
particular ways, choose particular pottery designs, or discard dung in
particular locations. Material traces and residues thus pose special problems for qualitative research. The main disciplines that have tried to
develop appropriate theory and method are history, art history, archaeology, anthropology, sociology, cognitive psychology, technology, and modern material culture studies, and it is from this range of disciplines that my
account is drawn.

◆ Written Documents and Records

Lincoln and Guba (1985, p. 277) distinguish documents and records on
the basis of whether the text was prepared to attest to some formal

110

transaction. Thus records include marriage certificates, driving licenses, building contracts, and banking statements. Documents, on the other hand, are prepared for personal rather than official reasons and include diaries, memos, letters, field notes, and so on. In fact, the two terms are often used interchangeably, although the distinction is an important one and has some parallels with the distinction between writing and speech, to be discussed below. Documents, closer to speech, require more contextualized interpretation. Records, on the other hand, may have local uses that become very distant from officially sanctioned meanings. Documents involve a personal technology, and records a full state technology of power. The distinction is also relevant for qualitative research, in that researchers may often be able to get access to documents, whereas access to records may be restricted by laws regarding privacy, confidentiality, and anonymity.

Despite the utility of the distinction between documents and records, my concern here is more the problems of interpretation of written texts of all kinds. Such texts are of importance for qualitative research because, in general terms, access can be easy and low cost, because the information provided may differ from and may not be available in spoken form, and because texts endure and thus give historical insight.

It has often been assumed, for example, in the archaeology of historical periods, that written texts provide a "truer" indication of original meanings than do other types of evidence (to be considered below). Indeed, Western social science has long privileged the spoken over the written and the written over the nonverbal (Derrida, 1978). Somehow it is assumed that words get us closer to minds. But as Derrida has shown, meaning does not reside in a text but in the writing and reading of it. As the text is reread in different contexts it is given new meanings, often contradictory and always socially embedded. Thus there is no "original" or "true" meaning of a text outside specific historical contexts. Historical archaeologists have come to accept that historical documents and records give not a better but simply a different picture from that provided by artifacts and architecture. Texts can be used alongside other forms of evidence so that the particular biases of each can be understood and compared.

Equally, different types of text have to be understood in the contexts of their conditions of production and reading. For example, the analyst will be concerned with whether a text was written as result of firsthand experience or from secondary sources, whether it was solicited or unsolicited, edited or unedited, anonymous or signed, and so on (Webb, Campbell, Schwartz, & Sechrest, 1966). As Ricoeur (1971) demonstrates, concrete texts differ from the abstract structures of language in that they are written to do something. They can be understood only as what they are—a form of artifact produced under certain material conditions (not everyone can write, or write in a certain way, or have access to relevant technologies of reproduction) embedded within social and ideological systems.

Words are, of course, spoken to do things as well as to say things—they have practical and social impact as well as communication function. Once transformed into a written text the gap between the "author" and the "reader" widens and the possibility of multiple reinterpretations increases. The text can "say" many different things in different contexts. But also the written text is an artifact, capable of transmission, manipulation, and alteration, used and discarded, reused and recycled—"doing" different things contextually through time. The writing down of words often allows language and meanings to be controlled more effectively, and to be linked to strategies of centralization and codification. The word, concretized or "made flesh" in the artifact, can transcend context and gather through time extended symbolic connotations. The word made enduring in artifacts has an important role to play in both secular and religious processes of the legitimation of power. Yet there is often a tension between the concrete nature of the written word, its enduring nature, and the continuous potential for rereading meanings in new contexts, undermining the authority of the word. Text and context are in a continual state of tension, each defining and redefining the other, saying and doing things differently through time.

In a related way, the written texts of anthropologists and archaeologists are increasingly coming under scrutiny as employing rhetorical strategies in order to establish positions of authority (e.g., Tilley, 1989). Archaeologists are used to the idea that their scientific activities leave traces and transform the worlds they study. Excavations cannot be repeated, and the residues of trenches, spoil tips, and old beer cans remain as specific expressions of a particular way of looking at the world. The past has been transformed into a present product, including the field notes and site reports. Ethnographic field notes (Sanjek, 1990) also transform the object of study into a historically situated product, "capturing" the "other" within a familiar routine. The field text has to be contextualized within specific historical moments.

I shall in this chapter treat written texts as special cases of artifacts, subject to similar interpretive procedures. In both texts and artifacts the problem is one of situating material culture within varying contexts while at the same time entering into a dialectic relationship between those contexts and the context of the analyst. This hermeneutical exercise, in which the lived experience surrounding the material culture is translated into a different context of interpretation, is common for both texts and other forms of material culture. I will note various differences between language and material culture in what follows, but the interpretive parallels have been widely discussed in the consideration of material culture as text (e.g., Hodder, 1991; Moore, 1986; Tilley, 1990).

◆ Artifact Analysis and Its Importance for the Interpretation of Social Experience

Ancient and modern buildings and artifacts, the intended and unintended residues of human activity, give alternative insights into the ways in which people perceived and fashioned their lives. Shortcuts across lawns indicate preferred traffic patterns, foreign-language signs indicate the degree of integration of a neighborhood, the number of cigarettes in an ashtray betrays a nervous tension, and the amount of paperwork in an "in" tray is a measure of workload or of work efficiency and priority (Lincoln & Guba, 1985, p. 280). Despite the inferential problems surrounding such evidence, I wish to establish at the outset that material traces of behavior give an important and different insight from that provided by any number of questionnaires.

"What people say" is often very different from "what people do." This point has perhaps been most successfully established over recent years by research stemming from the work of Bill Rathje (Rathje & Murphy, 1992; Rathje & Thompson, 1981). In studies in Tucson, Arizona, and elsewhere, Rathje and his colleagues collected domestic garbage bags and itemized the contents. It became clear that, for example, people's estimates about the amounts of garbage they produced were wildly incorrect, that discarded beer cans indicated a higher level of alcohol consumption than was admitted to, and that in times of meat shortage people threw away more meat than usual as a result of overhoarding. Thus a full sociological analysis cannot be restricted to interview data. It must also consider the material traces.

In another series of studies, the decoration of rooms as well as pots and other containers has been interpreted as a form of silent discourse conducted by women, whose voice has been silenced by dominant male interests. Decoration may be used to mark out, silently, and to draw attention to, tacitly, areas of female control, such as female areas of houses and the preparation and provision of food in containers. The decoration may at one level provide protection from female pollution, but at another level it expresses female power (Braithwaite, 1982; Donley, 1982; Hodder, 1991).

The study of material culture is thus of importance for qualitative researchers who wish to explore multiple and conflicting voices, differing and interacting interpretations. Many areas of experience are hidden from language, particularly subordinate experience. Ferguson (1991) has shown how study of the material traces of food and pots can provide insight into how slaves on plantations in the American South made sense of and reacted to their domination. The members of this normally silenced group expressed their own perspective in the mundane activities of everyday life.

Analysis of such traces is not a trivial pursuit, as the mundane and the everyday, because unimportant to dominant interests, may be of great importance for the expression of alternative perspectives. The material expression of power (parades, regalia, tombs, and art) can be set against the expression of resistance. The importance of such analysis is increased by the realization that material culture is not simply a passive by-product of other areas of life. Rather, material culture is active (Hodder, 1982). By this I mean that artifacts are produced so as to transform, materially, socially, and ideologically. It is the exchange of artifacts themselves that constructs social relationships; it is the style of spear that creates a feeling of common identity; it is the badge of authority that itself confers authority. Material culture is thus *necessary for* most social constructs. An adequate study of social interaction thus depends on the incorporation of mute material evidence.

◆ **Toward a Theory of Material Culture**

Having established that the study of material culture can be an important tool for sociological and anthropological analysis, it is necessary to attempt to build a theory on which the interpretation of material culture can be based. A difficulty here has been the diversity of the category "material culture," ranging from written texts to material symbols surrounding death, drama, and ritual, to shopping behavior and to the construction of roads and airplanes. As a result, theoretical directions have often taken rather different paths, as one can see by comparing attempts to build a comprehensive theory for technological behavior (Lemonnier, 1986) and attempts to consider material culture as text (Tilley, 1990).

Ultimately, material culture always has to be interpreted in relation to a situated context of production, use, discard, and reuse. In working toward that contextual interpretation, it may be helpful to distinguish some general characteristics and analogies for the different types of material culture. In this attempt to build a general theory, recent research in a range of disciplines has begun to separate two areas of material meaning.

Some material culture is designed specifically to be communicative and representational. The clearest example is a written text, but this category extends, for example, to the badge and uniform of certain professions, to red and green stop and go traffic lights, to smoke signals, to the images of Christ on the cross. Because this category includes written texts, it is to be expected that meaning in this category might be organized in ways similar to language. Thus, as with words in a language, the material symbols are, outside a historical context, often arbitrary. For example, any design on a flag could be used as long as it differs from the designs on other flags and is recognizable with its own identity. Thus the system of meanings in the case of flags is constructed through similarities and differences in a semiotic code. Miller (1982) has shown how dress is organized both syntagmatically and paradigmatically. The choice of hat, tie, shirt, trousers, shoes, and so on for a particular occasion is informed by a syntax that allows a particular set of clothes to be put together. On the other hand, the distinctions among different types of hats (bowler, straw, cloth, baseball) or jackets constitute paradigmatic choices.

The three broad areas of theory that have been applied to this first type of material meaning derive from information technology, Marxism, and structuralism. In the first, the aim has been to account for the ways in which material symboling can provide adaptive advantage to social groups. Thus the development of complex symboling systems allows more information to be processed more efficiently (e.g., Wobst, 1977). This type of approach is of limited value to qualitative research because it is not concerned with the interpretation and experience of meaningful symbols. In the second, the ideological component of symbols is identified within relations of power and domination (Leone, 1984; Miller & Tilley, 1984) and increasingly power and systems of value and prestige are seen as multiple and dialectical (Miller, Rowlands, & Tilley, 1989; Shanks & Tilley, 1987). The aim of structuralist analysis has been to examine design (e.g., Washburn,

1983) or spatial relationships (e.g., Glassie, 1975; McGhee, 1977) in terms of underlying codes, although here too the tendency has been on emphasizing multiple meanings contested within active social contexts as the various directions of poststructuralist thought have been debated (Tilley, 1990).

In much of this work the metaphor of language has been applied to material culture relatively unproblematically. The pot appears to "mean" in the same way as the word *pot*. Recent work has begun to draw attention to the limitations of this analogy between material culture and language, as will become clear in my consideration of the second type of material culture meaning. One can begin to explore the limitations of the analogy by considering that many examples of material culture are not produced to "mean" at all. In other words, they are not produced with symbolic functions as primary. Thus the madeleine cookie discussed in Proust's *A la recherche du temps perdu* (*Swann's Way*) was produced as an enticing food, made in a shape representing a fluted scallop. But Proust describes its meaning as quite different from this symbolic representation. Rather, the meaning was the evocation of a whole series of childhood memories, sounds, tastes, smells surrounding having tea with his mother in winter.

Many if not most material symbols do not work through rules of representation, using a language-like syntax. Rather, they work through the evocation of sets of practices within individual experience. It would be relatively difficult to construct a grammar or dictionary of material symbols except in the case of deliberately representational or symbolic items, such as flags and road signs. This is because most material symbols do not mean in the same way as language. Rather, they come to have abstract meaning through association and practice. Insofar as members of society experience common practices, material symbols can come to have common evocations and common meanings. Thus, for example, the ways in which certain types of food, drink, music, and sport are experienced are embedded within social convention and thus come to have common meaning. A garlic crusher may not be used overtly in Britain to represent or symbolize class, but through a complex set of practices surrounding food and its preparation the crusher has come to mean class through evocation.

Because objects endure, have their own traces, their own grain, individual objects with unique evocations can be recognized. The specific memory traces associated with any particular object (a particular garlic crusher) will vary from individual to individual. The particularity of material experience and meaning derives not only from the diversity of human life but also from the identifiability of material objects. The identifiable particularity of material experience always has the potential to work against and transform societywide conventions through practice. Because of this dialectic between structure and practice, and because of the multiple local meanings that can be given to things, it would be difficult to construct dictionaries and grammars for most material culture meanings.

Another reason for the inability to produce dictionaries of material culture returns us to the difficulty with which people give discursive accounts of material symbolism. The meanings often remain tacit and implicit. A smell or taste of a madeleine cookie may awake strong feelings, but it is notoriously difficult to describe a taste or a feel or to pin down the emotions evoked. We may know that in practice this or that item of clothing "looks good," "works well," or "is stylish," but we would be at a loss to say what it "means" because the item does not mean—rather, it is embedded in a set of practices that include class, status, goals, aesthetics. We may not know much about art, but we know what we like. On the basis of a set of practical associations, we build up an implicit knowledge about the associations and evocations of particular artifacts or styles. This type of embedded, practical experience seems to be different from the manipulation of rules of representation and from conscious analytic thought. Material symbolic meanings may get us close to lived experience, but they cannot easily be articulated.

The importance of practice for the social and symbolic meanings of artifacts has been emphasized in recent work on technology (Schlanger, 1990). Each technical operation is linked to others in operational chains (Leroi-Gourhan, 1964) involving materials, energy, and gestures. For example, some clays are better for throwing than others, so that type of clay constrains whether a manufacturer can make thrown pots or hand-built statuettes. Quality of clay is related to types of temper that should be used. All such operational chains are nondeterministic, and some degree of social choice is involved (Lemonnier, 1986; Miller, 1985). All operational chains involve aspects of production, exchange, and consumption, and so are part of a network of relations incorporating the material, the economic, the social, and the conceptual.

The practical operational chains often have implications that extend into not only social but also moral realms. For example, Latour (1988) discusses hydraulic door closers, devices that automatically close a door after someone has opened it. The material door closer thus takes the place of, or delegates, the role of a porter, someone who stands there and makes sure

117

that the door stays shut after people have gone through. But use of this particular delegate has various implications, one of which is that very young or infirm people have difficulty getting through the door. A social distinction is unwittingly implied by this technology. In another example, Latour discusses a key used by some inhabitants of Berlin. This double-ended key forces the user to lock the door in order to get the key out. The key delegates for staff or signs that might order a person to "relock the door behind you." Staff or signs would be unreliable—they could be outwitted or ignored. The key enforces a morality. In the same way "sleeping policemen" (speed bumps) force the driver of a car to be moral and to slow down in front of a school, but this morality is not socially encoded. That would be too unreliable. The morality is embedded within the practical consequences of breaking up one's car by driving too fast over the bumps. The social and moral meanings of the door closer, the Berlin key, or the speed bump are thoroughly embedded in the implications of material practices.

I have suggested that in developing a theory of material culture, the first task is to distinguish at least two different ways in which material culture has abstract meaning beyond primary utilitarian concerns. The first is through rules of representation. The second is through practice and evocation—through the networking, interconnection, and mutual implication of material and nonmaterial. Whereas it may be the case that written language is the prime example of the first category and tools the prime example of the second, language also has to be worked out in practices from which it derives much of its meaning. Equally, we have seen that material items can be placed within language-like codes. But there is some support from cognitive psychology for a general difference between the two types of knowledge. For example, Bechtel (1990, p. 264) argues that rule-based models of cognition are naturally good at quite different types of activity from connectionist models. Where the first is appropriate for problem solving, the second is best at tasks such as pattern recognition and motor control. It seems likely then that the skills involved in material practice and the social, symbolic, and moral meanings that are implicated in such practices might involve different cognitive systems than involved in rules and representations.

Bloch (1991) argues that practical knowledge is fundamentally different from linguistic knowledge in the way it is organized in the mind. Practical knowledge is "chunked" into highly contextualized information about how to "get on" in specific domains of action. Much cultural knowledge is nonlinear and purpose dedicated, formed through the practice of closely related activities. I have argued here that even the practical world involves social and symbolic meanings that are not organized representational codes but that are chunked or contextually organized realms of activity in which emotions, desires, morals, and social relations are involved at the level of implicit taken-for-granted skill or know-how.

It should perhaps be emphasized that the two types of material symbolism—the representational and the evocative or implicative—often work in close relation to each other. Thus a set of practices may associate men and women with different parts of houses or times of day, but in certain social contexts these associations might be built upon to construct symbolic rules of separation and exclusion and to build an abstract representational scheme in which mythology and cosmology play a part (e.g., Yates, 1989). Such schemes also have ideological components that feed back to constrain the practices. Thus practice, evocation, and representation interpenetrate and feed off each other in many if not all areas of life. Structure and practice are recursively related in the "structuration" of material life (Giddens, 1979; see also Bourdieu, 1977).

◆ Material Meanings in Time

It appears that people both experience and "read" material culture meanings. There is much more that could be said about how material culture works in the social context. For instance, some examples work by direct and explicit metaphor, where similarities in form refer to historical antecedents, whereas others work by being ambiguous and abstract, by using spectacle or dramatic effect, by controlling the approach of the onlooker, by controlling perspective. Although there is not space here to explore the full range of material strategies, it is important to establish the temporal dimension of lived experience.

As already noted, material culture is durable and can be given new meanings as it is separated from its primary producer. This temporal variation in meaning is often related to changes in meaning across space and culture. Archaeological or ethnographic artifacts are continually being taken out of their contexts and reinterpreted within museums within different social and cultural contexts. The Elgin Marbles housed in the British Museum take on new meanings that are in turn reinterpreted antagonistically in some circles in Greece. American Indian human and artifact remains may have a scientific meaning for archaeologists and biological anthropologists, but they have important emotive and identity meanings for indigenous peoples.

Material items are continually being reinterpreted in new contexts. Also, material culture can be added to or removed from, leaving the traces of reuses and reinterpretations. In some cases, the sequence of use can give insight into the thought processes of an individual, as when flint flakes that have been struck off a core in early prehistory are refitted by archaeologists today (e.g., Pelegrin, 1990) in order to rebuild the flint core and to follow the decisions made by the original flint knapper in producing flakes and tools. In other cases, longer frames of time are involved, as when a monument such as Stonehenge is adapted, rebuilt, and reused for divergent purposes over millennia up to the present day (Chippindale, 1983). In such an example, the narrative held within traces on the artifact has an overall form that has been produced by multiple individuals and groups, often unaware of earlier intentions and meanings. Few people today, although knowledgeable about Christmas practices, are aware of the historical reasons behind the choice of Christmas tree, Santa Claus, red coats, and flying reindeer.

There are many trajectories that material items can take through shifting meanings. For example, many are made initially to refer to or evoke metaphorically, whereas through time the original meaning becomes lost or the item becomes a cliché, having lost its novelty. An artifact may start as a focus but become simply a frame, part of an appropriate background. In the skeuomorphic process a functional component becomes decorative, as when a gas fire depicts burning wood or coal. In other cases the load of meaning invested in an artifact increases through time, as in the case of a talisman or holy relic. Material items are often central in the backward-looking invention of tradition, as when the Italian fascist movement elevated the Roman symbol of authority—a bundle of rods—to provide authority for a new form of centralized power.

This brief discussion of the temporal dimension emphasizes the contextuality of material culture meaning. As is clear from some of the examples given, changing meanings through time are often involved in antagonistic relations between groups. Past and present meanings are continually being contested and reinterpreted as part of social and political strategies. Such conflict over material meanings is of particular interest to qualitative research in that it expresses and focuses alternative views and interests. The reburial of American Indian and Australian aboriginal remains is an issue that has expressed, but perhaps also helped to construct, a new sense of indigenous rights in North America and Australia. As "ethnic cleansing" reappears in Europe, so too do attempts to reinterpret documents, monuments, and artifacts in ethnic terms. But past artifacts can also be used to help local communities in productive and practical ways. One example of the active use of the past in the present is provided by the work of Erickson (1988) in the area around Lake Titicaca in Peru. Information from the archaeological study of raised fields was used to reconstruct agricultural systems on the ancient model, with the participation and to the benefit of local farmers.

◆ Method

The interpretation of mute material evidence puts the interactionist view under pressure. How can an approach that gives considerable importance to interaction with speaking subjects (e.g., Denzin, 1989) deal with material traces for which informants are long dead or about which informants are not articulate?

I have already noted the importance of material evidence in providing insight into other components of lived experience. The methodological issues that are raised are not, however, unique. In all types of interactive research the analyst has to decide whether or not to take commentary at face value and how to evaluate spoken or unspoken responses. How does what is said fit into more general understanding? Analysts of material culture may not have much spoken commentary to work with, but they do have patterned evidence that has to be evaluated in relation to the full range of available information. They too have to fit different aspects of the evidence into a hermeneutical whole (Hodder, 1992; Shanks & Tilley, 1987). They ask, How does what is done fit into more general understanding?

In general terms, the interpreter of material culture works between past and present or between different examples of material culture, making analogies between them. The material evidence always has the potential to be patterned in unexpected ways. Thus it provides an "other" against which the analyst's own experience of the world has to be evaluated and can be enlarged. Although the evidence cannot "speak back," it can confront the interpreter in ways that enforce self-reappraisal. At least when a researcher is dealing with prehistoric remains, there are no "member checks" because the artifacts are themselves mute. On the other hand, material culture is the product of and is embedded in "internal" experience. Indeed, it could be argued that some material culture, precisely because it is not overt, self-conscious speech, may give deeper insights into the internal meanings according to which people lived their lives. I noted above some examples of material culture being used to express covert meanings. Thus the lack of spoken member checks is counteracted by the checks provided by unspoken material patterning that remain able to confront and undermine interpretation.

An important initial assumption made by those interpreting material culture is that belief, idea, and intention are important to action and practice (see above). It follows that the conceptual has some impact on the patterning of material remains. The ideational component of material patterning is not opposed to but is integrated with its material functioning. It is possible therefore to infer both utilitarian and conceptual meaning from the patterning of material evidence.

The interpreter is faced with material data that are patterned along a number of different dimensions simultaneously. Minimally, archaeologists distinguish technology, function, and style, and they use such attributes to form typologies and to seek spatial and temporal patterning. In practice, however, as the discussion above has shown, it has become increasingly difficult to separate technology from style or to separate types from their spatial and temporal contexts. In other words, the analytic or pattern-recognition stage has itself been identified as interpretive.

Thus at all stages, from the identification of classes and attributes to the understanding of high-level social processes, the interpreter has to deal simultaneously with three areas of evaluation. First, the interpreter has to identify the contexts within which things had similar meaning. The boundaries of the context are never "given"; they have to be interpreted. Of course, physical traces and separations might assist the definition of contextual boundaries, such as the boundaries around a village or the separation in time between sets of events. Ritual contexts might be more formalized than or may invert mundane contexts. But despite such clues there is an infinity of possible contexts that might have been constructed by indigenous actors. The notion of context is always relevant when different sets of data are being compared and where a primary question is whether the different examples are comparable, whether the apparent similarities are real.

Second, in conjunction with and inseparable from the identification of context is the recognition of similarities and differences. The interpreter argues for a context by showing that things are done similarly, that people respond similarly to similar situations, within its boundaries. The assumption is made that within the context similar events or things had similar meaning. But this is true only if the boundaries of the context have been correctly identified. Many artifacts initially identified as ritual or cultic have later been shown to come from entirely utilitarian contexts. Equally, claimed cross-cultural similarities always have to be evaluated to see if their contexts are comparable. Thus the interpretations of context and of meaningful similarities and differences are mutually dependent.

The identification of contexts, similarities, and differences within patterned materials depends on the application of appropriate social and material culture theories. The third evaluation that has to be made by the interpreter is of the relevance of general or specific historical theories to the data at hand. Observation and interpretation are theory laden, although theories can be changed in confrontation with material evidence in a dialectical fashion. Some of the appropriate types of general theory for material culture have been identified above. The more specific theories include the intentions and social goals of participants, or the nature of ritual or cultic as opposed to secular or utilitarian behavior.

In terms of the two types of material meaning identified earlier, rules of representation are built up from patterns of association and exclusion. For example, if a pin type is exclusively associated with women in a wide variety of contexts, then it might be interpreted as representing women in all situations. The aspect of womanhood that is represented by this association with pins is derived from other associations of the pins—perhaps with foreign, nonlocal artifacts (Sorensen, 1987). The more richly networked the associations that can be followed by the interpreter, and the thicker the description (Denzin, 1989) that can be produced, the subtler the interpretations that can be made.

For the other type of material meaning, grounded in practice, the initial task of the interpreter is to understand all the social and material implications of particular practices. This is greatly enhanced by studies of modern material culture, including ethnoarchaeology (Orme, 1981). Experimental archaeologists (Coles, 1979) are now well experienced in reconstructing past practices, from storage of cereals in pits to flaking flint tools. Such reconstructions, always unavoidably artificial to some degree, allow some direct insight into another lived experience. On the basis of such knowledge the implications of material practices, extending into the social and the moral, can be theorized. But again it is detailed thick description of associations and contexts that allows the material practices to be set within specific historical situations and the particular evocations to be understood.

An example of the application of these methods is provided by Merriman's (1987) interpretation of the intentions behind the building of a wall around the elite settlement of Heuneberg, Germany, in the sixth century B.C. (an example similar to that provided by Collingwood, 1956). In cultural terms, the Hallstatt context in central Europe, including Germany, can be separated from other cultural areas such as the Aegean at this time. And yet the walls are made of mud brick and they have bastions, both of which have parallels only in the Aegean. In practice, mud brick would not have been an effective long-term form of defense in the German climate. Thus some purpose other than defense is supposed. The walls are different from other contemporary walls in Germany and yet they are similar to walls found in the Aegean context. Other similarities and differences that seem relevant are the examples of prestige exchange—valuable objects such as wine flagons traded from the Aegean to Germany. This trade seems relevant because of a theory that elites in central Europe based their power on the control of prestige exchange with the Mediterranean. It seems likely, in the context of such prestige exchange, that the walls built in a Mediterranean form were also designed to confer prestige on the elites who organized their construction. In this example the intention of the wall building is interpreted as being for prestige rather than for defense. The interpretation is based on the simultaneous evaluation of similarities and differences, context and theory. Both representational symbolism (conferring prestige) and practical meanings (the building of walls by elites in a non-Mediterranean climate) are considered. For other examples of the method applied to modern material culture, see Hodder (1991) and Moore (1986).

◆ Confirmation

How is it possible to confirm such hypotheses about the meanings of mute material and written culture? Why are some interpretations more plausible than others? The answers to such questions are unlikely to differ radically from the procedures followed in other areas of interpretation, and so I will discuss them relatively briefly here (see Denzin, 1989; Lincoln & Guba, 1985). However, there are some differences in confirming hypotheses regarding material objects. Perhaps the major difficulty is that material culture, by its very nature, straddles the divide between a universal, natural science approach to materials and a historical, interpretive approach to culture. There is thus a particularly marked lack of agreement in the scientific community about the appropriate basis for confirmation procedures. In my view, an interpretive position can and should accommodate scientific information about, for example, natural processes of transformation and decay of artifacts. It is thus an interpretive position that I describe here.

The twin struts of confirmation are coherence and correspondence. Coherence is produced if the parts of the argument do not contradict each other and if the conclusions follow from the premises. There is a partial autonomy of different types of theory, from the observational to the global, and a coherent interpretation is one in which these different levels do not produce contradictory results. The partial autonomy of different types of theory is especially clear in relation to material culture. Because material evidence endures, it can continually be reobserved, reanalyzed, and reinterpreted. The observations made in earlier excavations are continually being reconsidered within new interpretive frameworks. It is clear from these reconsiderations of earlier work that earlier observations can be used to allow different interpretations—the different levels of theory are partially autonomous. The internal coherence between different levels of theory is continually being renegotiated.

As well as internal coherence there is external coherence—the degree to which the interpretation fits theories accepted in and outside the discipline. Of course, the evaluation of a coherent argument itself depends on the application of theoretical criteria, and I have already noted the lack of agreement in studies of material culture about foundational issues such as the importance of a natural science or humanistic approach. But whatever their views on such issues, most of those working with material culture seem to accept implicitly the importance of simplicity and elegance. An argument in which too much special pleading is required in order to claim coherence is less likely to be adopted than is a simple or elegant theory. The notion of coherence could also be extended to social and political issues within and beyond disciplines, but I shall here treat these questions separately.

The notion of correspondence between theory and data does not imply absolute objectivity and independence, but rather embeds the fit of data and theory within coherence. The data are made to cohere by being linked within theoretical arguments. Similarly, the coherence of the arguments is supported by the fit to data. On the other hand, data can confront theory, as already noted. Correspondence with the data is thus an essential part of arguments of coherence. There are many aspects of correspondence arguments that might be used. One is the exactness of fit, perhaps measured in statistical terms, between theoretical expectation and data, and this is a particularly important aspect of arguments exploiting the mute aspects of material culture. Other arguments of correspondence include the number of cases that are accounted for, their range in space and time, and the variety of different classes of data that are explained. However, such numerical indications of correspondence always have to be evaluated against contextual relevance and thick description to determine whether the different examples of fit are relevant to each other. In ethnographic and historical contexts correspondence with indigenous accounts can be part of the argument that supports contextual relevance.

Other criteria that affect the success of theories about material culture meaning include fruitfulness—how many new directions, new lines of inquiry, new perspectives are opened up. Reproducibility concerns whether other people, perhaps with different perspectives, come to similar results. Perhaps different arguments, based on different starting points, produce similar results. I have already noted that one of the advantages of material evidence is that it can continually be returned to, unexcavated parts of sites excavated and old trenches dug out and reexamined. Intersubjective agreement is of considerable importance although of particular difficulty in an area that so completely bridges the science-humanity divide. The success of interpretations depends on peer review (either informal or formally in journals) and on the number of people who believe, cite, and build on them.

But much depends too on the trustworthiness, professional credentials, and status of the author and supporters of an interpretation. Issues here include how long the interpreter spent in the field and how well she or he knows the data: their biases, problems, and unusual examples. Has the author obtained appropriate degrees and been admitted into professional societies? Is the individual an established and consistent writer, or has he or she yet to prove her- or himself? Does the author keep changing her or his mind?

In fact, the audience does not respond directly to an interpretation but to an interpretation written or staged as an article or presentation. The audience thus responds to and reinterprets a material artifact or event. The persuasiveness of the argument is closely tied to the rhetoric within which it is couched (Gero, 1991; Hodder, 1989; Spector, 1991; Tilley, 1989). The rhetoric determines how the different components of the discipline talk about and define problems and their solutions.

◆ Conclusion

Material culture, including written texts, poses a challenge for interpretive approaches that often stress the importance of dialogue with and spoken critical comment from participants. Material culture evidence, on the other hand, may have no living participants who can respond to its interpretation. Even if such participants do exist, they may often be unable to be articulate about material culture meanings. In any case, material culture endures, and so the original makers and users may be able to give only a partial picture of the full history of meanings given to an object as it is used and reinterpreted through time.

The challenge posed by material culture is important for anthropological and sociological analysis because material culture is often a medium in which alternative and often muted voices can be expressed. But the "reader" of material culture must recognize that only some aspects of material culture meaning are language-like. The meaning of much material culture comes about through use, and material culture knowledge is often highly chunked and contextualized. Technical operations implicate a wide network of material, social, and symbolic resources and the abstract meanings that result are closely tied in with the material.

The methods of interpretation of material culture center on the simultaneous hermeneutical procedures of context definition, the construction of patterned similarities and differences, and the use of relevant social and material culture theory. The material culture may not be able directly to "speak back," but if appropriate procedures are followed there is room for the data and for different levels of theory to confront interpretations. The interpreter learns from the experience of material remains—the data and the interpreter bring each other into existence in dialectical fashion. The interpretations can be confirmed or made more or less plausible than others using a fairly standard range of internal and external (social) criteria.

◆ References

Bechtel, W. (1990). Connectionism and the philosophy of mind: An overview. In W. G. Lycan (Ed.), *Mind and cognition: A reader.* Oxford: Basil Blackwell.

Bloch, M. (1991). Language, anthropology and cognitive science. *Man, 26,* 183-198.

Bourdieu, P. (1977). *Outline of a theory of practice.* Cambridge: Cambridge University Press.

Braithwaite, M. (1982). Decoration as ritual symbol. In I. Hodder (Ed.), *Symbolic and structural archaeology* (pp. 80-88). Cambridge: Cambridge University Press.

Chippindale, C. (1983). *Stonehenge complete.* London: Thames & Hudson.

Coles, J. M. (1979). *Experimental archaeology.* London: Academic Press.

Collingwood, R. (1956). *The idea of history.* Oxford: Oxford University Press.

Denzin, N. K. (1989). *Interpretive interactionism.* Newbury Park, CA: Sage.

Derrida, J. (1978). *Writing and difference.* London: Routledge & Kegan Paul.

Donley, L. (1982). House power: Swahili space and symbolic markers. In I. Hodder (Ed.), *Symbolic and structural archaeology* (pp. 63-73). Cambridge: Cambridge University Press.

Erickson, C. L. (1988). Raised field agriculture in the Lake Titicaca Basin: Putting ancient agriculture back to work. *Expedition, 30*(3), 8-16.

Ferguson, L. (1991). Struggling with pots in Colonial South Carolina. In R. McGuire & R. Paynter (Eds.), *The archaeology of inequality* (pp. 28-39). Oxford: Basil Blackwell.

Gero, J. (1991). Who experienced what in prehistory? A narrative explanation from Queyash, Peru. In R. Preucel (Ed.), *Processual and postprocessual archaeologies* (pp. 126-189). Carbondale: Southern Illinois University.

Giddens, A. (1979). *Central problems in social theory.* London: Macmillan.

Glassie, H. (1975). *Folk housing in middle Virginia.* Knoxville: University of Tennessee Press.

Hodder, I. (1982). *Symbols in action.* Cambridge: Cambridge University Press.

Hodder, I. (1989). Writing archaeology: Site reports in context. *Antiquity, 63,* 268-274.

Hodder, I. (1991). *Reading the past.* Cambridge: Cambridge University Press.

Hodder, I. (1992). *Theory and practice in archaeology.* London: Routledge.

Latour, B. (1988). Mixing humans and nonhumans together: The sociology of a door closer. *Social Problems, 35,* 298-310.

Lemonnier, P. (1986). The study of material culture today: Towards an anthropology of technical systems. *Journal of Anthropological Archaeology, 5,* 147-186.

Leone, M. (1984). Interpreting ideology in historical archaeology. In D. Miller & C. Tilley (Eds.), *Ideology, power and prehistory* (pp. 25-36). Cambridge: Cambridge University Press.

Leroi-Gourhan, A. (1964). *Le geste et la parole.* Paris: Michel.

Lincoln, Y. S., & Guba, E. G. (1985). *Naturalistic inquiry.* Beverly Hills, CA: Sage.

McGhee, R. (1977). Ivory for the sea woman. *Canadian Journal of Archaeology, 1,* 141-159.

Merriman, N. (1987). Value and motivation in prehistory: The evidence for "Celtic spirit." In I. Hodder (Ed.), *The archaeology of contextual meanings* (pp. 111-116). London: Unwin Hyman.

Miller, D. (1982). Artifacts as products of human categorisation processes. In I. Hodder (Ed.), *Symbolic and structural archaeology* (pp. 89-98). Cambridge: Cambridge University Press.

Miller, D. (1985). *Artifacts as categories.* Cambridge: Cambridge University Press.

Miller, D., Rowlands, M., & Tilley, C. (1989). *Domination and resistance.* London: Unwin Hyman.

Miller, D., & Tilley, C. (1984). *Ideology, power and prehistory.* Cambridge: Cambridge University Press.

Moore, H. (1986). *Space, text and gender.* Cambridge: Cambridge University Press.

Orme, B. (1981). *Anthropology for archaeologists.* London: Duckworth.

Pelegrin, J. (1990). Prehistoric lithic technology. *Archaeological Review from Cambridge, 9,* 116-125.

Rathje, W., & Murphy, C. (1992). *Rubbish! The archaeology of garbage.* New York: HarperCollins.

Rathje, W., & Thompson, B. (1981). *The Milwaukee Garbage Project.* Washington, DC: American Paper Institute, Solid Waste Council of the Paper Industry.

Ricoeur, P. (1971). The model of the text: Meaningful action considered as text. *Social Research, 38,* 529-562.

Sanjek, R. (Ed.). (1990). *Fieldnotes: The makings of anthropology.* Albany: State University of New York Press.

Schlanger, N. (1990). Techniques as human action: Two perspectives. *Archaeological Review from Cambridge, 9,* 18-26.

Shanks, M., & Tilley, C. (1987). *Reconstructing archaeology.* Cambridge: Cambridge University Press.

Sorensen, M.-L. (1987). Material order and cultural classification. In I. Hodder (Ed.), *The archaeology of contextual meanings* (pp. 90-101). Cambridge: Cambridge University Press.

Spector, J. (1991). What this awl means: Toward a feminist archaeology. In J. M. Gero & M. W. Conkey (Eds.), *Engendering archaeology* (pp. 388-406). Oxford: Basil Blackwell.

Tilley, C. (1989). Discourse and power: The genre of the Cambridge inaugural. In D. Miller, M. Rowlands, & C. Tilley (Eds.), *Domination and resistance* (pp. 41-62). London: Unwin Hyman.

Tilley, C. (Ed.). (1990). *Reading material culture.* Oxford: Basil Blackwell.

Washburn, D. (1983). *Structure and cognition in art.* Cambridge: Cambridge University Press.

Webb, E. J., Campbell, D. T., Schwartz, R. C., & Sechrest, L. (1966). *Unobtrusive measures: Nonreactive research in the social sciences.* Chicago: University of Chicago Press.

Wobst, M. (1977). Stylistic behavior and information exchange. *University of Michigan Museum of Anthropology, Anthropological Paper, 61,* 317-342.

Yates, T. (1989). Habitus and social space. In I. Hodder (Ed.), *The meanings of things* (pp. 248-262). London: Unwin Hyman.

5

On the Authority
of the Image

Visual Methods at
the Crossroads

Douglas Harper

◆ Visual sociology is primarily a subfield of qualitative sociology—the
recording, analysis, and communication of social life through photographs, film, and video. Visual sociology is related to visual ethnography
as it developed in anthropology, and to documentary photography, which
has existed largely outside the university. At the present time, ethnography
and documentary photography, the two sources for visual sociology, are
being questioned and fundamentally recast. Thus visual sociology has one
foot in a set of traditional approaches (visual ethnography and documentary photography) and the other in the experiments of the new ethnography and postmodern versions of documentary photography. It is a tricky
position. Visual sociology must trace its roots to this shifting ground,
holding on to what is valuable in the traditional while adopting elements
of the new. In this chapter I will trace the origins and developments of
visual sociology, discuss the current debates among the postmodern critics,
and suggest an integrated approach for the future.

Visual Ethnography and the "Realist Tale"

Anthropology came into existence in the late decades of the nineteenth century and was first thought of as closely related to biology, at that time primarily a science of classification. Photography was useful in providing visual information for the classification of races used to support theories of social evolution, the main preoccupation of early anthropology. The story of photography's role in this early history is well told in a recent volume edited by Elizabeth Edwards (1992), who suggests that photography was first thought of "as a simple . . . truth-revealing mechanism" (p. 4) utilized throughout anthropology's worldwide research arena. By about 1920 photography had largely lost its importance in anthropology because research interests shifted to social organization, which was thought to be less visual, and because photography itself had begun to lose its mystique. By 1920, Edwards suggests, "photography had become just another ancillary tool in the fieldworker's arsenal. Photographs became . . . marginal to the process of explanation rather than becoming part of a centrally conceived resource . . . a technique perceived as recording surface rather than depth, which was the business of the anthropologist" (p. 4).

From this rather unpromising situation, Bateson and Mead, working in the 1930s, largely reinvigorated the use of visual methods in anthropology. But although their book, *Balinese Character* (Bateson & Mead, 1942), showed the potential of visual ethnography for a wide-ranging study of culture, it did not inspire a revolution in ethnographic methods. The importance of *Balinese Character* remains, however, for those seeking a current practice; I will examine it here in some detail.

Bateson and Mead had each studied and written about Balinese culture for nearly a decade when they turned to photographs:

> We were separately engaged in efforts to translate aspects of culture never successfully recorded by the scientist, although often caught by the artist, into some form of communication sufficiently clear and sufficiently unequivocal to satisfy the requirements of scientific enquiry . . . [our several monographs on the Bali] all attempted to communicate those intangible aspects of culture which had been vaguely referred as its *ethos*. As no precise scientific vocabulary was available, the ordinary English words were used, with all their weight of culturally limited connotations, in an attempt to describe the way in which the emotional life of these various South Sea people was organized in culturally standardized forms. (p. xi)

Finding words inadequate, they turned to a method whereby text and images mutually inform:

> We are attempting a new method of stating the intangible relationships among different types of culturally standardized behavior by placing side by side mutually relevant photographs. . . . By the use of photographs, the wholeness of each piece of behavior can be preserved, while the special cross-referencing desired can be obtained by placing the series of photographs on the same page. (p. xii)

The authors worked as a team, Bateson photographing as Mead directed. They made more than 25,000 photographs over a two-year field experience, from which they selected 759 for *Balinese Character*. These photographs were sorted into Balinese cultural categories: "spatial orientation and levels," "learning," "integration and disintegration of the body," "orifices of the body," "autocosmic play," "parents and children," "siblings," "stages of child development," and "rites of passage." Their book offered a new model for integrating images and text. For example, in the chapter on rites of passage, photographic plates (pages with between 6 and 10 photographs each) visualize subtopics such as tooth filing, marriage, funerals, exhumation, and other rituals. The photographs are in numbered sequence and face pages of detailed explanation, image by image. The analysis moves from the level of concept to detailed study of specific events, elements, or moments.

The significance of the Bateson and Mead project is that the photographs are regarded as a part of culturally informed observation. Bateson writes: "In general we found that any attempt to select for special details was fatal, and that the best results were obtained when the photography was most rapid and almost random" (Bateson & Mead, 1942, p. 50). The mass of visual data—25,000 images—were catalogued, studied, distilled, and sorted into themes that derived from the cultural knowledge of the anthropologists. The images were arranged in groups that allowed several perspectives on a single subject to be presented simultaneously, or in sequences that showed how a social event evolved through time. Single images are important primarily in how they become a part of more elaborate visual statements. Finally, the anthropologists explained the cultural meaning of the photographs in lengthy descriptions that they placed on facing pages, presenting a model for image/text balance and organization.

There have been no visual ethnographies that equal *Balinese Character* in depth or comprehensiveness. Several visual monographs have applied some of Bateson and Mead's working methods and presentational styles. These include Danforth and Tsiaras's (1982) study of death rituals of rural Greece, which follows the format of *Balinese Character* but concentrates on a single ritual; Cancian's (1974) visual ethnography of Mexican peasant culture, which studies deviance and social disorganization; and Gardner and Heider's (1968) visual ethnography of the largely ritualistic war of Dani of New Guinea. These and a small number of other visual ethnographies are at the more experimental end of what John Van Maanen (1988) calls the "realist tale" of ethnography.

The conventions of the "realist tale"—taken-for-granted aspects of traditional ethnography—obscure the problems inherent in the anthropologist's claims for scientific legitimacy. These conventions, according to Van Maanen (1988, pp. 46-49), define the author as scientific expert who, of course, uses technical language to communicate his or her findings. Thus the experiences or emotions of the author are as inappropriate in the conventional ethnography as they would be in a report of a genetics experiment. In the realist tale, the subject matter is a documentary accounting interpreted by theoretical concepts of anthropology. The point of view of the subjects is offered in quotes, separated from the rest of the text, keeping the voice of the author in control.

Photography had a natural place in these reports, regarded primarily as a *reflection* rather than as an *interpretation* of what was photographed. George and Louise Spindler (1967) in their foreword to John Collier's classic text on visual anthropology, comment:

> Usually an anthropologist takes a photograph to illustrate a finding that he has already decided is significant. . . . He waits until whatever it is happens, then points his camera at it. His camera then is incidental to his research activity and comes into use late in the fieldwork period. He uses the camera not as a research technique, but as a highly selective confirmation that certain things are so, or as a very selective sample of "reality." (p. x)

Spindler and Spindler later comment that Collier has argued for a more inductive photographic ethnography (particularly in the use of photographs to elicit interviews, which I will discuss later), but the table of contents of Collier's text shows photography in the service of the traditional ethnography. Collier argues that visual ethnography is an efficient way to survey and map material culture or social interaction, leading to techniques such as sociometric analysis.

Still photography in ethnography has not developed much beyond the handful of experiments cited here, which logically developed from the standard photographically illustrated ethnographic monograph. Visual anthropology has become mostly a discipline of film and video, as even a quick reading of the journals *Visual Anthropology* and *Visual Anthropology Review* attest. To the extent that anthropologists use photographs, they generally relegate them to record keeping or cataloguing.

Documentary Photography and the Development of Visual Sociology

Visual sociology began during the 1960s. The visual anthropology movement, centered in the Third World and increasingly concerned with film and video, had a minor impact on the parallel movement in sociology. Rather, the first visual sociologists tended to be inspired by documentary photographers working on many of the issues that sociologists felt ought to be on the sociological agenda. These included photographic studies of drugs and drug culture (Clark, 1971), black ghetto life (Davidson, 1970), small-town southern poverty and racism (Adelman, 1972), the southern civil rights movement (Hansberry, 1964), institutionalization (Jackson, 1977; Lyon, 1971), social class (Estrin, 1979; Owens, 1973), the unionization of migrant farmworkers (Fusco & Horowitz, 1970), the countercultural life (Simon & Mungo, 1972), the antiwar movement (Kerry, 1971), the free speech movement (Copeland, 1969), and the social irresponsibility of corporate capitalism (Smith & Smith, 1975). Aspiring visual sociologists drew inspiration from the liberal humanist tradition of documentary photography, which dated to Jacob Riis's (1890/1971) examination of the poverty of the urban immigrant, the Farm Security Administration photographic documentation of poverty during the 1930s (Agee & Evans, 1939; Stryker & Wood, 1973), and, more indirectly, Robert Frank's (1959/1969) photographic portrait of an alienated, materialistic American culture in the 1950s. These books were made up mostly of photographs, sometimes with a well-developed text (for example, in Smith & Smith, 1975) that generally provided background for the photos. The documentary photographers were not sociologists, and although their books lacked sociological frames or theories, the documentarians did have a great deal to offer sociologists seeking a more direct and critical sociology. Sociologists looking for a visual method recognized that the documentary photographers often had deep involvement with their subjects, and thus an insider's knowledge, much as would a sociological field-worker. Adelman's (1972) study of southern poverty and racism, for example, emerged from his experiences as a VISTA worker; Eugene and Aileen Smith (1975), while writing *Minamata,* lived for several years in the Japanese village poisoned by corporate mercury dumping. Some of these studies were autobiographical and showed the importance of subtle, cultural knowledge; Estrin (1979) photographed her upper-class family and friends, and Owens (1973) photographed his own suburban community. Others, like Robert Frank, a Swiss photographer, simply traveled around the United States making photographs, but his images (1959/1969) resonated with widely held sociological ideas. In the documentary movement there was very little, if any, discussion of the issues of representation, ideology, or how the relationships with subjects influenced these largely photographic studies. As mentioned, these studies were characterized by the sense that the photographer should expose social problems in order to educate the public in order to change society. This idea, we shall see later, has lost a great deal of its currency.

From this beginning Howard S. Becker's (1974) lead article in Volume 1, Number 1, of the first journal devoted to the study of visual communication defined the basis for a visual sociology. Becker noted that photography and sociology had about the same birth date and that they had both been concerned with, among other things, the exploration of society. Early issues of the *American Journal of Sociology* routinely used photographs; Lewis Hine's early twentieth-century photographic surveys of social problems such as child labor were supported by the Russell Sage Foundation. From the beginning of photography, however, there was a split between those who saw photography as description ("documentary" photography) and those who saw it as art. As sociology has become more like science, Becker points out, photography has become more like art. Thus sociology and photography had ceased, by the time of the writing of the article, to have much to do with each other; his article was intended to begin dialogue and cross-fertilization between the two. Sociologists should study photography, Becker suggests, because photographers have studied many of the same topics sociologists routinely study: communities, social problems, work, social class, the "ambience of urban life," and more abstract themes such as social types or modal personalities.

An important theme raised by Becker concerns the role of theory in photographic representation. Although photographs are potentially packed with information, photographers "tend to restrict themselves to a few reiterated simple statements. Rhetorically important as a strategy of proof, the repetition leads to work that is intellectually and analytically thin" (Becker, 1974, p. 11). To make the photographs "intellectually denser," Becker suggests that the photographer must become conscious of the theory that guides his or her photography. That theory may be "lay theory"—taken-for-granted assumptions about how the world is organized— or it may be "deep, differentiated and sophisticated knowledge of the people and activities they investigate . . . for photographic projects concerned with exploring society it means learning to understand society better" (p. 11). Recall that Bateson and Mead, both professional anthropologists, had spent several years in the field and had completed ethnographic studies of several aspects of the culture they then turned to with their cameras. Their theories of the group they photographed were correspondingly complex, and grounded in anthropological knowledge. Becker reminds us that photographs, often thought of as "truth," are more precisely reflections of the photographer's point of view, biases, and knowledge (or lack of knowledge). Thus the integration of photography and sociology must begin with the understanding of just how much *un*sociological photography we are accustomed to seeing. Sociological photography may be guided by sociological concepts, which grow inductively as one's theories are revised.

Becker addresses how issues of validity, reliability, and sampling are treated by the visual sociologist. In simple terms, these are the questions: Has the ethnographer reported accurately what she or he has seen? Is the event reported on repeated enough times so that the single event can be understood to stand for a regularly repeating class of events? Do the events reported characterize the behavior of the group?

The issue begins with the recognition that the photographic image is "true" in the sense (physical or electronic manipulation aside) that it holds the visual trace of the reality at which the camera was pointed. But the more fundamental issue is to recognize that all images, despite their relationship to the world, are socially and technically constructed. The credibility of an image should be based on commonsense reasoning and evidence, rather than on debates about the essential quality of the photograph. The more we know about how the photograph came into existence, the more we can judge its validity. Thus to the question of whether the photograph represents the *only* truth of a particular setting, the answer lies in "distinguishing between the statement that X is true about something and the statement that X is all that is true about something" (Becker, 1986, p. 252). The problem of validity and reliability is related to access: whether the photographer has been able to observe and photograph a full range of activities that explore the particular question he or she is interested in. The camera makes access more difficult; in some circumstances it makes it impossible. Because photographing is much more active than observing, it certainly influences how the field-worker is received in the field.

Because the camera portrays people clearly, the issue of fieldwork ethics has a special place in visual sociology. There is no formula that works in all situations, but the issue should be framed morally. Steven Gold (1989) suggests that for the visual ethnographer,

> sensitivity is rooted in a covenantal rather than contractual relationship between researcher and host. Unlike a contract that simply specifies rights and duties, a covenant requires the researcher to consider his or her relationship with subjects on a much wider level, accepting the obligations that develop between involved, interdependent persons. . . . For visual sociology, the concepts of sensitivity and covenantal ethics are clearly related. A researcher cannot engage in the reciprocal relationship required by the covenant without making efforts to understand his or her hosts' beliefs, values, and views of the world. Similarly, the covenantal ethnic reminds the researcher to consider his other subjects' needs when researching and publishing. (pp. 104-105)

Each project must be considered individually, and the researcher must apply all he or she knows from his or her own understanding of fieldwork methods to the visual project. Because the camera intrudes and reveals, it must be used with the wants, needs, and cultural perspectives of the subjects at the forefront of one's consciousness. Beyond that, each solution must be made individually.

Thus visual sociology draws on traditions of ethnographers using cameras to record what were thought to be exotic cultures and of concerned people photographing society for some of the same reasons sociologists study it, as well as from fieldwork practices in sociology. It has been said by many that the camera is a telling symbol of modernism: a machine that advances the purposes of an empirical science, of which sociology has traditionally been a part, a science whose existence itself is the result of the liberal agenda of social reform. But the assumptions that underlie sociology, documentary photography, and ethnography have shifted since Becker wrote what was a clarion call for sociologists to take up cameras. The larger mandate of science itself is questioned, as is sociology's status as a science; liberalism, for many, has lost its potency; photographs are seen as problematic and tentative statements rather than reflections of truth. Thus, although visual sociology must recognize its roots in the traditions of ethnography and documentary, it must acknowledge and integrate the insights of the new critical comment in these areas as well. I shall now introduce the critical takes on ethnography and photography.

New Ethnography

The idea of ethnography as "partial truth" rather than complete document lies at the basis of the new ethnography. The book or film (or other mode of communication) that represents culture is partial, or incomplete, because culture itself is not precisely boundaried and continually evolves. For example, Dorinne Kondo (1990), an American of Japanese descent who wrote an ethnography of a Japanese workplace through an analysis of her own complex, partially cross-cultural, experience, writes:

> Culture . . . is no reified thing or system, but a meaningful way of being in the world, inseparable from the "deepest" aspects of one's "self"—the trope of depth and interior space itself a product of our own cultural conventions. These cultural meanings are themselves multiple and contradictory, and though they cannot be understood without reference to historical, political and economic discourses, the experience of culture cannot be reduced to these nor related to them in any simple, isomorphic way. (pp. 300-301)

Kondo constructs cultural description through her own negotiation of a liminal status and thus teaches us as much by looking inward as through her interaction with her cultural others.

Ethnographic knowledge traditionally derives from the interaction between the subject and the researcher. The postmodern critique questions the normal assumptions surrounding this interaction. Stephen Tyler (1986), for example, suggests an ethnographic model consisting of "a cooperatively evolved text consisting of fragments of discourse intended to evoke in the minds of both reader and writer an emergent fantasy of a possible world of commonsense reality" (p. 125). Paul Stoller's account of his apprenticeship among sorcerers in western Niger (Stoller & Olkes, 1987) emerged from cultural collaboration of the deepest type imaginable, that of becoming a culturally alien spiritual being; the author's ethnographic presentation is novelistic—narrative, conversational, and personally probing. Other experiments are written in a way that intends to bring the reader to the cultural world, rather than to report on it from a distance. To communicate the essentially cyclical nature of the tramp experience, I describe six weeks on the road in the company of tramp workers (Harper, 1982). The book examines work and migration, elements of a repeating pattern in a migrant lifestyle, much as the experience itself unfolded. The center of the book is the relationship on the move between the writer and the tramp—a variation of a typical momentary but culturally organized social bond.

Finally, the new ethnography challenges the very idea of abstracted analysis: "Post-modern ethnography . . . does not move toward abstraction, away from life, but back to experience. It aims not to foster the growth of knowledge but to restructure experience; not to understand objective reality, for that is already established by common sense, nor to explain how we understand, for that is impossible, but to reassimilate, to reintegrate the self in society and to restructure the conduct of everyday life" (Tyler, 1986, p. 135). For example, David Sudnow's (1978) study of the organization of improvised conduct attempts to communicate what the hand feels or thinks as one plays keyboard jazz or types one's ideas. The language violates taken-for-granted assumptions about action and motive, and the description ventures into areas that had not been described before. Whether the inquiry is successful by the standards of traditional ethnography (speaking of demonstrable truth) is beside the point. We know a truth about the accomplishment of jazz through Sudnow's research, but this knowledge is more an empathic understanding than a basis for prediction.

From the vantage point of the new critique, then, ethnography is most usefully thought of as a created tale that comes a lot closer to describing reality if it is done without trying to fulfill the impossible and undesirable (for ethnography) standards of science. Ethnography should draw upon narrative; include the point of view, voice, and experience of the author; and experiment with ways of telling. Similar themes (with their own twists, of course) are found in critiques of photo documentary, which leaves visual ethnography in the position of drawing upon critical commentary from two very different locations, each suggesting change in a similar direction.

The Postmodernist Critique
of Documentary Photography

The postmodern critique of documentary photography begins with the idea that the meaning of the photograph is constructed by the maker and the viewer, both of whom carry their social positions and interests to the photographic act. We are often reminded that the powerful, the established, the male, the colonizer typically portray the less powerful, less established, female, and colonized. Even exceptions such as Hubbard's (1991) collection of photographs by homeless children or Ewald's (1985) portraits and stories by Appalachian children are still, one can argue, part of this configuration in that the money, support, and editorial control of these books remain in the established publishing world.

The postmodern critique reminds us that the meaning of the photograph changes in different viewing contexts. The history of photography shifts from a history of the images of great photographers to a history of the uses of photographs, and whole photographic traditions. Excellent contemporary examples are case studies in the above-cited history of anthropological photography (Edwards, 1992). These case studies are not interesting to the extent that they tell us the size, shape, and material culture of long-disappeared Third World peoples, but they are interesting because they tell us how the colonials portrayed the colonized.

These insights confront the idea that photographs carry documentary truthfulness in the manner taken for granted in early anthropological or documentary photography. They also challenge the oft-stated notion that documentary photographs show the human condition—something we all supposedly recognize but cannot define.

The second overarching concern in the postmodern critique of documentary is the assertion that even if documentary was once a part of liberal humanism, liberal humanism is now thought of as a failed program based on naive assumptions. In Martha Rosler's (1989) words:

> In the liberal documentary, poverty and oppression are almost invariably equated with misfortunes caused by natural disasters: causality is vague, blame is not assigned, fate cannot be overcome. . . . Like photos of children in pleas for donations to international charity organizations, liberal documentary implores us to look in the face of deprivation and to weep (and maybe to send money). (p. 307)

Documentary photography advances the causes of a liberal system because it does not see the ideological aspects of its own patterns of representation. As noted above, documentary typically focuses on the specific and thus hides or mutes the critiques of the system; social problems are seen as personal stories and social ugliness is made beautiful or provocative. All of these characteristics of documentary photography, says the postmodern critic, obscure the very social realities the documentarian wishes to portray. These critical themes may be uncomfortable for many, but they cannot be ignored.

◆ Building a Visual Sociology

What can we say about a visual approach for today's and tomorrow's sociology? The following will be relevant for sociologists who want to do research and/or to teach visually, often separate groups with related but slightly different orientations and goals. I will look at the contributions of the four elements discussed thus far: traditional visual ethnography, documentary photography, and postmodern critiques directed to both practices.

Although an emerging visual sociology cannot treat business as usual, there are many elements in traditional ways of doing things that remain useful. First is the realization that to accomplish in-depth understanding one must undertake long and intense periods of field research. In fact, in our own first experiences in the field we think and photograph from our own cultural lenses. We must learn to see through the lenses of the cultural Other—in the ways field-workers always have gained cultural knowledge. The irony for visual sociology is that one can take an extraordinary number of photographs in a very short time (*National Geographic* photographers, for example, routinely expose a hundred rolls of film—3,600 separate images—*per day*), and creating so much *information* tricks one into thinking one has created *knowledge*. I experienced this phenomenon when photographing the work of a backwoods mechanic (Harper, 1987b). The transition from images that communicated poverty and disorder to those that showed community and creative intelligence was made only with the spirited involvement of my subject/friend. Thus the first step to a vital visual ethnography is the same level of commitment that is necessary for all field research.

The second principle of traditional ethnography that must be retained is the indispensable role of theory in our work. This means simply that our

141

photographic work should be guided by ideas that, directly or indirectly, relate to sociology. There is probably no better example than *Balinese Character*, discussed above. I assign visual sociology students the task of photographing sociological ideas—often a simple idea such as social interaction—and the discussions that emerge from the class viewing of the images have been the richest I have had as a teacher. It is disarmingly difficult to answer the question, as the group gazes at a student's photos: What sociological idea are you exploring with these photographs? How might you have better explored these ideas? The discussions typically lead from a very simple idea to several levels of complexity. Student interaction is intense as students learn from each other's experiments and seek their own solutions. Sociological thinking becomes a kind of problem solving that makes the world increasingly intelligible.

The point must be carried into our own work. We must continually remember that while we are photographing we are, indeed, gathering information; but that information must be created, organized, and presented in terms of ideas that we can verbalize. If we do not work from such a perspective, we will create visual information that will unconsciously reflect our personal taken-for-granted assumptions—the very thing that sociologists should suspend as they enter and try to understand the worlds of others.

It may be that photography works better with microtheory than with macrotheory, but just because photography does not easily facilitate such standard procedures as variable analysis (images could be sorted, compared, or otherwise analyzed statistically, but it probably would not be the best use of photographic information), that does not mean that photography cannot confront critical questions about social structure or social organization. Photographers such as El Lissitzky and Alexander Rodchenko used photomontage in the 1920s in the Soviet Union to describe the evolving sensibilities of the revolution; John Heartfield, working in Germany in the years before World War II, used photomontage to debunk and unmask Nazism (Ades, 1976). Leo Frankenberger (1991), a contemporary student of visual sociology, built photomontages from documentary photographs of a neighborhood to be demolished, onto which he fastened images of the people who live and lived in the neighborhood. His photomontage takes us inside the exteriors of the soon to be destroyed buildings to understand the lives lived there. These kinds of projects may work mostly as metaphor; rather than making the kind of statement sociologists expect from statistical studies, they are suggestive, empathic, descriptive.

I am suggesting in these comments that visual sociology begin with traditional assumptions and practices of sociological fieldwork and socio-logical analysis. The photograph can be thought of as data; in fact, the unique character of photographic images forces us to rethink many of our assumptions about how we move from observation to analysis in all forms of sociological research. But note that I suggest that image making and analysis *begins* with these and other traditional assumptions and practices. It does not end there.

Visual sociology has probably the least connection to the traditional practice of documentary photography, partly because traditional photo documentary has lost much of the cultural influence it asserted through much of the twentieth century. Documentary projects have evolved more experimental, personal, or abstracted forms, which sometimes provide models for a visual sociology. Jacob Holdt's (1985) decades-long voyage through the American underclass, for example, radically confronts the practice of making social problems beautiful or artful—Holdt used a cheap pocket camera and drugstore developing and did not frame images with an artist's eye. The visual confrontation with the subject is intensely direct and is mated to a text that forcefully tells the story of the ongoing journey and the human dramas that unfold along the way. Nick Waplington (1991) takes us to the mundane events of British working-class weekends; his photographs document the energetic, chaotic, person-filled "back stage" of life—people lying around, bodies askew on rough and serviceable furniture; kids playing a hundred games of their own invention; families drinking beer and pinching each other; men fixing old cars on the streets in front of their flats; women shopping, laden with their kids. The emphasis on the mundane, for Waplington, vitalizes a documentary practice that has tended to emphasize the spectacular. The result is visual ethnography of daily life that directly explores concepts of front stage/back stage familiar to all students of social interaction.

In general, however, documentary practice has moved closer to fine arts photography—relying on more subtle and abstract forms of photographic expression—at the same time that much fine arts photography has evolved to a kind of diffused social criticism, much more suggestive than evidential or literal, emerging more from the photographer's *view* of society than from a sustained analysis. It is difficult to imagine that visual sociology borrows directly from these forms aside from experiments, as suggested above.

We turn next to insights and contributions from critiques of documentary and ethnography.

Crafting Tales

We begin with the traditional sociology report—the use of third person, the pretense of "objectivity," the language of analysis—qualified, dispassionate, precise, and arid. The new ethnography embraces diametric oppositions to these forms: the first person, the understanding that all presentation is subjective, the language of narrative—vibrant, suggestive, engaged, and passionate. Photographs can, of course, serve either function. The photo on one's driver's license, for example, objectively and dispassionately documents one's identity. And, as developed above, photography in the service of traditional ethnography has worked largely in this spirit. Our understanding of photography as constructed, embodying, in fact, the essence of our point of view, however, leads us to see photography as a natural part of a new ethnography. Tales can easily be visual; we are accustomed to the idea of images-through-time in film. Images can organized in sequences that explore sociological ideas; these visual narratives might explore cycles in a cultural life (Harper, 1987a)—the migration, work, and drinking sprees of migrant workers, or the peasant pilgrimages of Europe (Bot, 1985). Emmet (1989) uses a photo narrative to describe nearly 10 years in the lives of a family of migrant farmworkers. These experiments in visual narrative scratch the surface of a potential method in a new ethnography.

Photo Elicitation

The new ethnography seeks to redefine the relationship between the researcher and the subject. The ideal model suggests collaboration rather than the traditional sense of research as a one-way flow of information, from subject to researcher, on terms and in terms of the researcher. The technique of photo elicitation promises a particularly apt alternative: a model for collaboration in research. Photo elicitation, first described by Collier (1967), is a very simple variation on the theme of open-ended interviewing. The open-ended interview is an exchange initiated and guided by the researcher in which the subject, one hopes, provides in-depth responses to complex questions. The open-ended interview rests on the assumption that the researcher will ask questions that are culturally meaningful to the subject. As most people who have done this kind of research know, it is more easily described than accomplished. In the photo-elicitation interview, interview/discussion is stimulated and guided by images. Typically these are photographs that the researcher has made of the subject's world (Gold, 1991; Harper, 1987b). A shocking thing happens in this interview format; the photographer, who knows his or her photograph as its maker (often having slaved over its creation in the darkroom) suddenly confronts the realization that he or she knows little or nothing about the cultural information contained in the image. As the individual pictured (or the individual from the pictured world) interprets the image, a dialogue is created in which the typical research roles are reversed. The researcher becomes a listener and one who encourages the dialogue to continue. The individual who describes the images must be convinced that his or her taken-for-granted understanding of the images is not shared by the researcher, often a startling realization for the subject as well.

This method has yet to catch on as a frontline sociological method, yet its potential is nearly endless. The photo interview may take place with photographs people have in their home collections, as many of my students have done. The photos may come from a historical archive, and may be used to re-create a historical understanding, a method I am using in an ongoing study of a dairy farm community. Or the method may stretch the collaborative bond to the end that the subjects direct the making of photographs before interpreting them in interviews, as done in a study of a Dutch neighborhood by a group of Dutch students (van der Does, Edelaar, Gooskens, Liefting, & van Mierlo, 1992). The well-achieved photo-elicitation interview really redefines the essential relationships of research, and the natural form for presenting this research is that of evenly constructed conversations.

These sensibilities from the new ethnography open the door for a creative and engaged visual ethnography. Given the expressive potential of photography and the intellectual ferment surrounding experiments in ethnography, the marriage of visual methods and ethnography seems natural.

Postmodern Critique of Documentary

It is in the postmodern critique of documentary where perhaps the greatest challenges to and, at the same time, some of the most useful contributions to a developing visual sociology lie. At its extreme, this critique calls for the end of photography, linking the photographic gaze to politically reactionary voyeurism. As noted above, this critique has characterized traditional documentary as linked to the prevailing power centers, thus reinforcing existing social arrangements even when it attempts to criticize. Part of this comes from the fact that photography typically focuses on discernible individuals or events; the power arrangements of the society are visually abstract, perhaps invisible. A response is to create photographic/textual statements that are critiques of documentary—demasking how prevailing forms of documentary communicate (Rosler, 1989). These acts of deconstruction are defined as Marxist because they suggest how social groups gain and maintain control through cultural manipulation, and are informed by a Freudian critique that asserts that our own act of seeing in the traditional documentary is fueled by voyeuristic pleasure (Clough, 1992).

So the postmodern critic/"photographer" more typically appropriates images from the culture, usually from mass media, and juxtaposes these images (or parts of images) to other scraps from the culture; words, phrases from mass culture or other sources (at times, photographs by the critic, such as in the work of Burgin, 1986) that serve as metaphor rather than as analysis. These comments about the culture are seen as an act of deconstruction, much as were the collages of John Heartfield and other artists from eras in which art was a more progressive cultural force. Although some of the statements that emerge from these practices lead us to see class and gender relations and oppression in new and provocative ways, they are hardly revolutionary. The artist/critic has all too often withdrawn from society to offer a commentary on the nature of social life. If visual sociology follows this path, it will become the expression of artistic opinion rather than the study of social life.

Where, then, lies the contribution of the postmodern criticism of the documentary? First is the important shift from concern with the "great artists of the documentary" to the study of the history of the uses of photography. Here visual sociology becomes a form of critical history, well demonstrated by Edwards (1992), cited above. With this understanding comes a certain loss of naïveté and what has to be considered sociological understanding.

Second, and relatedly, the new criticism allows us to confront the problem of ideology, the manner in which unequal relationships are hidden or ignored in the practice of photography. Traditionally this has meant that photography has been implicated as part of the power and domination that lie behind the relationship of the colonized or the native (the subject of the ethnography) and the colonizing culture, that of the ethnographer, but it includes issues of gender and class. Noteworthy examples are Solomon-Godeau's (1991) several studies of gendered photography, including her deconstruction and reconsideration of erotic photography, her development of Jean Clair's characterization of "the gaze as erection of the eye" in order to "better understand—in order to combat effectively—the complex network of relations that meshes power, patriarchy, and representation" (p. 237), and her several essays that begin to define a feminist photographic aesthetic and practice.

The new ethnographers must understand power relationships outside of the small social units they study, and they need to see their own work in the context of larger frames of power. To these ends, the visual sociologist working in the area of social criticism has much to gain from the sensibilities of those working in what has come to be known as the postmodern left.

I take a practical attitude toward the future of visual sociology. Although visual sociology has not exactly become a mass movement, changes in sociology itself (including a growing criticism of traditional empiricism and the experimental movements in ethnography cited above) are taking place; there is a growing body of visual work (including a professional journal, *Visual Sociology*) and a sponsoring organization, the International Visual Sociology Association, which has held conferences on visual sociology for more than a decade and is doing quite well indeed. Those who have used and taught visual methods share an excitement of discovery and creation. It is clear that visual representations help us learn ourselves; they help us communicate to others; they help us teach our students to see and struggle through their own attempts at recording, analyzing, and communicating. Most fundamentally, images allow us to make kinds of statements that cannot be made by words; thus images enlarge our consciousness and the possibilities for our sociology. Click!

◆ References

Adelman, B. (1972). *Down home.* New York: McGraw-Hill.

Ades, D. (1976). *Photomontage.* New York: Pantheon.

Agee, J., & Evans, W. (1939). *Let us now praise famous men.* Cambridge, MA: Houghton Mifflin.

Bateson, G., & Mead, M. (1942). *Balinese character: A photographic analysis.* New York: New York Academy of Sciences.

Becker, H. S. (1974). Photography and sociology. *Studies in the Anthropology of Visual Communication, 1*(1), 3-26.

Becker, H. S. (1986). *Doing things together.* Evanston: Northwestern University Press.

Bot, M. (1985). *Misere: The great pilgrimages of penance in Europe.* Rotterdam, Netherlands: Marrie Bot.

Burgin, V. (1986). *Between.* London: Basil Blackwell.

Cancian, F. (1974). *Another place.* San Francisco: Scrimshaw.

Clark, L. (1971). *Tulsa.* New York: Lunstrum.

Clifford, J., & Marcus, G. E. (Eds.). (1986). *Writing culture: The poetics and politics of ethnography.* Berkeley: University of California Press.

Clough, P. T. (1992). *The end(s) of ethnography: From realism to social criticism.* Newbury Park, CA: Sage.

Collier, J., Jr. (1967). *Visual anthropology: Photography as a research method.* New York: Holt, Rinehart & Winston.

Copeland, A. (Ed.). (1969). *People's park.* New York: Ballantine.

Danforth, L., & Tsiaras, A. (1982). *Death rituals of rural Greece.* Princeton, NJ: Princeton University Press.

Davidson, B. (1970). *E100 Street.* Cambridge, MA: Harvard University Press.

Edwards, E. (Ed.). (1992). *Anthropology and photography 1860-1920.* New Haven, CT: Yale University Press.

Emmet, H. L. (1989). *Fruit tramps: A family of migrant farmworkers.* Albuquerque: University of New Mexico Press.

Estrin, M. L. (1979). *To the manor born.* Boston: Little, Brown.

Ewald, W. (1985). *Portraits and dreams.* New York: Writers & Readers.

Frank, R. (1969). *The Americans.* New York: Aperture. (Original work published 1959)

Frankenberger, L. (1991). Going out of business in Highland Park. *Visual Sociology Review, 6*(1), 24-32.

Fusco, P., & Horowitz, G. D. (1970). *La causa.* New York: Collier.

Gardner, R., & Heider, K. (1968). *Gardens of war: Life and death in the New Guinea stone age.* New York: Random House.

Gold, S. J. (1989). Ethical issues in visual field work. In G. Blank, J. McCarthy, & E. Brent (Eds.), *New technology in sociology: Practical applications in research and work* (pp. 99-112). New Brunswick, NJ: Transaction.

Gold, S. J. (1991). Ethnic boundaries and ethnic entrepreneurship: A photo-elicitation study. *Visual Sociology, 6*(2), 9-23.

Hansberry, L. (1964). *The movement.* New York: Simon & Schuster.

Harper, D. (1982). *Good company.* Chicago: University of Chicago Press.

Harper, D. (1987a). The visual ethnographic narrative. *Visual Anthropology, 1*(1), 1-19.

Harper, D. (1987b). *Working knowledge: Skill and community in a small shop.* Chicago: University of Chicago Press.

Holdt, J. (1985). *American pictures.* Copenhagen: American Pictures Foundation.

Hubbard, J. (1991). *Shooting back: A photographic view of life by homeless children.* San Francisco: Chronicle.

Jackson, B. (1977). *Killing time.* Ithaca, NY: Cornell University Press.

Kerry, J. (1971). *The new soldier.* New York: Macmillan.

Kondo, D. (1990). *Crafting selves.* Chicago: University of Chicago Press.

Lyon, D. (1971). *Conversations with the dead.* New York: Holt, Rinehart & Winston.

Owens, B. (1973). *Suburbia.* San Francisco: Straight Arrow.

Riis, J. A. (1971). *How the other half lives.* New York: Dover. (Original work published 1890)

Rosler, M. (1989). In, around and afterthoughts (on documentary photography). In R. Bolton (Ed.), *The contest of meaning: Critical histories of photography.* Cambridge: MIT Press.

Simon, P., & Mungo, R. (1972). *Moving on standing still.* New York: Grossman.

Smith, W. E., & Smith, A. (1975). *Minamata.* New York: Holt, Rinehart & Winston.

Solomon-Godeau, A. (1991). *Photography at the dock: Essays on photographic history, institutions and practices.* Minneapolis: University of Minnesota Press.

Spindler, G., & Spindler, L. (1967). Foreword. In J. Collier, Jr., *Visual anthropology: Photography as a research method.* New York: Holt, Rinehart & Winston.

Stoller, P., & Olkes, C. (1987). *In sorcery's shadow.* Chicago: University of Chicago Press.

Stryker, R., & Wood, N. (1973). *In this proud land.* Greenwich: New York Graphic Society.

Sudnow, D. (1978). *Ways of the hand: The organization of improvised conduct.* Cambridge, MA: Harvard University Press.

Tyler, S. A. (1986). Post-modern ethnography: From document of the occult to occult document. In J. Clifford & G. E. Marcus (Eds.), *Writing culture: The poetics and politics of ethnography* (pp. 122-140). Berkeley: University of California Press.

van der Does, S., Edelaar, S., Gooskens, I., Liefting, M., & van Mierlo, M. (1992). Reading images: A study of a Dutch neighborhood. *Visual Sociology, 7*(1), 4-68.

Van Maanen, J. (1988). *Tales of the field: On writing ethnography.* Chicago: University of Chicago Press.

Waplington, N. (1991). *Living room.* New York: Aperture.

6

Personal Experience Methods

D. Jean Clandinin & F. Michael Connelly

It will be hard to put into words but here goes . . . you and I were sitting on opposite sides of a huge room, it seemed like a loft or something huge like that . . . and all that was left around us were the rafters and beams and some of the boards on the wall. . . . we were calling across this long distance to each other, surrounded by this building that was coming down. . . . there seemed to be a sense of urgency for us and we were shouting, not angrily. . . . Somehow there was a sense that soon something was going to crash and we would have to leave or something . . . anyway a sense of the time running out. . . . When I woke up I was telling you that we should sit beside each other and talk rather than shout at each other across this huge room, at least for as long as we could still talk. . . . I don't know what it all means but I do think that perhaps if we sat beside each other we could go on talking until whatever was going to happen happened . . . and so I wonder if you would come and sit beside me (metaphorically speaking) so we could talk. . . . Do you think you could do that? . . . or would you like me to walk across the room to sit beside you. . . . I am walking now and saying that I wish we could spend whatever time we have left talking and working with each other. . . . I want to spend the time until the huge barn or whatever it was is gone. . . . I want to spend the time sitting next to you on the floor talking and working together.

◆ Suppose we were to ask you as reader to tell us the meaning of this passage. What would you say? Chances are you would either speak freely, treating the passage as a kind of inkblot test, or you would refuse to comment, not knowing the context. Either way, the status of the passage as representing experience would be minimal and the emphasis in your response would be on presenting your own experience. The situation is controlled by us because we have brought the passage forward, and its experiential status depends upon what we choose to convey contextually. Is the passage an excerpt from a work of fiction? A likely possibility, given its content. Is it derived from a study? A likely possibility, as this is a chapter on method. Or is it an artifact created by us to introduce the chapter? Still another likely possibility. You have no way of knowing, and the choice of whether to leave the statement ambiguous or clarify its context is ours, depending on our purpose.

The passage is a verbatim transcript taken from a letter from one of our research participants to another. Knowing this, the status of the passage is clarified in important ways. You know that it is a passage written by a person to another person and witnessed, though the timing is not clear, by two researchers. The fact that it is a participant's experience and not a researcher's interpretation or reconstruction of it makes a difference to your understanding of the passage. Still, our experience as researchers is clearly intermingled here, if not for the participants, at least for you as reader because you know only what we have chosen to tell and that is a highly selective constructive act on our part, depending on the stories we wish to convey about our participants, ourselves as researchers, and ourselves as methodologists writing to other researchers.

Let us back the inquiry up one step, and instead of asking you the reader to respond to our question, let us tackle it ourselves. You become an observer of the intertwined experience of researcher and participant. Before providing any further context, we feel there are several experiential features of the passage worth noting. First, the opening content of the passage is a dream. We shall not get into validity and reliability questions over the relationship of written dream text, dreams, and life experience. There is a clear-cut context assumed by the author, who speaks in two voices, both as dreamer and as dream narrator to the colleague. Both voices speak as directly as human beings can of experience and both texts spoken by each voice are shaped as a story. Though there is no indication of temporal location, there is a temporal quality to both stories. In the dream the characters are waiting not quite passively as the room around them disassembles, and it is implied that in due course the building will be gone and that this will influence the relationship. There is an implicit plot line that takes place over time. Likewise, the narrator imagines the dream somehow to parallel events in the ongoing life of the participants, and the narrator's story closely parallels the dream story. The two are so intimately linked that a reader has to watch closely for the transition from dream to waking life; indeed, both stories are part of the participant's life experience.

Though two stories are clearly visible in the passage, and though it is possible to create a researcher story of the meaning of each of the stories in isolation and in relation to one another, the larger life story context from which both of these stories derive their meaning is missing for readers, but not, of course, for the participants. To return the interpretive task to our readers for the moment, it is unclear, for you, whether we, as researchers, are mere voyeurs of a life drama that we have been privileged to record or whether the drama takes place within the context of our own story, whether as researchers who have created a research setting in which the text was generated or whether the story takes place within the context of our own larger life story, in which case we, as researchers, are observing ourselves in participation with participants. It is even possible that we are the participants and that the study in question is an autobiographical one, a possibility that especially sharpens Rose's (1990) ethnographic question, "What are we doing here?" in which he is concerned not merely with the prosaic matter of researchers writing for status, postgraduate degrees, promotion, and tenure, but in the broader sense of building links between experiential inquiry and life experience more generally. What is entailed in "experiencing the experience" is the question highlighted.

We hope that this passage, and our account of it so far, will serve to whet your imagination of what it means to study experience. From time to time throughout this chapter we will return to this passage.

Our imagination as educators has been captured by the possibility of studying experience rather than using experience as a contextual given for educational discourse. We have been impressed with how universal the word *experience* is in education. The word *experience* is found in homes, schools, higher education, and adult learning institutions. It is found in the most practical discussions of education, and it is found in the most revered theoretical texts. It is owned by no subject field and is found in virtually any community of educational discourse. But, to use Adler and Van Doren's (1972) distinction, it tends to function as a word, not a term. It is mostly used with no special meaning and functions as the ultimate explanatory context: Why do teachers, students, and others do what they do? Because of their experience.

When experience becomes more central to theorizing and to understanding practice, it is often criticized as providing inappropriate data. Others offer more ideological objection that, in the end, comes down to arguments over the appropriate form of educational reasoning. These criticisms are not, of course, ad hoc; they constitute the politics of epistemology. From Kuhn (1970) in the sciences to Schwab (1964) in educational studies to Crews (1992) in literary criticism to Taylor (1989, 1992) in moral theory and multiculturalism, we see the shifting frames of reference that define acceptable knowledge and inquiry.

The social sciences are concerned with humans and their relations with themselves and their environments, and, as such, the social sciences are founded on the study of experience. Experience is, therefore, the starting point and key term for all social science inquiry. But scientific, social, and philosophical conditions conspire to create frames of reference that shift the definitions of what is acceptable in the study of experience. One of the current frames is the epistemological notion that meaning is contained in texts and that the study of texts, particularly their deconstruction, is the primary focus for education, anthropology, sociology, linguistic studies, and so forth. Watts (1992) points out that the current conjunction of poststructuralism with "remnants of the new left" has created what he calls a "linguistic left that has moved to center stage in contemporary academic life." This is reflected in a current disposition toward studying texts rather than people and their experience as well as in researchers' explicit and implicit imposition of text forms on experience. In effect, text forms represented by experience rather than the reverse are what are under study. These dispositions are based on the argument that experience cannot speak for itself and the focus needs to be on the meaning contained in texts and the forms by which they are constructed. One such line of thinking is essentially sociological and critical in origin and, roughly speaking, comes from the view that social organization and structure rather than people and experience are the appropriate starting points for social science inquiry. Rose (1990), for instance, writes about "the social forms such as the incorporated university that literally, textually, and legally frame the way we do the business of ethnography today" (p. 10). Another, contrasting, epistemological frame of reference argues that experience is too comprehensive, too holistic, and, therefore, an insufficiently analytic term to permit useful inquiry. This argument tends to be given by those whom Schön (1983, 1991) and Oakshott (1962) call "technical rationalists."

Following Schwab (1964), we call the arguments expressed in these frames of reference, respectively, formalistic and reductionistic. In the light of these objections to the study of experience, the problem of studying experience is to lay claim to the integrity of experience itself and to fend off either its formalistic denial through abstraction and the hegemonies of social organization and structure or its reduction into skills, techniques, and tactics. To do so is partly a matter of participating in the politics of method (Eisner, 1988), a process both Eisner and Pinar (1988) claim "is gaining a foothold for the study of experience."

These various objections, of course, all contain elements of truth important to the study of experience. On the one hand, raw sensory experience is, if not meaningless, next to it. Likewise, the extremes of formalism remove the particulars of experience. For example, E. M. Bruner (1986) writes that "experience structures expressions . . . but expressions also structure experience" (p. 6). In our effort to find a middle ground—a place where we can both say that we are involved in the study of experience and recognize the truths and epistemological values of reductionism and formalism—we have come to the study of narrative and storytelling. We make the assumption that experience is both temporal (D. Carr, 1986; Ricoeur, 1984) and storied (D. Carr, 1986; Crites, 1971; Heilbrun, 1988).

For us, keeping experience in the foreground comes about by periodic returns to the works of Dewey (1916, 1934, 1938). For Dewey, education, experience, and life are inextricably intertwined. In its most general sense, when one asks what it means to study education, the answer is to study experience. Following Dewey, the study of experience is the study of life, for example, the study of epiphanies, rituals, routines, metaphors, and everyday actions. One learns about education from thinking about life, and one learns about life from thinking about education. Sarason's (1988) autobiography makes the point that his life as psychologist and his life at large are intertwined. It is not that he fails to make a distinction between his job as a psychologist and the rest of his life. Rather, it is impossible to separate them in practice: He is a human being as a psychologist and he is a psychologist as a human being. Keeping this sense of the experiential whole is part of the study of narrative.

Broadly speaking, we follow D. Carr's (1986) middle-ground argument, in which the case is made that when persons note something of their experience, either to themselves or to others, they do so not by the mere recording of experience over time, but in storied form. Story is, therefore, neither raw sensation nor cultural form; it is both and neither. In effect, stories are the closest we can come to experience as we and others tell of our experience. A story has a sense of being full, a sense of coming out of a personal and social history.

With this as our standpoint we have a point of reference, a life and ground to stand on, for both imagining what experience is and imagining how it might be studied and represented in researchers' texts. Experience, in this view, is the stories people live. People live stories, and in the telling of them reaffirm them, modify them, and create new ones. For example, in our opening scenario, stories are told by an individual struggling to live a collaborative story with another. Her telling of the stories is an attempt to reaffirm her life story and to modify its living. Stories such as these, lived and told, educate the self and others, including the young and those, such as researchers, who are new to their communities.

◆ A Note on Narrative

There is not space in this chapter to give a full account of narrative terms. We and others have provided extensive elaborations elsewhere (J. Bruner, 1990; Connelly & Clandinin, 1990; Denzin, 1989; Mishler, 1986; Polkinghorne, 1988). It is equally as correct to say *inquiry into narrative* as it is to say *narrative inquiry*. By this we mean that narrative is both phenomenon and method. Narrative names the structured quality of experience to be studied, and it names the patterns of inquiry for its study. To preserve this distinction, we use the reasonably well-established device of calling the phenomenon *story* and the inquiry *narrative*. Thus we say that people by nature lead storied lives and tell stories of those lives, whereas narrative researchers describe such lives, collect and tell stories of them, and write narratives of experience.

Some narrative terms important in our work are *temporality, scene, plot, multiple researcher "I's,"* and *character.* For us, time and place, plot and scene, work together to create the experiential quality of narrative. Scene or place is where the action occurs, where characters are formed and live out their stories and where cultural and social context play constraining and enabling roles. Time is essential to plot. From the point of view of plot, the central structure of time is past-present-future. D. Carr (1986) relates this three-part structure of time to three critical dimensions of human experience—significance, value, intention—and, therefore, of narrative writing. We have dealt with issues of author/researcher's voice as an issue of multiple "I's," drawing attention to the "I" who speaks as researcher, teacher, man or woman, commentator, research participant, narrative critic, and theory builder. Denzin (1989) outlines a similar set of narrative terms, such as *emplotment, text, plot, point of view, personal and impersonal narration,* and *author's voice.*

◆ Levels of Experience

Some terms and distinctions have the quality of repeating themselves by generating the distinction time and again in each of the classes created by the distinctions. Dewey's theory of experience has this quality. An organism, for Dewey, is both individual and social. An individual's experience simultaneously has what he calls internal and existential conditions. For Dewey, a person does not have social experience: An individual is social—no sociality, no person; and vice versa. This quality shows up again in Dewey's thought where community is conceived of as an organism. Thus a community has individual and social qualities. This quality repeats itself as the focus of research attention shifts, say, from individual child, to classroom, to school, to community, to local government, and so on. Whatever is taken to be the individual—for example, a school—defines the existential level of social experience.

The foregoing is important to our purpose because it reveals the conceptual, and constructive, complexity of experience. What is taken to be experience is a function of the observer's interest. At any level there are internal and existential dimensions to be thought through. Furthermore, these dimensions are separable only in thought. In the process of trying to understand and make meaning of the experiential situation, it is the internal and existential whole that is ultimately of interest. In our dream scenario, for example, we might focus our attention on the dream, its telling, the life experience of the dream characters, our research experience of the dreamer's experience, or you, our reader's experience of the scenario and our account of it. Focusing on the dream narrator's experience raises questions of how this person feels in the telling, the moral tone both of the telling and of the dream, specific events in the narrator's life to which it is imagined the dream attaches, and so on. Existentially, questions arise about the person to whom the dream is told, what it is in the two people's relationship that makes the telling worthwhile, who they are and what kind of life they lead, the difference this makes to the telling, and so on. If we

156

were, instead, to focus on our readers' experience, questions arise internally of your emotional, moral, and aesthetic reaction to the dream scenario, to the specific events that come to your mind as you read it, of why and what meaning it has for you, and so on. Existentially, questions arise about what you were doing reading this material, for what purpose, what sense it will make to whatever endeavors you are engaged in, and so on.

In the study of experience it is the researcher's intentionality that defines the starting and stopping points. One of the common laments of those who focus on experience in all its messy complexity is that they lose track of the forest for the trees and find it hard to draw closure to a study. There are no easy ways to sort this out beyond constantly attending to the researcher's purpose from beginning to end of the study. Constant attention to the why of the work goes beyond the simple matter of keeping the researcher's eye on matters of relevance. At least as important is the almost inevitable redefinition of purpose that occurs in experiential studies as new, unexpected, and interesting events and stories are revealed. This matter is often made painfully clear in collaborative work, where the shifting interests and intentions of more than one participant need to be kept in rhythmic balance if the study is to proceed. Suppose, for instance, that the dream scenario was revealed to one of us who thought it was important to our collaborative research story and, therefore, brought it forward for our research discussion. Suppose further that the other person saw little significance in it. In sorting out the matter, our collaborative intentions would be preeminent as we worked together to make sense of the dream scenario.

Situation, the central term in Dewey's theory of experience, is specified by two criteria, interaction and continuity. *Interaction* refers to the intersection of internal and existential conditions as recounted above. *Continuity* refers to the temporal positioning of every situation. Situations do not just happen; they are historical and temporally directional according to the intentionality of the organism undergoing experience. Thus to talk about experience is to talk temporally. D. Carr (1986), drawing on Husserl (1970) and other phenomenologists, lodges a situation in a past horizon called "retention" and a future horizon called "protention." Phenomenologically, according to this view, there is a sense of history even before there is a history. There are, of course, objections to the view that all experience has a temporal quality. Contemplation, for instance, is ordinarily thought of as nontemporal, and, of course, quite apart from theorizing on the matter, much research is concerned with generalizations and principles that are thought to be time independent. For our purposes, however, an adequate study of experience makes time subject to inquiry. Suppose, for example, a study is conducted of elementary school teachers' beliefs about language learning. One way of interpreting the results is to claim certain generalizations about elementary school teachers' beliefs. A narrative interpretation would understand the beliefs not so much as generalizations but as experiential artifacts: monuments constructed out of the internal and existential histories of the teachers involved. Following the first interpretation, the beliefs constitute a structure of generalizations normatively useful for school planners and reformers. On the second, experiential, interpretation the teachers' beliefs are a sign of personal and social historical conditions that convey meaning in the present and that point in different directions than did the first interpretation for school reform.

To summarize, methods for the study of personal experience are simultaneously focused in four directions: inward and outward, backward and forward. By *inward* we mean the internal conditions of feelings, hopes, aesthetic reactions, moral dispositions, and so on. By *outward* we mean existential conditions, that is, the environment or what E. M. Bruner (1986) calls reality. By *backward* and *forward* we are referring to temporality, past, present, and future. To experience an experience is to experience it simultaneously in these four ways and to ask questions pointing each way. The dream text raises questions about, for example, the dreamer's feelings (internal), the person to whom she is speaking and in what setting (external), their histories (backward), and where they are going (forward). Furthermore, each of the levels for possible stories (the dream, the dream text, the participants, their life experience, the researchers, the audience) can be experienced through the asking of questions in the four directions. In this way the experience of the experience, for example, the researchers' experience of the dream text experience, is multifaceted.

The stories that make meaning of the experience at any one of these levels are interrelated. This can be illustrated through a consideration of the duration of time appropriate to each possible inquiry into our dream scenario. (Time duration is only one among a variety of matters that a more comprehensive study of experience would consider.) The time of dreaming is unknown, possibly a few moments. The time it takes to read the dream text is, likewise, a matter of minutes. But the time to write the text is unknown and may have been no longer than the time it took to write or may have involved days or weeks as the dreamer deliberated on the meaning of the dream and whether or not to tell it to her colleague.

Temporal duration is significant to the meaning we might make of this event, and the inquiry would need to pursue these temporal matters. Likewise, the time interval between the dream's telling and the colleague's response, as well as the time it took to respond, would provide important material for telling the colleague's story and the participants' relationship generally. Even supposing that the dreaming, telling, and responding took place rapidly, over a short time span, the life context that gave meaning to the dreaming, telling, and responding might be years long. The duration of the life experience called up by the dream and by the participants' discussion would be significant to understanding what is happening here. The same line of thinking applies to us as researchers trying to make sense of the dream scenario, because we, too, need personal experiential referents to understand what is happening. Why are you (the reader) reading the dream text? The dreamer's story invokes experiential memories as we read the text and these memories, and their temporal duration relative to the life history of the participants, makes a difference to the research story we tell of the scenario. It is important, therefore, for us to understand the autobiographical quality of our own experience, the events and their temporal duration called up as we read and make meaning of the event. The same is true for you, our reader.

We have worked our way through the dream scenario and made use of Dewey's theory of inquiry because we believe it is important for those who study personal experience to be open to a rich and sometimes seemingly endless range of possible events and stories and to be prepared to follow leads in many directions and to hold them all in inquiry context as the work proceeds. Experience is messy, and so is experiential research. We shall now offer a structural simplification that should be of some help to those researchers who find themselves in a forest of events and stories pointing inward and outward, and backward and forward.

There are three sets of methodological questions that confront the researcher in finding his or her way through the forest. One set of questions has to do with the field of research experience, the second set with the texts told and written about the field experience, and the third set with the research account. Field, text, research account, and the relations among them, name primary kinds of decisions undertaken by those who study experience. The relations between researcher and field range from being a neutral observer to fully becoming part of the life of participants; the relations between researcher and text based on the field experience involve complex questions of the representation of experience, the interpretation and reconstruction of experience, and appropriate text forms. Questions of telling, that is, of the research account, come down to matters of autobiographical presence and the significance of this presence for the text and for the field. Matters of signature (Geertz, 1988) and voice are important.

We can ask all of these methodological questions of the dream text. The dream text, for example, stands between the field of experience of the participants and the texts that we researchers might write about it. For example, this chapter in which the dream text is now embedded raises questions about who we are within all three sets of questions: who we are in relation to the dream narrator and her colleague, who we are in relation to their text, and who we are as we interpret their text in our research accounts. These three sets of methodological questions serve as a structure for the remainder of this chapter.

◆ Experiencing the Experience

As we begin work on a research project, we often talk about beginning a new story, a story of inquiry. Thinking about an inquiry in narrative terms allows us to conceptualize the inquiry experience as a storied one on several levels. Following Dewey, our principal interest in experience is the growth and transformation in the life stories we, our students, and research participants author. Therefore, difficult as it may be to tell a story, the more difficult but important task in narrative is the retelling of stories that allow for growth and change. We imagine, therefore, that in the construction of narratives of experience, there is a reflexive relationship between living a life story, telling a life story, retelling a life story, and reliving a life story. As researchers, we are always engaged in living, telling, reliving, and retelling our own stories. Our narratives of experience as Jean and Michael are always ongoing ones. We live out stories in our experiences, tell stories of those experiences, and modify them through retelling and reliving them. The research participants with whom we engage also live, tell, relive, and retell their own stories.

As researchers and participants come together, we are all already engaged in these narrative processes. The preconditions for any inquiry are set by prior inquiries. What this means is that there are narratives of inquiry out of which any particular inquiry grows and takes on meaning. These conditioning inquiries also have their own internal and existential conditions. All inquiry may, therefore, be seen as interactions of experiences of participants in a field and researchers' experiences as they come to that field. When we begin experiencing the experience, we need to be sensitive to the stories already being lived, told, relived, and retold. For example, the research participant whose dream text we shared on the first page of this chapter may have been engaged in conversations about her collaborative relationship with the other participant whether or not they were engaged in a research project with us. Our relationship as researchers with them may or may not have changed their ongoing conversation.

It is clear, however, that when we come together in research projects, all of us begin to live and tell a new story of our collaborative work together. For example, we might imagine that because of our research focus on collaboration, the two participants in the conversation about the dream are more aware of living a collaborative story and more intent on trying to figure out how to tell one. These new collaborative stories being lived and told as we work together in a research study also influence our other stories.

As researchers, we also tell another kind of story; that is, we try to tell or represent the story of the research project. We say more about writing the research story in a subsequent section on the transition from field texts to research texts. This consideration of the end of the research process brings us full circle to the beginnings of the inquiry, because in personal experience methods we must acknowledge the centrality of the researchers' own experience: their own tellings, livings, relivings, and retellings. Therefore, one of the starting points is the researchers' own narratives of experience. We try to gain experience of our experience through constructing narratives of that experience. It is here that we deal with questions of who we are in the field and who we are in the texts we write on our experience of the field experience. What becomes apparent here is that many of the ways we come in touch with our own experience, come to know what we know of our experience, is through stories. The methods we use in telling our stories of experience are similar to the ones we use with other research participants. We will discuss several methods here. Story is, however, central to each.

◆ From Field to Field Texts

What are normally called data—journal entries, field notes, photographs, and so on—are, for us, better thought of as field texts. They are texts created by participants and researchers to represent aspects of field experience. Some documents that eventually became field texts may have been created prior to the inquiry, or even during the inquiry but for a different purpose. Such documents became field texts when they became relevant to the inquiry. The dream text is a case in point. How we get from field to field texts is a critical matter in personal experience methods. Central to the creation of field texts is the relationship of researcher to participant. We take for granted that all field texts are selectively chosen from field experience and thereby embody an interpretive process. Even audio and visual recordings are interpretive texts shaped by the recorder. What we want to add to this understanding is the importance of the relationship.

Researcher relationships to ongoing participant stories shape the nature of field texts and establish the epistemological status of them. We assume that a relationship embeds meaning in the text and imposes form on the research texts ultimately developed. A field note is not simply a field note; a photograph is not simply a photograph; an oral history is not simply an oral history. What is told, as well as the meaning of what is told, is shaped by the relationship. The field text created may be more or less collaboratively constructed, may be more or less interpretive, and may be more or less researcher influenced. It depends. For example, the dream text was earlier presented as if it were not collaboratively constructed, not highly interpretive, and without researcher influence. Without knowing the relationship between us as researchers and the participants, you, our reader, have no way of knowing any of these things. If the situation was as implied, then the dream text would be a "realistic" representation of an aspect of the dreamer's life. In effect, the text would be comparatively close to, and representative of, an aspect of the participant's ongoing life. On the other hand, if the text was collaboratively constructed with the researchers, then it would be representative of the research and not of ongoing life without the research. Furthermore, we do not know if the dream text was a faithful record of a dream as it occurred or if it was, instead, an imaginative reconstruction of the emotional quality of the colleagues' relationship. In the latter case, the dream is less a descriptive account than an interpretive, semitheoretical expression. The epistemological status of the stories in the dream text is, therefore, unclear. They may have a "life as it is without influence by the researcher" quality or they may have the quality of stories self-consciously told for consumption by a research audience. Under these two circumstances the status of the stories as representing the field is entirely different. Not to be sensitive to the centrality of relationship in research can, therefore, lead to serious deceptions (Crites, 1979). We may deceive ourselves and others into thinking we know more about the participants' ongoing lives than is epistemologically warranted by our relationship to the participants. There are also interpretive deceptions possible on the side of theoretical understanding of field events in that we may think we have constructed more generalizable categories than warranted. These comments apply to each one of the methods described below for moving from field experience to field text. This is not an all-inclusive list of methods. Readers should also note that each of the methods described has its own body of literature and could take up a chapter on its own.

Oral History

One method for creating field texts is oral history. There is a range of strategies for obtaining an oral history, ranging from the use of a structured set of questions, in which the researchers' intentions are uppermost (Thompson, 1978), to asking a person to tell his or her own story in his or her own way (Anderson & Jack, 1991), in which the participant's intentions are uppermost. In commenting on their own work, Anderson and Jack (1991) write that shifting attention "from information gathering where the focus is on the right questions, to interaction, where the focus is on the process" (p. 23), illustrates the dynamic potential of collaboratively constructed oral history field texts. Depending on the character of the research relationship, the oral history will vary in focus in detailed ways, such as in the particular events narrated and in the emotional quality that appears in the field text. Oral history as a method of getting in touch with another's experience is closely connected with the methods of annals and chronicles.

Annals and Chronicles

Another method for creating field texts is to have participants construct annals of their lives or parts of their lives. An annal, for us, is a line schematic of an individual's life divided into moments or segments by events, years, places, or significant memories. The construction of an annal allows researchers and participants to gain a sense of the whole of an individual's life from his or her point of view. Annals often allow individuals to represent visually something of the topography of their life experiences, the highs and lows, the rhythms they construct around their life cycles. We know, of course, that the way a person constructs an annal is only one representation of his or her life. The way each individual tells his or her own story not only depends upon the purposes and intentions he or she has at the time, but is also dependent upon how the individual is making sense of the researcher's intentions and purposes. Once again, the relationship between researcher and participant makes a difference to the annal constructed.

After a participant has constructed an annal, we ask him or her to tell stories, to construct chronicles around the points marked on the annal. To return for a moment to the opening sequence of this chapter, we might imagine that the research participant who narrated her dream would, if asked to construct an annal, mark the significant moments of what is clearly an important collaborative relationship on her annal. Further, if asked to tell stories, to chronicle these moments, she may tell of meeting her collaborator, of beginning to work collaboratively, of times of tension, and so on.

Frequently we involve participants in creating annals and chronicles as a way to scaffold their oral histories, of beginning the process of having them re-collect their experiences. Annals and chronicles are also a way to begin to hear a person's family stories.

Family Stories

A related method of creating field texts is the telling or writing of family stories. Family stories are stories handed down across generations about family members and family events. Through family stories, people learn self-identity. Phrases such as "You're just like your grandfather" evoke grandfather stories and identify the person with the storied grandfather. The experience of family stories has existential and internal conditions; as Stone (1988) notes:

> The family's first concern is itself, but its second realm of concern is its relation to the world. Family stories about the world are usually teaching stories, telling members still at home the ways of the world according to the experiences its elders have had. . . . Family stories seem to persist in importance even when people think of themselves individually, without

164

regard to their familial roles. The particular human chain we're part of is central to our individual identity. (p. 7)

Photographs, Memory Boxes, Other Personal/Family Artifacts

Many of us collect a variety of materials as we compose our lives. We may collect and save photographs of people remarkable to our lives in some way, of special events, of places. Each photograph marks a special memory in our time, a memory around which we construct stories. Other things find their way into what are sometimes called memory boxes. For instance, the first author's memory "box," not really a box at all, contains old ticket stubs, gifts and trinkets from friends, items made by her son in school, bits of jewelry, and so on. Each item marks a time, a person, an event. She constructs stories around the items. Other items belong more to her family and mark family moments and events. Her great-grandmother's worn quilt, handed down from daughter to daughter and now used to cover her son, the plates her grandmother gave to her mother, her grandfather's watch—all are items around which family stories are composed and told.

All of these items become triggers to our memories, to recollecting the "little fragments that have no beginning and no end" (O'Brien, 1991, p. 39) and around which we tell and retell stories. It is these artifacts collected in our lives that provide a rich source of memories.

Research Interviews

One widely used method of creating field texts is through interview (Mishler, 1986). Interviews can be turned into written field texts through transcription, note taking, and/or the selective use of interview segments. The way an interviewer acts, questions, and responds in an interview shapes the relationship and, therefore, the ways participants respond and give accounts of their experience. This point is illustrated in Anderson and Jack's (1991) commentary on an interview study, in which they write, "Interviewers had either ignored these more subjective dimensions of women's lives or had accepted comments at face value when a pause, a word, or an expression might have invited the narrator to continue" (p. 12). Furthermore, the kinds of questions asked and the ways they are structured provide a frame within which participants shape their accounts of their experience. For example, Belenky, Clinchy, Goldberger, and Tarule's (1986) question, "Looking back over your life, what relationships have been really important to you? Why?" (p. 232) creates a different frame from Mikel Brown's (1989) sequence of questions, "Could you describe to me a situation where you had to make a decision and you weren't sure what was the right thing to do? . . . When you were trying to decide what to do, what was the conflict in this situation?" (pp. 88-89).

In our work with research interviews, we have become aware that there are gender and culture differences in the way individuals experience research interviews. Minister (1991) makes the point that "topic selection determined by interviewer questions, one person talking at a time, the narrator 'taking the floor' with referential language that keeps within the boundaries of selected topics" (p. 35) makes a difference to the content of field texts. In our work, particularly with children and with individuals from other cultures, we have noticed similar effects.

Journals

A powerful way for individuals to give accounts of their experience is through journal writing. May Sarton (1982), poet, novelist, and writer of journals, notes that "journals are a way of finding out where I really am. . . . They have to do with encounters with people who come here, who talk to me, or friends whom I see, or the garden. They sort of make me feel that the fabric of my life has a meaning" (p. 25). E. Carr (1966), another writer of journals, notes that her journals seem to be "made up of scraps of nothing" (p. v). She likens her journal entries to the small English candies called Hundreds and Thousands, which are "so small that separately they are not worth eating" (p. v). However, she writes that "it was these tiny things that, collectively, taught me how to live. Too insignificant to have been considered individually, but like the Hundreds and Thousands lapped up and sticking to our moist tongues, the little scraps and nothingnesses of my life have made a definite pattern" (p. v).

Journals, mostly unpublished, are another method of creating field texts. Many individuals write journals in which they try to keep "ongoing records of practices and reflections on those practices" (Connelly & Clandinin, 1988, p. 34). Children and adolescents often write journals of their thoughts, activities, and stories in attempts to make sense of their experiences. We have also found many journal writers among the teachers with whom we work. In their journals they weave together their accounts of the private and the professional, capturing fragments of experience in attempts to sort themselves out.

Autobiographical Writing

Closely linked to journal writing is autobiographical writing (Grumet, 1988; Olney, 1980; Pinar, 1981). Our journals become a kind of autobiographical writing, but, as Carr and Sarton point out, journals capture the small fragments of experience and not so much a sense of the whole. Autobiographical writing is a way to write of the whole context of life. Molloy (1991) notes that autobiography "is always a re-presentation, that is, a retelling, since the life to which it supposedly refers is already a kind of narrative construct. Life is always, necessarily, a tale" (p. 5). The retelling of a life through autobiographical writing is another method of creating field texts that capture "a tension between self and others, of generating a reflection on the fluctuating place of the subject within its community" (p. 9).

As researchers of personal experience, we recognize that any piece of autobiographical writing is "a particular reconstruction of an individual's narrative, and there could be other reconstructions" (Connelly & Clandinin, 1988, p. 39). There can always be a rich array of possible field texts created as we write autobiographically. For us, however, when autobiographical writing is shaped into an autobiography or memoir (Hampl, 1991), it is a research text.

Letters

We find letters a particularly interesting field text (White & Epston, 1990). Letters, unlike journals, are written to another person with the expectation of a response. In letters we try to give an account of ourselves, make meaning of our experiences, and attempt to establish and maintain relationships among ourselves, our experience, and the experience of another. For example, we opened this chapter with an excerpt from a letter. As presented, the letter is a fragment. There is no salutation and no closure to frame the letter. The salutation and closure of a letter often define the relationship—that is, in Sarton's (1984) words, they "give the reader the sense of a whole moment in time and place" (p. 289). Excerpts, writes Sarton, "lack continuity and appear to take place in some literary limbo" (p. 289). The dream text has this character. In order for us to understand the meaning embedded in the dream text, we need, in addition to the contextual matters described earlier in the chapter, the salutation and the closure that would give some sense of the ongoing relationship as the other is addressed.

In personal experience research, letters, as a research method, may be used among participants, among research collaborators, or among researchers and participants. In each case one of their merits is the equality established, the give and take of conversation.

Conversations

Conversation is a generic term covering many kinds of activities. For example, letter writing is a kind of written conversation. However, the more common kind is oral conversation, between pairs or among groups of individuals. As researchers become aware of the ways research interviews have constrained participants' texts of their experience, some have started to set up more conversational forms as a personal experience method (Oakley, 1981). As with letter writing, conversations are marked by equality among participants and by flexibility to allow group participants to establish the form and topics important to their inquiry. Conversation entails listening. The listener's response may constitute a probe into experience that takes the representation of experience far beyond what is possible in an interview. Indeed, there is probing in conversation, in-depth probing, but it is done in a situation of mutual trust, listening, and caring for the experience described by the other. Once again, we see the centrality of relationship among researchers and participants.

Field Notes and Other Stories From the Field

A great deal has been written about field notes, the mainstay ethnographic data collection method (Sanjek, 1990; Van Maanen, 1988). Field notes may be written by researchers or by participants, and they may be written in more or less detail with more or less interpretive content. In each of the choices, there are consequences for the kind of field text created. Researchers need to be self-conscious about the kind of field record created. Field notes become an important field text in personal experience methods when we acknowledge the relationships we have as researchers with our participants. The nature of these relationships shape the construction of the records. It makes a great deal of difference if we distance ourselves from events in order to record notes or if we actively participate in events as a partner. Similarly, it makes a difference as we create field notes if we see ourselves as recorders of events "over there" or if we see ourselves as characters in the events.

In our opinion, researchers are often more reluctant than necessary to use field records. They worry that field notes will be insufficient to capture field experience adequately. When this happens, tape recorders and videotape tend to be overused, with severe transcription penalties later as field notes are made on the basis of the transcripts. In any event, it is the fear that somehow experience will be lost that drives researchers to try to record or tape all of experience. What we fail to acknowledge clearly enough is that all field texts are constructed representations of experience.

◆ A Note on Ethics

In personal experience methods the ethical dimensions of researcher-participant relationships are highlighted. When we enter into a research relationship with participants and ask them to share their stories with us, there is the potential to shape their lived, told, relived, and retold stories as well as our own. These intensive relationships require serious consideration of who we are as researchers in the stories of participants, for when we become characters in their stories, we change their stories. In other places we have written that personal experience methods have the potential to generate new shared stories for participants and researchers in relationships that are akin to friendships (e.g., Clandinin & Connelly, 1988). As researchers we are also changed, but because we enter the relationships with certain intentions and purposes and, as the ones most often initiating the research relationship, our care and our responsibility is first directed toward participants. Autobiographical studies pose a somewhat unique case within this general point. In autobiographical studies, we must consider issues of care for those field texts and research texts we create about ourselves.

As we move from field texts to research texts, ethical issues remain of great importance. Because personal experience methods involve "real" people, and not just texts, we need to pay the closest attention to the aftermath of the research (Lightfoot, 1983). As personal experience researchers, we owe our care, our responsibility, to the research participants and how our research texts shape their lives. We all can find ourselves in the eventually constructed research texts. If as participants we are portrayed in an unexpected (for us) story, the research text may raise questions about the retelling and reliving of our stories. For researchers these issues of responsibility are always foregrounded as we construct research texts. Anonymity and other ways of fictionalizing research texts are important ethical concerns in personal experience methods. Even in an autobiographical work such as Oakley's (1992) *Taking It Like a Woman*, she cares for herself and other characters in her research text by fictionalizing sections of the work. In the dream text that opened this chapter, we too considered the aftermath of the research text by carefully fictionalizing the field text.

◆ From Field Texts to Research Texts

Sometimes our field texts are so compelling that as researchers we want to stop and let them speak for themselves. Field texts may consist of inviting, captivating family stories, conversations, and even dream texts. But researchers cannot stop there, because the task is to discover and construct meaning in those texts. Field texts need to be reconstructed as research texts. To return to the dream text, for example, the stories told there, along with an array of associated field texts, might seem sufficient because of the coherence of their story lines and their interest to readers. But those texts with their various story lines, though interesting, tend only to define and set the terms for an inquiry. They are the texts of which one asks questions of meaning and social significance. What is the meaning(s) of the dream text and why does it make a difference to figure it out? These are the general questions that drive the transition from field texts to research texts. Responses to these inquiries ultimately shape the research text. Field texts are not, in general, constructed with a reflective intent; rather, they are close to experience, tend to be descriptive, and are shaped around particular events. They have a recording quality to them, whether auditory or visual. Research texts are at a distance from field texts and grow out of the repeated asking of questions concerning meaning and significance. Like Carr's (1966) *Hundreds and Thousands*, a research account looks for the patterns, narrative threads, tensions, and themes either within or across individuals' personal experience. It would be tempting to view this overall process as a series of steps. However, because collaboration occurs from beginning to end, plot outlines are continually revised as consultation takes place over written materials and as further field texts are collected to develop points of importance in the revised story.

The search for these patterns, narrative threads, tensions, and themes that constitutes the inquiry that shapes field texts into research texts is created by the writer's experience. And the researcher's experience, like experience generally, has internal and existential conditions. Just as the researcher's relationship to participants shaped the field text, the researcher's relationship to the inquiry and to the participants shapes the research text. It makes a difference whether the researcher imagines her- or himself as having an emotional and ethical relationship to the participant and to the inquiry. If the researcher cares about the ongoing relationship to the participants as well as to the ways the research account is read and for what purpose, it will make a difference to the way the research account is written. For instance, our collaborative relationships with teachers are carefully negotiated with an eye both to present relationships and to the ways the proposed collaboration will affect our future relations. As noted above, these concerns play out in the emotional and ethical aspects of living as well as in the research text.

Though researchers' internal conditions of experience have tended not to play an important role in research and have often been consciously silenced through such conventional writing expressions as "this research" or "the researcher," researcher voice and signature are now recognized terms in personal experience methods. Who the researchers are makes a difference at all levels of the research, and the signature they put on their work comes out of the stories they live and tell. Existential conditions have been much more acknowledged in research, although we find them played out somewhat differently in personal experience methods. The conditions of most interest to us for this chapter are the inquiry purposes, available forms for expression of the research text, and the audience and the researcher's imagined relations to the audience. Let us turn first to a discussion of the internal conditions of voice and signature.

◆ Internal Conditions

Voice

There is a rich, developing literature on voice. In personal experience methods where there is a relationship between researcher and participants, there are issues of voice that arise for both. For many, especially for women being educated as researchers, voice is an acknowledgment that they have something to say. The methods of writing in liberal arts and science programs tend to emphasize accurate, summative readings of the works of others. But in research it is what the writer has to say, independently and not by way of summary, that matters. We think of this as the development of voice after silence. It is, perhaps, one of the most difficult transitions budding researchers need to make. Without a sense of voice, a researcher is bound to the ever-refined writing and rewriting of field texts at a time that calls for research texts.

But even when one has gained the confidence to inquire, rather than merely to summarize and interpret others, there is still, even for experienced researchers, a dilemma of voice in moving from field texts to research texts. This struggle for research voice is captured by the analogy of living on a knife edge as one struggles to express one's own voice in the midst of an inquiry designed to capture the participants' experience and represent their voices, all the while attempting to create a research text that will speak to, and reflect upon, the audience's voices. This sense of voice, and the dilemma that creates it, can never be sorted out except judicially. The researcher is always speaking partially naked and is genuinely open to legitimate criticism from participants and from audience. Some researchers are silenced by the invitation to criticism contained in the expression of voice.

There are other issues around voice. As we write our research texts, we need to consider the voice that is heard and the voice that is not heard. We may, for example, include the voice of a participant in such a way that she speaks her stories of teaching but not include her voice when she speaks her stories of being abused. Or, to look at the issue of voice in another way, we may include the voice of a participant in such a way that the context of the research text obscures or silences important parts of that participant's voice. There are multiple questions about voice, both our voices as researchers and the voices of participants as we construct our research texts. As researchers, we too struggle to speak our research texts in our multiple voices. Our silences, both those we choose and those of which we are unaware, are also issues of voice in our research texts.

Temporality is linked to voice. The question of who speaks in a text becomes important as we, and the stories we tell of our experience, change over time. An adult person speaking of her experience as a child raises the who speaks question. Is it the adult interpreting the childhood experience, in which case it is the adult speaking? Or is it the adult expressing the child's story as the child would have told the experience, in which case it is the child speaking? Field texts play a key role in sorting this out. Memory, unaided by field texts—for instance, a child's journal; parents', friends', and others' remembrances; photographs of the child—has an uncertain status and, for the most part, expresses a current voice rather than a historical voice.

Signature

Voice and signature are closely connected in the writing that transforms field texts into research texts. When a veil of silence is lifted and the writer knows he or she has something to say and feels the power of voice, that person still must find a way of saying what he or she wishes to speak. There is, says Geertz (1988), no more difficult dilemma for a writer than sorting out how to be in the text. "Being there in the text," he says, is even more difficult than "being there in the field." For Geertz, there are multiple forms for being there in the field as well as multiple forms for being there in the text. "Being there" in the special way that marks each of us as writers constitutes our research signature. The dilemma to which Geertz refers is the dilemma of how lively our signature should be: Too vivid a signature runs the risk of obscuring the field and its participants; too subtle a signature runs the risk of the deception that the research text speaks from the point of view of the participant.

The risks of an overly vivid signature are well-known in the literature and come under the heading of the abuses of subjectivity. The risks of too flimsy a signature are not as well thought through, and it is here that modern-day researchers of personal experience need to pay close attention to their writing. The signature can be too thin because other texts and other theories, rather than the writer, sign the work. Equally, the signature can be too thin because the researcher imagines that the participants and their field texts author the work. Both ways of thinning the signature need to be guarded against. In gaining a voice and a signature for it, the researcher puts his or her own stamp on the work.

The text that follows from the signature has rhythm, cadence, and expression that marks the signature and makes the work readily identifiable as the work of a certain author or set of collaborators. This expression of the signature is called "discourse" by Geertz. The signature and its expression in discourse creates an author identity.

173

◆ Existential Conditions

Three existential conditions of importance to personal experience methods in the movement from field texts to research texts are inquiry purposes, narrative forms, and audience and the researcher's imagined relations to them. We discuss each of these in turn.

Inquiry Purposes

The question raised earlier—What are we doing here?—comes to the forefront in the construction of research texts. Some argue that the act of working with participants in aid of their, and our, growth and transformation is sufficient justification for research work. But in research our responsibility goes beyond those with whom we work to a larger field and research community. Field texts will not adequately influence the discourse or the practices of those beyond the immediate research field. The research text performs this function. The temptation to conclude an inquiry at the stage of field texts combined with productive ongoing relationships with participants is vividly seen in autobiographical works where the construction of stories and their endless refinement into themes of control, power, expression, and so on are often felt to be so meaningful for the author that the question of who cares or who would want to read the autobiographical stories tends to be dismissed. Even in an autobiographical work it is crucial to write not only for the self but also for others. Writing for others takes place in the research text. In a fortuitous twist of fortune, the expressions of meaning contained in research texts are often profound for the self. Just as serving the self serves the community, so too serving the community in research texts also serves the self.

One of the special powers of personal experience methods is that their connection goes beyond theories, researchers, and practitioners, to the life community within which these traditional parties to inquiry relate. Personal experience research is a form of public inquiry that has the potential for transcending the specialties of research in particular subject fields. It does this because personal experience methods connect with fundamentally human qualities of human experience. Personal experience methods are human methods. For this reason the narrative form of the research texts is crucial to the texts' finding a place in public discourse.

Narrative Form

This book is being written at an important time in the development of personal experience methods. Marcus and Fischer (1986) call this time an "experimental moment." There is a willingness to experiment with narrative form. Literary (Bakhtin, 1981), visual (Chatman, 1980), poetic (Rose, 1990), dramatic (Turner, 1980), and other modes of expression are evident. These, and other, forms have recently been set out by Eisner (1991). Without going into detail, it is, perhaps, worth noting that just as painters learn to paint by adopting a painter's style so, too, one of the ways a person may experiment with narrative form is by adopting the signature of a favorite author. A writer might, for instance, experiment with research texts written in Virginia Woolf's or James Joyce's signature. Just as painters often develop their own styles as an outgrowth of experimentation with the signatures of well-known, accomplished painters, so, too, this experimentation eventually may lead to an individual's own research signature as narrative form is adapted to who he or she is. In this process of adaptation and the creation of signature, we are well advised to listen to the remnants of narrative form handed down to us by our own personal narrative histories.

Audience

Everything so far said here bears on the audience and our relationship to it. It makes a great deal of difference how we intend to interact with our audience through the research text. Following Chatman (1990), texts may be descriptive, expositional, argumentative, or narrative. All of these kinds of texts can be used in the service of others. For example, our narrative dream text could be used in a research text to "explain" to an audience how a collaborative relationship and the tensions within it function in inquiry. The dream text could also be part of a larger narrative research text that would invite members of the public to share in a collaborative inquiry relating communities of research and public communities. In the creation of research texts, researchers need to imagine themselves in conversation with an audience. What voice and signature mark the imagined audience? What voice and signature shall we adopt? What kind of conversation do we imagine will ensue?

◆ Relationships Across the Boundaries

Our task in this chapter has been to set forth a discussion of personal experience methods. Inevitably, in doing so, we have transcended our task. What first appears as methods of collecting data turns out to involve an inquiry into the field, field texts, research texts, audience, and the larger community beyond the world of theory and practice defined in any particular study. Earlier we noted that the whole of the social sciences are founded on the study of experience. In our view, experience is the starting point and key term for all social science inquiry. We see personal experience methods as a way to permit researchers to enter into and participate with the social world in ways that allow the possibility of transformations and growth. Personal experience methods offer all of us, not only we as chapter authors, but you as reader, the opportunity to create a middle ground where there is a conversation among people with different life experiences. Personal experience methods inevitably are relationship methods. As researchers, we cannot work with participants without sensing the fundamental human connection among us; nor can we create research texts without imagining a relationship to you, our audience. Voice and signature make it possible for there to be conversations through the texts among participants, researchers, and audiences. It is in the research relationships among participants and researchers, and among researchers and audiences, through research texts that we see the possibility for individual and social change.

◆ References

Adler, M., & Van Doren, C. (1972). *How to read a book*. New York: Simon & Schuster.

Anderson, K., & Jack, D. (1991). Learning to listen: Interview techniques and analyses. In S. Gluck & D. Patai (Eds.), *Women's words: The feminist practice of oral history* (pp. 11-26). New York: Routledge.

Bakhtin, M. M. (1981). *The dialogic imagination*. Austin: University of Texas Press.

Belenky, M., Clinchy, B., Goldberger, N., & Tarule, J. (1986). *Women's ways of knowing: The development of self, voice, and mind*. New York: Basic Books.

Bruner, E. M. (1986). Experience and its expressions. In V. Turner & E. Bruner (Eds.), *The anthropology of experience* (pp. 3-30). Chicago: University of Illinois Press.

Bruner, J. (1990). *Acts of meaning*. Cambridge, MA: Harvard University Press.

Carr, D. (1986). *Time, narrative, and history*. Bloomington: Indiana University Press.

Carr, E. (1966). *Hundreds and thousands: Journal of an artist*. Toronto: Irwin.

Chatman, S. (1980). What novels can do that films can't (and vice versa). In W. J. T. Mitchell (Ed.), *On narrative* (pp. 117-136). Chicago: University of Chicago Press.

Chatman, S. (1990). *Coming to terms: The rhetoric of narrative in fiction and film.* Ithaca, NY: Cornell University Press.

Clandinin, D. J., & Connelly, F. M. (1988). Studying teachers' knowledge of classrooms: Collaborative research, ethics, and the negotiation of narrative. *Journal of Educational Thought, 22,* 269-282.

Connelly, F. M., & Clandinin, D. J. (1988). *Teachers as curriculum planners: Narratives of experience.* New York: Teachers College Press.

Connelly, F. M., & Clandinin, D. J. (1990). Stories of experience and narrative inquiry. *Educational Researcher, 19*(5), 2-14.

Crews, F. (1992). *The critics bear it away: American fiction and the academy.* New York: Random House.

Crites, S. (1971). The narrative quality of experience. *Journal of the American Academy of Religion, 39,* 391-411.

Crites, S. (1979). The aesthetics of self-deception. *Soundings, 62,* 107-129.

Denzin, N. (1989). *Interpretive biography.* Newbury Park, CA: Sage.

Dewey, J. (1916). *Democracy and education.* New York: Macmillan.

Dewey, J. (1934). *Art as experience.* New York: Capricorn.

Dewey, J. (1938). *Experience and education.* New York: Collier.

Eisner, E. (1988). The primacy of experience and the politics of method. *Educational Researcher, 17*(5), 15-20.

Eisner, E. (1991). *The enlightened eye: Qualitative inquiry and the enhancement of educational practices.* New York: Macmillan.

Geertz, C. (1988). *Works and lives: The anthropologist as author.* Stanford, CA: Stanford University Press.

Grumet, M. (1988). *Bitter milk.* Amherst: University of Massachusetts Press.

Hampl, P. (1991). The need to say it. In J. Sternberg (Ed.), *The writer on her work* (Vol. 2). New York: W. W. Norton.

Heilbrun, C. (1988). *Writing a woman's life.* New York: W. W. Norton.

Husserl, E. (1970). *The crisis of European sciences and transcendental phenomenology* (D. Carr, Trans.). Evanston: Northwestern University Press.

Kuhn, T. S. (1970). *The structure of scientific revolutions* (2nd ed.). Chicago: University of Chicago Press.

Lightfoot, S. (1983). *The good high school.* New York: Basic Books.

Marcus, G. E., & Fischer, M. J. M. (1986). *Anthropology as cultural critique: An experimental moment in the human sciences.* Chicago: University of Chicago Press.

Mikel Brown, L. (1989). When is a moral problem not a moral problem? In C. Gilligan, N. Lyons, & T. Hanmer (Eds.), *Making connections: The relational worlds of adolescent girls at Emma Willard School.* Cambridge, MA: Harvard University Press.

Minister, K. A. (1991). A feminist frame for the oral history interview. In S. Gluck & D. Patai (Eds.), *Women's words: The feminist practice of oral history* (pp. 27-44). New York: Routledge.

Mishler, E. (1986). *Research interviewing: Context and narrative.* Cambridge, MA: Harvard University Press.

Molloy, S. (1991). *At face value: Autobiographical writing in Spanish America.* New York: Cambridge University Press.

Oakley, A. (1981). Interviewing women: A contradiction in terms. In H. Roberts (Ed.), *Doing feminist research* (pp. 30-61). London: Routledge & Kegan Paul.

Oakley, A. (1992). *Taking it like a woman.* London: Flamingo.

Oakshott, M. (1962). *Rationalism in politics.* London: Methuen.

O'Brien, T. (1991). *The things they carried.* Toronto: McClelland & Stewart.

Olney, J. (1980). *Autobiography: Essays theoretical and practical.* Princeton, NJ: Princeton University Press.

Pinar, W. F. (1981). Whole, bright, deep with understanding. *Journal of Curriculum Studies, 13*(3), 173-188.

Pinar, W. F. (1988). Preface. In W. F. Pinar (Ed.), *Contemporary curriculum discourse* (pp. v-vii). Scottsdale, AZ: Gorsuch Scarsdale.

Polkinghorne, D. E. (1988). *Narrative knowing and the human sciences.* Albany: State University of New York Press.

Ricoeur, P. (1984). *Time and narrative* (Vol. 1). Chicago: University of Chicago Press.

Rose, D. (1990). *Living the ethnographic life.* Newbury Park, CA: Sage.

Sanjek, R. (Ed.). (1990). *Fieldnotes: The makings of anthropology.* Albany: State University of New York Press.

Sarason, S. B. (1988). *The making of an American psychologist.* San Francisco: Jossey-Bass.

Sarton, M. (1982). *May Sarton: A self-portrait* (M. Simpson & M. Wheelock, Eds.). New York: W. W. Norton.

Sarton, M. (1984). *At seventy: A journal.* New York: W. W. Norton.

Schön, D. A. (1983). *The reflective practitioner: How professionals think in action.* New York: Basic Books.

Schön, D. A. (1991). *The reflective turn: Case studies in reflective practice.* New York: Teachers College Press.

Schwab, J. J. (1964). The structure of the disciplines: Meanings and significances. In G. W. Ford & L. Pugo (Eds.), *The structure of knowledge and the curriculum* (pp. 1-30). Chicago: Rand McNally.

Stone, E. (1988). *Black sheep and kissing cousins: How our family stories shape us.* New York: Times Books.

Taylor, C. (1989). *Sources of the self: The making of the modern identity.* Cambridge, MA: Harvard University Press.

Taylor, C. (1992). *Multiculturalism and "the politics of recognition."* Princeton, NJ: Princeton University Press.

Thompson, P. (1978). *The voice of the past: Oral history.* Oxford: Oxford University Press.

Turner, V. (1980). Social dramas and stories about them. In W. J. T. Mitchell (Ed.), *On narrative* (pp. 137-154). Chicago: University of Chicago Press.

Watts, S. (1992, April 29). Academic leftists are something of a fraud. *Chronicle of Higher Education,* pp. A40-A43.

White, M., & Epston, D. (1990). *Narrative means to therapeutic ends.* New York: W. W. Norton.

Van Maanen, J. (1988). *Tales of the field: On writing ethnography.* Chicago: University of Chicago Press.

7

Data Management
and Analysis Methods

A. Michael Huberman & Matthew B. Miles

◆ Definitions and Assumptions

Discussions of qualitative data management and analysis have become more differentiated and integrated over the past decade. In 1976, Sieber's review of seven well-respected texts on field methods found that less than 5-10% of their pages were devoted to analysis as such; in 1979, Miles noted that the qualitative analyst had few guidelines for protection against self-delusion, let alone against unreliable or invalid conclusions more generally. We also commented that analysis methods were rarely reported in enough detail for readers to follow how a researcher got from 3,600 pages of field notes to the final conclusions (Miles & Huberman, 1984).

Today we have come far from that state of affairs. The database we consulted in the preparation of the 1994 edition of *Qualitative Data Analysis: An Expanded Sourcebook* had more than tripled since publication of the first edition (Miles & Huberman, 1984, 1994). There are new journals, several handbooks, innumerable conferences on qualitative issues, special interest groups, and new software packages. It is a growth industry. As a result, many new texts, including the present one, have by now made Sieber's finding obsolete. Gradually, the craft of data management and analysis is becoming explicitly shared. Still, much remains to be done. Competing, polemical arguments are rampant. It is still unlikely that a researcher could write a case study from a colleague's field notes that would be plausibly similar to the original.

In this chapter we focus on data management and analysis methods, aiming to point to useful work as well as to unsolved issues. In turn, we will outline some basic assumptions and definitions, discuss systematic data collection and management issues, and then turn to data analysis concerns—those occurring before and early during data collection, as well as later on, both within and across cases. We conclude with some general issues in analysis: the importance of data displays, threats to analytic validity, and the importance of "transparency"—shareability—of management and analysis procedures themselves.

Working Definitions

In this chapter, we define *data management* pragmatically as the operations needed for a systematic, coherent process of data collection, storage, and retrieval. These operations are aimed at ensuring (a) high-quality, accessible data; (b) documentation of just what analyses have been carried out; and (c) retention of data and associated analyses after the study is complete.

Our definition of *data analysis* contains three linked subprocesses (Miles & Huberman, 1984, 1994): data reduction, data display, and conclusion drawing/verification (see Figure 7.1). These processes occur *before* data collection, during study design and planning; *during* data collection as interim and early analyses are carried out; and *after* data collection as final products are approached and completed.

With *data reduction,* the potential universe of data is reduced in an anticipatory way as the researcher chooses a conceptual framework, research questions, cases, and instruments. Once actual field notes, interviews, tapes, or other data are available, data summaries, coding, finding themes, clustering, and writing stories are all instances of further data selection and condensation.

Data display, defined as an organized, compressed assembly of information that permits conclusion drawing and/or action taking, is a second, inevitable, part of analysis. The researcher typically needs to see a reduced set of data as a basis for thinking about its meanings. More focused displays may include structured summaries, synopses (Fischer & Wertz, 1975), vignettes (Erickson, 1986), networklike or other diagrams (Carney, 1990; Gladwin, 1989; Strauss, 1987; Werner & Schoepfle, 1987a, 1987b), and

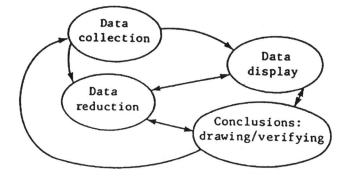

Figure 7.1. Components of Data Analysis: Interactive Model

matrices with text rather than numbers in the cells (Eisenhardt, 1989a, 1989b; Miles & Huberman, 1984, 1994).

Conclusion drawing and verification involve the researcher in interpretation: drawing meaning from displayed data. The range of tactics used appears to be large, ranging from the typical and wide use of comparison/contrast, noting of patterns and themes, clustering, and use of metaphors to confirmatory tactics such as triangulation, looking for negative cases, following up surprises, and checking results with respondents (Miles & Huberman, 1994). Many accounts of this aspect of analysis demonstrate that there is a multiple, iterative set of tactics in play (Chesler, 1987; Fischer & Wertz, 1975; Schillemans et al., n.d.) rather than one or two central ones. In this sense we can speak of "data transformation," as information is condensed, clustered, sorted, and linked over time (Gherardi & Turner, 1987).

Some Epistemological Assumptions

It is healthy medicine for researchers to make their preferences clear. To know how researchers construe the shape of the social world and how they mean to give us a credible account of it is to know just who we have on the other side of the table. When, for example, a realist, a critical theorist, and a social phenomenologist are competing for our attention, it matters a good deal to know where each is coming from. They will have diverse views of what is real, what can be known, and how these social facts can be rendered faithfully (Guba, 1990; Phillips, 1990; Ratcliffe, 1983).

In our case, we have advertised as "realists" (Huberman & Miles, 1985), but more precisely as "transcendental realists" (Bhaskar, 1978, 1989; Harré & Secord, 1973; Manicas & Secord, 1982). Fundamentally, we think that social phenomena exist not only in the mind, but in the objective world as well, and that there are some lawful, reasonably stable relationships to be found among them. The lawfulness comes from the sequences and the regularities that link phenomena together; it is from these that we derive the constructs that account for individual and social life.

This stance acknowledges the historical and social nature of knowledge, along with the meaning making at the center of phenomenogical experience (Packer & Addison, 1989; Polkinghorne, 1988). Our aim is to "transcend" these processes by carefully constructing explanations that can account for them in plausible ways. Thus transcendental realism calls both for causal explanation and for the evidence to show that each entity or event is an instance of that explanation. So there is a need not only for an explanatory structure, but also for a careful descriptive account of each particular configuration. This is one reason we and others have tilted toward more descriptive yet also more inductive methods of study.

◆ Data Management

Qualitative studies—especially those done by inexperienced or lone-wolf researchers—are vulnerable when it comes to data management. Kvale (1988) provides a wry analysis of the naive question, "How shall I find a method to analyze the 1,000 pages of interview transcripts I have collected?" His first answer is, "Never conduct interview research in such a way that you arrive at a situation where you [have to] ask such a question" (p. 90).

What sort of data are we talking about? Abstractly, qualitative data refer to essences of people, objects, and situations (Berg, 1989). Essentially, a raw experience is converted into words, typically compiled into extended text.

A portion of the raw experience may also be captured as still or moving images; these images can be used in a variety of ways, most of them also involving conversion or linkage to words. See especially Harper (1989) on diverse modes of image analysis. Ball and Smith (1992) also help us see that images are not more "realistic" than words, and are as subject as language to interpretation and captioning, are context dependent, can be faked, and so on.

The words involved are typically based on *observations, interviews,* or *documents* (as Wolcott, 1992, notes, "watching, asking or examining") and carried out close to a local setting for a sustained period. These modes of collecting data may be largely open, unstructured, and event driven, or more tightly defined, structured, and researcher driven.

Normally, the immediately collected information is not immediately available for analysis, but requires some *processing*; raw field notes can be indecipherable scribbles to anyone but the researcher, and must be corrected, extended, edited, and typed up. Audiotapes need to be transcribed, corrected, edited. Similar processing may be required for videotapes.

The "quality" of qualitative data aside, the quantity can be daunting, if not overwhelming. Depending on the level of detail, a day's processed field notes of, say, six interviews may easily run 50-100 single-spaced pages. And as needed site visits pile up, and multiple sites may be involved, the researcher is soon confronted with far more than Kvale's "1,000 pages."

Finally, we need to note here that unless a reasonably coherent system is in place for collecting information from a range of informants, across a potential range of sites, in a roughly comparable format, the researcher will be in data management limbo very quickly. This brings us to issues of storage and retrieval.

Storage and Retrieval

How data are stored and retrieved is the heart of data management; without a clear working scheme, data can easily be "miscoded, mislabeled, mislinked and mislaid" (Wolfe, 1992, p. 293). A good storage and retrieval system is critical for keeping track of what data are available; for permitting easy, flexible, reliable use of data—often by several members of a research team—at different points in time over a project's life; and for documenting the analyses made so that the study can, in principle, be verified or replicated.

There have actually been few detailed discussions of storage and retrieval systems for qualitative data. One is provided by Werner and Schoepfle (1987b), who correctly note that a system needs to be designed far prior to actual data collection. They distinguish among the raw field notes (journals), transcriptions, documents, and interpretive/analytic materials produced by the researcher, and stress the importance of a clear indexing system.

Levine (1985) proposes five general storage and retrieval functions: formatting (how materials are laid out, physically embodied, and structured into types of files), cross-referral (linkage across different files), indexing (defining codes, organizing them into a structure, and pairing codes with specific parts of the database), abstracting (condensed summaries of longer material, such as documents or extended field notes), and pagination (numbers and letters locating specific material in field notes—for example, B J K 1 22 locates for Brookside Hospital the first interview with Dr. Jameson by researcher Kennedy, page 22).

These functions, historically accomplished with notebooks, index cards, file folders, and edge-punch cards, can be carried out far more easily and quickly with computer software (for many specific suggestions, see Weitzman & Miles, 1993; see also Richards & Richards, Chapter 8, this volume). Even so, a physical filing system is also needed for raw field notes, hard copies of transcriptions, audiotapes, memos, and the like. We have proposed a checklist of what information needs to be stored, retrieved, and, usually, retained for a number of years afterward for a qualitative study (Miles & Huberman, 1994; see Table 7.1).

A final remark: A data management system and its effective revision and use over time do not occur in a social vacuum, but in the context of a real project staff, working over a projected and actual total of person-days (which typically amounts to 5-10 times as much time as in the field), and connected by a set of working agreements with study participants (informants, respondents) about the time, energy, information flow, and products that will be involved. (Specific suggestions on these topics appear in Miles & Huberman, 1994.)

◆ Analysis

Analysis via Study Design

Because this material is covered elsewhere in this series (see Janesick, Chapter 2, Volume 2), we will be brief. First, the design of qualitative studies can in a real sense be seen as analytic. Choices of conceptual framework, of research questions, of samples, of the "case" definition itself, and of instrumentation all involve anticipatory data reduction—which, as we have noted, is an essential aspect of data analysis. These choices have

TABLE 7.1 What to Store, Retrieve From, and Retain

1. *Raw material:* field notes, tapes, site documents.
2. *Partially processed data:* write-ups, transcriptions. Ideally, these should appear in their initial version, and in subsequent corrected, "cleaned," "commented-on" versions. Write-ups may profitably include marginal or reflective remarks made by the researcher during or after data collection.
3. *Coded data:* write-ups with specific codes attached.
4. *The coding scheme or thesaurus,* in its successive iterations.
5. *Memos or other analytic material:* the researcher's reflections on the conceptual meaning of the data.
6. *Search and retrieval records:* information showing which coded chunks or data segments the researcher looked for during analysis, and the retrieved material; records of links made among segments.
7. *Data displays:* matrices, charts, or networks used to display retrieved information in a more compressed, organized form, along with the associated analytic text. Typically, there are several revised versions of these.
8. *Analysis episodes:* documentation of what the researcher did, step by step, to assemble the displays and write the analytic text.
9. *Report text:* successive drafts of what is written on the design, methods, and findings of the study.
10. *General chronological log or documentation* of data collection and analysis work.
11. *Index* of all the above material.

a focusing and bounding function, ruling out certain variables, relationships, and associated data, and selecting others for attention. They also call for creative work. In effect, qualitative designs are not copyable, off-the-shelf patterns, but normally have to be custom-built, revised, and "choreographed" (Preissle, 1991).

Second, there is merit in both "loose," inductively oriented designs, and "tight," more deductively approached ones. The former work well when the terrain is unfamiliar and/or excessively complex, a single case is involved, and the intent is exploratory and descriptive. Tighter designs are indicated when the researcher has good prior acquaintance with the setting, has a good bank of applicable, well-delineated concepts, and takes a more explanatory and/or confirmatory stance involving multiple, comparable cases.

Qualitative studies ultimately aim to describe and explain (at some level) a pattern of relationships, which can be done only with a set of conceptually specified analytic categories (Mishler, 1990). Starting with them (deductively) or getting gradually to them (inductively) are both legitimate and useful paths. The components of such designs are described in the appendix to this chapter.

Interim Analysis

Unlike survey and experimental research, qualitative studies tend to have a peculiar life cycle, one that spreads collection and analysis throughout a study, but that calls for different modes of inquiry at different moments. This has some advantages. For one thing, errors in the field can be undone the next time out; there is always a second chance. Second, instrumentation can be adjusted and added to. In fact, unlike experimental studies, changes in observational protocols or interview schedules in a field study usually reflect a better understanding of the setting, thereby heightening the internal validity of the study.

But there are also some disadvantages. For example, the researcher is faced with the task of trying to reduce the amount of data taken in while still gathering more. The idea here is to focus much of the data collection on emergent themes or constructs (see below) yet still collect additional data. Ongoing analysis is inflationary. Typically, too, the more one investigates, the more layers of the setting one discovers.

Iterative Research

Most of these procedures call for the use of analytic induction. At the heart of analytic induction is the thesis that there are regularities to be found in the physical and social worlds. The theories or constructs that we derive express these regularities as precisely as possible. To uncover these constructs, we use an iterative procedure—a succession of question-and-answer cycles—that entails examining a given set of cases and then refining or modifying those cases on the basis of subsequent ones. Traditionally, the resulting inferences are deemed "valid," in the relaxed sense that they are probable, reasonable, or likely to be true (Robinson, 1951; Znaniecki, 1934).

In qualitative research, these procedures correspond to the "grounded theory" approach (Glaser & Strauss, 1967), which itself shares important features with other approaches to interim analysis (generative analysis, constructive analysis, "illuminative" analysis). In all these cases, however, inductive and deductive analyses are mixed. When a theme, hypothesis, or pattern is identified inductively, the researcher then moves into a verification mode, trying to confirm or qualify the finding. This then keys off a new inductive cycle.

Grounded theory acknowledges one important point: Analysis will be undifferentiated and disjointed until the researcher has some local acquaintance with the setting. This is also the case for theory-driven approaches (e.g., Miles & Huberman, 1994). Seeing how a construct works in the field takes time, especially because its instances are often fleeting, masked by other features, or take shapes different from those found in the research literature or in the lab.

In the typical inductive approach, analysis is set into motion with the first site visits. *Margin notes* are made on the field notes, more *reflective passages* are reviewed carefully, and some kind of *summary sheet* is drafted. At the next level are *coding* and *memo writing,* both handled elsewhere in this series (see Strauss & Corbin, Chapter 7, Volume 2).

With these caveats in mind, we have derived a set of "tactics" for generating meaning (Miles & Huberman, 1994). Numbered 1 to 13, they are roughly arranged from the descriptive to the explanatory, and from the concrete to the more abstract: *Noting patterns and themes* (1), *seeing plausibility*—making initial, intuitive sense (2)—and *clustering* by conceptual grouping (3) help one to see connections. *Making metaphors,* a kind of figurative grouping of data (4), is also a tactic for achieving more integration among diverse pieces of data. *Counting* (5) is a familiar way to see "what's there"—and to keep oneself honest.

Making contrasts and comparisons (6) is a classic tactic meant to sharpen understanding by clustering and distinguishing observations. Differentiation is also needed, as in *partitioning variables,* unbundling variables that have been prematurely grouped, or simply taking a less monolithic look (7).

More abstract tactics include *subsuming particulars into the general, shuttling back and forth between first-level data and more general categories* (8); *factoring* (9), an analogue of a familiar quantitative technique, allowing the analyst to move from a large number of measured variables to a smaller set of unobserved, usually hypothetical, variables; *noting relations between variables* (10); and *finding intervening variables* (11). Finally, assembling a coherent understanding of a data set is helped through *building a logical chain of evidence* (12) and *making conceptual/theoretical coherence,* typically through comparison with the referent constructs in the literature (13).

◆ Within-Case Analysis: General Issues

There are no fixed boundaries separating "interim" analysis, later analysis, or indeed final analysis. A series of issues appear, however, as particular cases are examined—and prior to the work of cross-case analysis (see the next section). These include the distinction between description and explanation, the general logic of analysis, the importance of data displays, the role of theory, and a workable view of causality.

Description and Explanation

Within-case analysis will invariably come to grips with two levels of understanding. The first is descriptive. The primitive questions of *what* is going on and *how* things are proceeding call for a reasonable accounting of the phenomena observed. This is description; as Bernard (1988) puts it, such analyses "make complicated things understandable by reducing them to their component parts" (p. 317). In effect, as Rein and Schön (1977) suggest, one vehicle for description of local actors, events, and settings is to tell a story (what happened, and then what happened next). Storytelling—a sense-making construction of a "scenario"—seems deeply pervasive in human thought (Goleman, 1992; Read, Druian, & Miller, 1989), but it is also shot through with interpretive shortcomings.

One of the more frequent queries in daily life, and one that invariably gets an answer, is, Why? But that familiar process masks the fact, as Draper (1988) points out, that "explaining" may also include providing requested information, justifying an action, giving reasons, supporting a claim, or making a causal statement. "Scientific" explanation falls in a narrow band of "why" questions, notably the last two. As Kaplan (1964) suggests, an explanation—whether cast in "purposive" or straightforwardly historical terms—is in effect a "concatenated description" that puts one fact or law in relation to others, making the description intelligible. Kaplan also helpfully points out that explanations are always condition and context dependent, partial, inconclusive, and indeterminately applicable—features that are not limited to qualitative studies.

The Importance of Displays in Analysis

To reiterate: Valid analysis is immensely aided by data displays that are focused enough to permit viewing of a full data set in one location and are systematically arranged to answer the research questions at hand. The "full" data set is at hand, albeit in a condensed mode, and can be interrogated. These are not selectively drawn "stacks" or "insights" or "key incidents." The analogue is to the output of statistical packages, which (a)

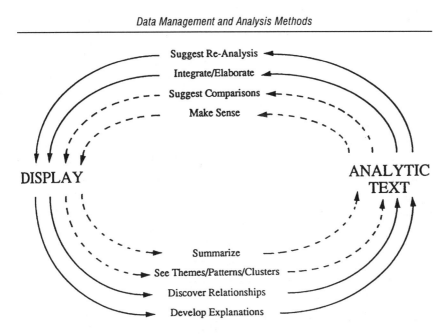

Figure 7.2. Interaction Between Display and Analytic Text

permit analysis to be conducted in close conjunction with the displayed data, (b) allow the analyst to see what further analyses are called for, (c) make for easy comparability across data sets, and (d) heighten credibility in the research report, where data displays normally accompany conclusions.

Here, too, analysis is sequential and interactive. Displayed data and the emerging written text of the researcher's conclusions influence each other. The display helps the writer see patterns; the first text makes sense of the display and suggests new analytic moves in the displayed data; a revised or extended display points to new relationships and explanations, leading to more differentiated and integrated text, and so on. Displays beget analyses, which then beget more powerful, suggestive displays (see Figure 7.2).

The Role of Theory in Within-Case Analysis

Virtuous claims about conclusions are usually supported by three meta-claims: (a) that the researcher has evolved, or has tested, a theory; (b) that all of the relevant data have been examined, and irrelevant data have not sneaked in; and (c) that there has been a steady and explicit "dialogue" (Ragin, 1987) between ideas and evidence.

Good theory, Glaser (1978) suggests, has categories that fit (or have come to fit) the data; is relevant to the core of what is going on; can be used to explain, predict, and interpret what is going on; and is modifiable. So much for the classical view. In practice, theory has a darker side that crops up during analysis. A good exhibit is the comparison between Everhart's (1985a, 1985b) and Cusick's (1985a, 1985b) studies on the meaning of schooling, as analyzed by Noblit (1988). Though both studied American high schools, Noblit shows that their interpretations varied widely. Everhart's critical theory assumptions led him to focus on students, and on schooling as a way to "proletarianize" students and reproduce the structures of capitalism through hierarchy and the passing out of reified information to students as "empty vessels." Cusick's structural-functional assumptions led him to focus on the school as created by staff, and on schooling as driven by an "egalitarian ideal," compromised by racial animosity, with "unappealing knowledge" taking second place to "friendly relations" with students. Each researcher, not surprisingly, saw the other's formulations as "ideological." Allegiance to preexisting "grand theory" led each to drastically different conclusions about very similar phenomena.

Furthermore, the theory-data boundary is permeable. As Van Maanen (1979) notes, there are actually only first-order concepts—the so-called facts of a study, which never "speak for themselves"—and second-order concepts—the "notions used by the researcher to explain the patterning of the first-order concepts" (pp. 39-40). Thus the "facts" one discovers are already the products of many levels of interpretation (Van Maanen, 1988).

At the least, qualitative researchers need to understand just how they are construing "theory" as analysis proceeds, because that construction will—consciously or not—inevitably influence and constrain data collection, data reduction, data display, and the drawing and verification of conclusions. Some alternate constructions include the following:

- "grand theory," as above: a congeries of a few major, well-articulated constructs
- a "map" aiming to generalize the story (or stories) told about a case (Rein & Schön, 1977)
- a predicted pattern of events, to be compared with what is actually observed (Yin, 1991)
- a model, with a series of connected propositions that specify relations, often hierarchical, among components (Reed & Furman, 1992)
- a network of nonhierarchical relationships, expressed through statements defining linkages among concepts (Carley, 1991)

Being clear about such constructions is also important because of the growing use of qualitative analysis software to accomplish the core functions noted above. They too have built-in assumptions about "theory" (see Weitzman & Miles, 1993). For example, programs such as Ethnograph (Qualis Research Associates, 1990) and NUD•IST (Richards & Richards, 1989) help the user develop theory through hierarchically related codes (*A* is an instance of a higher-level concept *B*, which in turn is subsumed in a more general *C*), whereas others, such as ATLAS/ti (Mühr, 1991), Hyper-RESEARCH (Hesse-Biber, Dupuis, & Kinder, 1990), and MECA (Carley, 1991), focus on theory as a connected network of links among entities (*A* promotes *B*, is part of *C*, hinders *D*, precedes *E* [which is also part of *B*], and so on).

A View of Causality

Finally, within-case analysis frequently confronts the question of understanding causality. Can qualitative studies establish causal relationships at all? That possibility is often attacked from both the right ("Only controlled quantitative experiments can do that") and the left ("Causality is an unworkable concept in human behavior—people are not billiard balls"). In line with our epistemological stance, mentioned at the outset, the position we take here is that qualitative studies (see Van Maanen, 1979, 1983) are especially well suited to finding causal relationships; they can look directly and longitudinally at the local processes underlying a temporal series of events and states, showing how these led to specific outcomes, and ruling out rival hypotheses. In effect, we get inside the black box; we can understand not just that a particular thing happened, but how and why it happened.

The credibility of such claims depends on how one views causality. Herewith we provide a brief summary of ours. First, causality necessarily brings in the question of time as part of an explanation; prior events are assumed to have a connection, more or less clear, with later events. Temporality is crucial (Faulconer & Williams, 1985); assessing causality requires us to understand the "plot"—events arranged in a loose order (Abbott, 1992). Though a variable-oriented viewpoint will always show a looping back of assorted effects onto causes that produce new effects (Eden, Jones, & Sims, 1983; Weick, 1979), the "plots" still unfold over time and must be understood that way at the case level. This is where the more narrative versions of causal analysis find their place (Abbott, 1992).

It is worth pointing out here that we confront one of the most likely threats to conventional causality: that, looked at closely, or "deconstructed," much causal analysis is generated rhetorically, as a series of textual devices, genres, tropes, figures of speech. Narrative accounts, for example, are made up almost exclusively of these figurative devices (Atkinson, 1992; Clough, 1992). Should we assess them in conventional terms? Or should we have specific canons for rhetorical causality that can, in some way, be separated from the logic of evidence we use for analytic explanations? Geertz (1983) has put the problem well in noting the slow movement in explanatory devices from social laws to metaphors of theater and games: "What the lever did for physics, the chess move promises to do for sociology" (p. 22).

Another key characteristic: Causality is local; distant and abstract forces such as "gravity" pale beside the immediate events and processes that occur when one deliberately drops a pencil (the friction between the fingers and the pencil, the decision to open one's fingers, the outward movement of the fingers). The immediate causal nexus is always in front of us, in a particular setting and at a particular time.

Third, a determination of causality cannot be precisely rule bound: to Hume's classical criteria of temporal precedence (A before B), constant conjunction (when A, always B), and contiguity of influence (a plausible mechanism links A and B) we have to add others, such as some of those proposed by Hill (1965) in epidemiology: strength of association (much more B with A than with other possible causes), biological gradient (if more A, then more B), coherence (the A-B relationship fits with what else we know about A and B), and analogy (A and B resemble the well-established pattern noted in C and D).

Fourth, there is always causal multiplexity: Causes are always multiple and "conjunctural," combining and affecting each other as well as the supposed effects (Ragin, 1987). Causes and effects must be seen as config-ured in networks—themselves deeply influenced by the local context.

Finally, assessing causality is of necessity a retrospective matter, requir-ing us to note how "some event has occurred in a particular case" (House, 1991). Thus we need the historian's method of "followability" (Abbott, 1992), and will typically be making "a retrospective gathering of events into an account that makes the ending reasonable and believable . . . con-figur[ing] the events in such a way that their part in the whole story becomes clear" (Polkinghorne, 1988, p. 171; compare Scriven's [1974] discussion of the "modus operandi" approach).

The commonsense causal questions derived here are largely those posed by Lofland and Lofland (1984): What are the conditions under which [X] appears? What facilitates its occurrence? What are circumstances in which it is likely to occur? In the presence of what conditions is it likely to become an outcome? Upon what factors does variation in it depend? Under what conditions is it present and under what conditions is it absent?

Of course, a useful causal explanation should necessarily apply to more than one case. Through analytic induction (Manning, 1982; Miller, 1982) a causal account obtained in one case can be tested elsewhere, be it supported, qualified, or subjected to revision. We now turn to the question of approaches to cross-case analysis.

◆ Cross-Case Analysis

The traditional mode of qualitative analysis has been the single-case study. In most ethnographic research, for example, "cases" are individuals or more molar units meant to share several common characteristics—a family, a tribe, a small business, a neighborhood, a community. Cases can also be instances of a larger phenomenon (e.g., "cases" of bribery, "cases" of learning to fight fires), usually of an important social process.

Such molar units are essentially multiples of individuals: firefighters, teachers, criminals, and so on. Whereas these individuals have typically been aggregated within their settings (e.g., firehouses, schools, particular neighborhoods), we are now seeing studies that focus on sets of individuals within several settings (schools, special programs, businesses), and doing this work with multiple methods (Firestone & Herriott, 1983; Louis, 1982; Schofield, 1990).

One objective here is to extend external validity. For example, looking at multiple actors in multiple settings enhances generalizability; the key processes, constructs, and explanations in play can be tested in several different configurations. And each configuration can be considered a replication of the process or question under study. Multiple cases also identify configurations (of actors, of working arrangements, of causal influences) that hold in some settings but not in others. We thus come out with distinct "clusters" or "families" of cases.

But cross-site analytic work is not so simple. As it turns out, Alcoholic A has a very different profile from Alcoholic B, as Denzin (1989) has pointed out, and the two cannot readily be compared unless we choose to focus on more abstract common characteristics. Thus there is a danger that multiple cases will be analyzed at high levels of inference, aggregating out the local webs of causality and ending with a smoothed set of generalizations that may not apply to any single case. This happens more often than we care to remember.

The tension here is that of reconciling the particular and the universal: reconciling an individual case's uniqueness with the need to understand generic processes at work across cases (Silverstein, 1988). Silverstein argues that each individual has a specific history—which we discard at our peril—but it is a history contained within the general principles that influence its development. Similarly, Noblit and Hare (1983) make a strong case for preserving uniqueness, yet also making comparisons. More recently, they have also cautioned against aggregating or averaging results across cases, in order to avoid misinterpretation and superficiality (Noblit & Hare, 1988).

A Crucial Distinction: Variables and Cases

Consider a typical study, one trying to predict the decision to attend college, with a sample of 300 adolescents and the following set of predictors: gender, socioeconomic status, parental expectations, school performance, peer support, and decision to attend college.

In a variable-oriented analysis, the predictor variables are intercorrelated and the key dependent variable, "decision to attend college," is regressed on the six others. This might show us that deciding to attend college is mainly influenced by school performance, with additional influences from parents' expectations and SES. We see how the variables as concepts are related, but we do not know the profile of any one individual.

In a case-oriented analysis, we would look more closely into a particular case, say, Case 005, who is female, middle-class, has parents with high expectations, and so on. These are, however, "thin" measures. To do a genuine case analysis, we need to look at a full history of Case 005: Nynke van der Molen, whose mother trained as a social worker but is bitter over the fact that she never worked outside the home, and whose father wants Nynke to work in the family florist shop. Chronology is also important: two years ago, Nynke's closest friend decided to go to college, just before Nynke began work in a stable and just before Nynke's mother showed her a scrapbook from social work school. Nynke then decided to enroll in veterinary studies.

These and other data can be displayed in matrix form (see Miles & Huberman, 1994), where the flow and configuration of events and reactions leading to Nynke's decision would come clear. It would also help to "incarnate" what the five predictors look like singly and how they interact collectively. That, in turn, would surface recurrent patterns, "families" or "clusters" of cases with characteristic configurations.

As Ragin (1987) notes, such a case-oriented approach looks at each entity, then teases out configurations *within* each case and subjects them to comparative analysis. In these comparisons (of a smaller number of cases), underlying similarities and systematic associations are sought out with regard to the main outcome variable. From there, a more explanatory model can be explicated, at least for the cases under study.

Each approach has its pluses and minuses. Variable-oriented analysis is good for finding probabilistic relationships among variables in a large population, but has difficulties with causal complexities, or dealing with subsamples. Case-oriented analysis is good at finding specific, concrete, historically grounded patterns common to small sets of cases, but its findings remain particularistic, although several case writers speciously claim greater generality.[1]

Strategies for Cross-Case Analysis

There are many ways to proceed with multiple-case data, or data coming from several sources. Below is a brief sampler, building on the case versus variable orientation we have just reviewed.

Case-oriented strategies. Yin (1984) advocates a *replication* strategy. A conceptual framework oversees the first case study, then successive cases are examined to see whether the new pattern matches the one found earlier. The "grounded theory" approach (e.g., Glaser, 1978) uses the same principle, but builds up the framework inductively, then tests and refines it with recourse to multiple comparison groups.

Denzin (1989) approaches the problem through multiple exemplars. After deconstructing prior conceptions of a particular phenomenon (such as "the alcoholic self"), multiple instances (cases) are collected, then "bracketed," in a phenomenological sense, and are then inspected for essential elements or components. The elements are then rebuilt into a reordered whole and put back into the natural social context.

195

Many researchers approach cross-case comparison by forming "types" or "families." Cases in a set are inspected to see if they fall into clusters that share certain patterns or configurations. Sometimes the clusters can be arrayed along some dimension (low to high conformity, vague to specific career ambitions, and so on).

Variable-oriented strategies. An often-used approach is *finding themes* that cut across cases. For example, Pearsol (1985) looked at interviews about sex equity programs with 25 teachers. After careful inductive coding, he found recurring themes such as "concern for students," "activist view of change," and "barriers to innovation." (Later he turned to a case-oriented approach, sorting the teachers into six types based on the initial configuration of themes.)

Often a key variable comes clear only during cross-site analysis. The strategy here might be called *pattern clarification.* For example, Eisenhardt (1989a) found evidence for the construct of "power centralization" by looking at data on CEO behavior in 10 microcomputer firms. Her matrix display included adjectives describing decision style, quantitative measures, organizational functions performed by the CEO, and some cameo descriptors (e.g., "[He] depends on picking good people and letting them operate").

Mixed Strategies

A more phenomenological approach, described by Fischer and Wertz (1975), might be called *interactive synthesis.* In studying the meaning of being a crime victim, these authors first wrote individual case synopses, then wrote a cross-case narrative based on a series of themes. They then composed a "general condensation" depicting the essential personal meanings, then cycled back to the case synopses to see how the condensation was exemplified there. Finally, they wrote a "general psychological structure" describing what seems essential in the temporal process of victimization. The sequence is carefully assembled. In particular, it includes an analytic mixture that *combines* methods, rather than relying on one and adding others essentially as appendages. Other examples of mixed strategies can be found in the work of Abbott (1992), Gladwin (1989), and Huberman (1991).

Technically, cross-case analyses are most easily made with "displays": matrix or other arrays of the data that allow the researcher to analyze, in a condensed form, the full data set, in order to see literally what is there.

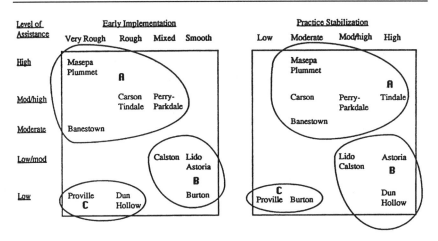

Figure 7.3. Scatterplot Over Time: The Consequences of Assistance

From there, several things can happen: The researcher may go back out in the field to retrieve missing data; other arrays may be made for a better look; or columns or rows, or all entries, within the arrays may be reconfigured.

Typically, the researcher begins with *a partially ordered metamatrix*, which brings the basic information from several cases into one big chart. Then come *descriptive or conceptually ordered displays, time-ordered matrices, effects matrices,* and *composite sequence analyses,* showing the flux of different cases through a generally framed flow of events and conditions.

Let us look at the scatterplot display matrix for 12 cases (school districts) shown in Figure 7.3. Note that this is simply a contingency table, crossing two variables ("early implementation" and "practice stabilization") with a third ("level of assistance"). In addition, each of the variables in play is scaled, so that the cases can be arrayed and examined in a roughly comparable way.

Typically, this kind of chart, which *follows* careful case-oriented work, constitutes a variable-oriented analytic sortie. With this display in hand, the researcher usually goes back again to the case-level data. What does "rough" early implementation correspond to at Masepa and Plummet, and are the two cases comparable? Did "assistance" actually seem to have little effect on "early implementation," and, if so, why? And what about the countervailing cases in cluster B? What was the pattern of assistance, the flow over time, the relationship between assistance and stabilization as perceived by informants? This examination then leads to another display, typically in a different form, that arrays the cases according to the forms in which these questions have been posed. In other words, displays come typically in a sequence: unordered, ordered by case on one or several dimensions of interest, regrouped by families of cases that share some characteristics, and displayed again as an interlocking set of more explanatory variables, ones that undergird the clusters of cases that have been identified.

◆ Verifying Conclusions and Threats to Analytic Validity

The "Cohabitation" of Realist and Interpretivist Canons

As we have noted, until recently there were virtually no canons, decision rules, algorithms, or even any agreed-upon heuristics for the conduct of qualitative research. This is less a developmental problem than an absence of consensus in deciding the grounds upon which findings are considered plausible or convincing and procedures are viewed as legitimate ones.

There do appear, however, to be some *procedural* commonalities, in the sequential process of analyzing, concluding, and confirming findings in a field study format. In both cases, the researcher shifts between cycles of inductive data collection and analysis to deductive cycles of testing and verification. As noted, exploratory and confirmatory sampling drive the collection of data that, once analyzed, lead to decisions on which data to collect next. Gradually, these data assemblies become more "conclusive." Roughly put, most "naturalistic" researchers subscribe to this basic analytic cycle.

Verification

Verification entails checking for the most common or most insidious biases that can steal into the process of drawing conclusions. Some of the most frequent shortcomings include the following (Douglas, 1976; Krathwohl, 1993; Miles & Huberman, 1984; Nisbett & Ross, 1980):

- ◆ data overload in the field, leading to the analysts thus missing important information, overweighting some findings, skewing the analysis

- salience of first impressions or of observations of highly concrete or dramatic incidents

- selectivity, overconfidence in some data, especially when trying to confirm a key finding

- co-occurrences taken as correlations, or even as causal relationships

- false base-rate proportions: extrapolation of the number of total instances from those observed

- unreliability of information from some sources

- overaccommodation to information that questions outright a tentative hypothesis

The term most often used in connection with analysis and confirmation issues is *triangulation*—a term with multiple meanings. The origin of the term is probably "multiple operationalism" (Campbell & Fiske, 1959): multiple measures that ensure that the variance reflected is that of the trait or treatment and not that associated with the measures. This is best done, for example, by multiplying independent measures and sources of the same phenomenon—for example, informants make the same claim independently, and the researcher observes the phenomenon; test scores back up work samples and observations. "Grounded" theorists have long contended that theory generated from one data source works less well than "slices of data" from different sources (Glaser, 1978).

But triangulation has also come to mean convergence among researchers (agreement between field notes of one investigator and observations of another) and convergence among theories. A general prescription has been to pick triangulation sources that have different biases, different strengths, so they can complement one another.

In the disorderly world of empirical research, however, independent measures never converge fully. Observations do not jibe completely with interview data, nor surveys with written records. In other words, sources can be inconsistent or even conflicting, with no easy means of resolution. In such cases, in fact, we may need to initiate a new way of thinking about the data at hand (Rossman & Wilson, 1985).

Beyond this, triangulation is less a tactic than a mode of inquiry. By self-consciously setting out to collect and double-check findings, using multiple sources and modes of evidence, the researcher will build the triangulation process into ongoing data collection. It will be the way he or she got to the finding in the first place—by seeing or hearing multiple instances of it from different sources, using different methods, and by squaring the finding with others with which it should coincide.

With this logic in mind, we have generated a list of "tactics" for testing or confirming conclusions (Miles & Huberman, 1984, 1994). The tactics meant to ward off the most obvious biases are the following: checking for representativeness, checking for researcher effects (reactivity), and triangulating and weighing the evidence (relying on more robust measures). Tactics for testing the viability of patterns turn around the active search for contrasts, comparisons, outliers, and extreme cases. More elaborate tests of conclusions call for attempts to rule out spurious conclusions, to replicate key findings, to check out rival explanations, and to look for negative evidence. Finally, feedback from informants can be used at any point in the cycle.

A more general and comprehensive approach to the verification of findings and conclusions is "auditing" (see the next section; see also Schwandt & Halpern, 1988). Applied to empirical research, auditing is an accounting metaphor for the systematic review of a given study on the part of an external examiner. Its main interest may be less the quality of an external review than the possibility for qualitative researchers to have a list of analytic bases to touch, so that interested and rigorous peers can determine whether the sampling, measurement, and analyses leading to the main conclusions and explanations stand up to the most common sources of bias and error.

On "Transparency" of Method

The conventions of quantitative research require clear, explicit reporting of data and procedures. That is expected so that (a) the reader will be confident of, and can verify, reported conclusions; (b) secondary analysis of the data is possible; (c) the study could in principle be replicated; and (d) fraud or misconduct, if it exists, will be more trackable. There is an added, internal need: keeping analytic strategies coherent, manageable, and repeatable as the study proceeds. That is, the reporting requirement encourages running documentation from the beginning. In our view, the same needs are present for qualitative studies, even if one takes a more interpretive stance (note, for example, the ideas about "confirmability" and "dependability" proposed by Lincoln & Guba, 1985). As we have written in previous work:

We have the unappealing double bind whereby qualitative studies can't be verified because researchers don't report on their methodology, and they don't report on their methodology because there are no established canons or conventions for doing so. (Miles & Huberman, 1984, p. 244)

Solutions

The most basic solution has already been discussed (see Table 7.1): careful retention, in easily retrievable form, of all study materials, from raw field notes through data displays and final report text. That solution, however, rests on another: a reflexive stance to the conduct of the study that assumes regular, ongoing, self-conscious documentation—of successive versions of coding schemes, of conceptual arguments among project staff, of analysis episodes—both successful ones and dead ends. We have reported a detailed documentation form for tracking data reduction, data display, and conclusion-drawing operations (Miles & Huberman, 1984), but we are not aware of instances of its use by other researchers. Carney (1990) advocates a "reflexivity journal" for the same purposes.

Recently, however, there has been movement toward more explicit, complete accounts. Some examples include the methodological accounts of phenomenological studies by Bartlett (1990) and Melnick and Beaudry (1990), the "data analysis chronology" in a hermeneutic study by Pearsol (1985), the detailed diary of ethnographic biographical research by L. M. Smith (1992), the careful reporting of case study research methods by Merryfield (1990), the account of "constant comparative" methods by Hodson (1991), and the details of data displays by Eisenhardt (1989a, 1989b). Still, not a few studies restrict their "methods" sections to statements such as "The study employed the constant comparative method," with no further explanation.

Part of the difficulty is that, given the diversity of approaches to qualitative work, there is no standard set of expectations for what a qualitative methods section should look like. As a minimum set, we would propose the following:

- ◆ sampling decisions made, both within and across cases
- ◆ instrumentation and data collection operations
- ◆ database summary: size, how produced
- ◆ software used, if any

- overview of analytic strategies followed
- inclusion of key data displays supporting main conclusions

A fourth solution is that of preparing for, and/or actually carrying out, an "audit" of the entire study being conducted. The first feasibility applications were by Halpern (1983); since then, Schwandt and Halpern (1988) have extended the audit idea, applying it to the review of evaluation studies. They suggest six levels of required attention:

- Are findings grounded in the data? (Is sampling appropriate? Are data weighted correctly?)
- Are inferences logical? (Are analytic strategies applied correctly? Are alternative explanations accounted for?)
- Is the category structure appropriate?
- Can inquiry decisions and methodological shifts be justified? (Were sampling decisions linked to working hypotheses?)
- What is the degree of researcher bias (premature closure, unexplored data in field notes, lack of search for negative cases, feelings of empathy)?
- What strategies were used for increasing credibility (second readers, feedback to informants, peer review, adequate time in the field)?

Such audits do not seem to be widely used, but when they are (e.g., Merryfield, 1990), they seem to have decidedly salutary effects, notably the encouragement of systematic record keeping and reflexivity.

Some Problems

The time and energy costs for adequate methodological documentation and/or auditing are not small. We have estimated a 20% increment in analysis time in the use of our documentation log (Miles & Huberman, 1984). Schwandt and Halpern (1988) give no cost figures, but the researcher's work in preparing an "audit trail" and the auditor's analysis, with its very detailed procedures, are at least as expensive. Careful computerization of a study will help, of course, but this carries its own costs. We should probably expect that detailed documentation and auditing will continue to be restricted to high-stakes studies, or to those in which the researcher has a special interest in documentation or auditing as such.

Study documentation and full reportage may also encourage a mechanistic, obsessive approach (see Marshall, 1990, and Noblit, 1988, who worry about the "bureaucratization" of data analysis). Or it may lead to abstract formulations of method that do not quite speak to the realities of qualitative research (see, for example, Constas, 1992, on the documentation of category development procedures). In any case, we need to be realistic about "reproducibility"; even in the field of synthetic chemistry, Bergman (1989) reports that nearly half of studies could not be reproduced, even by the original researchers. So we need a reasonable standard, not an abstractly demanding one.

Finally, we must remember that "transparency" has its risks. For example, maintaining detailed field notes in computer files, and making them available for reanalysis, even with supposed deidentification, raises questions about invasion of privacy and about potential harm to informants (see the very thoughtful discussion by Akeroyd, 1991). Any reasonable approach to methodological transparency must deal with ethical, not just technical, issues.

On balance, these problems do not seem insuperable, and the basic need for transparency remains. We see no reason not to keep advancing the state of the art—probably incrementally—through routinization of running documentation, the evolution of clearer reporting standards, and—now and then, when it matters—the in-depth analysis of method that a strong audit can bring. Given the care and scrupulousness with which qualitative research is meant to be conducted, as much in the ethnographic tradition as in the interpretive tradition, it should be possible to negotiate a minimal set of conventions for the conduct of qualitative research. Given that these traditions do have different frames for ensuring validity and dependability of study findings, there might well be a shared set of conventions along with specific rules for researchers working in different areas. We are getting there. Still, transparency does not come easily when it brings in its wake an added burden and a greater exposure to the judgments of one's professional peers.

Appendix: The Main Conceptual and Analytic Aspects of Design

Conceptual framework. This lays out the key factors, constructs, or variables, and the presumed relationships among them. We have argued that graphic displays of "bins" (main variables) connected by directional arrows specifying intervariable relationships are useful in making researchers' frameworks clear (Miles & Huberman, 1994). Conceptual frameworks, even in a "tight" design, are normally iterated over the life of the study.

Research questions. A set of defined questions (not necessarily "hypotheses") represents the facets of an empirical domain the researcher wants to explore, setting priorities and foci of attention and implicitly excluding a range of unstudied topics. They may be defined causally or noncausally, and deal with research, policy, evaluation, or management issues (N. L. Smith, 1981, 1987; see also Dillon's [1984] application of alternative schemata to a sample of more than 900 research questions). They usually represent a more detailed operationalization of the study's conceptual framework.

Case definition. Essentially, a "case" is a phenomenon of some sort occurring in a bounded context—the unit of analysis, in effect. Normally, there is a focus of attention and a more or less vaguely defined temporal, social, and/or physical boundary involved (e.g., a bypass surgery patient, before, during, and six months after surgery, in the family and hospital context). Foci and boundaries can be defined by social unit size (an individual, a role, a small group, an organization, community, nation), by spatial location, or temporally (an episode, an event, a day). Cases may have subcases embedded within them (Yin, 1984). As with the other conceptual aspects of study design, the definition of the "case" is a strongly analytic, data-selective choice, whether single or multiple cases are involved.

Sampling. Sampling choices within and across cases are powerfully determinative of just which data will be considered and used in analysis. Quantitative researchers often think randomly, statistically, and in terms of context-stripped case selections. Qualitative researchers must characteristically think purposively and conceptually about sampling (see Miles & Huberman, 1994, for specific suggestions).

In addition, within each case (even when the case is an individual), the researcher needs to sample an intricately nested range of activities, processes, events, locations, and times (Bogdan & Biklen, 1982; Lofland & Lofland, 1984; Schwartzman & Werner, 1990; Woods, 1979); such choices are theory driven (Glaser & Strauss, 1967), not driven by a concern with "representativeness." Sampling choices also typically evolve through successive waves of data collection. This is also true of cross-case sampling. Here again, the issue is not so much the quest for conventional generalizability, but rather an understanding of the conditions under which a particular finding appears and operates: how, where, when, and why it carries on as it does. Multiple cases are especially important as "comparison groups" (Glaser & Strauss, 1970); they also permit a "replication" strategy (Yin, 1991), where single-case findings are successively tested in a following series of cases. When multiple cases are carefully ordered along a key dimension, powerful explanations are more likely (see Eisenhardt, 1989b, for a compelling example).

Instrumentation. Other chapters in this volume deal explicitly with this theme, but a few remarks, in keeping with our approach, are in order. The general issue, as put by Warner (1991), is this: How can we maximize construct and descriptive-contextual validity, assure ourselves that our interpretations connect with people's lived experience, and minimize researcher impact? The answers, we think, usually lie in the direction of minimally predesigned instrumentation.

Similarly, how can we enhance internal validity, generalizability to other cases and settings, not to mention sheer manageability of data collection? Here, too, the answers lead us toward more fully predesigned instrumentation.

◆ Note

1. This is a crucial distinction, and it has been handled in several ways. For recent treatments, see Maxwell and Miller (1992) and Runkel (1990).

◆ References

Abbott, A. (1992). From causes to events: Notes on narrative positivism. *Sociological Methods and Research, 20,* 428-455.

Akeroyd, A. V. (1991). Personal information and qualitative research data: Some practical and ethical problems arising from data protection legislation. In N. G. Fielding & R. M. Lee (Eds.), *Using computers in qualitative research* (pp. 88-106). London: Sage.

Atkinson, P. A. (1992). *Understanding ethnographic texts.* Newbury Park, CA: Sage.

Ball, M. S., & Smith, G. W. H. (1992). *Analyzing visual data.* Newbury Park, CA: Sage.

Bartlett, L. (1990). *The dialectic between theory and method in critical interpretive research.* Queensland, Australia: University of Queensland.

Berg, B. L. (1989). *Qualitative research methods for the social sciences.* Boston: Allyn & Bacon.

Bergman, R. G. (1989). Irreproducibility in the scientific literature: How often do scientists tell the whole truth and nothing but the truth? *Ethical and Policy Perspectives on the Professions, 8*(2), 2-3.

Bernard, H. R. (1988). *Research methods in cultural anthropology.* Newbury Park, CA: Sage.

Bhaskar, R. (1978). *A realist theory of science.* Leeds, UK: Leeds.

Bhaskar, R. (1989). *Reclaiming reality: A critical introduction to contemporary philosophy.* London: Verso.

Bogdan, R. C., & Biklen, S. K. (1982). *Qualitative research for education: An introduction to theory and methods.* Boston: Allyn & Bacon.

Campbell, D., & Fiske, D. (1959). Convergent and discriminant validation by the multitrait-multimethod matrix. *Psychological Bulletin, 56,* 81-105.

Carley, K. (1991). *Textual analysis using maps.* Pittsburgh, PA: Carnegie Mellon University, Department of Social and Decision Sciences.

Carney, T. F. (1990). *Collaborative inquiry methodology.* Windsor, Ontario: University of Windsor, Division for Instructional Development.

Chesler, M. (1987). *Professionals' views of the "dangers" of self-help groups* (CRSO Paper 345). Ann Arbor, MI: Center for Research on Social Organization.

Clough, P. T. (1992). *The end(s) of ethnography: From realism to social criticism.* Newbury Park, CA: Sage.

Constas, M. A. (1992). Qualitative analysis as a public event: The documentation of category development procedures. *American Educational Research Journal, 29,* 253-266

Cusick, P. (1985a). Review of *Reading, writing and resistance. Anthropology Quarterly, 16,* 69-72.

Cusick, P. (1985b). Commentary on the Everhart/Cusick reviews. *Anthropology and Education Quarterly, 16,* 246-247.

Denzin, N. K. (1989). *Interpretive interactionism.* Newbury Park, CA: Sage.

Dillon, J. T. (1984). The classification of research questions. *Review of Educational Research, 54,* 327-361.

Douglas, J. (1976). *Investigative social research.* Beverly Hills, CA: Sage.

Draper, S. W. (1988). What's going on in everyday explanation? In C. Antaki (Ed.), *Analyzing everyday explanations: A casebook of methods* (pp. 15-31). Newbury Park, CA: Sage.

Eden, C., Jones, S., & Sims, D. (1983). *Messing about in problems: An informal structured approach to their identification and management.* Oxford: Pergamon.

Eisenhardt, K. M. (1989a). Building theories from case study research. *Academy of Management Review, 14,* 532-550.

Eisenhardt, K. M. (1989b). Making fast strategic decisions in high-velocity environments. *Academy of Management Journal, 32,* 543-576.

Erickson, F. (1986). Qualitative methods in research on teaching. In M. C. Wittrock (Ed.), *Handbook of research on teaching* (3rd ed., pp. 119-161). New York: Macmillan.

Everhart, R. (1985a). Review of *The egalitarian ideal and the American high school. Anthropology and Education Quarterly, 16,* 73-77.

Everhart, R. (1985b). Comment on the Everhart/Cusick reviews. *Anthropology and Education Quarterly, 16,* 247-248.

Faulconer, J. E., & Williams, R. N. (1985). Temporality in human action: An alternative to positivism and historicism. *American Psychologist, 40,* 1179-1188.

Firestone, W. A., & Herriott, R. E. (1983). The formalization of qualitative research: An adaptation of "soft" science to the policy world. *Evaluation Review, 7,* 437-466.

Fischer, C., & Wertz, F. (1975). Empirical phenomenological analyses of being criminally victimized. In A. Giorgi (Ed.), *Phenomenology and psychological research* (pp. 135-158). Pittsburgh, PA: Duquesne University Press.

Geertz, C. (1983). *Local knowledge: Further essays in interpretive anthropology.* New York: Basic Book.

Gherardi, S., & Turner, B. (1987). *Real men don't collect soft data.* Trento, Italy: Universita di Trento, Dipartimento di Politica Sociale.

Gladwin, C. H. (1989). *Ethnographic decision tree modeling.* Newbury Park, CA: Sage.

Glaser, B. G. (1978). *Theoretical sensitivity: Advances in the methodology of grounded theory.* Mill Valley, CA: Sociology Press.

Glaser, B. G., & Strauss, A. L. (1967). *The discovery of grounded theory: Strategies for qualitative research.* Chicago: Aldine.

Glaser, B. G., & Strauss, A. L. (1970). Discovery of substantive theory: A basic strategy underlying qualitative research. In W. Filstead (Ed.), *Qualitative methodology* (pp. 288-297). Chicago: Rand McNally.

Goleman, D. (1992, May 12). Jurors hear evidence and turn it into stories. *New York Times,* pp. C1, C11.

Guba, E. G. (1990). Carrying on the dialog. In E. G. Guba (Ed.), *The paradigm dialog* (pp. 368-378). Newbury Park, CA: Sage.

Halpern, E. S. (1983). *Auditing naturalistic inquiries, some preliminary applications. Part 1: Development of the process. Part 2: Case study application.* Paper presented at the meeting of the American Educational Research Association.

Harper, D. (1989). Visual sociology: Expanding sociological vision. In G. Blank et al. (Eds.), *New technology in sociology: Practical applications in research and work* (pp. 81-97). New Brunswick, NJ: Transaction.

Harré, R., & Secord, P. (1973). *The explanation of social behavior.* Totowa, NJ: Littlefield, Adams.

Hesse-Biber, S., Dupuis, P., & Kinder, T. S. (1990). *HyperRESEARCH.* Paper presented at the annual meeting of the American Sociological Association, Washington, DC.

Hill, A. B. (1965). The environment and disease: Association or causation? *Proceedings of the Royal Society of Medicine, 58,* 295-300.

Hodson, R. (1991). The active worker: Compliance and autonomy at the workplace. *Journal of Contemporary Ethnography, 20,* 47-78.

House, E. R. (1991). Realism in research. *Educational Researcher, 20*(6), 2-9.

Huberman, A. M. (1991). The professional life cycle of teachers. *Teachers College Record, 91*(1), 31-57.

Huberman, A. M., & Miles, M. B. (1985). Assessing local causality in qualitative research. In D. N. Berg & K. K. Smith (Eds.), *Exploring clinical methods for social research* (pp. 351-381). Newbury Park, CA: Sage.

Kaplan, A. (1964). *The conduct of inquiry.* Scranton, PA: Chandler.

Krathwohl, D. R. (1993). *Methods of educational and social science research: An integrated approach.* White Plains, NY: Longman.

Kvale, S. (1988). The 1000-page question. *Phenomenology and Pedagogy, 6*(2), 90-106.

Levine, H. G. (1985). Principles of data storage and retrieval for use in qualitative evaluations. *Educational Evaluation and Policy Analysis, 7*(2), 169-186.

Lincoln, Y. S., & Guba, E. G. (1985). *Naturalistic inquiry.* Newbury Park, CA: Sage.

Lofland, J., & Lofland, L. H. (1984). *Analyzing social settings: A guide to qualitative observation and analysis* (2nd ed.). Belmont, CA: Wadsworth.

Louis, K. S. (1982). Multisite/multimethod studies. *American Behavioral Scientist, 26*(1), 6-22.

Manicas, P. T., & Secord, P. F. (1982). Implications for psychology of the new philosophy of science. *American Psychologist, 38,* 390-413.

Manning, P. K. (1982). Analytic induction. In R. B. Smith & P. K. Manning, *A handbook of social science methods: Vol. 2. Qualitative methods* (pp. 273-302). Cambridge, MA: Ballinger.

Marshall, C. (1990). Goodness criteria: Are they objective or judgment calls? In E. G. Guba (Ed.), *The paradigm dialog* (pp. 188-197). Newbury Park, CA: Sage.

Maxwell, J. A., & Miller, B. A. (1992). *Two aspects of thought and two components of qualitative data analysis.* Cambridge, MA: Harvard University, Graduate School of Education.

Melnick, C. R., & Beaudry, J. S. (1990, April). *A qualitative research perspective: Theory, practice, essence.* Paper presented at the annual meeting of the American Educational Research Association, Boston.

Merryfield, M. M. (1990, April). *Integrating interpretation and description in case study reporting: Constructing dialogues and scenes.* Paper presented at the annual meeting of the American Educational Research Association, Boston.

Miles, M. B. (1979). Qualitative data as an attractive nuisance: The problem of analysis. *Administrative Science Quarterly, 24,* 590-601.

Miles, M. B., & Huberman, A. M. (1984). *Qualitative data analysis: A sourcebook of new methods.* Newbury Park, CA: Sage.

Miles, M. B., & Huberman, A. M. (1994). *Qualitative data analysis: An expanded sourcebook* (2nd ed.). Newbury Park, CA: Sage.

Miller, S. I. (1982). Quality and quantity: Another view of analytic induction as a research technique. *Quality and Quantity, 16,* 281-295.

Mishler, E. G. (1990). Validation in inquiry-guided research: The role of exemplars in narrative studies. *Harvard Educational Review, 60,* 415-441.

Mühr, T. (1991). ATLAS/ti: A prototype for the support of text interpretation. *Qualitative Sociology, 14,* 349-371.

Nisbett, R. E., & Ross, L. (1980). *Human inference: Strategies and shortcomings of social judgment.* Englewood Cliffs, NJ: Prentice Hall.

Noblit, G. W. (1988, February). *A sense of interpretation.* Paper presented at the Ethnography in Education Research Forum, Philadelphia.

Noblit, G. W., & Hare, R. D. (1983, April). *Meta-ethnography: Issues in the synthesis and replication of qualitative research.* Paper presented at the meeting of the American Educational Research Association.

Noblit, G. W., & Hare, R. D. (1988). *Meta-ethnography: Synthesizing qualitative studies.* Newbury Park, CA: Sage.

Packer, M. J., & Addison, R. B. (1989). Evaluating an interpretive account. In M. J. Packer & R. B. Addison (Eds.), *Entering the circle: Hermeneutic investigation in psychology* (pp. 275-292). Albany: State University of New York Press.

Pearsol, J. A. (1985). *Controlling qualitative data: Understanding teachers' value perspectives on a sex equity education project.* Paper presented at the annual meeting of the American Educational Research Association, Chicago.

Phillips, D. C. (1990). Subjectivity and objectivity: An objective inquiry. In E. W. Eisner & A. Peshkin (Eds.), *Qualitative inquiry in education: The continuing debate* (pp. 19-37). New York: Teachers College Press.

Polkinghorne, D. E. (1988). *Narrative knowing and the human sciences.* Albany: State University of New York Press.

Preissle, J. (1991). *The choreography of design: A personal view of what design means in qualitative research.* Paper presented at the Qualitative Research Conference, University of Georgia, Athens.

Qualis Research Associates. (1990). *The Ethnograph: A program for the computer-assisted analysis of text-based data.* Corvallis, OR: Author.

Ragin, C. C. (1987). *The comparative method: Moving beyond qualitative and quantitative strategies.* Berkeley: University of California Press.

Ratcliffe, J. W. (1983). Notions of validity in qualitative research methodology. *Knowledge: Creation, Diffusion, Utilization, 5,* 147-167.

Read, S. J., Druian, P. R., & Miller, L. C. (1989). The role of causal sequence in the meaning of actions. *British Journal of Social Psychology, 28,* 341-351.

Reed, D. B., & Furman, G. C. (1992). *The 2 × 2 matrix in qualitative data analysis and theory generation.* Paper presented at the annual meeting of the American Educational Research Association, San Francisco.

Rein, M., & Schön, D. (1977). Problem setting in policy research. In C. Weiss (Ed.), *Using social policy research in public policy making.* Lexington, MA: D. C. Heath.

Richards, L., & Richards, T. (1989). *Old goals, new goals: Toward the next generation of qualitative analysis programs.* Bundoora, Victoria, Australia: La Trobe University.

Robinson, W. S. (1951). The logical structure of analytic induction. *American Sociological Review, 16,* 812-818.

Rossman, G. B., & Wilson, B. L. (1985). Numbers and words: Combining quantitative and qualitative methods in a single large-scale evaluation study. *Evaluation Review, 9,* 627-643.

Runkel, P. J. (1990). *Casting nets and testing specimens: Two grand methods of psychology.* New York: Praeger.

Schillemans, L., et al. (n.d.). *Treating victims of incest.* Antwerp, Belgium: Flemish Institute for General Practice and University of Antwerp, Department of Family Medicine.

Schofield, J. W. (1990). Increasing the generalizability of qualitative research. In E. Eisner & A. Peshkin (Eds.), *Qualitative inquiry in education: The continuing debate* (pp. 201-232). New York: Teachers College Press.

Schwandt, T. A., & Halpern, E. S. (1988). *Linking auditing and metaevaluation: Enhancing quality in applied research.* Newbury Park, CA: Sage.

Schwartzman, H., & Werner, O. (1990). Census, taxonomies, and the partition of ethnographic tasks. *Cultural Anthropology Methods Newsletter, 2*(3), 8-9.

Scriven, M. (1974). Maximizing the power of causal investigations: The modus operandi method. In W. J. Popham (Ed.), *Evaluation in education: Current perspectives* (pp. 68-84). Berkeley, CA: McCutchan.

Sieber, S. D. (1976). *A synopsis and critique of guidelines for qualitative analysis contained in selected textbooks.* New York: Center for Policy Research, Project on Social Architecture in Education.

Silverstein, A. (1988). An Aristotelian resolution of the ideographic versus nomothetic tension. *American Psychologist, 43,* 425-430.

Smith, L. M. (1992). Ethnography. In M. C. Alkin (Ed.), *Encyclopedia of educational research* (Vol. 2, 6th ed., pp. 458-462). New York: Macmillan.

Smith, N. L. (1981). Noncausal inquiry in education. *Educational Researcher, 10*(3), 23.

Smith, N. L. (1987). Toward the justification of claims in evaluation research. *Evaluation and Program Planning, 10,* 309-314.

Strauss, A. L. (1987). *Qualitative analysis for social scientists.* Cambridge: Cambridge University Press.

Van Maanen, J. (Ed.). (1979). *Qualitative methodology.* Beverly Hills, CA: Sage.

Van Maanen, J. (Ed.). (1983). *Qualitative methodology* (updated reprint). Beverly Hills, CA: Sage.

Van Maanen, J. (1988). *Tales of the field: On writing ethnography.* Chicago: University of Chicago Press.

Warner, W. (1991). *Improving interpretive validity of camera-based qualitative research.* Paper presented at the Qualitative Health Research Conference, Edmonton, Alberta.

Weick, K. (1979). *The social psychology of organizing.* Reading, MA: Addison-Wesley.

Weitzman, E., & Miles, M. B. (1993). *Computer-aided qualitative data analysis: A review of selected software.* New York: Center for Policy Research.

Werner, O., & Schoepfle, G. M. (1987a). *Systematic fieldwork: Vol. 1. Foundations of ethnography and interviewing.* Newbury Park, CA: Sage.

Werner, O., & Schoepfle, G. M. (1987b). *Systematic fieldwork: Vol. 2. Ethnographic analysis and data management.* Newbury Park, CA: Sage.

Wolcott, H. F. (1992). Posturing in qualitative inquiry. In M. D. LeCompte, W. L. Millroy, & J. Preissle (Eds.), *The handbook of qualitative research in education* (pp. 3-52). New York: Academic Press.

Wolfe, R. (1992). Data management. In M. C. Alkin (Ed.), *Encyclopedia of educational research* (6th ed., pp. 293-299). New York: Macmillan.

Woods, P. (1979). *The divided school.* London: Routledge & Kegan Paul.

Yin, R. K. (1984). *Case study research: Design and methods.* Beverly Hills, CA: Sage.

Yin, R. K. (1991). *Applications of case study research.* Washington, DC: Cosmos Corporation.

Znaniecki, R. (1934). *The method of sociology.* New York: Farrar & Rinehart.

8

Using Computers in Qualitative Research

Thomas J. Richards & Lyn Richards

◆ Most qualitative researchers now work with computers, but relatively few use software designed for qualitative analysis. This is not because they see no need for help in handling rich, complex, or messy data. Rather, computers offer no instant solutions to the problems faced by qualitative researchers, because the data they handle are particularly resistant to tidy processing methods and the methods they use are very unlike the techniques computers easily support. The past decade has produced a plethora of software packages that seem as though they should help, but these are packages designed for executives, librarians, and banks. There is now a much smaller group of programs designed for particular approaches to qualitative research, but they are less accessible and less professionally presented. Thus the researcher is offered a bewildering range of ways of handling textual data on computers, and many of these are quite different from the methods found in qualitative texts. The computer method can have dramatic implications for the research process and outcomes, from unacceptable restrictions on analysis to unexpected opening out of possibilities.

Our purposes in this chapter are to look at methodological features of qualitative data analysis (QDA) to consider how, and how much, and how well, it can be computerized; to give an overview of general-purpose packages that can be used in QDA, and some types of special-purpose QDA packages; to discuss how they can be used and how well they work; to

211

provide some pointers to future software developments; and to stimulate methodological debate on computational QDA. We have written elsewhere of our concerns about the impacts of computing techniques on method and the real dangers of software constraining and distorting research (Richards & Richards, 1991a, 1991b), and of our experiences as researchers making the transition to computers (Richards & Richards, 1994). The first remains a background theme in this chapter.

Most reports on software options are accounts of particular programs, usually by their developers and/or marketers. We ourselves are, *inter alia,* developers. (NUD•IST, the software we developed in our research, is now marketed by a company at our university.) Like literary critics who are also novelists, we have a methodological position and a commitment to its products. The reader, thus informed, can evaluate our arguments.

Both as researchers and as software designers, we started from the research processes involved in relating data and theory in qualitative data analysis and the different ways software might support or distort them. This chapter starts there. We then describe and critique a series of types of software in terms of purposes and design, examining the implications of the method supported by each. Thus we offer a methodological map, and, like all maps, it selects the features to be presented. Our goal is to emphasize the new frontiers, rather than to offer a list of product descriptions.

Product descriptions are readily available from developers (to counter our standpoint): For a special journal issue on this topic, see the November 1991 issue of *Qualitative Sociology*; for conference papers, see Fielding and Lee (1991). Most contributions to those collections (including ours) are arguments for particular software approaches. For penetrating comparative reviews by a nondeveloper and nonmarketer, see Miles and Huberman (1994, Appendix A) and, for more depth, Weitzman and Miles (1994). For earlier partial surveys, compare Tesch (1990) with Pfaffenberger (1988) on sociological approaches, and both with Bailey (1982), Hockey (1980), and Miall (1990) on related software for humanities.

Here instead we offer the researcher a comparative account of software architectures and of the directions of developments. We encourage readers to evaluate software packages in terms of what they propose to do (Did you *want* to do that?) and what new techniques might or might not enhance analysis or restrict method. Having chosen a software approach, the best way to get up-to-date information on software is to send for current product descriptions and demonstration disks and read the survey literature. A list of addresses for the developers of the programs discussed here is included in the appendix to this chapter.

◆ Theory and Data

Working "up" from data is often presented as what qualitative research is especially about. It is done in many ways: building new understandings from "thick descriptions"; reflecting on and exploring data records; discovering patterns and constructing and exploring impressions, summaries, pen portraits. All such efforts have theoretical results. They produce new ideas and new concepts, which are sometimes linked and presented more formally as new theories. Most approaches to qualitative research also work "down" from theory. They incorporate, explore, and build on prior theoretical input, on hunches or ideas or sometimes formal hypotheses. Many also stress the testing of theory derived from the project's data.

Computers easily offer assistance in the management of complex data. They also, with more difficulty, can be used in the discovery and management of unrecognized ideas and concepts, and the construction and exploration of explanatory links between the data and emergent ideas, to make fabrics of argument and understanding around them.

Managing Data

Ideas are produced in qualitative research in heterogeneous ways, many of which are not given the august title of "theorizing." It is not our purpose to survey the range of those methods; rather, we simply note that there is a range and that these methods are supported by software. As other chapters in this volume indicate, different researchers have different methods (and terms) for the exploration and understanding of rich data; production of "thick descriptions" (Geertz, 1973, p. 26); discovery and uses of patterns; construction of new concepts and testing of old; linking of these into theoretical frameworks, explanations, and models; and validating of impressions and conclusions. Nor are these unchanging. Theory testing is emphasized increasingly even in recent writings in the "grounded theory" tradition (Glaser & Strauss, 1967; see also Strauss & Corbin, 1990), which is often, in our view mistakenly, presented as the dominant approach to theorizing in qualitative research.

All these processes involve the recognition of categories *in the data,* generation of ideas about them, and exploration of meanings *in the data.* Because the categories and meanings are found in the text or data records, this process demands data management methods that support insight and discovery, encourage recognition and development of categories, and store them and their links with data. Ease of access to data is important to support recognition of the surprising and unexpected, construction of coherent stories, and exploration of sought patterns, as well as construction and testing of hypotheses (Bogdan & Taylor, 1975). But those methods also must not get in the way, by distorting rich records, diluting "thick descriptions," or demanding routines that destroy insight.

When these theorizing processes were done using manual data-handling methods, researchers often (though by no means always) managed their data by coding for retrieval. The *code-and-retrieve* process consists of labeling passages of the data according to what they are about or other content of interest in them (*coding* or *indexing*), then providing a way of collecting identically labeled passages (*retrieving*). Collecting photocopied segments into labeled hang files and writing text references onto labeled index cards are two obvious noncomputational code-and-retrieve techniques. The technique of annotating passages in page margins is code only.

Before computers, many researchers did not code segments of text. Rather, they felt through, explored, read and reread, "worked and reworked the particulars of ethnographic inquiry" (Kirk & Miller, 1986, p. 32). This required a simpler and more complex form of data management, as researchers compared and systematically built upon data records, keeping growing memo records about the accruing evidence and their exploration of its narrative and convincing body. Theory was arrived at and tested not through the retrieval of text chunks but through complex processes of evidence analysis, including consideration of knowledge about the site or story that is not in the text. For an eloquent account of why code-and-retrieve methods can fail the ethnographer, and of how computing technology rather than the research subject can determine ethnographic method, see Agar (1991)—an autobiography that is the more important because Agar himself is a user of computers and "select-and-sort" techniques.

Many researchers still do not use the code-and-retrieve method. Possibly fewer would use the method now if the software they bought did not support it. But it is certainly the most widely recommended technique for management of rich and complex records. (For different approaches, see,

214

e.g., Hammersley & Atkinson, 1983; Lofland & Lofland, 1984; Lincoln & Guba, 1985; Miles & Huberman, 1984.) However, despite its popularity, the code-and-retrieve method has rarely been examined as a *method*. The literature contains many lucid descriptions of how data records were handled, but reveals little serious debate over what that method of data handling does to data or how it contributes to analysis.

This taken-for-granted method was easily supported by computers and became the basis of most specialist QDA software. Computers, moreover, offered the possibility of addressing its limitations and adapting the code-and-retrieve mode of organization to assist with other theorizing activities. The method was thus subjected to debate in the new context of computing. An odd result of these developments was that the code-and-retrieve method for the first time was treated as in some way atheoretical, merely "descriptive-analytical" (Tesch, 1990). The creation of this dichotomy both underestimates the method and skews critiques of software based on it. One of our arguments below is that all of the specialized software we describe is so based. All of these software packages can be used just for coding and retrieval. And far from merely supporting description, techniques of coding for retrieval strongly support some ways of making ideas, and of constructing and testing theories.

First, the generation of categories, even the simplest descriptors, whether arrived at prior to data reading or by discovery of recurrent topics (Bogdan & Taylor, 1975) or *in vivo* categories in text (Strauss, 1987), is a contribution to theory. Decisions are being made about what is a category of significance to the study, what questions are being asked, what concepts developed, what ideas explored, and whether these categories should be altered, redefined, or deleted during analysis. Second, decisions about what text segments are relevant to a category are never merely clerical decisions; they always involve some theoretical consideration. Third, the viewing of segments from many documents on one topic or selected topics always offers a new way of seeing data. This is the major claim of the method to support analysis, and researchers using it clearly engage in the building up of theories. Moreover, the method supports pursuit of patterns by comparison of text segments on that topic from different sources (e.g., Did the young women have different ideas about domestic duties from women of other age groups?). Such questions may be crucial for locating patterns and are sometimes formally portrayed by presentation of data in qualitative matrices (Miles & Huberman, 1984).

So it is misleading to label the code-and-retrieve method as not theory building. But the challenge remains to adapt it to ways of recording, linking, exploring, testing, and building cumulatively on the insights derived from data. To draw on a distinction first made by Turner (1981), theory *emergence* in qualitative research is interlinked with processes of theory *construction*. Ideas, concepts, and categories discovered in the data are woven by researchers into fabrics of theory. These processes offer greater challenges to software designers.

Theory Construction

Theory *construction* in qualitative research (the exploration and linking of theoretical and other organizing and explanatory concepts and statements) is creative, not merely mechanical. The data-handling tasks associated are thus highly complex. And theory *testing* is usually part of theory construction, not a subsequent stage. Concepts are captured; links are explored, created, and tested; ideas are documented and systematically reworked, in textual memos, models, and diagrams expressing the specification, explication, exploration, and elaboration of theories. How can computers support this?

The code-and-retrieve method, we have argued, supports theory emergence. It also expresses theories that can be represented by codes and then tested by looking for codes in text and studying the relationships of codes. Computer-based code-and-retrieve will do this better, because computers are good at working with structure, not content. In a code-and-retrieve system, we express or define content by coding the text.

Suppose, for example, you have a hypothesis that people of a certain type and in a certain situation will behave in a certain way, and you have comprehensive interviews with individuals that check in each case for the types and conditions and the behavior, and the interview transcripts are coded for these. An example is "Young mothers who are reluctant to return to work explain it in terms of a woman's duty to stay at home." Then a simple study of coding patterns in the interview texts can be used to confirm the theory's *correctness* (check if there are any interviews coded for all the types and conditions but not for the behavior) and *completeness*—"*Only* young mothers . . . "—(check if there are any interviews coded for the behavior but not for all the types and conditions).[1] Note that what we are doing here is successfully using co-occurrences of codes within interview documents as evidence for features of theories: *Textual structure* as delineated by code-and-retrieve methods can be related to *theoretical content* (including information about the world). If this were not so, we would not use code-and-retrieve methods.

But this is not always so. Most social science theories find their support in the *content of the data,* not the *structure of textual records.* Management of records by use of code-and-retrieve in such cases offers help, but that help is limited to retrieving all passages coded with something relevant to the theory in question, so that the researcher can reflect on them all together.

This is not an insignificant contribution. The ability to retrieve all the text about a certain topic or topics strongly supports the development of new insights. The computer can do this quickly and efficiently. Sophisticated programs offer a wide range of ways of selecting retrievals according to co-occurrence or non-co-occurrence of codes in text, allowing the researcher to "fracture" the data (Strauss, 1987) and see it anew. But this contribution to the researcher's ability to access data should not obscure an important distinction: that between the *textual level* of work, which is where code-and-retrieve methods operate, where we code for talk-about-return-to-work and talk-about-mothering, and the *conceptual level* of work, where theories about people and the world are expressed, where evidence and argument are brought to bear, and where returning to work and mothering are explored.

The code-and-retrieve method we have described applies only to text. That which is coded and retrieved is the document. Literally, one codes talk-about-mothering (the text passages), not mothering (the concept). But no researcher stops there. What one would *also* like to do with software is to support directly conceptual-level work, not just textual-level work—that is, to have software that could directly represent the concept of equality and how it gets related to the concept of parenting.

So the dichotomy that matters is not descriptive-analytic versus theoretical: All data management methods involve theorizing. Rather, in assessing what computers contribute we need to distinguish textual-level operations from conceptual-level operations. Whereas code-and-retrieve as we have described it is a textual-level operation, one's codings and retrievals are guided by theoretical interests, are used to shape and test theory, and (inevitably) put theoretical blinkers on one's access to the text. Textual-level operations are theoretically relevant, but they do not construct or operate on theories.

Finding ways of supporting theoretical-level operations in qualitative research offers a major challenge to software designers. Consider, for example, how we work when developing theory from the text. We often get going by finding little things that relate in some meaningful way—perhaps, if our interest is in stress, that certain topics get discussed in anxious ways (and that is something that good coding and retrieval can find for us). So then we start looking for components in those topics that might cause anxiety, often by studying the text, finding or guessing the components and coding for them, recalling situational facts not in the text, and looking for suggestive co-occurrences of codes. We might on a hunch start looking at text passages on people's personal security and how they arrange it (research on background theory here, and lots of coding again), to see if there is some possible connection between components occurring in the anxiety topics and security arrangements. If we find one, the theory is still thin, so we embark on a search for others, and thereby look for a pattern. The result of this is a little group of chunked-together coded text, ideas and hypotheses that, provided they can be kept and accessed as a chunk, can become an ingredient in further more abstracted or wide-ranging explorations. This chunk is said to be of larger "grain size" than its component codings, and it may in turn become an ingredient of a later theorizing of larger grain size still that is built out of existing chunks. (Big fleas are made out of smaller fleas.)

And so the web—of code, explore, relate, study the text—grows, resulting in little explorations, little tests, little ideas hardly worth calling theories but that need to be hung onto as wholes, to be further data for further study. Together they link together with other theories and make the story, the understanding of the text. The strength of this growing interpretation lies to a considerable extent in the fine grain size and tight interknittedness of all these steps; and the job of qualitative data handling (and software) is to help in the development of such growing interpretations.

This network of concepts, evidence, relations of concepts, coordinations of data, of hierarchies of grain size where the theory/data/explanation chunks of one grain size are the data for the work of the next grain size up, is a good fractal-like model of people's explanatory belief systems (belief systems are explanation systems). This is how a person (e.g., a social scientist) reflectively constructs an explanation, a story, for and from data.

The process is not all bottom-up, however. The researcher uses at each stage expectations, prior theories, hunches, experience, and a good education (as with the theoretical determination of textual codes). The network builds up from the bottom, guided by a vision of the structure of a larger-scale network into which these small empirical gleanings must fit.

When one gets there, the larger-scale structure is likely to be different in many ways from the early ghostly vision; were it not so, the constructed theory would be quite unempirical, quite unconditioned by one's data. And if one's prior ideas are wildly out, then that will show up in the increasingly procrustean strains of trying to build the anticipated larger structures from the small, heavily data-conditioned ones. Here is where one's critics will show one a more amenable approach to interpreting the data, fewer exceptions requiring fewer ad hoc justifications, more meaningful relationships binding cases and patterns together, more elegance.

We will call this description of building relations between data and theory *data-theory bootstrapping*. Providing direct conceptual-level support for this process puts some interesting demands on software design. Coding for retrieval seems to be basic to such procedures, but researchers also want to hold their growing nets or hierarchies of concepts, evidence links, groupings of ideas, and so on that make up the explanatory structure in an accessible way that will help them see where they have been and give access to the fine grains out of which we build the larger grains. The software system that would help with this would hold not just the data and tools for manipulating it, but also in some sense the growing analysis and explanation system.

And because, in that recursive fractal-like way we have described, the partial results and little theories become part of the data for the next move in the analysis, that software would treat the analysis/explanation material added to the database as more data alongside the original textual material. The very analytic structures, the explanations, become more data. Indeed, the very processes of analysis (the computations) should be fed back in as data. That is, we want to save as data the theory/data/explanation chunks of one grain size so they can be explored as data for explanations at the next level up. Methodologically, this is known as *system closure*: Results obtained about the system, analytic techniques used on the system, become part of the system. A hallmark of qualitative social science research (but not of physics) is that the data being researched in a project are closed over its own techniques and results. System closure is the software feature needed to support directly the conceptual process of data-theory bootstrapping. (Needed, yes, but not sufficient—system closure will not necessarily give you a leg up on direct conceptual-level software operations.)

Qualitative researchers also need to jump from one code to a *conceptually* related one (to explore theory) or to a *factually* related one (to explore patterns in the world the research is about). So the database should maintain and exploit theoretical links between concepts, and the real-world facts about and links among people, places, actions, and so on, not just explore *textual* links between codes representing those concepts, people, and so on. If, for example, we store that John is married to Mary, that John is a blue-collar worker, and that John has been out of work (note that these are facts that might not be expressed in the text at all), we should then be able to ask for all the remarks of women married to out-of-work blue-collar people on some coded topic and *automatically* get Mary's remarks.

The procedures of theory construction described here require above all a very flexible, very easy-to-modify database, that will shift, reorganize, undo, and backtrack to earlier states. This is because the process of constructing an understanding is tentative, involving the exploration and testing of hunches at all grain size levels, hanging onto them if they look good for now, throwing them away when they no longer fit, while maintaining the rest of the growing structure.

Can computers assist with, even improve on, the ways we construct and test theory? Can they go further, and support the *explicit formulation of theory*? What of the explicit *finding and recording of knowledge* about the situation being studied, the putting of data to theory?

◆ Current Situation in Qualitative Software

In the following sections we explore the architecture and purposes of available software. We start with types aimed at a broad class of users, but that can offer advantages not available in specialist packages. This provides a basis for understanding why special-purpose packages arose and what they try to do. We then deal with those, considering first software that adapts the traditional code-and-retrieve method, and then approaches that combine that method with new ways of constructing the links among theories, knowledge, and text, testing them and modeling them.

General-Purpose Software Packages

Word Processors

Apart from the obvious and familiar advantages (such as ability to inspect an entire document, collate and explore selected extracts in a new document, print it out, line number it, edit it), the modern word processor

(WP) offers some features unmatched in most specialist QDA software. If the data are textual (e.g., interviews) and in WP document form, these features include the following:

- The ability to handle multiple documents on-screen in separate windows at the same time, which facilitates comparing thematically similar passages in different documents and copying segments of one document to another.

- The ability to handle formatted files (using the WP program's own format conventions) so that tables, diagrams, and the like can be included. Most special-purpose QDA packages work only with text-only ASCII files.

- The ability to include static pictures, charts, tables, and so on as illustrations or as editable models of the emerging ideas and diagrams of the theories. These need not be computer generated, but can be documents of any sort read into a disk file by use of a scanner, and may be in color.

- The ability to include video and audio data, accessible via icons in the WP text.

- Generally good text-search facilities, which in some WP programs support the use of patterns in text search.

- A *publish-and-subscribe* facility, in which a passage from one document is marked as available for inclusion in others (published). When included in another (subscribed to) it is not copied; rather, it is as if the published portion of the first document is visible directly in the second document. In this way, if the published passage is edited at any future time in the first document, those changes show up in the subscribing document.

- A *linking* or *hypertext* facility by which the user can select the subscribed passage and so open a new window into the publishing document at the published text, for inspection and editing. An elegant application of linking, for QDA purposes, is to mark passages in a (publishing) document with keywords or icons, and link the keywords through to the subscribing documents. Selecting the keywords in the subscribing documents will then open a window into the publishing document at the position of the keyword, so the user can see the keyed passage. In this way groups of related passages, in the same or different documents, can get linked together and the user can jump from one to the other.

- An *annotation* facility, in which an icon is inserted in the text and clicking on it opens a text window in which one can read and write memos. The annotations can optionally be printed with the WP file at the point they annotate.

These relatively recent features, such as publish/subscribe, linking, incorporation of video/audio data, and annotations, powerfully extend the more traditional WP features such as text search. For the qualitative analyst they provide imaginative ways of linking data, combining different media appropriately, and relating commentary and theoretical memos.

The main problem with WPs is what they do not do, or support badly. They do not automate the grouping of similarly coded passages—one must copy and paste, or link, them oneself (or at best write a macro). They become very clumsy if one tries to use them to handle large numbers of codes or many references from codes to text. They will not provide text searches for co-occurrences of codes (more on these in later sections). And they will not provide clerical and management tools (e.g., What codes have I used? What do they mean?). In WP programs, clerical data must be stored separately to prevent it getting lost in the data documents, whereas good special-purpose QDA software will hold and retrieve clerical data where and when wanted, to facilitate database exploration.

Nevertheless, smaller projects in particular may welcome the modern word processor as a flexible and full-featured tool for document exploration and the construction of analysis documents that relate themselves neatly to source documents and other media, which can be only a mouse click away. And specialist software packages too often lag way behind in these features.

Text Search Packages

Text search, long ignored by qualitative researchers, offers much more than useful tools for linguistic or protocol analysis. It can find themes in the text, gain instant access to occurrences of a newly discovered theme in text already coded, and locate topic markers such as question numbers.

The principles of most text search tools are much the same, and extend the text search facilities found in WPs. The simplest will search for a string (sequence of characters) in files of text and report each find in some way, such as displaying it in context and outputting its character or line position in the file. A more sophisticated type will support search for Boolean co-occurrences of strings (*and, or,* and *not* searches) within some stated unit of text, such as a line or paragraph, or even allow one to express complex *patterns* in the search, and will report and save every string in the text that matches the pattern. The common grammar used to express patterns is called *regular expression syntax* and is embodied in the famous Unix utility called grep (global regular expression printer), which is usually available as freeware for other types of computers, and is more powerful than most proprietary text search packages.

Text search packages search files (they do not need to be open in a window) and sometimes have special facilities for fast searching for user-supplied keywords in documents and then providing statistically useful results of various sorts on keyword co-occurrences and correlations.

Text search alone is not a sufficient tool for most qualitative researchers, because they also want, among other things, to store finds at a code (a system closure feature). But it is a necessary tool for gaining direct access to data records, rather than accessing them only through codes expressing the researcher's interpretation. When words of the text matter, or codes fail, text search is essential, and the computer searches text much faster than one can code it. Hence software supporting other QDA methods is greatly strengthened if it includes text search facilities.

In addition to general text search packages such as GOfer™ and ZyINDEX™, a number of concordance and similar content-analysis programs have been developed, primarily for literary studies, that will carry out word frequency counts, provide listings of chosen words embedded in a line of context and with a references to where they occur (KWIC—keyword in context—indexes), spot grammatical styles, and usually provide statistics on their finds. Some of these packages are extremely sophisticated (for further details, see Bailey, 1982; Hockey, 1980; Miall, 1990).

Relational Database
Management Systems

Relational database management systems (RDBMSs) can undoubtedly be very useful in a social science project, for both management of project information and analysis of research data. However, their powers are often misunderstood and misapplied in the QDA context.

Suppose you have a card file of your interviewees, each card containing name, address, gender, birth date, and date of interview. These cards can be easily replaced in an RDBMS by a two-dimensional table, with one row per card and columns for name, address, and so on. The rows are called *records,* corresponding to each card in the original stack. The columns are called *fields*. You define the fields for each table, then create as many records with those fields as you need. Typically, fields can be defined as *numeric* (holding a number), *Boolean* (holding *true* or *false*), *character* (holding a few words of text, such as a name), *date,* and *memos* (holding your notes on the record). You have to specify how many characters each character field occupies (except memos, which is usually set to some upper limit, such as 800 characters). Whether or not a field is filled in for a given record, it will still occupy that number of characters in disk storage (except for memos, which can grow up to the limit).

The power of database systems comes from tools to *sort* records on any numeric, Boolean, or text field, or combinations thereof, and to *filter* records, extracting certain ones with desired values in various fields. If you think of other fields you want after you have created your database, it is usually easy to add them in. Some RDBMSs also specialize in handling text rather than fixed-size numeric or character fields; these can be of advantage for QDA purposes. Facilities are often provided for text search on text or character fields, but note that text sectors of these fields cannot be coded for retrieval of the coded segments.

In your interview project, having created the database table described above to manage biographical data about interviewees, you could then create further ones to handle data about what they said in the interviews. If the interview comprises a number of questions, with free text answers to each question, a common procedure is to create a database table for each question, one record per interviewee, with a field for the interviewee's name, another containing the entire text of his or her response, and further ones labeled with topic codes containing the portions of the response germane to each topic code.

These database systems are called *relational* because the researcher can relate one such table to another. All he or she needs is to have a field in common. Any of the tables above can be related if they all have the interviewee name field in common. Similarly, tables with a topic field in common can be related through the common topic field, allowing the easy extraction of what an interviewee, or selected interviewees, said on that topic in answer to different questions. The result is that the researcher can use tables jointly to extract interesting data. One could, for example, list all married female interviewees who have a certain attitude toward alcoholism. This enables numerical and comparative studies—What fraction of all married female interviewees are they? Are unmarried females rather different in their attitudes?

So how useful are these systems to a qualitative researcher? They work best for discrete structured data, rather than for long, unstructured textual data requiring close study of content and data-theory bootstrapping. The attempt to create fields corresponding to topic codes, and putting text in those fields, is extremely expensive of storage. Moreover, if one uses many codes, more code fields per record tend to be empty, leading to sparsely filled tables that are hard to work with. RDBMSs work well for such purposes as analyzing the results of structured questionnaires that get discrete data as answers—names, places, and so on—or for analyzing social systems that can be described in discrete terms (participants, objects, transactions between, and so on). After all, RDBMSs have grown up to handle the discrete data of businesses—employee data, inventory, sales transactions, and the like—for purposes of analysis of business trends.

Like many general-purpose tools, however, they can be ingeniously extended. One such extension is a powerful technique for the construction of comprehensive relational databases known as the entity-relationship approach (ERA) (Chen, 1976). This approach comes into its own when the subject of the research project can be characterized as a system whose operation is to be studied, such as a classroom situation, a workplace, or a household. The user draws up a network diagram in which the *nodes* (the "knots" in the network that the lines join) are the various entities under study, such as the personnel and departments and functions in the company, the means of communication used in the company. Any relations among these entities are drawn as labeled lines (*arcs*) linking the nodes, for example, "reports to," "communicates with," "uses."

In this way the network diagram will specify and relate the major activities and entities in the system, such as the people involved, their tools, their goals within the system, their choices among tools, their actions. If the qualitative data about each of these features (nodes and arcs in the net) tend to be discrete rather than narrative (e.g., for an activity: type of activity, date and time of its occurrence, tools used, participants, its goals), then a whole database table can be set up for that node, whose records hold data about each item of that type that is observed in the study. Observation of the system (studying classroom activities, observing the shuffling of information around the office, and so on) then provides the data that go into the records.

The links in the network diagram show how to relate the database tables in the linked nodes to each other (the *relational* aspect of an RDBMS), and then the very powerful browsing features of a good RDBMS package can be applied to study and find patterns in the operation of the system under study. Winer and Carrière (1991) provide a very instructive and lucid account of a highly innovative system using RDBMSs in this way.

Where data are often discrete and the subject of study can be thought of as a system, the ERA diagrams provide a powerful discipline for creating semantically clear and precise network diagrams describing the system. No meaningless arrows or confused categories here. Then, using the ERA to create a relational database for the data provides a powerful data analysis system for the researcher. But a word of warning: You will want on your research team a computer scientist trained in *data modeling* (construction of ERA diagrams that can be turned neatly into an RDBMS system); the task of system analysis necessary to set up the database system is a skilled professional process. A better idea might be to start teaching data modeling in sociological methods courses—that might help to critique the current often meaningless use of diagrams in sociological literature, and to develop powerful skills in representing social systems and modeling theories.

HyperCard® and Hypermedia

The popular Apple® product HyperCard is a nonrelational database management system with an appealing user interface. A table of records is represented as a "stack" of file cards, only the top one of which (i.e., one record) is visible at a time. One can easily design the visual appearance of card stacks using HyperCard's simple drawing and design facilities. Typically, this is done by designing "fields" to hold the desired data on each card. "Buttons" can be added to the cards that, when selected by mouse click, carry out some predefined actions, such as displaying the next card in the stack. A simple and rather weak programming language allows "stackware authors" (don't call them programmers) to program the behavior of cards, especially button actions.

This simple software metaphor lends itself to some clever applications for QDA. You can tell the products by their Hyper-names, but don't assume they all do the same thing. Hyperqual is a simple code-and-retrieve program (Tesch, 1990). A sophisticated Scottish newcomer, HyperSoft, ingeniously addresses modeling tasks. HyperRESEARCH, discussed below, takes a specific approach to hypothesis testing. These all have in common the restriction of displaying only one record at a time, and none can act as a *relational* database, because there is no simple way in HyperCard of relationally linking stacks by common data fields.

HyperCard is very good at storing text, as one can add scrolling text fields to cards. These fields can support text code-and-retrieve facilities, with the advantage of "one-step" coding (no need to code paper records and then input coding data). Moreover, by positioning buttons over words or phrases and programming the button action to go to other cards with the same words or phrases, one can provide a sort of *hypertext* facility—a way of linking similar text passages so that one can move from one to the other. (Where the links are not just with text, but, for example, with audio and video media, we call this facility *hypermedia*.) The hypermedia facilities of HyperCard can be exploited to link field data text to the researcher's memos about it, or to records of associated factual data, or to link the passages of the research report to evidence material relevant to each passage. Other packages, such as StorySpace™, are designed to support these facilities directly, and should be taken seriously as tools for imaginative exploration (and creation) of text. For an example of such work using another such package, NoteCards™, see Halasz, Moran, and Trigg (1987). For a general survey of hypertext principles and software, see Conklin (1987).

Conclusion

Software not designed for QDA can be useful for certain purposes, but it can also constrain researchers who need flexibility and multiple methods. However, a study of how these systems work is essential if researchers are to know what they might expect of specialist software. From these general-purpose approaches, specialist qualitative research software should now gain such features as the following:

- ◆ publish-and-subscribe facility as a way of maintaining segmentation (coding) of text that changes; for example, as one adds commentary directly into the field notes
- ◆ pattern-based text search, *plus* the ability to code the finds automatically
- ◆ the way RDBMS packages organize discrete qualitative data; sort, filter, and make reports on it; and can be used to find patterns in the data
- ◆ hypermedia features that support "commenting" on segmented text and other media data directly, associating database material and audio/video playback with text, and storing memos linked to text, then moving easily among memos, data, and text

Special-Purpose Software for QDA

The 1980s delivered a collection of QDA software tools designed to address the peculiar needs of QDA work. Recent software systems build on the techniques developed by the pioneer programs, and incorporate both their ability to do the tasks of coding for retrieval and, we would argue, the disadvantages of that method. We distinguish five types of specialist software, each identified by its information representation and processing methods. The first, code-and-retrieve, is a form of information processing that is incorporated in each of the other four. All of the later types provide other ways of storing and accessing knowledge and constructing, exploring, and testing data and theory. In each case we describe one (sometimes the only) software example.

Code-and-Retrieve Software

This type of software was the first development for QDA, created by social scientists attempting to replicate the code-and-retrieve techniques that they had used manually. It has been around long enough for studies by or of its users to appear (e.g., Tallerico, 1991), and the range and operation of packages then available has been fully described by Tesch (1990).

Code-and-retrieve packages, all in different ways, allow one to enter (and change) coding of specified text segments of documents into a database, then collect and display all text segments marked by the same code. Some have enhancements that improve considerably on manual methods. The first available and best-known example of this type of software is the Ethnograph (Seidel & Clark, 1984). In its forthcoming version 4, the Ethnograph will do the following:

- retrieve on presence or absence of two (or more) codes; that is, report and optionally display all text portions indexed by all of the nominated codes, or by one but not the second—doing so-called Boolean searches using logical *and* and relative *not* or searches for sequences or proximity of codes
- support the collection of documents into sets, called *catalogues*; retrieval operations can then be restricted to a chosen catalogue
- do text search
- store memos
- display the occurrences of codes in files or specified text portions
- display subheaders to identify speakers or context
- display statistics about the number of retrievals
- hold factual information about each document as codes applying to the whole document (called *face-sheet variables*) or to individuals (in a *speaker sheet,* recording religion, gender, age group, and so on) (These codes can be used in multicode retrieval. Note that a face- sheet variable, though conveniently indexing a whole document, is actually coding a *fact,* and so operates at the conceptual level as well as the textual level. Imaginatively used in

228

retrievals, this provides a powerful way of relating conceptual-level operations to textual- level ones.)

The method thus offers much assistance in managing data, and also, as we argued above, in building and using theoretical categories. But it also has major problems, and software developments have sought to address these. First, the method "decontextualizes" (Seidel's term, used in Tesch, 1990, p. 115). Stripping the segment out of context is necessary and desirable if it is to be "recontextualized" in the new category context. But the context of data is essential to any "holistic" interpretation. Second, the method always threatens with rigidity. All code-and-retrieve software permits introduction and deletion of codes at any time, but this leaves problems in constructing new categories after the coding of many records without those categories; for example, how to return to the passages previously missed? And third, this method tends to impose on qualitative research a chronology more like that of survey research: sequential stages of data collection, data coding, then data analysis. Analysis is postponed if researchers find difficulty in keeping the ideas and insights emerging while clerically coding (and computers will do much more coding, so the task can become more dominating).

Developers of software supporting code-and-retrieve usually and rightly deplore these effects, particularly the last, and attribute them, particularly the last, to bad habits in the user rather than the software. Each of these problems is accessible to computer solution, but, like most manual systems, software systems do not easily support the integration of the process of coding (often perceived as dreary and clerical) with the (tentative, exciting) processes of discovery and surprise, or recording of new ideas and exploration of links between emerging categories. Developers make no claim that code-and-retrieve software supports anything like the entire qualitative research process, but minimally that it speeds up and extends the common clerical business of document coding, and makes the clerical business of retrieval guaranteed complete relative to the coding (unlike flicking through pages of transcript looking for marginal annotations). It is probably this perception of code-and-retrieve software that has led to the mistaken view that it has no theory-finding, theory-building, or theory-testing ramifications.

Software is certainly responding to these challenges. "Decontextualized" text collected at a code was always easy to chase back to the original context via information about the location of segments; but software using multiple window interfaces will allow the original documents to be viewed alongside the grouped retrievals. Limits on the number of codes available and/or the number of times a given rich passage can be coded are being extended or even removed. Considerable effort has gone into making the codes and their contents flexible, so data segments can be easily recoded and inconsistencies in coding discovered, and codes viewed, redefined, amalgamated, deleted, and duplicated *safely*. Retrieval styles are now more flexible and include exploration of context by sequencing or proximity of codes in the text. Questioning is no longer limited to the *intersection* of codes at particular text segments. (*In document co-occurrence* is often more important, to find documents coded somewhere with specified codes, though the segments coded do not intersect.) Storing *knowledge* about the situations or people or behaviors studied is often supported, even if that knowledge does not refer to whole documents. And recent software assists researchers, as filing cabinets never did, in managing codes and in the storage of ideas *about* codes and data, in memos, related both to the codes and to the data, as well as in checking reliability and consistency of coding and coders. Some systems combining code-and-retrieve with text search allow automatic indexing of text finds, and a few offer pattern-based text search, essential if the text does not conveniently always offer exactly the characters sought.

Coding for retrieval is one procedure incorporated, increasingly with extra facilities, in virtually all sophisticated QDA software, because it is one very major type of software support that most forms of QDA need, and that general-purpose software cannot provide easily if at all. But the method retains the limitation we stressed in the early sections, that the code-and-retrieve method directs analysis to occurrence or not of specified codes at selected portions of text.

Rule-Based Theory-Building Systems

One direction has been to seek ways of more explicitly specifying, developing, and, especially, testing theory. In commercial expert system software, this is often done using the idea of a *production-rule system*. An example of this genre is HyperRESEARCH, a tool that shows what HyperCard can do if you really work at it (Hesse-Biber, Dupuis, & Kinder, 1991). In its fundamentals this is a code-and-retrieve system, but it exploits the Macintosh^{TM} computer and HyperCard to include pictures and audio- and videotapes among the documents it can index. It also contains many of the desirable enhancements to code-and-retrieve technology we nominated above. It will do text search with "autocoding" of the finds. It will do Boolean searches for in-document co-occurrences of codes, not just for places in the documents where codes intersect. But, significantly, it allows one to retain retrievals in the system. Like autocoding of text search finds, this is a significant system closure feature.

It does this through the use of *production rules*. A production rule is an if-then rule of the form "If conditions C_1 to C_n hold for some data, then perform action A on the data." In HyperRESEARCH, the form is "If a case is coded as C_1 . . . and C_n, then code it also as A." (HyperRESEARCH looks at its data in terms of *cases*, rather than documents, and tries to find theories that explain all the cases studied. Textual data for the cases could be split across different documents.) The new code A (called the *goal*) is then added to the database, referencing the cases coded with *all* of C_1 to C_n. Once the conclusion code A is in the database, it can be used as a condition for another rule, which the user can then begin constructing.

Alternatively, one can build up rule sets "backward," beginning with a rule expressing one's overall hypothesis, then trying to find rules whose conclusions are the conditions of the hypothesis. This process is repeated until one arrives at rules whose conditions are all codes in the textual database. Running the rules forward then enables one to find cases where, by virtue of having all the right initial conditions in their text, the conclusion of the ultimate (initial) hypothesis also holds, even though it is not coded in the text. In the example given by the developers (Hesse-Biber et al., 1991), the overall hypothesis is that if a mother has a negative influence on her daughter's self-image (C_1) and the daughter dislikes her appearance (C_2), then the mother has damaged the daughter's self-image (A, the goal of the research). Then if this C_1 and C_2 are not codes used in the research, they may be defined as goals of further rules, such as, if the mother is critical of the daughter's body image and the mother-daughter relationship is strained, and the daughter is experiencing weight loss, then add that the mother has negatively influenced the daughter's self-image (C_1). In this way one creates "chains" of rules backward from the goal until one is using only conditions that are already codes in the case documents. At that stage the rule set can be "run" to find how many of the cases end up with the goal statement added to them.

This sounds rather like a knowledge-based expert system in artificial intelligence, in that it contains qualitative production rules. But taking the rules together, it amounts to a search for the cases that have coded *somewhere in them* all the conditions of all the rules that are actual indexing codes (i.e., in-case co-occurrences). If (continuing the example of the previous paragraph) the initial codes in the documents used in the rule set are K_1 to K_m, we are doing an in-case co-occurrence search for these codes, nothing more. Cases where the search succeeds are treated as confirming the final hypothesis "If C_1 and C_2, then A," and those where it fails as (presumably) disconfirming it.

But be careful of the methodology here! The *disconfirming* instances of a hypothesis "If C_1 to C_n hold, then A holds" are cases where *all* the conditions hold and the goal, A, *does not* hold. Cases where not all the conditions hold are not disconfirming instances at all. Typically, C_1 to C_n are a mixture of theoretical statements and specific conditions that hold for a given case, and A is an *observable* feature of the case. In other words, *it must be possible* to evaluate whether the goal holds in a case *independent* of whether the conditions all hold. But given that there is no independent coding of cases for A (rather, A is added whenever C_1 to C_n hold), we can never find a case in which C_1 to C_n hold but A does not—the hypothesis is a tautology. What we *can* find is cases where not all of C_1 to C_n hold, but that proves nothing about the hypothesis. In fact, what the running of the whole rule set boils down to is simply looking for cases where the original codes K_1 to K_m occur!

What, then, is the value of production-rule systems for QDA? These rules are certainly an intuitive way of articulating at least some sorts of theory. They do provide a way of bridging the gap between textual-level analysis and the representation and analysis of facts and theories to which we have drawn attention. Starting at the textual level, the production rules allow the definition of increasingly abstract and theoretical concepts in terms initially of the textual codings (K_1 to K_m in the above example) and ultimately whole theories as the later production rules. This conforms closely to the model of data-theory bootstrapping, and provides an elegant way of relating textual-level and conceptual-level operations. But for the process to be of any value in theory testing, as distinct from theory construction, the cases must *independently* be coded with all the rule goals, and the rules run as a search procedure for cases where all conditions of a rule hold but the goal does not.

A methodological difficulty with this is that production rules are supposed to bridge the textual/conceptual divide by making their goals (A's) be more theoretical concepts defined in terms of less theoretical existing ones (the C's). Now we are saying the A's must be observable features already coded into the text.

Note carefully that this argument is not so much critical of Hyper-RESEARCH, which provides powerful additions to code-and-retrieve and the incorporation of production rules, as it is of thoughtless ways of employing the production-rule facility. In qualitative research, such misuses could contradict the central goals of building up understanding from data by forever returning to it. This is not easily achieved by getting a machine to insert new codes when it finds others, without care to see if the insertion of the new code is justified by the text. There are also dangers of building, in any software, an edifice of sophisticated reasoning on textual-structure coding. A weak link will always be the adequacy of the coding process, and this caution applies to all the following sections.

Logic-Based Systems

Discussion of production-rule systems leads naturally to logic-based systems. These use if-then rules for their representation of hypotheses, as the production-rule systems do, but the type of rule and the way it works is very different and more sophisticated. The rules are those of *clausal form logic,* a computationally useful way of expressing and computing with the standard calculus of formal logic (Richards, 1989). A useful fragment of clausal form logic lends itself well to computer implementation, both to represent data in a way that is an alternative to RDBMSs and to compute with those data using logical deduction. This computational paradigm is known as *logic programming* and is realized in the computer language Prolog (Clocksin & Mellish, 1984). The best-known examples of its employment for QDA purposes are in AQUAD for IBM-PC computers (Huber & Garcia, 1991) and QUALOG for mainframes (Shelly & Sibert, 1985), on which AQUAD was based. AQUAD is not only written in Prolog, but makes Prolog available to users to express hypotheses and compute with them. QUALOG uses a different logic programming language, LogLISP. We will discuss only AQUAD here as our exemplar of this genre.

Like nearly all QDA systems, AQUAD supports code-and-retrieve. However, it provides a sophisticated set of retrieval patterns, called hypothesis structures, used in *linkage analysis.* Although some of these retrieval patterns are Boolean, such as looking for one code or another in a text, many are more interesting, such as searching for positive *and negative* cases of one code occurring *within a certain distance* of another in the text. The output of such searches is typically numerical tables showing cases where the searched-for linkage did hold and, for instance, the textual distance between the codes. This is why the linkage analyses are seen as hypothesislike, and not just bare retrievals of text. The flavor of linkage analysis is not "Show me all text of codes A and B within textual distance d," but "To what extent do codes A and B occur within textual distance d—is it a significant association?" This is a very powerful feature that helps link qualitative and quantitative analysis in one research project.

Where the 12 provided hypothesis patterns are insufficient, the user can access the Prolog language and program the hypothesis structure he or she wishes to use, as a Prolog procedure, then run it to get the desired retrieval. This facility is challenging for nonprogrammers, and even for programmers unfamiliar with Prolog, as is plain from the user manual examples (at least to one of us, TJR, who has been teaching Prolog for more than a decade). This is where the logic-based nature of AQUAD shows up—hypotheses simply are statements of clausal form logic embedded in Prolog procedures, along with control structures, print control statements, string search commands, and the other paraphernalia of a program; and these are what the user must write to extend the power and expressiveness of AQUAD.

Two other built-in features of AQUAD should be mentioned for their general utility in QDA work. The first is the support of qualitative matrices. The user nominates two sets of related codes, such as a range of emotions and a range of personal data on the interviewees (e.g., age group), as columns and rows. Each cell in the resulting table contains the text segments indexed by both the column and row codes for the cell, that is, the result of a Boolean intersection or AND retrieval. Inspection of the resulting matrix is a powerful heuristic in QDA.

The second feature is the *configuration analysis.* This derives from a powerful technique in formal logic, the Quine-McClusky algorithm (McDermott, 1985), which was introduced to QDA by Ragin (1987). Suppose you guess that the presence or absence of conditions C_1 to C_n may be causally relevant to the occurrence of outcome A. Then, where C_1 to C_n and A are codes that can be found in a case (e.g., interview) in AQUAD, you can use configuration analysis to see which of the C's really are relevant to the occurrence or prevention of A, whether by their presence or absence, and what those combinations of the C's are. As a simple example, hypothesize that whenever C_1, C_2, and C_3 occur in a case, so does A. And suppose your data show this is perfectly correct, but *also* show that whenever C_1

234

and C_2 occur but C_3 does not, A still occurs. Then in the presence of C_1 and C_2, C_3 is irrelevant to the occurrence of A. Configuration analysis detects all such cases automatically. Note how powerfully this method extends the easy code-and-retrieve ability to check the correctness and consistency of hypotheses, discussed earlier. This is an elegant example of how computerization can enhance precomputational techniques. In AQUAD, the C's and the A can be not just codes, but any of the linkage structures expressible in the system or constructible in Prolog by the user.

Configuration analysis is one of several types of *induction* techniques used in artificial intelligence to find necessary or sufficient conditions of outcomes or, equivalently, to find the simplest set of if-then rules predicting a given outcome. These induction techniques deserve far more exploitation in computational QDA than they have received, because (a) they are almost impossible to use manually; (b) they are of great power and reliability in finding and simplifying associations of codes; (c) they are qualitative in nature, relying on presence/absence of codes, Occam's razor, and Popperian falsification of hypotheses by single counterinstances (rather than the relativistic quantification of acceptability of hypotheses that occurs in statistical analyses); and (d) they are a powerful way of making textual-level code-and-retrieve methods highly relevant to theorizing.

So how does logic fare as a tool in computational QDA? We have said that induction techniques deserve much development. Logic programming, on the other hand, although highly expressive, is at least currently a tool of such complexity that many users will be unwilling to learn it. Moreover, it is used entirely, at present, to express textual relations between codes (this code following that one in the text, and so on), and not the conceptual relations between the coded entities (person C_1 knows person C_2, the greeting protocol C_3 is a functional component of establishing social relationship C_4, and so on). Undoubtedly one of the research directions of the coming decade is the idea of writing and testing hypotheses based on codes at the conceptual-relation and not the textual-relation level, and using formal logic to do it, and making the logic available in a way that is habitable by the average user of QDA software. In the section below on conceptual networks we will see one partial approach to this.

An Index-Based Approach

We turn now with some trepidation to describing a design approach used in our own rather hybrid software system, NUD•IST™ version 3.0.

This system combines and relates many of the features in other specialized designs described here. Like them, it is based on a code-and-retrieve facility and endeavors to go beyond simply retrieving text according to how it was coded. It can be thought of as having two major components for managing not only documents but also ideas. The first, a *document system,* holds textual-level data about documents, which may be on-line disk files or off-line documents such as books or anything else that can be sequentially segmented for coding (videotapes are supported directly via a link to the CVideo™ system). These documents may be indexed by typing in codes or by text search and autoindexing. On-line documents can be edited at any time, even after indexing. Use of multiple windows allows views into many documents or their indexing at once. Retrievals can be done by a wide range of Boolean, context, proximity, and sequencing searches, and grouped into qualitative matrices. Results of retrievals can be stored as index codes, as can the results of text searches, which can be regular expression pattern based. All NUD•IST operations can be executed in batch mode if desired, to automate repetitive work. Thus far NUD•IST is a code-and-retrieve system, and many users, we find, use it only in this way.

But the codes and references are kept in an *index system* designed also to allow the user to create and manipulate concepts and store and explore emerging ideas. The *nodes* of the index system, where indexing is kept, are optionally organized into hierarchies, or *trees,* to represent the organization of concepts into categories and subcategories, a taxonomy of concepts and index codes. Trees, of which there may be any number, are visually represented on the screen. The user can select a node, explore or change it, or move it elsewhere in the tree system. The trees and the nodes in them can represent anything the user wishes, such as people, objects, emotions, or ideas. They can store factual data (about cases, data types, settings, and so on), if nodes represent values of variables. Links between ideas, such as *causes, talked about, married,* can be represented in further nodes or in the node linkages in the trees. In this way the nodes in the index system can be treated as both textual level (coding documents) and conceptual level (recording things about the world and storing theory). This duality is made possible by the tree structure, which can represent conceptual relations, hence permitting nodes to be treated as concepts, not just as index codes into text. This is aided by being able to give nodes definitions and textual memos that the user can write and edit. (Documents can have memos too.) Document and node memos can also be treated as data documents and indexed like any other documents, so the index searching tools can be applied to them like any other documents, to explore the interrelationships of ideas being created.

Thus the index system approach builds on and extends the code-and-retrieve technique, emphasizing system closure. The user can explore the document and index systems and the relations between the two provided by the coding of documents. As theoretical-level structures change, the user can alter the index system without losing the references to documents supporting analysis at the textual level (groupings of text references by subjects). When such operations are carried out, NUD•IST adds to the node memo a log of what was done. Thus each node has a documented history, helping the user in auditing the research process as well as aiding interpretation of the index system as a structure of theoretical-level concepts and assertions. Where the index trees are used taxonomically, higher nodes automatically represent meaningful groupings of the textual data indexed at lower-level nodes, thus assembling and retrieving textual references for the generic concepts out of references for more specific ones. Techniques exploiting the tree structuring of the index system allow theory testing as well as the representation of facts and hypotheses.

As its authors, we find it easy and necessary to criticize NUD•IST: Criticisms feed back as future design features. First, NUD•IST appears, compared with the other systems described here, as a rather awkward hybrid, containing features of code-and-retrieve, ways of handling production-rule and other types of conceptual-level reasoning, conceptual representations alternative to conceptual network systems, and database storage facilities, all interacting through interlocking tools. NUD•IST was designed originally for provision of a range of software tools, from which users could choose according to their theoretical and methodological needs. We have learned that merely providing such varied tools can be confusing; tool sets must be integrated and easily accessible if they are to be used skillfully by the very wide range of researchers seeking QDA software.

Second, the system removes so many constraints, of size and variety of records and indexes, that a sort of methodological anomie can result. We have learned too that novice researchers, who may find their own rich and messy records to be alarming in their diversity, may be further alarmed by software that seems designed to celebrate diversity. User reports make it clear that the full implications of system closure are not easily grasped early. And, perhaps most important, the software offers many ways for a researcher never to finish a study. Novices too are often stalled by anxiety about creating a perfect index system up front, not trusting the promise that they can create and re-create the index system as they develop theories and discover patterns.

Third, the approach lacks visual display of conceptual-level diagrams and models, such as conceptual networks, that researchers may need in order to see their emerging theories before they can confidently continue with theory construction. They can see and manipulate visual models of their index systems, but not models of their emerging theories. They have to go to graphics programs (or even pencil and paper) to do that. Or, if their theories are of the right type, they can use conceptual network systems instead.

Conceptual Network Systems

Concept diagrams, conceptual graphs, semantic nets, and *conceptual networks* are all (roughly) different names given to the same idea, of representing conceptual information in a graphic manner, as opposed to production rules or the symbolic approach of formal logic. They appeal initially to researchers who have worked pictorially, by doodling diagrams on blackboards, or more formally in an attempt to give graphic representation to emerging theory and thereby draw out discovered linkages.

The objects in one's conceptual system (people, groupings of people, properties such as age or being a vegetarian, places, emotions—essentially anything one might code for a QDA project) are represented by little boxes on a sheet of paper. (Put them in alphabetical order and one has one's code list.) Now one joins various boxes with labeled arrows to indicate relationships between them; for instance, a *loves* arrow from the *John* box to the *Mary* box to indicate that John loves Mary, a *causes* arrow from the *anger* box to the *violence* box, and so on. Technically, the boxes are called *nodes,* the arrows joining them are *directed arcs,* and the whole resulting network is a *directed graph.* The arrows represent relationships and the boxes represent objects, properties, and concepts. An introduction to semantic nets, which also discusses their limitations compared with logic, may be found in Richards (1989, chap. 1); Sowa (1991) provides a full treatment. Semantic nets have also been discussed above, as the *entity-relationship approach* to designing an RDBMS.

Commonly occurring arcs are *isa* ("is a") and *ako* ("a kind of"); for example, [Mary]—isa→ [Protestant]—ako→[Christian]—ako→[religious believer]. Others are *belongs-to* (class membership) and *case-of,* such as

[Mary]—belongs- to→ [20s]—case-of→[age group]. These often have useful logical properties that can be exploited to do reasoning about the knowledge in the graph. Ako for example is *transitive,* that is, if A ako B, and B ako C, then A ako C. Thus, above, we infer [Protestant]—ako→[religious believer]. Rather similarly, we can infer [Mary]—isa→[religious believer].

Semantic nets make for intuitive and logically rich representation systems that have, like production rules and formal logic, been widely exploited in artificial intelligence work. If one wants to see all the relationships an object in one's system has, for instance, one need only look at its node in the graph and follow the arcs to and from it. But semantic nets have their limits. One cannot use an arc to represent a three-place relation or greater, such as Reverend A married Miss B to Mr. C, or person A sold item B to person C for $D. And if one wishes to represent the fundamental logical ideas of *not, or* and *all, some,* the tricks one needs to get up to can make the graphs quite unintuitive.

Semantic nets are meant to be used with some semantic rigor, like any precise language. When a node is drawn, it is meant to be clear what that node represents (Is it a concept, the objects falling under the concept, the common property of those objects, or the collection of those objects?); when an arrow is drawn, the relationship the arrow represents is meant to be clear (What does it mean? Does it relate the two node categories as a whole or the objects categorized in the two nodes?), as is the reason for the sense of the arrow (Why not double-headed? Why not the other way? Why have it at all?).

Several researchers have recommended the use of commercial computer drawing packages for qualitative model building (e.g., Padilla, 1991), and many use such diagrams as pictorial props in their publications. But what computing, and the literature on conceptual graphs, offers is the chance to be systematic and rigorous in the construction of these graphs so that they represent knowledge that can be searched for, extracted, and reasoned with.

One systematic and advanced approach to conceptual graphs is ATLAS/ti (Mühr, 1991). Again, the basis is code-and-retrieve functions in text, and these are reasonably sophisticated, with interesting ideas, particularly the idea of being able to group codes into "families." To code-and-retrieve is added an admirable memoing facility, and codes can apply to memos as well as to the original documentary text—a system closure feature. A particularly useful retrieval idea is ordering codes by date of last use, number of references, and the like. There is a good pattern-based text search facility, the finds of which can be coded—as in HyperRESEARCH and NUD•IST, this is another system closure feature.

Conceptual graphs are supported by an on-screen "intelligent" editing facility (i.e., the system makes the drawing of nodes, arcs, and their labels trivially easy, and also makes an internal logical representation of the graph one is drawing—it is not just a picture). Nodes can be codes (and hence have associated text). Arcs can be given one of a built-in set of relation names, such as *causes, isa, part-of, contradicts,* so that when such a relation is set up, its built-in logic, such as transitivity, becomes available for the system's reasoning about the network. Alternatively, a user can choose a name of his or her own for an arc (e.g., *supports position*) and provide a logic for that relation in a simple way. ATLAS will redraw a graph if it becomes too tangled.

These graphs operate at a conceptual level, not at the textual level. That is, the relationships between the nodes (codes) relate what the nodes represent (e.g., [anger]—causes→[violence]) rather than the nodes' textual references (e.g., passages about violence follow passages about anger). Thus, like NUD•IST but in a different and more visually direct way, ATLAS represents theory and factual knowledge, not relying on its indirect representation through textual relations that might be held relevant to a conceptual linkage.

What is the value of a conceptual graph representation of a project and its information? Networks are best seen as a tremendous generalization of the rather primitive information representation available in a code-and-retrieve system, which comprises simply an unstructured set of codes plus support for exploring their textual relations. Here we have a rich representation system for using nodes not just as textual codes, but as parts of graphs modeling systems in the world being studied, theories, and so on. Allied with ATLAS's sophisticated text retrieval system, the graphs support subtle exploration of text via a visually immediate interface that relates the text to the systems or theories in the world being studied. In cases such as evidence analysis, for example, facts gleaned about the historical situation under study can be represented directly into the network, for example, [Macbeth]—killed→[Duncan], and the study of the text coded at [Macbeth] and [Duncan] provides evidence for the claim. Standard semantic network techniques (which the ATLAS system will support, although it does not seem to exploit them) even permit the relations, such as killing, to be treated as nodes and so have associated text, which adds to the richness of the representation and subtlety of the exploration.

So, how useful are semantic networks? They are certainly, in ATLAS, very easy to construct and rich to explore. They lack the "intelligence" of production rules or formal logic as being "runnable" theories whose execution has some definite useful result, and they (at least in the ATLAS form) lack the power to represent crucial logical concepts that a logic system has, such as expressing generality, negation or absence, and alternativeness. It is very hard to see, for example, how configuration analysis, such as in AQUAD, could be represented, let alone executed, via ATLAS semantic nets.

The type of qualitative research project involved tends to dictate whether a semantic network approach such as ATLAS will be useful. It would be much better than code-and-retrieve at data-theory bootstrapping work. Its main value is where the subject of investigation can be seen as comprising a number of topics with some major characteristics of note and relationships to each other (a system). Then it can be of considerable heuristic value to draw that up in a semantic net and use the resulting nodes and arc labels as the basis for text segmentation or other data organization. (See our remarks above about the types of projects for which the entity-relationship approach to RDBMSs applies.)

For researchers wishing to organize concepts, the tree structures of an index system approach and the semantic net modeling of theories offer related but different advantages. Trees have the advantage that their structure is uniform and easily comprehensible. But that can also be a disadvantage, as the real world is often neither uniform nor comprehensible. Semantic nets directly and visually offer more forms of concept organization. Both methods support the most common form, the taxonomic tree, in which the children of any node can be treated as specializations, in some sense, of their parent concept: a kind of, a part of, is a, member of a group, case of, and so on. These are the main types of link used in semantic nets to convey logical properties of concept relations such as transitivity, and hence to support reasoning. But semantic nets represent relations between concepts that go beyond a thesauruslike taxonomy. The trees of NUD•IST are more restricted, but NUD•IST uses index system search plus the saving of search results as nodes as an alternative to semantic nets (worse for some things—it is less visual—and better for others—the system, not the user, looks for the links, and it is flexible).

As taxonomy structures, both have limitations. Semantic nets encourage researchers to keep the number of nodes small: (a) Computer screens cannot display more than a few tens, (b) the number of links (and hence the complexity) increases with the square of the number of nodes, and (c) big networks just look confusing. ATLAS offers a number of techniques for managing that sort of growing complexity, and future research in this field must concentrate on this issue. Index trees offer a different limitation for taxonomies, given that they impose hierarchy. Some concepts can be treated as specializations of several more general ones, not just one. Allowing a node to have multiple parents could handle this, but may prove confusing. Moreover, although trees offer the user the ability to structure data and ideas about data, they do not allow him or her to name links. One purpose of naming links is to associate logical properties with the links of a given name, for example, transitivity for *a kind of.* In an index structure approach, links are recorded and explored not by dragging and naming arrows but by creating and shifting nodes, a less visual and immediate process.

◆ Conclusions

Artificial intelligence research has thus contributed to qualitative analysis powerful techniques for managing not only documents but also concepts, and for constructing and expressing theories. Many researchers may of course never want these features, and will use computers for enhanced code-and-retrieve for collecting related passages for their contemplation. One needs indeed to avoid the danger that the style of the software one uses can coerce a project along a particular direction.

However, coercion is not a function of sophistication—the simpler code-and-retrieve packages can coerce a project into particular directions just because of their lack of support of various analyses that can be done on retrieved codes, such as co-occurrence patterns. And it is very hard to see how features such as configuration analysis, or organization of concepts into hierarchies or nets, or indeed the very provision of conceptual-level tools, can be other than powerful heuristics for qualitative researchers—if well used. The secret is, of course, not to force a feature onto a researcher if it is not appropriate for a particular task—and to provide flexibility and a "light touch" in the more powerful features so that they do not run away with their users.

In terms of research directions, look for developments in the logic programming approach, to make its power more accessible to the nonprogrammer and to extend its rules to express more directly conceptual-level structures and knowledge about the world under study. Look for wider deployment of configuration analysis and ways of generalizing that technique, and other methods of supporting inductive searches. The entity-relationship approach needs cross-breeding with good solid code-and-retrieve facilities, to provide relational database systems more attuned to text-based QDA work. Look too for ways of supporting project management, in particular (given the tentative, cut-and-try nature of a lot of QDA exploration), support for forking research work at a point in time into several future paths, pruning the unpromising ones, backtracking to earlier forks, and pursuing more alternatives within the promising paths. The growing bridges between qualitative and quantitative research are demanding software support, so look for innovative research on how to support that computationally.

Above all, look for ways of developing computer support of conceptual-level work in text-based research, not just textual-level work. That is the very hard research, for, as we hope this chapter makes clear, although software designs imported from artificial intelligence and database research are providing the breakthroughs, none of them is exactly what QDA needs. The problem and the excitement is that QDA is probably the most subtle and intuitive of human epistemological enterprises, and therefore likely to be the last to achieve satisfactory computerization.

Appendix:
Software Developers

AQUAD. G. L. Huber, Universität Tübingen, Institut für Erziehungswissenschaft I, Münzgasse 2230, 7400 Tübingen 1, Germany.

ATLAS/ti. Thomas Mühr, Technische Universität Berlin, Project Public Health A4, Hardenbergstrasse 4-5, 10623 Berlin, Germany.

CVideo. Knowledge Revolution, 15 Brush Place, San Francisco, CA 94103, USA.

The Ethnograph. Qualis Research Associates, P.O. Box 2070, Amherst, MA 01004, USA.

HyperCard 2.0. Manufactured by Apple® Corp., available from any Apple retail outlet.

HyperRESEARCH. S. Hesse-Biber, Department of Sociology, Boston College, Chestnut Hill, Boston, MA 02167, USA.

NoteCards. Xerox Palo Alto Research Center, 3333 Coyote Hill Road, Palo Alto, CA 94304, USA.

NUD•IST. Qualitative Solutions and Research, Box 171, La Trobe University Post Office, Vic 3083, Australia. Fax (+61-3) 479-1441.

StorySpace. Central Services, 1703 East Michigan Avenue, Jackson, MI 49202, USA.

◆ Note

1. Formally, if you have an if-then hypothesis of the form "If C_1 and C_2 and . . . hold, then A holds," then it is shown to be *correct* if no case is found of all the C's occurring without the A occurring; and it is shown to be *complete* if in every case where A occurs, all the C's occur too. A correct hypothesis shows that A always occurs under these conditions, whereas a complete one shows there is no other set of conditions under which A occurs— both relative to the data, of course. Plainly, code-and-retrieve methods can easily test correctness and completeness of if-then statements.

◆ References

Agar, M. (1991). The right brain strikes back. In N. G. Fielding & R. M. Lee (Eds.), *Using computers in qualitative research* (pp. 181-194). Newbury Park, CA: Sage.

Bailey, R. W. (Ed.). (1982). *Computing in the humanities.* Amsterdam: North-Holland.

Bogdan, R. C., & Taylor, S. J. (1975). *Introduction to qualitative research methods: A phenomenological approach to the social sciences.* New York: John Wiley.

Chen, P. (1976). The entity-relationship model: Toward a unified view of data. *ACM Transactions on Database Systems, 1,* 19-36.

Clocksin, W. F., & Mellish, C. S. (1984). *Programming in Prolog* (2nd ed.). Berlin: Springer.

Conklin, J. (1987). Hypertext: An introduction and survey. *IEEE Computer, 20,* 17-41.

Fielding, N. G., & Lee, R. M. (Eds.). (1991). *Using computers in qualitative research.* Newbury Park, CA: Sage.

Geertz, C. (1973). *The interpretation of cultures: Selected essays.* New York: Basic Books.

Glaser, B. G., & Strauss, A. L. (1967). *The discovery of grounded theory: Strategies for qualitative research.* Chicago: Aldine.

Halasz, F. G., Moran, T. P., & Trigg, R. H. (1987). *NoteCards in a nutshell.* Paper presented at the ACM Conference on Human Factors in Computing Systems, Toronto.

Hammersley, M., & Atkinson, P. (1983). *Ethnography: Principles in practice.* London: Tavistock.

Hesse-Biber, S., Dupuis, P., & Kinder, T. S. (1991). HyperRESEARCH: A computer program for the analysis of qualitative data with an emphasis on hypothesis testing and multimedia analysis. *Qualitative Sociology, 14,* 289-306.

Hockey, S. (1980). *A guide to computer applications in the humanities.* London: Duckworth.

Huber, G. L., & Garcia, C. M. (1991). Computer assistance for testing hypotheses about qualitative data: The software package AQUAD 3.0. *Qualitative Sociology, 14,* 325-348.

Kirk, J., & Miller, M. L. (1986). *Reliability and validity in qualitative research.* Newbury Park, CA: Sage.

Lincoln, Y. S., & Guba, E. G. (1985). *Naturalistic inquiry.* Beverly Hills, CA: Sage.

Lofland, J., & Lofland, L. (1984). *Analyzing social settings* (2nd ed.). Belmont, CA: Wadsworth.

McDermott, R. M. (1985). *Computer-aided logic design.* Indianapolis: Sams.

Miall, D. S. (Ed.). (1990). *Humanities and the computer: New directions.* Oxford: Clarendon.

Miles, M. B., & Huberman, A. M. (1984). *Qualitative data analysis: A sourcebook of new methods.* Beverly Hills, CA: Sage.

Miles, M. B., & Huberman, A. M. (1994). *Qualitative data analysis: A new sourcebook of methods* (2nd ed.). Newbury Park, CA: Sage.

Mühr, T. (1991). ATLAS/ti: A prototype for the support of text interpretation. *Qualitative Sociology, 14,* 349-371.

Padilla, R. (1991). Using computers to develop concept models of social situations. *Qualitative Sociology, 14,* 263-274.

Pfaffenberger, B. (1988). *Microcomputer applications in qualitative research.* Beverly Hills, CA: Sage.

Ragin, C. C. (1987). *The comparative method: Moving beyond qualitative and quantitative strategies.* Berkeley: University of California Press.

Richards, L., & Richards, T. J. (1991a). Computing in qualitative analysis: A healthy development? *Qualitative Health Research, 1,* 234-262.

Richards, L., & Richards, T. J. (1991b). The transformation of qualitative method: Computational paradigms and research processes. In N. G. Fielding & R. M. Lee (Eds.), *Using computers in qualitative research* (pp. 38-53). Newbury Park, CA: Sage.

Richards, L., & Richards, T. J. (1994). From filing cabinet to computer. In A. Bryman & R. G. Burgess (Eds.), *Analyzing qualitative data.* London: Routledge.

Richards, T. J. (1989). *Clausal form logic: The elements of computer reasoning systems.* London: Addison-Wesley.

Seidel, J. V., & Clark, J. A. (1984). The Ethnograph: A computer program for the analysis of qualitative data. *Qualitative Sociology, 7,* 110-125.

Shelly, A., & Sibert, G. (1985). *The QUALOG users' manual.* Syracuse, NY: Syracuse University, School of Computer and Information Science.

Sowa, J. F. (Ed.). (1991). *Principles of semantic networks: Explorations in the representation of knowledge.* San Mateo, CA: Morgan Kaufmann.

Strauss, A. L. (1987). *Qualitative analysis for social scientists.* New York: Cambridge University Press.

Strauss, A. L., & Corbin, J. (1990). *Basics of qualitative research: Grounded theory procedures and techniques.* Newbury Park, CA: Sage.

Tallerico, M. (1991). Applications of qualitative analysis software: A view from the field. *Qualitative Sociology, 14,* 275-285.

Tesch, R (1990). *Qualitative research: Analysis types and software tools.* London: Falmer.

Turner, B. A. (1981). Some practical aspects of qualitative data analysis. *Quality and Quantity, 15,* 225-247.

Weitzman, E., & Miles, M. B. (1994). *Computer programs for qualitative data analysis.* Newbury Park, CA: Sage.

Winer, L. R., & Carrière, M. (1991). A qualitative information system for data management. *Qualitative Sociology, 14,* 245-262.

9

Narrative, Content, and Semiotic Analysis

Peter K. Manning & Betsy Cullum-Swan

◆ Documentary data have always been central to social science, but
   modes of analyzing them vary, and the centrality of documentary
evidence also varies within the social sciences and in subfields within them.[1]
Some of these shifts are the topic of this chapter. We intend to chart the
relationships among narrative, content, and semiotic analysis, illustrating
the changing meanings of texts (written documents) and their role in social
research and theorizing.

In the early part of this century, social scientists studied people, trying
to extract from written materials the patterns, orders, senses, and meanings
of their life experiences. Documents, almost from the beginning of empirical work in sociology, have been controversial (Blumer, 1939; Gottschalk,
Kluckhohn, & Angell, 1945). The first major American empirical study,
the classic by W. I. Thomas and Florian Znaniecki, *The Polish Peasant*
(1918), relied upon diaries, letters, and other personal documents to
characterize the impact of immigration to the United States upon Polish
immigrants. However, since Emile Durkheim's *Suicide* (1951) established
sociology as a discipline, sociology and other social sciences have been
wedded to positivistic methods (methods that take the external world as
extant and reproducible through scientific or logical means) and associated
concepts of validity, reliability, generalization, prediction, and control

(Denzin, 1989). They combine these methodological and often technical concerns (based on the canons of statistical measurement) somewhat uneasily with often subtle interpretive theoretical frameworks.

In many respects, the debate over the use of documents in social science concerns validity, reliability, representativeness, and generalizability of findings drawn from textual evidence. Ironically, the question of which methodology is superior for interpreting words, rather than numbers, has not been debated. The social sciences, with the possible exception of content analysis, have not developed systematic evaluative techniques for documentary analysis (see Berelson, 1952; Holsti, 1969). The dominance of quantitative methods has resulted in an underdeveloped theory of qualitative textual analysis and heavy reliance on literary criticism, linguistics, computer science, and cognitive psychology for models for assessing the quality of documents.

✧ This Chapter's Focus

We begin with a brief history of documentary or textual analysis, outlining the changing paradigms within which these research approaches are used, including documentary research and narrative, discourse, and content analysis. We then introduce semiotics, which brings us to examples of the varieties of structuralist and semiotic analysis. Structuralists assume that content is a function of form and code and meaning is a product of a system of relationships. Documents are "products," like speech itself, of a system within which they are defined and made meaningful. Documents so defined are converted into "texts" to be read and interpreted (Foucault, 1973, p. 47).

This radical redefinition of documents, we argue in the penultimate section of the chapter, changes methodological stances. The impact of independent and "exogenous variables" on the meaning, content, or structure of documents, and their validity or reliability, becomes a background, whereas the foreground is the relationship between the "text" as a social construction and its form or its imputed audience-derived meanings. In the final section of the chapter we address selected consequences of the radical relativism produced by structuralism and semiotics. We illustrate these consequences with examples of ethnographic, or culturally descriptive, semiotic research. We end the chapter with two forms of semiotic analysis of McDonald's.

247

◆ Content and Narrative Analysis

Content Analysis

After World War II, sociologists and students of mass communications refined content analysis. Content analysis is a quantitatively oriented technique by which standardized measurements are applied to metrically defined units and these are used to characterize and compare documents (Berelson, 1952; Kracauer, 1993). Content analysis has been used to characterize the content of popular magazines (Lowenthal, 1962) and other documents. Content analysis was massively facilitated by the electronic computer and computer-based programs such as the General Enquirer (Stone, Dunphy, & Kirsch, 1967). Recently, its use has been most popular in cultural studies and mass communications research.

Aside from the methodological problems associated with any quantitative technique (sampling, generalization, validity, especially external validity, and reliability), content analysis has been unable to capture the *context* within which a written text has meaning. Context has been variously defined, in terms of an ongoing narrative ("plot"), the immediate semantic environment, the literary tropes operating, and connections between the text and experience or knowledge (Eco, 1979). Ethnomethodological approaches (see Holstein & Gubrium, Chapter 6, Volume 2, this series) attempt to understand context as the taken-for-granted knowledge brought to the experience and displayed in the talk. Levinson (1983) defines context as a matter of pragmatics, "what the reader brings to" the utterance or, in this case, the text. The microinteractional aspect of content analysis has never been fully solved. That is, what is brought to a reading by a reader can be estimated using panels or samples of readers or coders, or by literary or social science experts who define meaning authoritatively. Barthes (1975b), in urging consideration of the "readerly text," highlights the subtle interactions among reading, the text, and the reader. This remains an open or moot point.

Narrative Analysis

Narrative analysis takes a number of analytic forms. We discuss them here in declining level of formality, that is, the degree to which the internal coherence of the text is defined in advance with reference to codes, syntax, grammar, or forms.

Russian formalism, associated with the works of R. Jakobson, V. Sklovskij, M. Bakhtin, B. Uspensky, and V. Propp, and the Rumanian-French writer Tzvetan Todorov, emphasizes the role of form in conveying meaning in a narrative (see Jameson, 1972). Perhaps the most famous example of formalist-structuralism is Propp's (1968) elegant propositional quasi-algebraic analysis of the Russian fairy tale. Propp claims the Russian fairy tale can be understood using only four principles: The functions of characters are stable elements in a tale; the functions known in a fairy tale are limited; the sequence of functions is always identical; and fairy tales are of one type with regard to structure (our paraphrase from Propp, 1968, chap. 2). Lévi-Strauss's (1963) analysis of myth (based in Roman Jakobson's structural linguistics) uses binary oppositions, a closed system of relations, a synchronic model, and standardized units. Lévi-Strauss, unlike Propp, argues that a story ("myth") unfolds paradigmatically in terms of oppositions, rather than linearly in terms of functions. Other variants on structuralist semiotics are found in the works of Lotman (1990) and Griemas (1966), which can be summarized by the semiotic square that combines opposition and contradiction to analyze the structure of social systems (e.g., law; see Jackson, 1986).

Systematic forms of narrative analysis, "top-down" or "bottom-up" approaches, make quite different assumptions about the organization of cognitive meaning. Top-down versions have had considerable influence in education and cognitive psychology (Rumelhart, 1977; Rumelhart & Norman, 1981). The investigator begins with a set of rules and principles and seeks to exhaust the meaning of a text using the rules and principles (see Boje, 1991; Heise, 1992). In using the Ethnograph, a program for narrative analysis, an event such as the Russian Revolution is first reduced to a series of propositions. Events require prerequisites (preconditions such as those leading to the Russian Revolution—hunger); events must exhaust the conditions that the prerequisites created (all conditions must be related to an outcome—hunger leads to riots); events' prerequisites must be subsequently exhausted before they can be repeated. Thus what is "tested" is the preconceived closed and logically constrained binary model (events either happened or they did not) of the researcher. This approach is influenced by cognitive psychology and artificial intelligence, and such analyses are made possible by the memory capacity and flexibility of computers and software. Bottom-up versions, found in most ethnographic work, on the other hand, derive context-dependent units to produce an infrastructure that explains the tale's effect. Dwyer (1982), for example, presents his material as a dialogue between himself and the other, a Faquir, whereas Crapanzano (1980) interpolates and comments on Moroccan culture. Often such reports rely on personal interviews or documents, and the translation of these materials into parts of a coherent argument remains fuzzy (Atkinson, 1992; Riessman, 1993).

Some studies contrast narratives, self-formatted stories, with formal, externally formatted narratives, such as medical interviews. Cicourel (1973, 1982, 1985, 1986) demonstrates that neither approach adequately captures human information processing and sense making. Furthermore, he questions the assumption of both of these models that views human reasoning as algorithmic and linear. The basic distinction between a preformatted interaction with an instrumental purpose, such as a medical or survey research interview, and a personal story, with its wandering, complex, sensate, and expressive forms, is a primary contrast in the literature on narratives. Whereas the life situation of the person, the embodied here-and-now reality, is looked at from the body's perspective, the medical interview looks at the body as an objective, functioning machine.

Medical writing on stories is revealing. Diverse writers, many of them medically trained, such as Kleinman (1988), Brody (1987), Coles (1989), Mishler (1984), and Paget (1988) in medical social science, argue for the utility of narrative analysis but share no common definition, purpose, method or technique, or mode of analysis. They assert that stories reflect human feelings and lived experience, and that healing necessarily involves the telling, hearing, and unraveling of stories. However, each presents a unique, appealing, aesthetic, and humanistic rationale for his or her approach and weaves it into the logic of the medical interview.

The concern with lives and lived experience resurfaced relatively late in narrative analysis. The emphasis in contemporary anthropology and feminism is upon the study of lives from the narrator's experience, as a shared production with social scientists. These stories are seen as real, yet with a tenuous grip on a consensually defined social reality that can be validly and reliably reproduced by social scientists. Emphasizing the role of these narratives in empowering persons through more subtle understandings of their life situations stands the structuralist concern with the power of codes, rules, and social functions of texts on its head.[2]

To a striking extent, narrative analysis is rather loosely formulated, almost intuitive, using terms defined by the analyst (see Riessman, 1993). Narrative analysis typically takes the perspective of the teller, rather than that of the society, as in Propp's and Lévi-Strauss's models. If one defines narrative as a story with a beginning, middle, and end that reveals someone's experiences, narratives take many forms, are told in many settings, before many audiences, and with various degrees of connection to actual events or persons. Thus themes, principal metaphors, definitions of narrative, defining structures of stories (beginning, middle, and end), and conclusions are often defined poetically and artistically and are quite context bound (Atkinson, 1990; see also Potter & Wetherell, 1987). For example, using a small number of stories, or even one, organizational analysts assert the importance of stories in organizations (Martin, 1990; Martin, Feldman, Hatch, & Sitkin, 1983). These approaches are little shaped by the traditions of content analysis or the coding used in quantitative sociological work, and are used to contrast the "human" or "cultural" dimension of organizations rather than to illuminate personal lives.

At the extreme, macrotextual analysis sees the verbalization and representation of society and groups through words. These representations are seen as marking, dramatizing, and constructing often complex social relations. Macrotextual work draws on the ideas of Kenneth Burke—dramaturgy (1966; Gusfield, 1989), Hugh D. Duncan—dramatism (1962, 1968, 1969), and Murray Edelman—symbolic analyses of politics (1966, 1977, 1992; Merelman, 1984, 1992). This approach views texts as symbolic action, or means to frame a situation, define it, grant it meaning, and mobilize appropriate responses to it. Burke, for example, uses five basic terms of dramatism for analysis of any discourse: act, scene, agent, agency, and purpose (these ideas are paralleled in Goffman's early work; see Perinbanayagam, 1991). This scheme has been well applied to the assessment of the effectiveness of court stories (Bennett & Feldman, 1986). Societal-level analysis of discourse, such as of anti-drunken driving messages (Gusfield, 1966, 1986; Jacobs, 1989), tourism (MacCannell, 1976/ 1989), and comparative societal representation (Lincoln, 1992), works by identifying broad themes, audiences, and symbols used to persuade and mobilize groups. In this sense, macrotextual or narrative analysis sees society as a "speaker" and social signs, including words, as texts (Brown, 1987, 1989, 1992).

◆ Semiotics

Semiotics, or the science of signs, provides a set of assumptions and concepts that permit systematic analysis of symbolic systems. The Swiss linguist Ferdinand de Saussure (1857-1913) founded semiotics (Culler, 1977). Saussure's (1915/1966) work and writings of the American pragmatist Charles Peirce (1931) and Charles Morris are the primary sources of the theory underlying semiotics. Although semiotics is based on language, language is but one among many sign systems of varying degrees of unity, applicability, and complexity. Morse code, etiquette, mathematics, music, and even highway signs are examples of semiotic systems. Sign systems can be loosely or tightly connected or articulated, and the relations within them can be various: homological, analogical, even metaphoric. Social semioticians see social life, group structure, beliefs, practices, and the content of social relations as functionally analogous to the units that structure language. By extension of this semiotic position, all human communication is a display of signs, something of a text to be "read." Disagreement remains about the utility of semiotics and the relevance of the linguistic conceit or analogy to social analysis (see, for example, Noth, 1990).

A *sign* is something that represents or stands for something else in the mind of someone. A sign is composed in the first instance of an *expression,* such as a word, sound, or symbol, and a *content,* or something that is seen as completing the meaning of the expression (Hjemslev, 1961). For example, a lily is an expression linked conventionally with death, Easter, and resurrection as a content. Smoke is linked to cigarettes and to cancer, and Marilyn Monroe to sex. Each of these connections is social and arbitrary, so that many kinds of links exist between expression and content.[3]

The process of linking or connecting expression and content is social and depends upon the perspective of the observer. A sign is essentially incomplete because it requires an *interpretant,* or context. That which links the expression and the content is brought to the signifying event. When the interpretant changes, signs change meaning. Behind any idea or feature of the social world is yet another interpretant. This the basis for the radical claim that no reality lies under or behind a sign, and no "real world" exists. Semiotics, in short, studies whatever can be taken to be a sign, or against which any sign can be checked. The interpretant of a sign is another sign, and that sign is validated as it were by yet another sign, and so on without end (Eco, 1979, p. 7).

The connections made between expression and content and among signs are mental. Thus semiotics depends upon a "primitive phenomenology"; that is, meaningful connections between the expression and content are socially created and maintained (Culler, 1975). Typically, these connections are shared and collective, and provide an important source of the ideas, rules, practices, codes, and recipe knowledge called "culture" (Barley, 1983; Culler, 1975). Culture is a reference point—a means by which one comes to believe in the reality of the expression (Eco, 1979, pp. 71-72). These connections between clusters of signs are sometimes called *paradigms*. Several paradigms or domains of meaning, when collected, constitute a *field* (Bourdieu, 1977, p. 47). A field may be created or constituted by discourse, as for example in an artistic or scientific field, by practices, or by material objects. Of particular interest here are discourse fields that can be mapped onto larger social structures of signs. Organizations, for example, can be characterized by logic that is constituted of fields of argumentation. That which provides the social connection among the components of a sign, a set of signs clustered as texts, and even assembled as discourse, is a *code*.

Sign functions are important in social analysis because signs, and signs about signs, that represent social differentiation mark and reinforce social relations (Guiraud, 1975). To some degree, the potentially volatile contextual nature of meaning is reduced by shared knowledge, rules and codes employed within a culture to make sense of fields of signs. More often, the understandings are a function of "knowledgeability" (Giddens, 1984) or tacit, nonverbal meanings, taken for granted and unrecognized even by participants. Nevertheless, these are powerful constraints upon meaning.

The connections among signs are variable, and the resultant meanings are variable as well. It has been conventional to restrict the range of meanings of expression content to three levels: denotative, connotative, and mythological or allegorical. Denotative meaning is seen in connections between a grade and a level of school performance. We read one as the other: 4.0 = excellent; 3.5.= very good, and so on. A connotation is created when "honors" are conferred on those scoring above a given GPA level. This status becomes "mythical" if the label "honors" is taken to indicate "knowledge." The connotative and mythical level of interpretation, as Barthes (1967, 1972, pp. 115ff.) illustrates, results from the unexamined nonempirical or belief-based connections drawn between denotative and connotative meanings. Signs, whatever the context, can also produce or express emotions as well as cognitions or logical formulations.

As meanings collect under an ideological canopy, unpacking them becomes more complex and problematic, and knowing the culture becomes essential. Culture is sedimented in institutions that "pin down" and stabilize the links between expression and content and contain the codes that anchor the potentially migratory expression (Bourdieu, 1977). Thus, within a given cultural system, power and authority stabilize floating and arbitrary expressions to establish and generate structurally dictated sign concreteness.

As a result of semiotics, theoretic influences now flow from structural linguistics, pragmatics, phenomenological sociology, and, most notably, varieties of "structuralism," poststructuralism, and postmodernism (Borgmann, 1992; Culler, 1975; Denzin, 1986; Guiraud, 1975; Hawkes, 1977; Kurzweil, 1980; Rose, 1992; Rosenau, 1992; Sturrock, 1979). Let us review them.

◆ Structuralism

Structuralism, both a theoretical perspective and methodological approach in contemporary social sciences, combines a formal model of explanation found in math, economics, and psychology, and an analytic approach derived from semiotics. Structuralism, a formal mode of analysis derived from Saussurian linguistics, sees social reality as constructed largely by language, and language forms as the material from which social research is fashioned. A major shift in social theory resulted in the 1960s from popularization of structuralism in social science initiated by the anthropologist Claude Lévi-Strauss (1963, 1966). Structuralism produced the "linguistic turn" in social theory, reshaping American social thought. Structuralism sees "documents," once viewed as actual physical or concretely assessable objects, as "texts," analytic phenomena produced by definitions and theoretical operations (Barthes, 1975b; Foucault, 1973, p. 47). Texts, previously considered self-writings for others' readings, become real and decipherable through a set of institutionally generated codes, or interpretive frames.

Structuralism seeks to identify the elements of a whole through systematic procedures "the method of analysis is structuralist when meaning, in the object analyzed, is taken to be dependent on the arrangement of its parts" (Descombes, 1980, p. 84). Structuralism is essentially a comparative method, because it seeks isomorphism in two or more contents. Once these units, parts, or elements are analytically sorted out, they can be combined, recombined, and transformed to create new models.

Structural explanation seeks to identify and array the units in a system to discover the "deeper" relationships or pattern(s) underlying an event or series of events. The explanation sought for observed phenomena is in terms of underlying rules, principles, or conventions that produce surface meanings. Structuralism relies on tautology, not causal explanations, synchronic analyses that obviate history (except as a signified representation). In theory, structuralism works with a closed system of meanings in which elements can be derived and sorted according to some principles or rules, and some calculus of possibilities can be derived (Ricoeur, as quoted in Culler, 1975, p. 26). Explanation is "a semantic process that generates a certain type of statement: namely, one that *meaningfully* encodes already encoded . . . values" (Lemert, 1979a, p. 944).

Structuralism is called "dehumanizing" in its drift and implications. It rejects the "homocentric" subjectivism and metaphysics of theories such as existentialism and pragmatism: Persons are not seen as bundles of sentiments or investigated "with reference to inner subjective and cultural meanings" (Lemert, 1979b, p. 100). Experience is secondary to systems of order, such as kinship, or law, or education. The person is merely the "speaking object," a user of codes and symbols who selects among preconstituted options, voices, and programs. Structures exist as the organizing centers of social action; persons are in every sense not only the creations of such structures, but manifestations of elements and rules created by social structures.

Poststructuralism

Poststructuralism, illustrated in the works of Lacan, Kristeva, Barthes, Foucault, Bourdieu, Touraine, Ricouer, and Guattari and Deleuze, contains modifications of structuralist themes. The philosopher Jacques Derrida, who developed Heidegger's notion of deconstruction, is "poststructuralist" in chronological terms, but in many respects he interpolates between the varieties of structuralism (Lemert, 1981, 1990). Poststructuralism contains some elements of the original Saussurian model and elaborates others that emerged after the decline in interest in the rigid program of Lévi-Strauss.

The "undecidable" or the uncertainty in meaning that arises from changes in context is an irreducible and a given in all texts. One must accept the difficulty of reading intentions from speech acts or texts and eschew final answers through philosophical analysis. Formal models of meaning cannot be forced into simple matrices based on a series of binary oppositions. Barthes has sought to elevate the importance of pleasure, sexuality, and the emotions. The "irrational" has a new place in analyses of political myth (Barthes, 1972) and sexuality (Barthes, 1975a; Foucault, 1978). The decentered subject reemerges (Lemert, 1979b) now as an empty, noncontrolling *object* of actions, something merely acted upon (Milovanovic, 1993). This theme of passivity and objectification is central in Baudrillard's work, although it is also emergent in Derrida's and Foucault's.

Poststructuralists urge careful reconsideration of written texts and their formulation, constitution, and conventional interpretation. To some extent, because the conventional canons of interpretation reflect dominant values (and writers), they obscure the virtues of writers, ideas, perspectives, and values deemed "marginal." In this sense, poststructuralism turns attention to the margins and reverses the usual adherence to dominant cultural values. The literature of the Third World, of people of color, of writers from non-European countries, is to be read and understood within the given cultural context, rather than from the perspective of Western European or Greco-Roman traditions. A text, in poststructuralist terms, is not an object or thing, but an occasion for the interplay of multiple codes and perspectives. One must seek to extract and examine the operations or means by which meaning is conveyed (see Derrida, 1976; Kristeva, 1980, p. 37). Reading a novel is an occasion for semiotic practice in which the synthesized patterns of several utterances can be read (our paraphrase of Kristeva, 1980, p. 37). Any writing contains multiple codes and times, and may even frame other writing within it (see Barthes, 1975b).

Once the field is a text itself, the previous anchoring of anthropology and sociology in "facts" and "data" vanishes, and authors speculate about fundamental issues of epistemology (Tyler, 1987), literary forms, and genres (Atkinson, 1990, 1992; Geertz, 1988); the senses arise as themes (Stoller, 1992), and individual speakers disappear into discourse patterns (Moerman, 1988).

◆ Some Analytic Consequences of the Semiotic/Linguistic Turn

A classic interactionist interpretation of the artistic process imagines it as a linear, "production line" process in which persons write documents for readers (see Clifford, 1988; Clifford & Marcus, 1986). Semiotics, and the structuralist model of social relations based upon it, is significant with

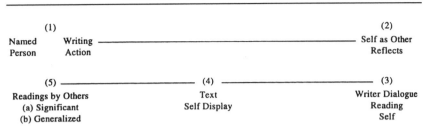

Figure 9.1. An Interactionist Model of Document Production

respect to documentary analysis because the imagery or model differs from the interactionist model. Figure 9.1 outlines the interactionist model.

The Interactionist Model

In the classic interactionist model of documentary analysis, a solitary internalized reflexivity takes place. An embodied person (1) (with a name, personal identity, and location in time and space) performs an action, "writing" (2). This action, reflecting a "self," including both an "I" and a "me," is reflected upon by the self as other. The writer (3) reflects upon the self writing and reads the product as an activity reflecting upon the role, or "writer." Writing represents an aspect of a writer's self. The writer's self is displayed in the text (4). The products of self-conscious writing activity, "texts" (diaries, stories, autobiographies, biographies, letters, novels, confessionals, depositions, and research) are read (5). These "readings" are re-presentations of the writer's documentary presentation of self.

Let us elaborate this model so as to contrast it better with a structuralist semiotic model. Reading entails an audience, some members of which are significant others for the writer, and for whom the person writes. Reading is done by scholars, critics, other writers, reviewers, historians, and related intellectuals. The serious critic intends to reconstruct the process of writing, reading, and reflection and to ruminate upon, according to the conventional canons of taste and the genre, the quality of the writing. The critic's task is to place the writing, the text, and its readings into alternative contexts or fields, or to recode the text. Adequate criticism should enable others to "penetrate" the author's intent and the tenor of the times within which the text existed, to strip away lies and stylistic obfuscations, and to discover therefore the deeper or "real" meaning of a written product.

Various levels of social reality can be explored, much as an archaeological expedition penetrates ever more deeply into a site.

A Structuralist Model

Structuralists modify Figure 9.1 (a model of artistic "production" generally, if one substitutes "plastic form" or "representation" for "text" in the figure). They make several radical disjunctive moves that alter many of the assumptions of objectivist/positivist social sciences as well as literary criticism. Fundamentally, the assumed-to-be-intimate and indivisible connections among persons, bodies, selves, lives, experiences, and stories are made problematic (see Denzin, 1989, chap. 2). Reality is socially constructed, as are the signs that convey, indicate, or represent it. Structuralists assume the relativity of the expression (including the possibility of nonreferential expressions). Meaning is context dependent, a function of coding (Barthes, 1975b). Loose relationships exist between the surface features of a narrative and underlying code(s) for decoding or translating a text. Although, ironically, stories always have this loose connection to the world—that is, they are not always referential to actual events—the elision of forms in the narrative model makes judgments of the meaning of a "story" problematic. A text can always be rendered in another code, another voice can be heard, a new standpoint illuminated (Clifford, 1988; Tyler, 1987; Van Maanen, 1988).

All texts metaphorically speak with many voices and contain within them many potential alternative readings. Within any story, the narrative line can be distinguished from the subject of the story. Reading as an activity creates another representation and shifts the field of the text. The unity of embodied self-writer-text-audience is analytically strewn asunder. Even the modes of discourse of science and history are seen as problematic (H. White, 1978).

But this repositioning of meaning as a function of codes has even more radical variants. A "crisis in representation" is precipitated by structuralism and semiotics. Consider these examples.

Frequently seen now is the journalistic conceit of wholly fabricating quotes, persons, scenes, long dialogues, and even events as a means of dramatizing and integrating "truth" and "fiction." Popularized by Tom Wolfe, and displayed in *The Right Stuff* (1979), the "new journalism" stylishly integrates the discretion to create lives found in fiction with the appeal of characters who are real people making real decisions in real life

258

(see Agar, 1990). The consequences of these modes of fabrication are seen in the recent Masson-Malcolm trial (in May 1993), in which damaging quotes alleged to be from Masson and used by Malcolm were contested by Masson.

Media logic suffuses all media forms and confounds experienced reality with the artifices of the media. Fiction, news, and current events are collapsed in TV programs such as *Top Cops, Cops,* and *Rescue 911.* All produce versions of reality. Altheide (1993) notes that the elision of social control through the media with entertainment is rapidly escalating. A current television show, *Case Closed,* employs private investigators to hunt clues and pursue cases abandoned by the police. Further, the integration of advertising, news, and drama is now proceeding. Real-life events (e.g., the invasion and fire at the Branch Davidian compound in Waco, Texas; the explosion of a Pan Am jet over Lockerbie, Scotland) are "news" and "advertisements" for forthcoming television films (Altheide, 1993).

The media influence the diffusion of rapid-fire collage, atemporal, surreal, vividly colored, and fragmented imagery, almost a visual explosion, associated with many music videos, into television news, melodrama, and advertising. The model is MTV (Kaplan, 1987). These sound fragments and geometric distortions of faces and figures have largely displaced films with a logical progression, a story line, and a narrative structure (beginning, middle, and end, or opening, crisis, resolution, and closing).

These manifestations of structuralism's influence move a considerable distance from the classic interactionist model of reading and meaning. These changes in form result because social relations produce similar modes of experiencing and analysis of such experiencing for media, the public, and scholars. Highly reflexive societies reflect on and analyze that preoccupation with reflection.

◆ Two Semiotic Approaches to McDonald's

Structuralist semiotics is not without weaknesses. It has limited capacity to explain change, the interaction of self and group, the history of an individual or group experience with a symbol system, or changes in sign systems themselves. Change in the meaning of signs over time, semiosis, is best revealed through in-depth interviewing and systematic observation. The interpretant, perspective, or standpoint of the observer from which the system is constructed must be identified in social and cultural context.

In this sense, a social semiotics requires (or assumes) a rich ethnographic texture within which the semiotic analysis can be socially embedded. To analyze a menu, for example, semiotically and out of ethnographic context is sensible only if a reader is a sophisticated and experienced observer of the same "facts."

We contend that a *semiotic discourse analytic* (Cullum-Swan, 1989) provides a history and context for understanding meaning that is congruent with a symbolic interactionist perspective. Meaning is derived or accomplished from an understanding of cultural knowledge and social forms rather than from personal knowledge gained through reflexive communication with others (Mead, 1934). The purpose of such an analysis is to place signs in context with the relevant interpretants over time. This permits analysis of differential meaning by demographic features, such as gender, race, and class, and by personal elements, such as self, role relations, and group membership (Blumer, 1969). Our examples illustrate the utility of both a semiotic method (an analysis of the codes that organize the menu) and semiotic discourse analysis. We believe they are complementary methods that together provide a more complete understanding of how personal experience and cultural milieus contribute to sign interpretation.

A Menu: The Structuralist View

McDonald's is perhaps the world's best-known business, and among the most successful (Peters & Waterman, 1982). Its success is related to its fit with many contemporary urban lifestyles: it is fast, efficient, predictable, standardized, routinized, and bureaucratically organized (Ritzer, 1993). Its logic is apparent and seems to tap into basic understandings of categories, classifications, boundaries and frames, associations, and meaningful divisions among foods and drinks. Perhaps two generations have been socialized to the McDonald's experience, and the menu needs little explanation for the typical American child (who can connect the pictures to the physical objects to which they refer). The conventions connecting expression and content are known; the McDonald's sign system is known and well embedded in the culture. With the exception of a few local variations, the menu is standardized to facilitate rapid decisions at any McDonald's. Below, we attempt to show *how* these signs convey meaning in a particular context.[4]

The first task is to discover the political and social *field,* the set of objective and subjective pressures giving meaning to the structure and codes to be studied. We call this the "fast food" field.[5] The signs and sign vehicles (which carry the abstract sign) speak to rapidity of transaction (the cash registers are built into the counters). The modes of service available to the customer—drive through, take out, or eat in—range from fast to faster.

Taking the menu, a central symbol or collective representation, as primary data, we ask: What principles organize it? How does it convey constraint and order choice? The menu is divided into colored panels. These are devoted to types of items, some of which are clustered into "meals." This suggests that a color and meal-based *code,* or principle for assembling meaning and constituting messages (Eco, 1979), orders the menu. Shown above and in front of the customer and extending from left to right are 13 plastic boxes: 8 panels list food or drink items and 5 show pictures. Pictures contrast with, mark, and dramatize the information-laden panels. The panels, from left to right, show the following:

1. picture (Egg McMuffin)
2. breakfast items—7
3. Extra Value (breakfast) Meals—5 (side items underneath)
4. picture (McChicken sandwich)
5. sandwiches (beef)—6
6. sandwiches (chicken and fish)—3 (french fries listed underneath)
7. picture (Extra Value Meals)
8. Extra Value (lunch or dinner) Meals
9. beverages—11 with size variations
10. picture (McDonald's Value Pack Meals and children's meals that include toys)
11. Happy Meals (children's) (salads listed underneath)
12. desserts (gift certificate listed underneath)
13. picture (ice cream sundae)

What do the colors on the panels mean? Above the colored panels are labels: over panels 1-3, "breakfast" (yellow); over 5, 6, and 8, "sandwiches," "french fries," and "Extra Value Meals" (red); over 9, "beverages" (blue); over 11, "Happy Meals" and "salads" (brown); and over 12, "desserts" (purple). Primary colors (yellow, red, and blue), divide and mark core items, whereas subdued colors (brown and purple) mark peripheral items (drinks and desserts are not included in combination meals). In addition to marking core and periphery items, the colors indicate courses, if one considers salads and desserts as such in an Anglo-American meal. The color-coded panels mark a basic division in the United States between breakfast and lunch or dinner. The color code divides breakfast (yellow) from lunch and dinner (red) for adults. No such distinction is made for children (brown—Happy Meals are served for either lunch or dinner).

The horizontal panels are also coded by individual (à la carte items) and three combination "meals": "Happy Meals" for children and "Extra Value" breakfast and lunch/dinner combinations. Meals include base items plus a core item. For example, breakfast value meals include hash browns, a large coffee or an orange juice, and one of the five (sausage or egg, biscuit or muffin) breakfast core items. Extra Value Meals include a medium drink, large fries, and a sandwich or Chicken McNuggets. Combinations not only increase per person spending, but speed and simplify ordering and billing.

Having seen that colors and space are used to divide items and distinguish meals by time of day and age of consumer, we can look inside each panel to ask what orders the items (expressions) within it. Each panel is an *associative context* (paradigm) listing similar foods. The panels contain metonymic (part/whole) contrasts between substitutable items (e.g., panel 5 shows six types of beef sandwich: Big Mac, Quarter Pounder with Cheese, McLean burger, hamburger and cheeseburger [listed on the same line], and double cheeseburger). Is there a rationale for the vertical arrangement of the items, one on top of the other? What is it? What things does the menu not reflect? Price is not primary, but a secondary or tertiary code. The price is shown to the right of each sandwich in panels 5, 6, and 9, but is not the basis for their order. Nor are sandwiches listed in order of complexity (layers, sauces) or size. The menu is an advertisement. The most commonly ordered items are high on the list. Similarly, Coke, Diet Coke, and Sprite, followed by H-C Orange (all Coca-Cola products), are the first two lines, and decaffeinated coffee and orange juice are the bottom two.

Having seen the codes, what can one discover about the associations across items of the menu? Do they cohere as a sign system? Both connotative and denotative meanings are shared. The primary denotations of each item, as noted, are courses, prices, single and combination "meals," core and periphery of given meals, and adult/child. Adding the "Mc" prefix creates connotative unity: "Egg McMuffin," "McLean," "Big Mac," "Chicken McNuggets." These "Mcs" are institutional markers, or signs about signs, that collect disparate items into a unifying institutional theme. The links between these signs are analogical, or based on similarity.

In short, the semiotics of the McDonald's menu are well chosen for effect. They reflect knowledge of the content and timing of American meals as well as age and lifestyle distinctions, and employ spatial and visual organization that facilitates visibility, simplicity, and utilitarian orientation to the message (Jakobson, 1960). To summarize the coding of the McDonald's menu, the most important code is color/meal, followed by core/periphery (of meal items), adult/child, and individual/combination meals. A secondary code is vertical placement *within* a panel, a metonymic list of items. These placements reflect marketing aims and the popularity of items—that is, the higher, the more popular.[6]

This analysis suggests that the purpose of the sign system is to convey messages that enable fast decisions and increase turnover, and clusters that raise per person expenditure and minimize complex, ad hoc item selection. Colors, panels, clusterings of signs, and the simple, brief, evocative, and terse names coded into the menu and the cash register for billing and collection ease all bespeak efficient, routinized, fast-transaction-based food service.

A Semiotic Discourse Approach to McDonald's Experiences

We draw on focused, in-depth interviews to draw out the meaning of the McDonald's experience. Such interviews provide the best tool for eliciting data for a semiotic discourse analysis because they reveal the circumstances subjects recall in going to McDonald's and their associations with the visits. Selves, developed over time and reflecting the sedimentation of experience, are intertwined with McDonald's. These selves are linked to significant others lodged in the "me" and are part of the replaying of joint actions. Self, other, and experience are inextricably interwoven in a biographical and physical context. These associations are personal and historical but also organizationally generated; they explore the experiential meanings attached to individual visits to McDonald's rather than cultural knowledge displayed in a skillful order.

Biographical Associations

Any McDonald's visit may call up past visits with family, a team, friends, and personal associations. The following scenario typifies individual associations and experiences at McDonald's and suggest how two are woven together.

One example comes from a colleague. As a child, she had chronic health problems calling for regular and painful treatments at a doctor's office. A trip to McDonald's was the reward for being a "good girl." As an adult, she has extremely negative associations about McDonald's; she rarely enters its dreaded portals, and has been there only twice in the past 25 years. On the first of those two visits, she was sold a still-frozen "filet of fish" sandwich. On that visit, she was in line with a "regular" who was firmly entrenched in his customer role. It was clear from his affect and conversation that he was mentally retarded. He genuinely enjoyed his visits—they were the high point of his day! He came every day for dinner and systematically ate his way through the menu, eating one particular sandwich according to the day of the week. He knew all the employees by name, and they knew and could predict his order by the day of the week—for instance, fish on Friday, Big Mac on Sunday. This specific setting and employees were his home in symbolic terms, providing a routine in an otherwise empty life. On the second of her two visits, our colleague wisely purchased only coffee. The greasy smell of a McDonald's is firmly lodged in her memory and is sufficient to make her ill. Other negative associations arise in spite of the cheerful externalities of McDonald's.[7]

Organizationally Produced Meanings

Many people have negative or at least ambivalent associations with McDonald's. People choose it when they are disorganized, hurried, harassed or distracted, uncomfortably hungry, lonely and alone, and short of cash. Only children with no negative associations (going happily with friends or family) and disenfranchised, marginal adults—such as the homeless or the mentally ill or retarded—remain entirely positive, and anticipate, McDonald's. The corporation, through charitable activities and gaudy, enthusiastic, loud, family-focused ads, simulates happiness, togetherness, and "giving Mom a break" ("You deserve a break today, so get up and get away to McDonald's" was a recent ad jingle).

These are systematic attempts to replace or displace attention from the potentially ambivalent or negative significance of a McDonald's trip. The symbolization serves to defer focus from the reality of a visit. Organizational processes are linked to the creation of a consumer culture, marketing the positive experience of going to McDonald's, such as "happy" meals, clowns, playgrounds, golden arches—reminiscent of rainbows and heaven. Further organizational attempts to create a pseudo-gemeinschaft (Merton, 1961) environment are manifest in the physical and spatial attributes of the place and the "professional education" given to employees.

Many themes of American society—fast, cheap food, served by strangers with a minimal of interaction, obligation, and reciprocity—are displayed in the social organization of serving as well as in the well-recognized building (Ritzer, 1993). The rhetoric of space, spoken by convenient and capacious parking lots, broad, glass-enclosed buildings, semiopen kitchens, and abundant seating, is welcoming to Americans.

As in a Las Vegas casino, time is suspended in McDonald's. It is always daytime, and light and ambiance are not softened to romanticize the experience. Inside, one's gaze falls upon the huge, sunlike, lighted menu. The yellow brightness is almost overwhelming to burned-out, tired, and jaded "evening diners." The building conveys antiseptic cleanliness. The early original buildings were constructed of white, tilelike materials and resembled operating rooms. The severe simplicity of architecture and the interior decor do not connote any particular class or culture, except that of postindustrial society. There are no personal menus, maitre d's, waiters to tip, or preferred seating areas. All are treated equally, and "what you want is what you get." The only requirements are shoes, shirt, and a couple of bucks. One is not encouraged to eat at a leisurely pace. (In a London McDonald's near Marylebone Road, the molded plastic seats are slanted downward, so that one rests against them, but cannot really occupy them.)

The organization works efficiently and effectively to present a front-stage set of simulacra that communicate a fun and friendly, family-oriented, accessible, convenient setting for eating staffed by pleasant and tidy people. This is the public, advertised front. There is a systematic attempt to connote "home" as well. One can see backstage into the kitchen, which is the hub and heart of a home, and see and hear the cooking and compiling of food orders ("I need another Big Mac, please").

Public presentation and private reality differ. Supposedly, as at home, one can dash in and "grab something" or spend some time eating and relaxing. However, it is not a relaxing atmosphere: People rush in and out, babies cry, employees wash tables as one eats, and lonely diners sit silently, not participating in leisurely conversation with significant others. McDonald's confuses in other ways, claiming to be the world's biggest recycler of paper and waste, but not mentioning that it is also the world's biggest producer of trash. It displays pamphlets emphasizing nutrition, yet most of the entrées have dangerously high levels of fat and calories. "Environment-friendly" pamphlets written in 1990 project unfulfilled levels of recycling for 1991, and function ritually to show the organization's concern for health and the environment. Despite these apparent conflicts, the obvious appeal of McDonald's to many is that it offers cheap food, quick service, and instrumental modes of obtaining it.

McDonald's tries to ritualize the experience. A key ritual is the greeting, "Welcome to McDonald's. How may I serve you?" as if it were a home, not a restaurant. Ironically, choice and "having it your way" are extremely limited. Have you ever attempted to order a Big Mac without sauce? You wait—perhaps as punishment for interrupting the system. Or you may be informed that you must accept it as is. This does not mimic the indulgent mother who cooks for 10 years without onions to please a family member. The identification of food with mother, comfort, and love is implicit, even though the meals are not served by motherly people, but by a diverse lot of mostly young teenagers.

McDonald's efficient and democratic servers learn their trade at "Hamburger U." They learn the theory and practice of standardized food production, including such elements as the size of bag required for a given number of items, the ritual greeting, proper hygiene and attire, and the execution of snappy service. The best learners are inculcated with management skills and will acquire the nuances of supervising production. McDonald's promotes from within.

However, this apparent egalitarianism does not always work. Sometimes, the interactive effects among race, sex, age, and ethnicity of the servers, management, and customers can result in frustration and passive aggressive behaviors. Waiting 20 minutes for a Big Mac is considerably more annoying than a similar wait for cherries jubilee. One informant of ours recounted a McDonald's visit on an Ohio turnpike. The "management" was a Caucasian female; most of the employees were young Afro-American males. The entire crew claimed to be "on break," and was totally unresponsive to the manager's instructions and virtually ignored the milling and irritated customers.

McDonald's as a Dramatic Production

Impression management is essential to modern business success. Erving Goffman (1959) has alerted us to the importance of fronts, strategies, and impression management with reference to individuals, but organizations also manage impressions. The costumes and props of McDonald's have become more complex, elaborated, and expensive over time. The original "restaurant" was a small, boxy "drive-in" with two or three employees and no seating. This differed from the typical drive-in, which offered personalized curb service and delivery at the car. The primary innovation was the speed of service. This change in service, in reality extremely depersonalizing, required the customer to wait in line at a window with a tray, carry his or her own food to a table, and neatly clean the table and dispose of all trash at the completion of the meal. This was touted as an advance because it was *fast* (or faster).

As the organizational chart became more elaborate, so did the dramatic production of the McDonald's Corporation. Cast and setting were dramatically transformed! Indoor seating, increased menu items, fancy and colorful uniforms, drive-through windows, buildings with historical themes, children's accoutrements (highchairs, bibs, diaper changing areas), the cast of Ronald McDonald and Friends, attached indoor and outdoor playgrounds, and large, gleaming restrooms symbolized the new meaning attached to a McDonald's visit. These simple and powerful organizational signifieds become unconsciously combined with complex and sometimes conflicting personal associations.

These changes are indicative of semiosis, the changing meaning of the McDonald's sign production apparatus over time. Transformations in menu items, building form, seating arrangements, bathroom facilities, and the standardized cheerful affect of the employees are reactive to societal shifts as well as to changes in individual "taste." The continued worldwide growth and profitability of the organization testify to management's ability to "read" and manipulate the audience.

In this semiotic discourse analysis, ethnographic materials illuminate the signification process. A theme here is the complex interplay of private, experiential, and personal signifieds with public and organizationally constructed signifieds. This symbolic "struggle" is a function of the organizationally generated meanings, the elaborate and methodical cultural production of McDonald's, as well as personal meanings.

McDonald's is an example of an organizational culture that strategically facilitates management's aims: making profits and pleasing customers (Peters & Waterman, 1982). As we have attempted to show here, McDonald's is a brilliantly conceived dramatic production well designed to confuse. It manipulates people's sense of front- and backstage areas, public and private spaces, home and business, and instrumental and expressive aspects of food and eating, and subtly markets the creation and consumption of experience. As in the case of Disneyland, the fundamental purpose is to market experience at a profit (Van Maanen, 1992). The symbolizations employed by McDonald's serve to suppress and delay personal and group meanings contrary to the business purposes of the corporation and to elevate the connotations of "fun eating."

◆ Conclusion

We have argued that although documents have long occupied an important role in the social sciences, the perspectives within which they are viewed as data have changed significantly. The quest changed from the reconstruction of personal experience to the epistemology and production of a text. Content and narrative analysis struggle continuously with the problem of context or the embeddedness of a text or story within personal or group experience. Semiotics seizes on signs and how they mean, obviating the question of experience, the self, and much of the Western attitude toward literature and the social sciences. Emphasis shifts to codes, paradigms, and explanations for the ordered meaning of a text, rather than the character, biography, or intent of the writer or subject of the writing. We have also provided a brief example of semiotic discourse analysis, using the McDonald's menu and the McDonald's experience as topics.

It would appear that these points are consistent with the drift of postmodernist thinking. McDonald's exemplifies the postmodern idea of "floating signifiers," contents arbitrarily linked to expressions, and the generation of desire by sign manipulation (Baudrillard, 1979). Once the aim is selling experience, even the connotation or suggestion of desirability produced by associations with a signifier is a powerful tool. McDonald's is a vast enactment of commodified experience, and it is a "text to be read." Thus the humanistic concerns of the social sciences return, awkwardly, in the analysis of the structural sources of the production of experience and the simulation of culture.

◆ Notes

1. In psychology, for example, texts were analyzed with a combination of projective tests, clinical analyses, and more precise modes of assessing the content of written docu-

ments. Psychology essentially abandoned what Robert White (1963), following Henry A. Murray, called "the study of lives," autobiographical materials, history, and even the self as a fundamental concept (Gergen, 1991; Potter & Wetherell, 1987).

2. Some of these ideas are modified from Green (1993, p. 3, Table 1.1). *Semiotics* takes as its fundamental unit the sign and studies the types of coherence among signs and sign systems. Its pragmatic dimensions concern how signs are used and what they mean in context. Related areas of study (see Eco, 1979) are sign production (how new signs are developed), a theory of codes (how signs are understood as messages and the underlying principles organizing a given sign system), and signification and communication (the structure of information conveying systems and S-codes, or a system of elements that can be linked to others to communicate, e.g., information theory, physics, mathematics). *Speech act theory,* which is not discussed here, as it is not a textual analysis or production methodology, uses the "utterance" or speech act as a key unit, and studies language performance, the social organization of speech acts, and meaning as related to the cultural and social context in which they are uttered. *Textual analysis* uses sentences and larger fragments of texts as units of analysis, and studies the interaction between textual forms and genres and audience reactions or responses produced. Although heavily influenced by computer-generated content analysis, the original purpose was interpretation of the hermeneutics of texts. *Discourse analysis* takes as its unit longer segments of texts or rhetoric, oscillating between the structure of the argument to the impact or meaning of it.

3. All of our examples are "arbitrary," or based on cultural knowledge. C. S. Peirce (1931) argues that what we call sign-referent links are of three kinds: (a) iconic, based on the mode of representation; (b) indexical, based on natural or causal relations between expression and content; and (c) arbitrary, based on cultural knowledge. Eco (1979, p. 178) argues, and we agree, that Peirce's tripartite distinctions are based on the assumption that the "real" character of content can be known.

4. Our fieldwork was done previously. We refined our analytic focus and modes of data gathering and reduction. The fieldwork reported here, substantiated by some 40 years of McDonald's dining, was executed in two McDonald's in East Lansing, Michigan, on May 29-June 1, 1993.

5. Among the national organizations in this field are Arby's, Burger King, McDonald's, and Wendy's (see Feinstein, 1989). The "fast-food" field contrasts with other forms of restaurant dining. It is indicated by a brief, limited public menu, shown above the server as an overhead lighted display at the front of every store, uncomfortable seats, food dispensed at a counter (no table service), optional take-out service, and preprepared standardized food. The server, cashier, and cleaner roles are interchangeable. Customers dispose of their rubbish when finished, sharing the task with young workers.

6. Space does not permit a more detailed analysis of the coding of particular food and drink items using two oppositions to organize them (Lévi-Strauss, 1969): the raw versus the cooked, and hot and cold.

7. Another friend has a terrible fear of clowns and had recurrent childhood nightmares involving villainous clowns. As Ronald McDonald, a clown, is the personal representative of the corporation, and his frightening visage is omnipresent in the media and at the restaurant, our friend fears McDonald's. The prospect of a combination of a circus and a trip to McDonald's is enough to send him off the deep end. Similarly, many children of divorced families are taken to McDonald's because of chaos during the breakup of the

269

household and subsequently by their fathers during visitation. These children might also have very negative feelings about fast-food chains.

◆ References

Agar, M. (1990). Text and fieldwork: Exploring the excluded middle. In J. Van Maanen (Ed.), The presentation of ethnographic research [Special issue]. *Journal of Contemporary Ethnography, 19,* 73-88.

Altheide, D. L. (1993). *News as advertisement.* Unpublished manuscript, Arizona State University.

Atkinson, P. A. (1990). *The ethnographic imagination: Textual constructions of reality.* London: Routledge.

Atkinson, P. A. (1992). *Understanding ethnographic texts.* Newbury Park, CA: Sage.

Barley, S. (1983). Semiotics and the study of occupational and organizational cultures. *Administrative Science Quarterly, 28,* 393-413.

Barthes, R. (1967). *Elements of semiology and writing degree zero.* Boston: Beacon.

Barthes, R. (1972). *Mythologies* (A. Lavers, Trans.). New York: Hill & Wang.

Barthes, R. (1975a). *The pleasure of the text* (R. Miller, Trans.). New York: Hill & Wang.

Barthes, R. (1975b). *S/Z.* London: Jonathan Cape.

Baudrillard, J. (1979). *Seduction.* New York: St. Martin's.

Bennett, W. L., & Feldman, M. (1986). *Reconstructing reality in the courtroom.* New Brunswick, NJ: Rutgers University Press.

Berelson, B. (1952). *Content analysis in communication research.* Glencoe, IL: Free Press.

Blumer, H. (1939). *Critiques of research in the social sciences* (Vol. 1) (Bulletin 44). New York: Social Science Research Council.

Blumer, H. (1969). *Symbolic interactionism: Perspective and method.* Englewood Cliffs, NJ: Prentice Hall.

Boje, D. (1991). The story telling organization: A study of story performance in an office supply firm. *Administrative Science Quarterly, 36,* 106-126.

Borgmann, A. (1992). *Crossing the postmodern divide.* Chicago: University of Chicago Press.

Bourdieu, P. (1977). *Outline of a theory of practice.* Cambridge: Cambridge University Press.

Brody, H. (1987). *Stories of sickness.* New Haven, CT: Yale University Press.

Brown, R. H. (1987). *Society as text.* Chicago: University of Chicago Press.

Brown, R. H. (1989). *Social science as civic discourse.* Chicago: University of Chicago Press.

Brown, R. H. (1992). *Writing the social text.* Hawthorne, NY: Aldine.

Burke, K. (1966). *A rhetoric of motives and a grammar of motives.* Cleveland: World.

Cicourel, A. (1973). *Cognitive sociology.* New York: Free Press.

Cicourel, A. (1982). Language and belief in a medical setting. In H. Brynes (Ed.), *Contemporary perceptions of language: Interdisciplinary dimensions* (pp. 48-78). Washington, DC: Georgetown University Press.

Cicourel, A. (1985). Text and discourse. *Annual Review of Anthropology, 14,* 159-185.

Cicourel, A. (1986). Social measurement as the creation of expert systems. In D. Fiske & R. A. Schweder (Eds.), *Metatheory in social science* (pp. 246-270). Chicago: University of Chicago Press.

Clifford, J. (1988). *The predicament of culture: Twentieth-century ethnography, literature, and art.* Cambridge, MA: Harvard University Press.

Clifford, J., & Marcus, G. E. (Eds.). (1986). *Writing culture: The poetics and politics of ethnography.* Berkeley: University of California Press.

Crapanzano, V. (1980). *Tuhami: Portrait of a Moroccan.* Chicago: University of Chicago Press.

Coles, R. (1989). *The call of stories.* Boston: Houghton Mifflin.

Culler, J. (1975). *Structuralist poetics.* Ithaca, NY: Cornell University Press.

Culler, J. (1977). *Ferdinand de Saussure.* Harmondsworth: Penguin.

Cullum-Swan, B. (1989). *Behavior in pubic places: A frame analysis of gynecological exams.* Unpublished master's thesis, Michigan State University, Department of Sociology.

Denzin, N. K. (1986). Postmodern social theory. *Sociological Theory, 4,* 194-204.

Denzin, N. K. (1989). *The research act* (3rd ed.). Englewood Cliffs, NJ: Prentice Hall.

Derrida, J. (1976). *On grammatology* (G. C. Spivak, Trans.). Baltimore: Johns Hopkins University Press.

Descombes, V. (1980). *Modern French philosophy.* Cambridge: Cambridge University Press.

Duncan, H. D. (1962). *Communication and social order.* Totowa, NJ: Bedminster.

Duncan, H. D. (1968). *Symbols in society.* New York: Oxford University Press.

Duncan, H. D. (1969). *Symbols and social theory.* New York: Oxford University Press.

Durkheim, E. (1951). *Suicide.* Glencoe, IL: Free Press.

Dwyer, K. (1982). *Moroccan dialogue: Anthropology in question.* Baltimore: Johns Hopkins University Press.

Eco, U. (1979). *A theory of semiotics.* Bloomington: Indiana University Press.

Edelman, M. (1966). *The symbolic uses of politics.* Urbana: University of Illinois Press.

Edelman, M. (1977). *Political language.* New York: Academic Press.

Edelman, M. (1992). *Constructing the political spectacle.* Chicago: University of Chicago Press.

Feinstein, J. (1989). *Dining out.* New York: New York University Press.

Foucault, M. (1973). *The order of things: An archaeology of the human sciences.* New York: Vintage.

Foucault, M. (1978). *A history of sexuality.* New York: Pantheon.

Geertz, C. (1988). *Works and lives: The anthropologist as author.* Stanford, CA: Stanford University Press.

Gergen, K. J. (1991). *The saturated self: Dilemmas of identity in contemporary life.* New York: Basic Books.

Giddens, A. (1984). *The constitution of society: Outline of the theory of structuration.* Berkeley: University of California Press.

Goffman, E. (1959). *The presentation of self in everyday life.* Garden City, NY: Doubleday.

Gottschalk, L., Kluckhohn, C., & Angell, R. C. (1945). *The use of personal documents in history, anthropology and sociology* (Bulletin 53). New York: Social Science Research Council.

Green, B. S. (1993). *Gerontology and the construction of old age.* Hawthorne, NY: Aldine.

Griemas, A. J. (1966). *Structural semiotics.* Lincoln: University of Nebraska Press.

Guiraud, P. (1975). *Semiology.* London: Routledge & Kegan Paul.

Gusfield, J. (1966). *Symbolic crusade.* Urbana: University of Illinois Press.

Gusfield, J. (1986). *The culture of public problems.* Chicago: University of Chicago Press.

Gusfield, J. (1989). (Ed.). *Kenneth Burke on symbols and society*. Chicago: University of Chicago Press.

Hawkes, T. (1977). *Semiotics and structuralism*. Berkeley: University of California Press.

Heise, D. (1992). *Ethnograph* (2nd ed.). Chapel Hill: University of North Carolina Press.

Hjemslev, L. (1961). *Prolegomena to a theory of language* (rev. ed.). Madison: University of Wisconsin Press.

Holsti, O. (1969). *Content analysis for social sciences*. Reading, MA: Addison-Wesley.

Jackson, B. (1986). *Semiotics and legal theory*. London: Routledge & Kegan Paul.

Jacobs, J. (1989). *Drunk driving*. Chicago: University of Chicago Press.

Jakobson, R. (1960). Closing statement. In T. Seboek (Ed.), *The uses of language* (pp. 330-377). Cambridge: MIT Press.

Jameson, F. (1972). *The prison house of language*. Princeton, NJ: Princeton University Press.

Kaplan, E. A. (1987). *Rocking around the clock*. London: Methuen.

Kleinman, A. (1988). *The illness narratives*. New York: Basic Books.

Kracauer, S. (1993). The challenge to qualitative content analysis. *Public Opinion Quarterly, 16*, 631-642.

Kristeva, J. (1980). *Desire in language*. New York: Columbia University Press.

Kurzweil, E. (1980). *The age of structuralism*. New York: Columbia University Press.

Lemert, C. (1979a). Language, structure and measurement. *American Journal of Sociology, 84*, 929-957.

Lemert, C. (1979b). Structuralist semiotics. In S. McNall (Ed.), *Theoretical perspectives in sociology* (pp. 96-111). New York: St. Martin's.

Lemert, C. (1981). Reading French sociology. In C. Lemert (Ed.), *French sociology* (pp. 4-32). New York: Columbia University Press.

Lemert, C. (1990). Varieties of French structuralism. In G. Ritzer (Ed.), *Theoretical sociology* (pp. 230-254). New York: Columbia University Press.

Levinson, S. (1983). *Pragmatics*. Cambridge: Cambridge University Press.

Lévi-Strauss, C. (1963). *Structural anthropology*. New York: Basic Books.

Lévi-Strauss, C. (1966). *The savage mind* (2nd ed.). Chicago: University of Chicago Press.

Lévi-Strauss, C. (1969). *The raw and the cooked*. New York: Harper & Row.

Lincoln, B. (1992). *Discourse and the construction of society*. New York: Oxford University Press.

Lotman, Y. (1990). *Universe of the mind: A semiotic theory of culture*. Bloomington: Indiana University Press.

Lowenthal, L. (1962). *Literature, culture and society*. Englewood Cliffs, NJ: Prentice Hall.

MacCannell, D. (1989). *The tourist*. Boston: Schocken. (Original work published 1976)

Martin, J. (1990). Deconstructing organizational taboos. *Organization Science, 1*, 339-359.

Martin, J., Feldman, M. S., Hatch, M. J., & Sitkin, S. (1983). The uniqueness paradox in stories. *Administrative Science Quarterly, 28*, 438-453.

Mead, G. H. (1934). *Mind, self and society: From the standpoint of a social behaviorist*. Chicago: University of Chicago Press.

Merelman, R. (1984). *Making something of ourselves*. Berkeley: University of California Press.

Merelman, R. (1992). *Language, symbols and politics*. Boulder, CO: Westview.

Merton, R. K. (1961). *Social theory and social structure*. New York: Free Press.

Milovanovic, D. (1993). *Postmodern law and discourse*. Liverpool: Deborah Charles.

Mishler, E. (1984). *The discourse of medicine.* Norwood, NJ: Ablex.

Moerman, M. (1988). *Talking culture.* Philadelphia: University of Pennsylvania Press.

Noth, W. (1990). *Handbook of semiotics.* Bloomington: Indiana University Press.

Paget, M. (1988). *The unity of mistakes.* Philadelphia: Temple University Press.

Peirce, C. S. (1931). *Collected papers.* Cambridge, MA: Harvard University Press.

Perinbanayagam, R. (1991). *Discursive acts.* Hawthorne, NY: Aldine.

Peters, T. J., & Waterman, R. H., Jr. (1982). *In search of excellence.* New York: Harper & Row.

Potter, J., & Wetherell, M. (1987). *Discourse and social psychology.* London: Sage.

Propp, V. (1968). *The morphology of the folktale* (2nd ed., rev.). Austin: University of Texas Press.

Riessman, C. (1993). *Narrative analysis.* Newbury Park, CA: Sage.

Ritzer, G. (1993). *The McDonaldization of society.* Newbury Park, CA: Pine Forge.

Rose, M. (1990). *The post-modern and the post-industrial.* Cambridge: Cambridge University Press.

Rosenau, P. M. (1992). *Postmodernism and the social sciences.* Princeton, NJ: Princeton University Press.

Rumelhart, D. (1977). Understanding and summarizing brief stories. In D. LaBerge & J. Samuels (Eds.), *Basic processes in reading perception and comprehension* (pp. 265-303). Norwood, NJ: Ablex.

Rumelhart, D., & Norman, D. A. (1981). Analogical processes in learning. In J. R. Anderson (Ed.), *Cognitive skills and their acquisition* (pp. 335-359). Hillsdale, NJ: Lawrence Erlbaum.

Saussure, F. de. (1966). *Course in general linguistics* (C. Bally & A. Sechehaye, Eds.; W. Baskin, Trans.). New York: McGraw-Hill. (Original work published 1915)

Stoller, P. (1992). *The taste of ethnographic things.* Philadelphia: University of Pennsylvania Press.

Stone, P. J., Dunphy, D., & Kirsch, J. (1967). *The General Enquirer.* Cambridge: Harvard University Press.

Sturrock, J. (1979). *Structuralism and since.* London: Open University Press.

Thomas, W. I., & Znaniecki, F. (1918). *The Polish peasant* (Vols. 1-2). Chicago: University of Chicago Press.

Tyler, S. A. (1987). *The unspeakable: Discourse, dialogue, and rhetoric in the postmodern world.* Madison: University of Wisconsin Press.

Van Maanen, J. (1988). *Tales of the field: On writing ethnography.* Chicago: University of Chicago Press.

Van Maanen, J. (1992). Displacing Disney: Some notes on the flow of culture. *Qualitative Sociology, 15,* 31-45.

White, H. (1978). *Topics of discourse.* Baltimore: Johns Hopkins University Press.

White, R. (1963). *The study of lives.* New York: Atherton.

Wolfe, T. (1979). *The right stuff.* New York: Farrar, Strauss & Giroux.

PART II

◆ The Art of Interpretation, Evaluation, and Presentation

In conventional terms, the following section signals the terminal phase of qualitative inquiry. The researcher and evaluator now assesses, analyses, and interprets the empirical materials that have been collected. This process, conventionally conceived, implements a set of analytic procedures that produces interpretations, which are then integrated into a theory, or put forward as a set of policy recommendations. The resulting interpretations are assessed in terms of a set of criteria from the positivist or postpositivist tradition, including validity, reliability, and objectivity. Those that stand up to scrutiny are put forward as the findings of the study.

Part II explores the art and politics of interpretation and evaluation, arguing that the processes of analysis, evaluation, and interpretation are neither terminal nor mechanical. They are always ongoing, emergent, unpredictable, and unfinished. They are done through the process of writing, itself an interpretive, personal, and political act. They are like a dance, to invoke the metaphor used by Valerie Janesick in her chapter in Volume 2 of this series.

We begin by assessing a number of criteria that have been traditionally (as well as recently) used to judge the adequacy of qualitative research. These criteria flow from the major paradigms now operating in this field.

◆ Criteria for Evaluating Qualitative Research

There is considerable debate over what constitutes good interpretation in qualitative research (Hammersley, 1992, p. 57). Modifying Hammersley (1992, p. 57), there are four basic positions on this issue. First, there are those who apply the same criteria to qualitative research as are employed in quantitative inquiry. Here there is the belief that one set of criteria should be applied to all scientific research, that is there is nothing special about qualitative research that demands a special set of criteria. As we argued earlier, the positivist and postpositivist paradigms apply four standard criteria to disciplined inquiry: internal validity, external validity, reliability, and objectivity. The use of these criteria, or their variants, is consistent with this first position, which we label *positivist*.

The second position, *postpositivist*, argues that a set of criteria unique to qualitative research needs to be developed. This is so because it represents "an alternative paradigm to quantitative social research" (Hammersley, 1992, p. 57). Although there is considerable disagreement over what these criteria should be, there is agreement that they should be different (see Lincoln & Guba, 1985). In practice, this position has often led to the development of criteria that are in agreement with the postpositivist criteria; they are merely fitted to a naturalistic research context (see, for example, Kirk & Miller, 1986). Hammersley (1992, p. 64) summarizes postpositivist criteria in the following way. Such researchers assess a work in terms of its ability to (a) generate generic/formal theory; (b) be empirically grounded and scientifically credible; (c) produce findings that can be generalized, or transferred to other settings;

and (d) be internally reflexive in terms of taking account of the effects of the researcher and the research strategy on the findings that have been produced.[1]

The *constructivists* offer an important departure from postpositivism. They argue for quality criteria that translate internal and external validity, reliability, and objectivity into trustworthiness and authenticity. These criteria are different from those employed by *critical theorists,* who stress action, praxis, and the historical situatedness of findings. In contrast, *feminist scholarship,* in the three traditions outlined by Olesen (empiricist, standpoint, cultural studies), works, respectively, within the traditional positivist, postpositivist, and postmodern (and poststructural; see below) models of evaluation. Ethnic, critical theory, and cultural studies models of inquiry are similarly so aligned. As one moves from the postpositivist to the postmodern and poststructural positions, increased importance is attached to such antifoundational criteria as emotionality, caring, subjective understanding, dialogic texts, and the formation of long-term, trusting relationships with those studied.

The third position, *postmodernism,* argues that "the character of qualitative research implies that there can be no criteria for judging its products" (Hammersley, 1992, p. 58). This argument contends that the very idea of assessing qualitative research is antithetical to the nature of this research and the world it attempts to study (see Smith, 1984, p. 383). This position doubts all criteria and privileges none, although those who work within it favor criteria like those adopted by some poststructuralists.

The fourth position, *poststructuralism,* contends that an entirely new set of criteria, divorced from the positivist and postpositivist traditions, needs to be constructed. Such criteria would flow from the qualitative project, stressing subjectivity, emotionality, feeling, and other antifoundational factors (see Ellis & Flaherty, 1992, pp. 5-6; Richardson, 1991; Seidman, 1991).

◆ Reflective, Reflexive Ethnography

The above discussion frames the first chapter in this section. Reflective, reflexive ethnography examines the criteria it uses when interpretive, explanatory statements are made. David Altheide and

John Johnson review the recent literature on this topic, including the nonpositivist search for validity. They identify several different perspectives on validity, including validity as culture, ideology, gender, language, relevance, standards, and reflexive accounting. As their referents indicate, these seven positions read validity through lenses that are no longer confined to pure knowledge, or truth claims. Thus validity is seen as a process shaped by culture, ideology, gender, language, and so on.

Altheide and Johnson prefer to conceive of validity as reflexive accounting. They connect this position to a framework they call "analytic realism." This perspective assumes the researcher interprets the world, and this interpretive process rests on an ethnographic ethic. This ethic directs attention to the situated, relational, and textual structures of the ethnographic experience. Researchers are obliged to delineate clearly the interactions that have occurred among themselves, their methodologies, and the settings and actors studied.

Validity-as-reflexive-accounting works from the postpositivist position, as presented by Hammersley. Altheide and Johnson believe that a set of criteria unique to qualitative research needs to be developed. The reflexive spirit of their ethnographic ethic implements the call for internal reflexivity that Hammersley associates with the postpositivist paradigm.

◆ The Art and Politics of Interpretation

Working from the poststructural and postmodern positions, Norman Denzin argues that interpretation is an artful political process. There is no single interpretive truth. Interpretations are narrative, or storied, accounts. Interpretation-as-storytelling may privilege any of a number of different narrative positions. These positions refer back to the major paradigms and interpretive positions discussed above (positivism, postpositivism, constructionism, critical theory, feminism, cultural studies, ethnic models of inquiry). Separate interpretive styles are associated with these traditions, including the theoretical form of the text (substantive, formal, critical) and its narrative structure (essay, experimental, and so on).

Denzin predicts the continued production of more elaborate interpretive epistemologies based on race, class, gender, and ethnicity. Such moves will continue to privilege the personal and the political in the qualitative text. This will increase the importance of such work for social change.

◆ Writing as Inquiry

Writers interpret as they write, so writing is a form of inquiry. Laurel Richardson explores new writing and interpretive styles that flow from what she calls the contemporary or postmodern sensibility. These new forms include narratives of the self, fiction, poetry, drama, performance science, polyvocal texts, responsive readings, aphorisms, comedy and satire, visual presentations, and mixed genres. Richardson then discusses in detail one class of experimental genre, which she calls "evocative representations." Work in this genre includes narratives of the self and ethnographic fictional representations.

A central image in her text is the crystal, which she contrasts to the triangle. Traditional postpositivist research has relied upon triangulation, including the use of multiple methods, as a method of validation. This model implies a fixed point of reference that can be triangulated. Postmodernist, mixed-genre texts do not triangulate. The central image is the crystal, which "combines symmetry and substance with an infinite variety of shapes, substances, transmutations, . . . and angles of approach." Crystals are prisms that reflect and refract, creating ever-changing images and pictures of reality. Crystallization deconstructs the traditional idea of validity, for now there can be no single, or triangulated, truth.

◆ The Practice and Promise of Qualitative Program Evaluation

Program evaluation is, of course, a major site of qualitative research. Evaluators are interpreters. Their texts tell stories. These stories, Jennifer Greene argues, are inherently political. Greene examines this political process in terms of the postpositivist, pragmatic, interpretivist, and critical paradigms. She reviews the work of the major figures in this area, including Guba and Lincoln, Patton, Stake, and Eisner. In her conclusion she calls for more morally engaged evaluation practices that are responsive to the feminist, emancipatory, and critical inquiry traditions. She seeks an explicit political agenda for program evaluation, and finds the means for that agenda in the qualitative research tradition.

◆ Influencing Policy With Qualitative Research

Qualitative researchers can influence social policy, and Ray Rist shows how they do this. He shows how qualitative research has pivotal relevance in each stage of the policy cycle, from problem formulation to the implementation and accountability stages. Qualitative researchers can isolate target populations, show the immediate effects of certain programs on such groups, and isolate the constraints that operate against policy changes in such settings. Unlike others, who relegate qualitative research to a secondary position in this process, Rist's model gives it a central part in the shaping of social policy.

The Greene and Rist texts connect back to applied research traditions. They show how the interpretive, qualitative text can morally empower citizens and shape government policies. At the same time, they chart new lines of action for evaluators who are themselves part of the ruling apparatuses of society (Ryan, 1993). Rist and Greene reclaim a new moral authority for the evaluator. This claim can also empower the qualitative researcher who does not engage in direct program evaluation.

◆ Conclusion

The readings here affirm our position that qualitative research has come of age. Multiple discourses now surround topics that in earlier historical moments were contained within the broad grasp of the positivist and postpositivist perspectives. There are now many ways to write, read, assess, evaluate, and apply qualitative research texts. This complex field invites reflexive appraisal, which is the last topic of this volume.

◆ Note

1. Hammersley's own criteria, as we have previously discussed, collapse this list into two dimensions: credibility and relevance.

◆ References

Ellis, C., & Flaherty, M. G. (1992). An agenda for the interpretation of lived experience. In C. Ellis & M. G. Flaherty (Eds.), *Investigating subjectivity: Research on lived experience* (pp. 1-16). Newbury Park, CA: Sage.

Hammersley, M. (1992). *What's wrong with ethnography? Methodological explorations.* London: Routledge.

Kirk, J., & Miller, M. L. (1986). *Reliability and validity in qualitative research.* Beverly Hills, CA: Sage.

Lincoln, Y. S., & Guba, E. G. (1985). *Naturalistic inquiry.* Beverly Hills, CA: Sage.

Richardson, L. (1991). Postmodern social theory: Representational practices. *Sociological Theory, 9,* 173-179.

Ryan, K. E. (1993, November 5). *Evaluation ethics: Contributions from forms of feminine moral thinking.* Paper presented at the annual meeting of the American Evaluation Association, Dallas.

Seidman, S. (1991). Postmodern anxiety: The politics of epistemology. *Sociological Theory, 9,* 180-190.

Smith, J. K. (1984). The problem of criteria for judging interpretive inquiry. *Educational Evaluation and Policy Analysis, 6,* 379-391.

10

Criteria for Assessing
Interpretive Validity in
Qualitative Research

David L. Altheide & John M. Johnson

◆ Pogo could have had students of ethnography in mind when he stated,
"We has met the enemy, and it is us." After decades of academic and
paradigmatic politics, ethnographic and qualitative research finds itself in
an astonishing position. This is unanticipated by all, especially by those
closest to it, who were for so many decades accustomed to its devalued,
unappreciated, marginal status. There is a remarkable new interest in
ethnographic and qualitative research. It occurs even in disciplines (such
as education, justice studies, clinical work, legal studies, policy analysis)
where the practice is underdeveloped. This growing interest has been
observed by others. Evidence for the trend can be gleaned from many
sources. Yet, as Pogo suggests, students of ethnography have become their
own worst critics, often resurrecting epistemological issues about the
problematics of "objectivity," "purpose of knowledge," and filtering through
new insights about communication contexts, logic, and formats.

Unprecedented criticism of ethnographic or qualitative method, substance, style, practice, and relevance has emerged. The criticism emerges
not from the traditional enemies, the positivists who fault qualitative
research for its failure to meet some or all of the usual positivistic criteria
of truth, but from the insiders to the ethnographic movement. This trend

is consistent with a newer and more extreme "reflexive turn" by ethnographic practice about 20-25 years ago. This reflexive turn has added much to our understanding of how qualitative research is actually done, but has additionally raised hitherto unanticipated dilemmas about representation and legitimation (standpoint or voice). More specifically, important questions have been raised about the role of the ethnographer in the reports produced, the basis for knowledge claims, and how a relativistic perspective in ethnography can produce solid findings.

Our purpose in this chapter is to address some of these dilemmas as we have encountered them in our work, and to offer suggestions for judging ethnographic products. Our purpose of clarifying the domain of meaningful existence poses special problems, as we have abandoned the positivists' formula for objective knowledge. A critical question is, How should interpretive methodologies be judged by readers who share the perspective that *how* knowledge is acquired, organized, and interpreted is relevant to *what* the claims are? Our position is this: As long as we strive to base our claims and interpretations of social life on data of any kind, we must have a logic for assessing and communicating the interactive process through which the investigator acquired the research experience and information. If we are to understand the "detailed means through which human beings engage in meaningful action and create a world of their own or one that is shared with others" (Morgan, 1983, p. 397), we must acknowledge that "insufficient attention has as yet been devoted to evolving criteria for assessing the general quality and rigor of interpretive research" (Morgan, 1983, p. 399).

Our main conceptual vehicle is "validity" and related issues. We set forth a perspective for assessing qualitative research, but our main interest is in establishing some working boundaries for approaching the problem. We examine points raised by a number of thoughtful critiques, particularly some of the more recent writings of "postmodernist" scholars. Following an overview of some alternative views about validity offered by these critics, we set forth a different position on the issue of validity. We suggest some general guidelines for assessing ethnographic research and examine a key issue for grounding alternative plans for this classical approach to social science, establishing a goal/purpose/grounding for an *ethnographic ethic* that can be located within an ecology of knowledge. We then focus on a model of ethnography, *analytic realism,* based on the view that the social world is an interpreted world, not a literal world.

◆ Ethnography in Perspective

For as long as scholars have conducted qualitative or ethnographic research, they have studied the research process. At the turn of the century and in the decades immediately following it, knowledge and insights about the processes and problems of qualitative research were published, but were also communicated orally. In anthropology, Franz Boas and his students orally communicated their vigorous and vibrant ethnographic traditions. Indeed, anthropologists and sociologists, although differing historically in their respective preferences for "exotic/foreign" peoples or "the urban underclass," nevertheless were quite similar in their approaches. In sociology, Robert Park and the many qualitative researchers of the Chicago school communicated their insights and reflections to insiders and neophytes. During the 1960s and 1970s, there was a more pointed critique and analysis of ethnography, *a reflexive turn in qualitative research.*

One meaning of *reflexivity* is that the scientific observer is part and parcel of the setting, context, and culture he or she is trying to understand and represent. After the reflexive turn, increasing numbers of qualitative researchers began to appreciate what this meant for the validity of ethnographic or qualitative research. There was a new appreciation of the older problems and issues in ethnography, as more and more scholars began to realize that the traditional problems of entrée or access to a setting, personal relations with the members in a setting, how field research data were conceived and recorded, and a host of other pragmatic issues had important implications for what a particular observer reported as the "findings" of the research. This growing recognition contributed to a vibrant and creative period of self-criticism and self-reflection among ethnographers.

For the contemporary qualitative researcher who is sensitive to the research process, the past 25 years, in particular, have included many publications that seek to analyze the intimate relationship between the research process and the findings it produces. There are numerous reports dealing with research processes, from "membership roles in fieldwork" (see Adler & Adler, 1987) to "leaving" a research setting (Altheide, 1980). Many ethnographers have addressed these problems of validity and verisimilitude with straightforward honesty and integrity. As a result, we now understand much more about the complexities and nuances of the qualitative research process, and how the resolution of pragmatic research questions bears upon the important issues of validity and field research (see Clifford & Marcus, 1986; Geertz, 1973). John Van Maanen's contribution *Tales of the Field* (1988) reflects an effort to do for sociological ethnographies what the Clifford and Marcus collection *Writing Culture* (1986) has done for anthropological ethnography.

These works and others have led to heated debates about the nature of ethnography, particularly as they are read by younger scholars and others unfamiliar with many of the groundbreaking analyses of reflexivity that were published by symbolic interactionists, ethnomethodologists, and phenomenologists in the 1970s (see Jorgensen, 1989). Included among the more recent issues concerning ethnographic research are *representation*, or the problems of showing the realities of the lived experiences of the observed settings, and *reporting*, or how the language used by a social scientist may necessarily include rhetorical features. Cutting through both are related issues of *interpretation* and *voice*, or whose point of view is taken to report the findings (Snow & Morrill, 1993, p. 8). From this vantage point, ethnographies represent "stories" or narrative "tales" that are told, in part, to fit the genre of storytelling. The problem, then, is that if a different style or genre is selected in giving an ethnographic account, we have a different view or story presented. What, in short, ethnographers are claimed to be doing in such cases is providing a "text," which in turn is read and interpreted by readers or audiences, who, because of their own interpretive and sense-making capacities, will derive their own unique meanings or "readings" of the text.

Taken as a whole, we can say with confidence that these more recent writings have sensitized us to the fact that there is more to ethnography than "what happens in the field." Another important part of it is what takes place "back in the office" when the observer or researcher is "writing it up."

◆ The Quest for an Interpretive Validity

The traditional criteria of methodological adequacy and validity were formulated and essentially "owned" by positivism, the philosophical, theoretical, and methodological perspective that has justified the use of quantitative methods in the social sciences for most of the twentieth century. Promoting the nineteenth-century model of science-as-the-physical-sciences, positivism seeks the development of universalistic laws, whereby actual or real events in the world are explained in a deductive fashion by universal laws that assert definite and unproblematic relationships. Through the use of techniques that produce the numerical data presumed to reflect true measures of objective categories, the positivist opts for sense-directed data, giving the "empirical science" its meaning. The perspective includes the common assertion that "reliability," or the stability of methods and findings, is an indicator of "validity," or the accuracy and truthfulness of the findings.

Ethnographers usually took a different approach. Few doubted that there was a reality that could be known. Most ethnographers focus on the processes that members used in constructing or creating their activities, and how they found or established order in their activities. This focus on what some have termed the "definition of the situation" was oriented to meanings and interpretations of members who lived in specific historical, social, and cultural contexts, and faced numerous practical challenges and limitations. It was on descriptions—including descriptions of language, nuances, and, of course, routines—that ethnographers based their reports. As the anthropologist Laura Nader (1993) comments about a collection of field studies:

> The concept "ethnography" has been gradually reduced in meaning in recent years and in proportion to its popularity. . . . Ethnographic is not ethnography. . . . Anthropologists are less preoccupied with being scientific than are their social science colleagues, more intent on recording and interpreting another people's way of life—ethnography we call it. Ethnography entails deep immersion and is seldom accomplished in short periods of time. It is a special kind of description, not to be confused with qualitative and descriptive studies of another kind. The goal of ethnography, as Malinowski put it, is "to grasp the native's point of view, his relation to life, to realize his vision of his world." Anthropology *is* a feat of empathy and analysis. (p. 7)

A key part of the method, then, is to see firsthand what occurs; failing that, ethnographers would ask informants and others for their recollections, points of view, and interpretations. Although the predictability sought by positivists was not the issue, ethnographers argued that their approach provided knowledge as understanding, rather than control. Even though ethnographers realized that the contextual and often emergent nature of their work made precision beyond a reasonable expectation impractical, they wrote—and spoke—authoritatively about their accounts before sympathetic audiences.

The nature of these contexts, goals, and perspectives, and the nature of relevant audiences have been questioned in recent years. The social fact of ethnography is that it is conducted by human beings who witness numerous contexts, layered one upon—and through—the other. Time, purpose, approach, language, styles, and loyalties are all implicated. A small but growing number of critics argue, therefore, that the essential reflexive character of all ethnographic accounts renders them not only "nonobjective" but partisan, partial, incomplete, and inextricably bound to the contexts and rationales of the researcher, contexts he or she may represent (albeit unknowingly) and the rhetorical genres through which the flawed ethnographic reports are manifested and held forth.

Positivism answered the validity question in terms of reliability: Reliable (repeatable, generalizable) methods and findings were valid ones. The current widespread awareness of the social construction of reality, the confusion in coming to grips with "reflexivity," has ironically led to a radical antifunctionalist position. This stance claims that knowledge, even the knowledge process, is without grounding, without authority, and therefore, many things "go." That is, "knowledge" itself is no loner the criterion, because all "knowledge claims" are based on various assumptions. Most critics would agree that an "assumptionless" science is not possible, while they would also maintain that research and inquiry are desirable. What has changed is the purpose of research, and what those standards for assessing the purpose might be. Research is no longer coupled with knowledge, but has been given multiple choices (such as liberation, emancipation, programmatic politics, expressive "art"). Depending on one's choice, research is defined accordingly. For many scientific ethnographers, however, Hammersley's (1992) view remains cogent: "An account is valid or true if it represents accurately those features of the phenomena that it is intended to describe, explain or theorize" (p. 69). For many others, however, this vision of "realism" is no longer compelling.

All knowledge and claims to knowledge are reflexive of the process, assumptions, location, history, and context of knowing and the knower. From this point of view, validity depends on the "interpretive communities," or the audiences—who may be other than researchers and academics— and the goals of the research. Validity will be quite different for different audiences. From another point of view, the one we suggest, a narrower conception of validity is tied more to the researcher/design/academic audience(s).

Different moments in the validity quest/critique have been examined by observers stressing *power,* including culture, ideology, gender, language/text, relevance/advocacy. Numerous writings by students of culture, including those associated with ideologies, including feminism, have sought to identify the unstated grounding and assumptions of validity/knowledge claims. Sharing in more ways than they differ, these points of departure often converge. Central to many of these arguments is that validity should be either abandoned altogether as a viable concept or radically qualified, or "hyphenated." Many of the following depictions have been cast in such phrases as *successor validity, catalytic validity, interrogated validity, transgressive validity, imperial validity, simulacra/ironic validity, situated validity,* and *voluptuous validity* (see Atkinson, 1990, 1992; Eisner & Peshkin, 1990; Guba, 1990; Hammersley, 1990, 1992; Lather, 1993; Wolcott, 1991). The main positions on validity are depicted below.

Validity-as-culture (VAC) is well-known to social science students. A basic claim is that the ethnographer reflects, imposes, reproduces, writes, and then reads his or her cultural point of view for the "others." Point of view is the culprit in validity. The solution entails efforts to include more points of view, including reassessing how researchers view the research mission and the research topic. Atkinson (1992) suggests that ethnographies can be mythologized, "but the sense of class continuities is hardly surprisingly stronger in the British genre than in the American which is more preoccupied with a sense of place" (p. 34).

Validity-as-ideology (VAI) is very similar to VAC, except the focus is on the certain specific cultural features involving social power, legitimacy, and assumptions about social structure, such as subordinate/superordinate.

Validity-as-gender (VAG), like VAC and VAI, focuses on taken-for-granted assumptions made by "competent" researchers in carrying out their conceptual and data collection tasks, including some issues about power and domination in social interaction. One concern is that these asymmetrical aspects of social power may be normalized and further legitimated.

Validity-as-language/text (VAL) resonates with all the validities described above, particularly how cultural categories and views of the world, as implicated in language and, more broadly, "discourse," restrict decisions and choices through how things are framed.

Validity-as-relevance/advocacy (VAR) stresses the utility and "empowerment" of research to benefit and uplift those groups often studied—relatively powerless people, such as the poor, or peasants.

Validity-as-standards (VAS) asserts that the expectation about a distinctive authority for science, or the researchers legitimated by this "mantle of respectability," is itself suspect, and that truth claims are so multiple as to evade single authority or procedure. In the extreme case, science ceases to operate as a desirable model of knowledge, because it is, after all, understanding rather than codified, theoretically integrated information—as knowledge—that is to be preferred.

The hyphenated validities described above are offered as illustrations of the range of attention the "problem of validity" has received. Common to most formulations is an abandonment of any pretense of linkage or adequacy of representations of a life world within a broader context. Rather, the general model seems to be that validity should be relevant and serviceable for some application of knowledge: Is knowledge useful? Does it, for example, liberate, or empower? These, in our view, are useful arguments to clarify issues and to caution researchers, subjects, and readers (audiences) alike. Insofar as they enable audience members to engage in the dialogue of evaluating and reflecting on research reports, this is good. However, there will be no satisfactory view about quality ethnography without a clear statement about validity that goes beyond the researcher's purpose or ideology.

Qualitative research, as many of the chapters in this volume make clear, is carried out in ways that are sensitive to the nature of human and cultural social contexts, and is commonly guided by the ethic to remain loyal or true to the phenomena under study, rather than to any particular set of methodological techniques or principles. Although the positivists' experience is now widely acknowl- edged even by its practitioners to have serious shortcomings in being unable to produce valid results through their quantitatively driven methods, it has been the notion of validity (especially external validity) that has contributed to current "major reconsiderations" by its staunchest supporters. Hammersley (1992) notes some of these relationships in ethnographic research:

> For me, research is a process of inquiry which is collective not individual; and it is geared towards the production of valid and relevant knowledge, rather than to the solution of practical problems. . . . The great value of

research on this model is that it produces knowledge that, on the average, is likely to contain fewer errors than knowledge from any other source. This arises from the role of the research community in checking the results of particular studies, and the fact that it deploys, or should deploy, a more skeptical form of assessment than is typical elsewhere. The orientation to routinely skeptical colleagues is the main distinguishing characteristic of research, as compared with other sorts of inquiry including the sorts of everyday inquiry that we all occasionally engage in as practitioners of one sort or another. (p. 131)

Any attempt to set forth meaningful criteria for assessing the adequacy of qualitative research must begin with a sense of the goals of ethnography. What is ethnography committed to, and what forms might this take? The frame we choose to delineate our perspective on these important topics is an ethical and humanistic one, rather than conventional scientific parameters of idealism or realism. In short, before setting forth "how to assess" ethnography, we prefer to set forth "what we intend by ethnography."

◆ Principles of an Ethnographic Ethic

An ethnographic ethic calls for retaining many long-standing and taken-for-granted canons of ethical ethnography, including the critical commitment to search for the members' understandings, contexts, and so on, of the settings studied. *Validity-as-reflexive-accounting* (VARA) is an alternative perspective to those noted above. It places the researcher, the topic, and the sense-making process in interaction. Works and criteria suggested by Dingwall (1992), Hammersley (1990), Athens (1984), Lincoln and Guba (1985), and Guba (1990) have been particularly helpful. In keeping with the position of analytic realism, based on the view that the social world is an interpreted world, not a literal world, always under symbolic construction (even deconstruction!), the basic idea is that the focus is on the process of the ethnographic work (see Athens, 1984; Dingwall, 1992):

1. the relationship between what is observed (behaviors, rituals, meanings) and the larger cultural, historical, and organizational contexts within which the observations are made (the substance);
2. the relationships among the observer, the observed, and the setting (the observer);

3. the issue of perspective (or point of view), whether the observer's or the members', used to render an interpretation of the ethnographic data (the interpretation);

4. the role of the reader in the final product (the audience); and

5. the issue of representational, rhetorical, or authorial style used by the author(s) to render the description and/or interpretation (the style).

These five dimensions of qualitative research include problematic issues pertaining to validity. Each of these areas includes questions or issues that must be addressed and pragmatically resolved by any particular observer in the course of his or her research. The ethnographic ethic calls for ethnographers to substantiate their interpretations and findings with a reflexive account of themselves and the processes of their research.

Analytic realism is an approach to qualitative data analysis and writing. It is founded on the view that the social world is an interpreted world. It is interpreted by the subjects we study. It is interpreted by the qualitative researcher. It is based on the value of trying to represent faithfully and accurately the social worlds or phenomena studied. Analytic realism rejects the dichotomy of realism/idealism, and other conceptual dualisms, as being incompatible with the nature of lived experience and its interpretation. Like pragmatism, it cuts across conventional questions about ontology, truth, and method, and instead redirects such concerns to the empirical world of lived experience. Analytic realism assumes that the meanings and definitions brought to actual situations are produced through a communication process. As researchers and observers become increasingly aware that the categories and ideas used to describe the empirical (socially constructed) world are also symbols from specific contexts, this too becomes part of the phenomena studied empirically, and incorporated into the research report(s).

Our general approach to evaluating ethnographic work can be stated as follows: The process by which the ethnography occurred must be clearly delineated, including accounts of the interactions among context, researcher, methods, setting, and actors.[1] Hammersley's (1992) notion of "subtle realism" is akin to our analytic realism in terms of the stronger emphasis we put on verifiable knowledge about the interpretive process as a way of knowing:

This subtle realism retains from naive realism the idea that research investigates independent, knowable phenomena. But it breaks with it in denying that we have direct access to those phenomena, in accepting that we must always rely on cultural assumptions, and in denying that our aim is to reproduce social phenomena in some way that is uniquely appropriate to them. Obversely, subtle realism shares with skepticism and relativism a recognition that all knowledge is based on assumptions and purposes and is a human construction, but it rejects these positions' abandonment of the regulative idea of independent and knowable phenomena. Perhaps most important of all, subtle realism is distinct from both naive realism and relativism in its rejection of the notion that knowledge must be defined as beliefs whose validity is known with certainty. (p. 52)

This approach, tied to naturalism, identifies four general criteria of ethnographic quality: plausibility, credibility, relevance, and importance of the topic. Hammersley (1992, p. 62) appears to be more comfortable with the first two, committed to the third as a way of justifying our public response, and quite ambivalent about the fourth, importance. Notwithstanding the political contextuality of each, his explication of scientific—that is, disciplined—research as distinctive from everyday thinking and observing is noteworthy.[2]

Within the province of analytic realism, an ethnographic ethic encompasses these dimensions. Distinct from "ethical ethnography," an ethnographic ethic integrates many of the traditional concerns and perspectives of ethnography with more recent insights gleaned from the reflexive turn noted above, as well as tacit knowledge and reflexive accountability, which we will examine below. Throughout, an ethnographer's commitment is to obtain the members' perspectives on the social reality of the observed setting. Of course, we now know that many settings in modern life have many perspectives and voices, which means that ethnographers should faithfully report this multivocality (or cacophony) and, if possible, show where the author's voice is located in relation to these.

Central to this ethic is the renewed realization that all knowledge is perspectival, so the ethical practice of ethnography demands that the author's perspective be specified. Ever since the Enlightenment, there has been a long-standing ambivalence and tension between "scientific" and "historicist" perspectives (Diamond, 1964; Maquet, 1964), which essentially involves where a given observer puts the decisive weight or emphasis on the contextually particular or more general patterns of a particular observed setting. Many of our most famous ethnographers (including Kroeber, Sapir, Benedict, Mead, and Tyler) have decidedly straddled the fence on this issue, wanting to have both substantive particularity and processual abstraction, and usually concluding with neither. The perspectival nature of knowledge is an obdurate fact of ethnography. The approach of the ethnographic ethic acknowledges this, and provides the reader with an explicit statement about "where the author is coming from," which is the ethnographic version of truth in advertising, an ethical responsibility for those who elect to exercise the social science power and authorial voice. The tension inherent in this problem is useful, inevitable, and provides floating stepping-stones for the creative investigator, not unlike the "science/art" tension celebrated by theoretical physicists.

> In my view, the immediate audience for research must be the research community, even though the ultimate aim is to produce knowledge that is of value to others. Therefore, communications to policy-makers from researchers should draw on multiple studies and on the necessarily always provisional conclusions of the research community about their validity, rather than reporting the outcome of a particular piece of research. (Hammersley, 1992, p. 132)

This audience has special interests, including the necessity of distinguishing data from analysis, a capacity to promote theoretical sampling (e.g., comparisons and contrasts) as well as an accounting of its research design (see Dingwall, 1992).

The classical ethic in ethnography begins and ends with commonsense members of the settings studied, with real persons (not "Man/Woman" in the abstract), which is why many ethnographies are so commonsensically appealing to laypersons and nonethnographic social scientists alike. The goal of an ethnography is understanding, and a corollary assumption is that understanding is ultimately useful, even in some unknown or unknowable sense. But this classical ethic is no longer shared, as the ethical pluralism so evident in the larger society now characterizes scientific practice as well, embodied in the theoretical and paradigmatic specialization of the latter. With the newly legitimated agendas of theory-driven and action-driven ethnography, ethical practice asks a specification of these purposes so that readers and audiences (who no doubt approach such works at this moment in historical time with assumptions and expectations of descriptive realism and externality) will have a more truthful introduction to what they are about to buy.

◆ Research Design, Methods, and Problems

How a researcher accounts for his or her approach to certain aspects of research, including the routine sources of problems, is key for evaluating the work substantively and methodologically. The existing methods literature shows that certain problems are inevitable and unavoidable in the conduct of ethnographic research, problems that inevitably influence the observations, findings, and analyses (see Hammersley & Atkinson, 1983). Any particular observer must achieve some pragmatic resolution of these dilemmas, and his or her research observations and field experiences are thereby influenced in some unknown manner by whatever practical resolution is achieved. Given that the society we seek to study and understand is so complex, pluralistic, and changing, and as so few of us have any personal experience in the wide range of settings we read about in ethnographic reports, one criterion of verisimilitude useful in assessing ethnographic reports is learning about how a given observer resolved the inevitable field problems.

For example, reflexive ethnographies illustrate that each and every setting, without exception, is socially stratified. The stratified hierarchies vary from one setting to another, and the stratification has different consequences in one setting compared with others, but all settings are stratified in some manner, and commonly on the basis of gender, age, race, and/or ethnicity, or social class/education/occupation. Because a setting's stratification will be related to its categories and classification of membership groups and alliances, the personal qualities of a given ethnographer will "fit" or "not fit" somewhere in this schema. The quality and validity of the information thus obtained from ethnographic research will be related to how a given observer met and resolved these issues for the particular setting studied. The problem is, in some manner, inevitable and unavoidable, and cannot be transcended by the ethnographer's heroic diligence or empathic virtue. As we discuss more fully below, claims of full membership or "becoming the phenomenon" do not adequately resolve this dilemma, except perhaps in the most narrowly homogeneous social groups, as in small cults, for example, which are highly exceptional rather than commonplace in contemporary society. Most of the settings of our ethnographic interest are very complex and stratified, with differing and shifting member perspectives, allegiances, and loyalties. For this reason we continue with some criteria for accounting for ourselves, which will then be followed by some notes about accounting for the substantive findings.

◆ Reflexive Accounting for Substance

As we learn more about other significant and essentially invariable dimensions of settings, such as hierarchical organization, these are added. In order to satisfy the basic elements of the ethnographic ethic, the following "generic" topics should be included in ethnographic reports:

- ◆ the contexts: history, physical setting, and environment
- ◆ number of participants, key individuals
- ◆ activities
- ◆ schedules, temporal order
- ◆ division of labor, hierarchies
- ◆ routines and variations
- ◆ significant events and their origins and consequences
- ◆ members' perspectives and meanings
- ◆ social rules and basic patterns of order

These dimensions provide a template for the investigator as well as framework in which a prospective reader of the report can understand what contributes to the *definition of the situation,* its nature, character, origin, and consequences.

Our experience suggests that the subjects of ethnographic studies are invariably temporally and spatially bounded. That the range of activities under investigation occurs in time and space (which becomes a "place" when given a meaning) provides one anchorage, among many others, for penetrating the hermeneutic circle. A key feature of this knowledge, of course, is its incompleteness, its implicit and tacit dimensions. Our subjects always know more than they can tell us, usually even more than they allow us to see; likewise, we often know far more than we can articulate. Even the most ardent social science wordsmiths are at a loss to transform nuances, subtleties, and the sense of the sublime into symbols! For this reason we acknowledge the realm of *tacit knowledge,* the ineffable truths, unutterable partly because they are between meanings and actions, the glue that joins human intentionality to more concretely focused symbols of practice. As we will discuss further below, the key issue is not to capture the informant's voice, but to elucidate the experience that is implicated by the subjects in the context of their activities as they perform them, and as they are understood by the ethnographer. Harper's (1987) explanation of how he used a photographer in a study of a local craftsman illustrates this intersection of meaning:

> The key, I think, is a simple idea that is the base of all ethnography. I want to explain the way Willie has explained to me. I hope to show a small social world that most people would not look at very closely. In the process I want to tell about some of the times between Willie and me, thinking that at the root of all sociology there are people making connections, many like ours. (p. 14)

The ethnographer, of course, would add that what one sees and directly experiences is also important.

◆ Tacit Knowledge and an Ecology of Understanding

Good ethnographies display tacit knowledge. With apologies to William James, Alfred Schutz, and others, we focus on the dimensions of "an ecology of knowing." Contextual, taken-for-granted, tacit knowledge plays a constitutive role in providing meaning. Social life is spatially and temporally ordered through experiences that cannot be reduced to spatial boundaries as numerous forms of communication attempt to do, especially those based on textual and linear metaphors. More specifically, experience is different from words and symbols about those experiences. Words are always poor representations of the temporal and evocative life world. Words and texts are not the primary stuff of the existential moments of most actors in what Schutz (1967) terms the "natural attitude." They are very significant for intellectuals and wordsmiths who claim to represent such experiences. Yet, as those word workers have come to rely on and represent words and other texts for the actual experiences, their procedures of analysis have been reified to stand for the actual experience. Therein lies much of the problem that some have termed the "crisis in representation."

Capturing members' words alone is not enough for ethnography. If it were, ethnographies would be replaced by interviews. Good ethnographies reflect tacit knowledge, the largely unarticulated, contextual understanding that is often manifested in nods, silences, humor, and naughty nuances. This is the most challenging dimension of ethnography, and gets to the core of the members' perspective or, for that matter, the subtleties of membership itself. This is the stuff of ethnography referred to above in the quote from Laura Nader (1993): "Anthropology is a feat of empathy and analysis"

(p. 7). But, without doubting the wisdom of Professor Nader, it is necessary to give an accounting of how we know things, what we regard and treat as empirical materials—the experiences—from which we produce our second (or third) accounts of "what was happening." [3]

One approach to making ourselves more accountable, and thereby sharing our experience and insights more fully with readers, is to locate inquiry within the process and context of actual human experience. Our experience suggests that researchers should accept the inevitability that all statements are reflexive, and that the research act is a social act. Indeed, that is the essential rationale for research approaches grounded in the contexts of experience of the people who are actually involved in their settings and arenas.

The context of experience is our domain. Tacit knowledge exists in that time when action is taken that is not understood, when understanding is offered without articulation, and when conclusions are apprehended without an argument. The nature of meaning and its unfortunate location between language and experience produces an imperfect fit. The issue was cast by William James (and by others, in different terms) as the interplay between the "kernel" of an idea or experience and its "fringe," or the symbolic awareness that helped define borders of an experience as part of others. Thunder, James wrote, is recognized as "contrasting-with-silence." We do not apprehend anything without connecting it to something else, and that "else" turns out to be everything in our life world and its appropriate zones of relevance.

The array of contextual understanding and information is always simultaneously too much and too little for optimum intersubjective understanding. As Schutz argued, we rely on certain routines to connect various finite provinces of meaning to a situation, and mine may not be commensurate with yours. Over time, however, we concede the differences for the purpose at hand, a project of action, and we draw on recipes, typifications, and taken-for-granted understandings and assumptions. These, Schutz taught, constitute the world of the natural attitude, the basic wide-awake orientation of how we engage the world and others.

◆ The Implications of Tacit Knowledge

Words are like weapons that can be used to produce discontinuities in our experience. The equation of meaning and text destroys the ineffable linkages between our raw experiences and their poetic interpretations (see Bauman, 1988). Tacit knowledge includes what actors know, take for granted, and leave unexplicated in specific situations, things that may have been "learned" in some formal or semiformal sense at some earlier time, both substantively and procedurally. Tacit knowledge may also include deep structures from the *emotional memory* of past generations, enabling responses and actions deeply ingrained in human emotional and physical survival. Social scientists share with societal members some or all of these features of tacit knowledge, those aspects of *common sense* that provide the deep rules and deep substantive or cultural background critical for understanding any specific utterance or act. Social scientific analyses not only make use of these commonsense resources, but often analyze them as topics, too.

There are varieties of tacit knowledge, of course. Two general distinctions can be offered between general cultural knowledge and more specific situational and experiential knowledge. Our intent is not simply to list a variety of examples, but rather to suggest some analytic elements of tacit knowledge that may be useful in the current debate about the nature of our subject matter as social observers, or the "knowers," on the one hand, and the subject matter, or the "known," on the other. It is our contention that any claim to treat the subject matter of social science as merely "discursive" or "textual" materials overlooks the subtle and significant role of tacit knowledge. Indeed, we would further suggest that often such errors of omission are made because the observer takes for granted the central role of tacit knowledge that joins him or her to the subject matter. As it is not regarded as problematic, its constitutive role is not considered, and therefore remains outside of the central discourse of analysis, despite its significance for the subject and topic under investigation.

The most critical component of tacit knowledge is what it contributes to the definition of a situation. The temporal and spatial components are clear. For example, is this a new or different situation from the one I was in a moment ago, or is it quite similar? Has this changed? This largely nondiscursive knowledge is employed in an instant and shapes the discourse about a topic or situation that will follow. For example, bureaucratic settings have numerous occasions for what could be termed "bureaucratic tacit knowledge." This includes understandings about written and verbal communications, different accounting schemes and language. Any experienced bureaucratic worker recognizes, for example, that control is communicated in various ways, including the amount of talk one performs in

299

certain settings, such as meetings. Moreover, anyone recognizes that there is a directory of legitimate and illegitimate terminology. For example, within social science departments today, any discussion regarding hiring someone almost never includes an explicit statement that "hiring this person will make us look good to the central administration," or "I will support this hiring decision in order to gain points with my colleagues, whose support I will need soon on another matter." In short, the language is always one of quality and excellence, even though, in numerous instances, faculty members and others who publicly postured one way will admit that the "discussion" was a ruse for another purpose. It is this sense of "other purposes" that directs our sociological gaze to tacit knowledge.

An issue related to tacit knowledge is the problem of communication. By and large, tacit knowledge is nondiscursive, whereas textual and many other symbolic forms of communication are discursive. The problem, then, is how to talk about what is seldom spoken about, and, indeed, one of its features is that it is beyond words, seemingly more basic and pervasive than the spatial configuration of spoken words, and especially written words, allows. More is involved here than simply positing that "to speak of something changes it"; we believe that, but this is a different issue. The issue, again, is how something that operates in existential moments and has a distinctive temporal form can be adequately communicated.

The difficulty with tacit knowledge is that it is not easily compatible with what we term the *bias of communication*. We refer to the more public and shareable communication form and logic. In general, this means that time is replaced by spatial assignment of symbols; space and place come to supersede temporal dimensions of the subject matter. More specifically, communication permits—indeed, demands—that shareable and nonidiosyncratic understandings and meanings be constructed through rules of grammar, syntax, and orderly formats of expression. The communication form, like all formats of communication, makes the invisible visible, reproducible, and memorable. The mechanisms and procedures have their own logic, and press content into its shape. Make no mistake, this process has such an impact on subsequent behavior and communication that it has been heralded as the foundation of the symbolic interaction process, with which we are so familiar. This has implications for how we might assess the appropriateness of the reporting style and approach of an ethnography.

It is the nature of different kinds of experience in everyday affairs that is important for current debates about the relationship between the knower and the known. This nexus between what we know and how we know it forges a critical linkage for the analytic realist seeking to fulfill the ethnographic ethic to turn his or her attention to the nature and criteria for assessing the adequacy of the research process itself. Accordingly, we approach the researcher's activities and perspectives.

◆ Accounting for Ourselves

A key part of the ethnographic ethic is how we account for ourselves. Good ethnographies show the hand of the ethnographer. The effort may not always be successful, but there should be clear "tracks" indicating the attempt has been made. We are in the midst of a rediscovery that social reality is constructed by human agents—even social scientists!—using cultural categories and language in specific situations or contexts of meaning. This interest is indeed welcome, because it gives us license to do yet another elucidation of the "concept of knowing."

There is a distinction to be drawn between interesting, provocative, and insightful accounts of ethnographic research and high-quality ethnographic work. Given our emphasis on the reflexive nature of social life, it will not surprise the reader that we prefer those studies that enable the ethnographic audience to engage the researcher symbolically, and enter through the research window of clarity (and opportunity). Although no one is suggesting a "literal" accounting, our work and that of many others suggests that the more a reader (audience member) can engage in a symbolic dialogue with the author about a host of routinely encountered problems that compromise ethnographic work, the more our confidence increases. Good ethnographies increase our confidence in the findings, interpretations, and accounts offered.

Our collective experience in reading a literature spanning more than 50 years, along with our own work on numerous topics and projects, suggests that there is a minimal set of problem areas likely to be encountered in most studies. We do not offer solutions to the problems we discuss below, but only suggest that these can provide a focus for a broader and more complete account of the reflexive process through which something is understood (Altheide, 1976; Denzin, 1992; Douglas, 1976; Johnson, 1975). Such information enables the reader to engage the study in an interactive process that includes seeking more information, contextualizing findings, and reliving the report as the playing out of the interactions among the researcher, the subjects, and the topic in question.

Suggested items for locating and informing the role of the researcher vis-à-vis the phenomenon include a statement about topics previously delineated in other work (Altheide, 1976, pp. 197ff.):

- entrée—organizational and individual
- approach and self-presentation
- trust and rapport
- the researcher's role and way of fitting in
- mistakes, misconceptions, surprises
- types and varieties of data
- data collection and recording
- data coding and organization
- data demonstration and analytic use
- narrative report

More detailed accounts could be offered as a subset of several of the above. Consider problems of communication with informants: misinformation, evasions, lies, fronts, taken-for-granted meanings, problematic meanings, self-deceptions. We do not claim that attending to the relevance of these issues in a study makes the study more truthful, but only that the truth claims of the researcher can be more systematically assessed by readers who share a concern with the relationship between *what* was observed and *how* it was accomplished.

The idea for the critical reader of an ethnography is to ask whether or not any of the above were likely to have been relevant problems, whether they were explicitly treated as problematic by the researcher, and, if so, how they were addressed, resolved, compromised, avoided, and so forth. Because these dimensions of ethnographic research are so pervasive and important for obtaining truthful accounts, they should be implicitly or explicitly addressed in the report. Drawing on such criteria enables the ethnographic reader to approach the ethnography interactively and critically, and to ask, What was done, and how was it done? What are the likely and foreseen consequences of the particular research issue, and how were they handled by the researcher? These dimensions represent one range of potential problems likely to be encountered by an ethnographer.

No study avoids all of these problems, although few researchers give reflexive accounts of their research problems and experiences. One major problem is that the phenomenon of interest is commonly multiperspectival; there is usually a multiplicity of modes of meanings, perspectives, and activities, even in one setting. Indeed, this multiplicity is often unknown to many of the official members of the setting. Thus one does not easily "become the phenomenon" in contemporary life. As we strive to make ourselves, our activities, and our claims more accountable, a critical step is to acknowledge our awareness of a process that may actually impede and prevent our adequate understanding of all relevant dimensions of an activity.

◆ Ethnographic Writing

Ethnographic reports reflect some of the criteria the researcher had in mind when the research began. One of our aims in this chapter has been to set forth one distinction based on an ethnographic ethic and grounded in what we term analytic realism. One of the points stressed above is the narrative account, or style, of the report. In a sense, the "type of story" told, as Van Maanen (1988) and others have noted, can essentially "frame" the work and take it over; the content of the ethnographic report may be racing to keep up with the story structure. As Fine and Martin's (1990) analysis of Erving Goffman's classic *Asylums* suggests, humor as a form can show the horrific sadness of everyday routines:

> We read *Asylums* as a political tract, aimed, in part, as unmasking the "fraud" of mental hospitals and psychiatric practice. It does not aim to demean individuals, but it does take on this system and those elements of the outside world that are being convenienced by the existence of the system. The mental institution is functional like the institution of slavery is functional, it makes life easier for some at the expense of others. (p. 110)

Underlying analytic realism is the assertion that the perspectival nature of knowledge is an obdurate fact of all ethnography, and thus an ethical approach acknowledges this and provides the audience with explicit statements about "where the author is coming from." For those who choose to exercise the social science power and authorial voice, this is one of the moral imperatives of ethnographic reportage.

◆ Ethnography as Text: Interpretive Validity

Within the ecology of knowledge, analytic realism acknowledges that how findings are represented is very important for claims making and assessment. The broad issue is "representation" and in what form or genre the ethnographic report is presented—for example, in a "realist" tale, "confessional" tale, or "impressionist" tale (Van Maanen, 1988). It is also important to note, as Dingwall (1992) advises, that there is a clear distinction apparent in the text between the data or materials and the analysis. The nature and process by which communication is organized is central to how ethnography is produced as a document. Fortunately, previous work (see Altheide, 1985; Altheide & Snow, 1979, 1991) in the area of *media logic* and especially the nature and use of *formats,* or how experience is defined, recognized, organized, selected, and presented, helps us anticipate many of the problems that have been noticed in recent years by postmodern writers and others.

Postmodern critics, apparently in agreement with some of the literature noted above, observe that the most critical feature of representations (e.g., reports, data) are their logics, metanarratives by which they are presented as though derived independent of a researcher's context, rhetoric, discipline, and narrative style. This, of course, is an issue of format. What many of the changes in representation essentially amount to are different formats. One of the recent students of ethnographic writing to notice this is Paul Atkinson, whose *Understanding Ethnographic Texts* (1992) cleverly applies many of the arguments presented above about formats of ethnographic writing. After noting that "society is not a kind of text" and that "textual formats make the social world reliable" (p. 11), Atkinson writes about how postmodern ethnographic accounts challenge conventional formats for order, representation, and integration:

> The standard literary formats of academic monographs (chapters, sub-headings, titles, indexes, etc.) are also arbitrary forms of classification and codification. . . . Postmodern tendencies replace the familiar formats of realist writing with a range of different types. (p. 14)

After noting that some ethnographic accounts, such as M. J. Mulkay's *The Word and the World: Explorations in the Form of Sociological Analysis* (1985), are presented through one-act plays and giving the book its own "voice," Atkinson nevertheless urges caution, advising researchers not to go to extremes. Implicit in his insights is the critical point that we can say something narratively only through metanarratives, and these are, essentially, formats. Even though postmodern writers often aspire to be "evocative," they do so by implicitly being representational (e.g., people have to have some idea about a common referent to participate in irony): "From the point of view of the extreme 'textualist,' ethnographic writing refers to itself and to other texts. It does not report a social world that is independent of its textual representations" (p. 51). Atkinson (1992) then adds, "But we should not and need not therefore assume that they have no capacity to represent and reveal aspects of the social world."

For Atkinson and others, then, formats as metanarratives are important to identify in our efforts to "unpack" ethnography, but it is neither intellectually cogent nor practical to suggest that "all is text."

It would therefore be quite wrong for a reader of this book to leave it with the view that there is "nothing beyond the text." Such a view capitulates the mistaken separation of Science and Rhetoric. It was wrong to celebrate science and ignore rhetoric. It is equally wrong simply to reverse the emphasis. Scholarship is rhetorical in the sense that its arguments are shaped, illustrated, and explained to audiences of readers. Its practitioners must use the methods of representation that are to hand. But that is not a dispensation for irresponsibility. On the contrary, just as the researcher must take responsibility for theoretical and methodological decisions, so textual or representational decisions must be made responsibly. We do not have perfect theoretical and epistemological foundations; we do not have perfect methods for data collection; we do not have perfect or transparent modes of representation. We work in the knowledge of our limited resources. But we do not have to abandon the attempt to produce the disciplined accounts of the world that are coherent, methodical, and sensible. (Atkinson, 1992, p. 51)

Analytic realism acknowledges that the anticipation of reporting (and even narrative frameworks) can inform what it is one "grasps" in a setting, and "how" that is to be done. The ethnographer is not committed to "any old story," but wants to provide an account that communicates with the reader the truth about the setting and situation, as the ethnographer has come to understand it. For the ethnographer, the notion of validity does count, although it is acknowledged that other researchers at different times may come away with different interpretations. However, not all observations and interpretations will be equally problematic; any ethnographer will be able to identify those features of the setting that became a conceptual grounding for the work, such as perhaps some physical settings, demographic foundations, or scheduling of particular activities. Given these considerations, and prior to more detailed discussion about the problem areas of ethnographic work, some discussion about related dimensions of validity may be helpful, particularly sorting out the relationship between what we find and how we report it.

Another important problem has less to do with avowed similarities and differences between social science and literature, and that is the distinction between the writer and the audience. All accounts are produced with some audience in mind. (A writer cannot neatly be separated from "the audience" because he or she was an audience member before becoming a writer.) Thus, in a sense, every writer presumes some version of a "generalized other" for whom the account is intended. However, elementary social psychological research has confirmed what the Scottish moralists and others have argued quite eloquently: Because perception is active and thereby contributes to any experience, everyone may see and interpret things a bit differently. In terms of reading, this means that each reader will bring a context of meaning and interpretation to an account, or text, and will interpret it accordingly. This interpretation or "reading" may or may not be commensurate with what the writer intended. In this regard, the social scientist is no different from the novelist. Both produce texts for others to interpret and re-create. The upshot is that social scientists are also claims makers and "tellers of stories," albeit of a different sort. We insist that what separates ethnographers from the others is not so much the objective truth of what is being stated as it is the *process* or *way of knowing*. We should continue to be concerned with producing texts that explicate *how* we claim to know *what* we know. It is precisely the difficulty of intersubjective understanding that demands that social scientists as claims makers be clear and precise in delineating the basis for their claims.

Cultural messages are made meaningful within situations of use. A valid interpretation of text without a context is impossible. Symbols and their meanings are interpretive and relational. Although few would deny this claim, there does seem to be some clear disagreement about the notion of relational, in terms of what, extent, and significance. For example, any account of the "meaning of *Dallas*" or some other cultural product, whether a TV show, an icon, a commercial advertisement, or something else, without some general location of a point of reference is interesting, but always incorrect. If any such interpretation strikes a chord in us it is because we can locate it within our own experience. To make general claims without knowing how the message was produced or, probably more significantly, how the audience member was situated to interpret it, is to make a gross, but interesting and often provocative, error.

It is the context that provides for interpretive meaning. Good sociological accounts point out the multiplicity of meanings and perspectives, and the rationality of these perspectives, by setting forth the context(s). This is not obvious, particularly when more and more scholars are taking it for granted—indeed, insisting—that text can be "read" through a set of interpretive procedures and decoding books, usually produced in the confines of academic offices or libraries. But we do not want to imply that one cannot generalize beyond situations. Rather, there is a more fundamental point that should not be misunderstood: Meaning is put together and packaged, as it were, through nonverbal, usually nonlinear, and "invisible" features of context, often commonsensically referred to as tone, emotion, history, or experience.

Understanding context is important for intelligibility and comprehension. The significance of context for interpretation and understanding, and the inevitability of reflexivity for all sense making, offers ethnography an additional resource for its authority. Field-workers place themselves in the contexts of experience in order to permit the reflexivity process to work. Experienced ethnographers, then, do not avoid reflexivity; they embrace it. A good example is Manning's (1987) study of police call codes. Although Manning does a sophisticated analysis of what certain codes reflexively index, it is only his in-depth awareness of the police and organizational culture that provides the knowledge for the meaning of the message. He knows the work, the language, and the situations, typical, routine, and unique. As he clearly acknowledges, he could not have rendered a valid sociological account without this awareness.

The general impact of the bias of communication is to disqualify anything that does not meet the requirements of the communication logic. There are numerous other communication logics that are less discursive, more private, and encoded as symbols within symbols. As Schutz and others have argued, intimates, especially lovers, have this unspeakable, nonpublic, and seemingly "electric" awareness of feeling and mood—all without a spoken word, even without a noticeable symbolic body-language shift. We would simply reiterate that the meanings of things are not always contained in what is communicated in a text, but rather, the context, awareness, and experience as tacit knowledge sets the tone.

The claim that we are all "telling stories" has led many analysts to move away from sociological analyses of topics in favor of looking at how we tell the stories, which, by implication, is more invariant and therefore more significant than the sociological experience of sense making. Moreover, the status of sociology, science, and any sense-making effort comes to stand or fall on the rising epistemic status of storytelling as a form of truth seeking. Although we certainly should reflect on how we make sense of our research experiences, and how we may transform them—indeed, constitute them— through the process of "telling" or "reporting" these experiences, we should not become trapped by sociological logic. For example, although we can analyze sociological accounts through story and narrative forms, it is equally true that we have for years analyzed narrative accounts—stories— through a sociological perspective.

We would like to offer a different slant on the problem of storytelling in order to improve our awareness of tacit knowledge. Our perspective is that we are not compelled to tell stories, but to give accounts of our research experiences and ideas. All accounts are not stories, unless we define them circularly as such. We can, of course, tell stories, realizing that the structure of such accounts may be analyzed through the logic of particular genres that are deemed to encompass our particular "stories." But we can also settle for clear, coherent accounts (reports, vignettes, findings, essays, or the like) that may be open to ambiguity and uncertainty while still making a claim. We should not, in other words, privilege a cultural format of communication—"the story" with capturing and misrepresenting other claims, including those of tacit knowledge.

◆ Conclusion

Reflexive ethnography has taught us much in two decades, and the next decade will undoubtedly offer more. But the lessons to be drawn from its teachings are not unambiguously clear. We have attempted to present some of the key issues and most engaging critiques of ethnography, along with a framework for reformulating validity, interpretive validity, as well as some general principles or rules of thumb for assessing qualitative and particularly ethnographic research. The literature points out, illustrates, and documents the wide range of personal, interpersonal, political, ethical, practical, economic, occupational, and rhetorical influences on scientific problems, research, and products. It is clear that individuals draw different conclusions from all of this, and make different commitments as a result. This is a chaotic but exciting and creative time for ethnography and all of its newly emergent forms. On the one hand, we wish to celebrate this period of creative endeavor and say, "Let a thousand blossoms bloom." On the other hand, our growing wisdom tells us that the new era requires a new skepticism in the reading of ethnographic research. As we have stressed, one is not logically driven to accept solipsism simply because research and reason indicate that "bedrock objectivity" is untenable when human beings driven by meanings and perspective—science—attempt to study systematically the activities and meanings of fellow humans! Nor do we accept the contention of some that the "problem of reflexivity," which has been seriously investigated by social scientists for at least 30 years (and quite longer by philosophers) denies the researcher superior authority over all knowers, even when specific criteria and questions direct inquiry.

Among the key problems to be discussed by ethnographers and all qualitative researchers are issues about ethnographic loyalty and commitment, whether this is to the people/settings we study or the audiences we seek to influence with our reports (e.g., policy makers) or an ideological commitment to "higher goals" ("liberation" of "oppressed" groups, relevance, and so forth). We anticipate additional discussion about issues involving the utility of "discourse analysis," "semiotics," deconstruction, and other methods for analyzing cultural symbols and markers of social life. Perhaps most challenging during the next decade will be careful analyses of the role of new formats for defining, selecting, organizing, and presenting information, as well as their relevance for communicating issues about validity. Will social science audiences, for example, extend poetic readings, one-act plays, and dramatic presentations the same legitimacy as "conventional" formats? These issues and many more now define the ongoing dialogue about ethnography.

The challenge remains to think about the work and how we do it, but, above all, still to do the work of understanding and presenting various life worlds and their important participants. Just as surely as everyday-life participants negotiate and resolve their uncertainties about their own knowledge and criteria of knowing, so, too, can ethnographers reflect on our purpose at hand and celebrate one of our meaningful activities, that of clarifying the nature, context, process, significance, and consequences of the ways in which human beings define their situations.

◆ Notes

1. This position is similar to formulations by other researchers who have pondered the criteria of good ethnography. A few whose insights we have found helpful include Hammersley (1990, 1992), Atkinson (1990, 1992), Dingwall (1992), Athens (1984), and Silverman (1989). However, our position differs in important ways from at least some of the criteria offered by others, such as Guba (1990), who calls for the reports to be meaningful ("demystifying") to the subjects themselves, for the researcher's prior theoretical understandings to be modified, and for the research to start with a realist ontology. Our elements also do not include a criterion of relevance or "importance" because we concur with Hammersley (1992, pp. 119, 124ff.) that the "policy criterion of validity for ethnography" is fraught with problems.

2. This is more significant in view of the claims of many postmodern detractors that all grounds of authority—expert and layperson—are plausible and, in the face of the problematics of validity, equally tenable.

The key difference [between science and everyday claim checking] . . . is that researchers specialise in inquiry, whereas in everyday life inquiry is a minor and subordinate element of other activities. And the other side of this is that the publication of research findings involves a claim to authority; and such publications are often accorded more authority than the judgements of nonresearchers. The justifications seem to me to lie in a form of social organisation that subjects claims to a more severe level of routine validity checking than is common in most other spheres of life and involves sustained attempts to resolve disagreements by debate and further inquiry, rather than by other means. (Hammersley, 1992, p. 62)

Hammersley then adds that all findings must be subject to communal assessment in an effort to resolve disagreements by seeking common grounds of agreement, that scientists must be willing to change their views, and that the scientific community must be inclusive, and open to anyone to participate who is able and willing to operate on the basis of these principles.

3. To do it well may be a gift, but to be able to account for how we did it, and to provide a broken line for others—such as students—to follow, is part of our challenge, and we must attend to the issue. In this sense, we think Snow and Morrill (1993) are correct, that sociologists have been more careful about some of our ethnographic claims, and have done better at "debriefing" our approaches—at least insofar as we put ourselves on the line—than have anthropologists. And it does matter. We need not assume our methods will be completely transparent, but we can at least take steps to cut through the professorial and perspectival haze that can choke future analyses and generations of field-workers as surely as Southern California smog can distort a Pacific vista.

◆ References

Adler, P. A., & Adler, P. (1987). *Membership roles in field research.* Newbury Park, CA: Sage.

Altheide, D. L. (1976). *Creating reality: How TV news distorts events.* Beverly Hills, CA: Sage.

Altheide, D. L. (1980). Leaving the newsroom. In W. B. Shaffir, R. A. Stebbins, & A. Turowetz (Eds.), *Fieldwork experience: Qualitative approaches to social research* (pp. 301-310). New York: St. Martin's.

Altheide, D. L. (1985). *Media power.* Beverly Hills, CA: Sage.

Altheide, D. L., & Snow, R. P. (1979). *Media logic.* Beverly Hills, CA: Sage.

Altheide, D. L., & Snow, R. P. (1991). *Media worlds in the postjournalism era.* Hawthorne, NY: Aldine de Gruyter.

Athens, L. (1984). Scientific criteria for evaluating qualitative studies. In N. K. Denzin (Ed.), *Studies in symbolic interaction* (Vol. 5). Greenwich, CT: JAI.

Atkinson, P. A. (1990). *The ethnographic imagination: Textual constructions of reality.* London: Routledge.

Atkinson, P. A. (1992). *Understanding ethnographic texts.* Newbury Park, CA: Sage.

Bauman, Z. (1988). Is there a postmodern sociology? *Theory, Culture & Society, 5,* 217-238.

Clifford, J., & Marcus, G. E. (Eds.). (1986). *Writing culture: The poetics and politics of ethnography.* Berkeley: University of California Press.

Denzin, N. K. (1992). Whose Cornerville is it, anyway? *Journal of Contemporary Ethnography, 21,* 120-132.

Diamond, S. (1964). The search for the primitive. In S. Diamond, *Man's image in medicine and anthropology* (pp. 27-66). New York: International Universities Press.

Dingwall, R. (1992). "Don't mind him—he's from Barcelona": Qualitative methods in health studies. In J. Daly, I. McDonald, & E. Willis (Eds.), *Researching health care* (pp. 161-174). London: Routledge.

Douglas, J. D. (1976). *Investigative social research.* Beverly Hills, CA: Sage.

Eisner, E. W., & Peshkin, A. (Eds.). (1990). *Qualitative inquiry in education: The continuing debate.* New York: Teachers College Press.

Fine, G. A., & Martin, D. D. (1990). A partisan view: Sarcasm, satire, and irony as voices in Erving Goffman's *Asylums. Journal of Contemporary Ethnography, 19,* 89-115.

Geertz, C. (1973). *The interpretation of cultures: Selected essays.* New York: Basic Books.

Guba, E. G. (1990). Subjectivity and objectivity, In E. W. Eisner & A. Peshkin (Eds.), *Qualitative inquiry in education: The continuing debate* (pp. 74-91). New York: Teachers College Press

Hammersley, M. (1990). *Reading ethnographic research: A critical guide.* London: Longman.

Hammersley, M. (1992). *What's wrong with ethnography? Methodological explorations.* London: Routledge.

Hammersley, M., & Atkinson, P. (1983). *Ethnography: Principles in practice.* London: Tavistock.

Harper, D. (1987). *Working knowledge: Skill and community in a small shop.* Berkeley: University of California Press.

Johnson, J. M. (1975). *Doing field research.* New York: Free Press.

Jorgensen, D. L. (1989). *Participant observation: A methodology for human studies.* Newbury Park, CA: Sage.

Lather, P. (1993). Fertile obsession: Validity after poststructuralism. *Sociological Quarterly, 35.*

Lincoln, Y. S., & Guba, E. G. (1985). *Naturalistic inquiry.* Beverly Hills, CA: Sage.

Manning, P. (1987). *Semiotics and fieldwork.* Newbury Park, CA: Sage.

Maquet, J. J. (1964). Objectivity in anthropology. *Current Anthropology, 5,* 47-55.

Morgan, G. (Ed.). (1983). *Beyond method*. Beverly Hills, CA: Sage.

Mulkay, M. J. (1985). *The word and the world: Explorations in the form of sociological analysis*. London: George Allen & Unwin.

Nader, L. (1993). Paradigm busting and vertical linkage. *Contemporary Sociology, 33*, 6-7.

Richardson, L. (1990). Narrative and sociology. *Journal of Contemporary Ethnography, 19*, 116-135.

Schutz, A. (1967). *The phenomenology of the social world*. Evanston, IL: Northwestern University Press.

Silverman, D. (1989). Six rules of qualitative research: A post-romantic argument. *Symbolic Interaction, 12*, 215-230.

Snow, D. A., & Morill, C. (1993). Reflections on anthropology's ethnographic crisis of faith. *Contemporary Sociology, 22*, 8-11.

Van Maanen, J. (1988). *Tales of the field: On writing ethnography*. Chicago: University of Chicago Press.

Wolcott, H. F. (1990). On seeking—and rejecting—validity in qualitative research. In E. W. Eisner & A. Peshkin (Eds.), *Qualitative inquiry in education: The continuing debate* (pp. 121-152). New York: Teachers College Press.

11

The Art and Politics of Interpretation

Norman K. Denzin

Once upon a time, the Lone Ethnographer rode off into the
sunset in search of his "native." After undergoing a series of
trials, he encountered the object of his quest in a distant land.
There he underwent his rite of passage by enduring the ultimate
ordeal of "fieldwork." After collecting "the data," the Lone
Ethnographer returned home and wrote a "true" account of "the
culture."

—Renato Rosaldo, *Culture and Truth,* 1989

I have been working to change the way I speak and write.

—bell hooks, *Yearning,* 1990

◆ In the social sciences there is only interpretation. Nothing speaks for
itself. Confronted with a mountain of impressions, documents, and
field notes, the qualitative researcher faces the difficult and challenging
task of making sense of what has been learned. I call making sense of what
has been learned *the art of interpretation.* This may also be described as
moving from the field to the text to the reader. The practice of this art

AUTHOR'S NOTE: I would like to thank Mitch Allen, Kenneth Gergen, Meaghan Morris, Laurel
Richardson, Katherine E. Ryan, and Yvonna Lincoln for their comments on earlier versions of this
chapter.

allows the field-worker-as-*bricoleur* (Lévi-Strauss, 1966, p. 17) to translate what has been learned into a body of textual work that communicates these understandings to the reader.

These texts, borrowing from John Van Maanen (1988), constitute tales of the field. They are the stories we tell one another. This is so because interpretation requires the telling of a story, or a narrative that states "things happen this way because" or "this happened, after this happened, because this happened first." Interpreters as storytellers tell narrative tales with beginnings, middles, and ends. These tales always embody implicit and explicit theories of causality, where narrative or textual causality is presumed to map the actual goings-on in the real world (Ricoeur, 1985, p. 4). How this complex art of interpretation and storytelling is practiced is the topic of this chapter.

The history of qualitative research in the social sciences reveals continual attempts to wrestle with this process and its methods. In this chapter I review several of these methods, or traditions, paying special attention to those that have been employed in the most recent past, including the constructivist,[1] grounded theory, feminist, Marxist, cultural studies, and poststructural perspectives.[2] I examine problems generic to this process, and briefly allude to my own perspective, interpretive interactionism (Denzin, 1989). I conclude with predictions concerning where the art and politics of interpretation will be 10 years from now.

◆ **The Interpretive Crisis
   in the Social Sciences**

The following assumptions organize my analysis. First, the social sciences today face a crisis of interpretation, for previously agreed-upon criteria from the positivist and postpositivist traditions are now being challenged (Guba, 1990b, p. 371; Rosaldo, 1989, p. 45). This crisis has been described as poststructural and postmodern, a new sensibility regarding the social text and its claims to authority. Describing this new situation, Richardson (1991) observes, "The core of [this] sensibility is doubt that any discourse has a privileged place, any method or theory a universal and general claim to authoritative knowledge" (p. 173).

Second, each social science community (Fish, 1980) has its own criteria for judging the adequacy of any given interpretive statement. These criteria will be grounded in the canonical texts the community takes to be central to its mission. What works in one community may not work in another. Patricia Hill Collins (1990) contends, for example, that the Eurocentric, masculine positivist epistemology asks African American women to "objectify themselves, devalue their emotional life, displace their motivations for furthering knowledge about Black women, and confront in an adversarial relationship those with more social, economic and professional power" (p. 205).

Third, this crisis can be resolved only from *within* social science communities. It is doubtful that a new set of criteria shared by all points of view will, can, or should be developed. This means that "once the privileged veil of truth is lifted, feminism, Afro-American, gay, and other disparaged discourses rise to the same epistemological status as the dominant discourse" (Richardson, 1991, p. 173).

Fourth, increasingly, the criteria of evaluation will turn, as Richardson notes, on moral, practical, aesthetic, political, and personal issues—the production, that is, of texts that articulate an emancipatory, participative perspective on the human condition and its betterment.

Fifth, as Clough (1992, p. 136) argues, the problems of writing are not different from the problems of method or fieldwork. It is not the case, as some may contend, that the above problems can be answered only through new forms of writing. As Yvonna Lincoln and I argue in Chapter 1 of this volume, these new writing forms function primarily as sources of validation for a reinvigorated empirical science. They direct attention away from the ways in which the experimental text can perpetuate new forms and technologies of knowledge and power that align qualitative research with the state. The insistence that writing and fieldwork are different cannot be allowed (Clough, 1992, p. 136).

The age of a putative value-free social science appears to be over. Accordingly, sixth, any discussion of this process must become political, personal, and experiential. Following John Dewey, I believe that the methods for making sense of experience are always personal. Life and method, as Clandinin and Connelly argue in Chapter 6 of this volume, are inextricably intertwined. One learns about method by thinking about how one makes sense of one's own life. The researcher, as a writer, is a bricoleur. He or she fashions meaning and interpretation out of ongoing experience. As a bricoleur, the researcher uses any tool or method that is readily at hand. I discuss, then, the politics, craft, and art of experience and interpretation.

◆ From Field to Text to Reader

Moving from the field to the text[3] to the reader is a complex, reflexive process. The researcher creates a field text consisting of field notes and documents from the field. From this text he or she creates a research text, notes and interpretations based on the field text, what David Plath (1990) calls "filed notes." The researcher then re-creates the research text as a working interpretive document. This working document contains the writer's initial attempts to make sense out of what has been learned, what Clandinin and Connelly (Chapter 26, this volume) term "experiencing experience." The writer next produces a quasi-public text, one that is shared with colleagues, whose comments and suggestions the writer seeks. The writer than transforms this statement into a public document, which embodies the writer's self-understandings, which are now inscribed in the experiences of those studied.[4] This statement, in turn, furnishes the context for the understandings the reader brings to the experiences being described by the writer. Reading and writing, then, are central to interpretation, for, as Geertz (1973, p. 18) argues, interpretation involves the construction of a reading of an event, both by the writer and by the reader. To paraphrase Geertz, a good interpretation takes us into the center of the experiences being described.

Such interpretations, however, may not take us to the heart of the matter, as these matters are understood in the everyday world. Here is Rosaldo (1989) describing, in anthropological terms, the daily family breakfast at the home of his prospective parents-in-law: "Every morning the reigning patriarch, as if just in from the hunt, shouts from the kitchen, 'How many people would like a poached egg?' Women and children take turns saying yes or no. In the meantime the women talk among themselves and designate one among them the toast maker" (pp. 46-47).

Rosaldo (1989) says of this account, "My rendition of a family breakfast in the ethnographic present transformed a relatively spontaneous event into a generic cultural form. It became a caricatured analysis . . . the reader will probably not be surprised to hear that my potential in-laws laughed and laughed as they listened to the microethnography . . . about their family breakfast" (p. 48). Rosaldo employs terms that Geertz (1983) would call experience-distant, or second order. Terms and phrases such as *reigning patriarch* and *in from the hunt* may work for the anthropologist talking to another anthropologist, but they lack relevance and meaning for Rosaldo's prospective new family.

Interpretation is an art; it is not formulaic or mechanical.[5] It can be learned, like any form of storytelling, only through doing. Indeed, as Laurel Richardson argues in Chapter 12 of this volume, writing is interpretation, or storytelling. Field-workers can neither make sense of nor understand what has been learned until they sit down and write the interpretive text, telling the story first to themselves and then to their significant others, and then to the public.

A situated, writing self structures the interactions that take place among the writer, the text, and the reader. The writer presents a particular and unique self in the text, a self that claims to have some authority over the subject matter that is being interpreted. However, the rules for presenting this self are no longer clear. Krieger (1991) comments: "The challenge lies in what each of us chooses to do when we represent our experiences. Whose rules do we follow? Will we make our own? Do we . . . have the guts to say, 'You may not like it, but here I am'?" (p. 244).

Interpretation as Storytelling

The storytelling self (see Manning & Cullum-Swan, Chapter 9, this volume) that is presented is always one attached to an interpretive perspective, an "espoused theory" (Argyris & Schön, 1974, p. viii) that gives the writer a public persona. Four major paradigms (positivist and postpositivist, constructivist, critical) and three major perspectives (feminist, ethnic models, cultural studies) now structure qualitative writing. The stories qualitative researchers tell one another come from one or another of these paradigms and perspectives.

These paradigms and perspectives serve several functions for the writer. They are masks that are hidden behind, put on, and taken off as writers write their particular storied and self-versions of a feminist, gay-lesbian, Afro-American, Hispanic, Marxist, constructionist, grounded theory, phenomenological, or interactionist text. They give the writer a public identity. These masks direct the writer into specific theoretical and research traditions, what Argyris and Schön (1974) call "theories-in-use" (p. viii). Each tradition has its own taken-for-granted and problematic writing style.

317

These masks offer scenarios that lead writers to impose a particular order on the world studied. For example, if the paradigm is positivist or postpositivist, the writer will present a text that stresses variables, hypotheses, and propositions derived from a particular theory that sees the world in terms of causes and effects (see Guba & Lincoln, 1989, p. 84). Strauss and Corbin (1990) offer a simple example: "Conditions of intense pain will be followed by measures taken to relieve pain" (p. 111). Here antecedent conditions (intense pain) produce subsequent actions (measures to relieve the pain).

If the paradigm is constructivist, the writer will present a text that stresses emergent designs and emergent understandings. An interpretive, or phenomenologically based, text would emphasize socially constructed realities, local generalizations, interpretive resources, stocks of knowledge, intersubjectivity, practical reasoning, and ordinary talk (Holstein & Gubrium, Chapter 6, Volume 2, this series).

A writer working from a feminist standpoint paradigm (see Olesen, Chapter 9, Volume 1, this series) will attempt to tell a situated story stressing gender, reflexivity, emotion, and an action orientation (Fonow & Cook, 1991, p. 2), examining, for example, how "the ideology of the 'single parent' [organizes] multiple sites (parent-teaching contact) in education" (Smith, 1992, p. 97). Similarly, a Marxist or emancipatory text will stress the importance of terms such as *action, structure, culture,* and *power,* which are then fitted into a general model of society (Carspecken & Apple, 1992, p. 513; see also, in Volume 1 of this series, Kincheloe & McLaren, Chapter 8, and Fiske, Chapter 11; and in Volume 2, Reason, Chapter 10).

Writing Issues: Sense Making, Representation, Legitimation, Desire

Any discussion of how the researcher moves from the field to the text must address a host of issues or problems closely related to storytelling traditions. These issues group into four areas. (Each problem works its effects on the field, research, and interpretive texts that lay the foundation for the writer's final, public document.) These problems may be conceptualized as phases, each turning on a different issue, and each turning back on the others, as in Dilthey's (1900/1976) hermeneutic circle. They may be named and called the interpretation, or sense-making, representation, legitimation, and desiring phases of moving from field to text to reader.

They interact with each other as the writer wrestles with them in the field, research, interpretive, and public phases of textual construction.

Sense Making

The first issue concerns how the writer moves from and through field notes into the actual writing process (into the research and interpretive texts), making decisions about what will be written about, what will be included, how it will be represented, and so on. A considerable literature surrounds this process (see Wolcott, 1990, for a review; see also Sanjek, 1990). For example, Strauss and Corbin (1990, p. 197) direct investigators in this field and research text phase to write memos, as well as theoretical, operational, and code notes concerning conceptual labels, paradigm features, emerging theoretical understandings, and visual representations of relationships between concepts and analytic terms. Richardson (Chapter 12, this volume) discusses other forms of anticipatory interpretive writing, including observation, methodological, theoretical, and personal notes that are kept in an ongoing journal.

Representation

The second area speaks to such topics as voice, audience, the "Other," and the author's place in the reflexive texts that are produced (see Geertz, 1988; Krieger, 1991; Richardson, 1990, 1992; Rose, 1990; Van Maanen, 1988; see also Richardson, Chapter 12, this volume). To paraphrase Brady (1991, p. 5), there is more than one way to do representation. Representation, of course, is always self-presentation. That is, the Other's presence is directly connected to the writers' self-presence in the text. The Other who is presented in the text is always a version of the researcher's self. Krieger (1991) argues: "When we discuss others, we are always talking about ourselves. Our images of 'them' are images of 'us' " (p. 5). This can occur poetically, as in Laurel Richardson's (1992) poem "Louisa May's Story of Her Life." Richardson has Louisa May say of herself:

> *I grew up poor in a rented house*
> *in a very normal sort of way*
> *on a very normal sort of street*
> *with some very nice middle-class friends.* (p. 127)

Here Richardson's poetic self poetically presents Louisa May's truncated life story.

Representation turns on voice and the use of pronouns, including first-person statements. Patricia Hill Collins (1990) describes her use of pronouns:

> I often use the pronoun "our" instead of "their" when referring to African-American women, a choice that embeds me in the group I am studying instead of distancing me from it. In addition, I occasionally place my own concrete experience in the text. To support my analysis, I cite few statistics and instead rely on the voices of Black women from all walks of life. (p. 202)

Frequently writers are positioned outside, yet alongside, those Others they write about, never making clear where they stand in these hyphenated relationships (see Fine, Chapter 4, Volume 1, this series) that connect the Other to them. When Others are not allowed to speak, they remain "an absent presence without voice" (hooks, 1990, p. 126). There are major problems with this approach to "Othering," and it has been extensively criticized (Denzin, 1990). In such situations it is best to let Others do their own talking. However, even when "we" allow the Other to speak, when we talk about or for them, we are taking over their voice. A multivoiced as opposed to single-voiced text can partially overcome this issue (see Bakhtin, 1986; also Collins, 1990).

Legitimation

The third problem centers on matters of epistemology, including how a public text legitimates itself, or makes claims for its own authority. Traditional foundationalist topics such as reliability, validity, and generalizability may be encountered here (see Hammersley, 1992; Lather, 1993; see also Altheide & Johnson, Chapter 10, this volume; Lincoln & Denzin, Chapter 13, Volume 1, this series; Stake, Chapter 4, Volume 2, this series). The postmodern sensibility doubts foundational arguments that seek to anchor a text's authority in such terms. A more local, personal, and political turn is taken. On this, Seidman (1991) is informative: "Instead of appealing to absolutist justifications, instead of constructing theoretical logics and epistemic casuistries to justify a conceptual strategy . . . I propose that we be satisfied with local, pragmatic rationales for our conceptual [interpretive] approaches" (p. 136; see also Lather, 1993).

Desire

There is still a fourth problem, or phase, in this project, given in the subtitle to Howard S. Becker's influential 1986 book, *Writing for Social Scientists: How to Start and Finish Your Thesis, Book, or Article.* This problem circles back on the first, making decisions about what will be written. But it goes deeper and refers to the writing practices that field-workers deploy: how one moves from a blank page (or screen) to a written text, one sentence after another, building an emergent, reflexive interpretation of the subject matter at hand (see Richardson, Chapter 12, this volume; also see Becker, 1986; for an interpretation of Becker's strategies, see Clough, 1992, chap. 5). The topic, to borrow Roland Barthes's (1975) phrase, is the pleasure of the text. Or, as Laurel Richardson (Chapter 12, this volume) says, "Can we create texts that are vital?"

A vital text is not boring. It grips the reader (and the writer). A vital text invites readers to engage the author's subject matter. Many qualitative research texts are boring. Writers have been taught to write in a particular style, a style that takes the "omniscient voice of science, the view from everywhere" (Richardson, Chapter 12, this volume). The postmodern sensibility encourages writers to put themselves into their texts, to engage writing as a creative act of discovery and inquiry. However, engaging or boring writing has more to do with the writer than with the paradigm or perspective that is employed.

I turn now to the problems generic to the sense-making, representation, legitimation, and desiring phases of writing. This will involve additional consideration of the relationship between the writer and the text.

◆ Two Models of the Writer

The foregoing discussion has separated, or isolated, four phases of writing. Although analytically useful, this formulation conveys a sometimes heroic, romantic picture of the writer and the text. It presumes a writer with the guts to tell it like it is, to put him- or herself on the line, so to speak. It presumes a socially situated (and isolated), unique writer who has the courage and authenticity to write a bold new text. This writer first experiences, feels, and thinks. Having had the experience, this bold writer then writes, deploying one or more narrative traditions in the story he or she tells.[6]

This model makes writing an expressive, and not a productive, process. It romanticizes the writer and his or her experiences. It distances experience from its expressions. Sense making, interpretation, representation, and claims for legitimacy are all part of the same process. They can be separated only artificially.

Interpretation is a productive process that sets forth the multiple meanings of an event, object, experience, or text. Interpretation is transformative. It illuminates, throws light on experience. It brings out, and refines, as when butter is clarified, the meanings that can be sifted from a text, an object, or a slice of experience. So conceived, meaning is not in a text, nor does interpretation precede experience, or its representation. Meaning, interpretation, and representation are deeply intertwined in one another.

Raymond Carver (1989), the short story writer, describes it this way. Writing is an "act of discovery" (p. 25). The writer deals with moments of experience. The writer brings all of his or her powers, "intelligence and literary skill" (p. 27) to bear on these moments to show how "things out there really are and how he [or she] sees those things—like no one else sees them" (p. 27). This is done "through the use of clear and specific language; language that will bring to life the details that will light up the story for the reader . . . the language must be accurately and precisely given" (p. 27).

Experimental writing, Carver argues, is "original." "The real experimenters have to Make It New . . . and in the process have to find things out for themselves. . . . writers want to carry news from their world to ours" (p. 24). This means that "absolutely everything is important" (p. 38), including where the writer puts the "commas and periods" (p. 38). The writer invests experience with meaning, showing how everything has suddenly become clear. What was unclear before has "just now become clear" (p. 23). Such understandings emerge in moments of sudden awakening. The writer brings this sense of discovery and awakening to the reader.

Writing, then, relives and reinscribes experience, bringing newly discovered meanings to the reader. No cheap tricks, Carver (1989, p. 23) says, no gimmicks. Writing must bring news of the world to the reader. In writing, the writer creates this world. He or she fills it with real and fictional people. Their problems and their crises are brought to life. Their lives gone out of control are vividly described. Their lives, suddenly illuminated with new meanings and new transformation of self, are depicted.

What is given in the text, what is written, is made up and fashioned out of memory and field notes. Writing of this order, writing that powerfully reinscribes and re-creates experience, invests itself with its own power and authority. No one else but this writer could have brought this new corner of the world alive in this way for the reader.

Thus are expressive (romantic) and productive views of writing mutually complementary. The field-worker must be a committed writer, but the stories that are boldly told are those that flow from a commitment not to shock, or brutalize, or alienate the reader (Carver, 1989, p. 24). Experimentation is not an excuse or a "license to be careless, silly or imitative" (p. 24).

◆ The Writing Process

Understanding and mystery are central to the writing project. Carver's writer unravels a mystery, discovering and then understanding what was previously hidden and unclear. He or she cuts to the heart of an experience, disclosing its immediate, as well as deep, symbolic and long-lasting meanings for the people involved. This suggests that the writer accurately describes a hidden or submerged reality that the text brings to light. So conceived, a text establishes its own verisimilitude. It tells the truth. But there are complicated relations among truth, reality, and the text (see also Lincoln & Denzin, Chapter 13, Volume 1, this series). Every writing genre has its own laws of verisimilitude.

For example, verisimilitude is the theme of the murder mystery. "Its law is the antagonism between truth and verisimilitude" (Todorov, 1977, p. 86). In a murder mystery, the murderer must appear to be innocent and the innocent person must be made to appear guilty. "The truth has no verisimilitude, and the verisimilitude has no truth" (Todorov, 1977, p. 86). The end of the narrative must, of course, resolve this tension or contradiction. It must show the apparently innocent person to be guilty, and the apparently guilty party to be innocent. Only in the conclusion to the mystery, as Todorov (1977) notes, do truth and verisimilitude coincide. Thus is truth only and always a "distanced and postponed verisimilitude" (p. 88). Truth is a textual production.

So in the end, clear description, as defined by a genre, provides the basis for interpretation, understanding, and verisimilitude. That is, an event or process can be neither interpreted nor understood until it has been well described. However, the age of "objective" description is over. We are, as Lather (1991, p. 91) argues, in the age of inscription. Writers create their own situated, inscribed versions of the realities they describe.

There is more than one way to do a description-as-an-inscription. Thin description simply states a set of facts (Geertz, 1973, pp. 9-10; Ryle, 1968, pp. 8-9), for example:

> X drank a cup of coffee at 9:30 a.m. on Wednesday February 3 as he e-mailed a message to his editor and co-editor.

Here is a thick description, taken from a Carver short story, "So Much Water So Close to Home" (1989). The action described in this passage sets the context for the nervous breakdown of the woman who narrates the story. Four men have gone to the mountains on a fishing trip.

> They parked the car in the mountains and hiked several miles to where they wanted to fish. They carried their bedrolls, food and cooking utensils, their cards, their whisky. The first evening at the river, even before they could set up camp, Mel Dorn found the girl floating face down in the river; nude, lodged near the shore in some branches. He called the other men and they all came to look at her. They talked about what to do . . . one of them thought they should start back to the car at once. The others stirred the sand with their shoes and said they felt inclined to stay. They pleaded fatigue, the late hour, the fact that the girl 'wasn't going anywhere.' In the end they all decided to stay. (pp. 186-187)

A thin description simply reports facts, independent of intentions or circumstances. A thick description, in contrast, gives the context of an experience, states the intentions and meanings that organized the experience, and reveals the experience as a process. Out of this process arises a text's claims for truth, or its verisimilitude.

Ethnography, Geertz (1973, p. 10) suggests, is thick description, a "written representation of a culture" (Van Maanen, 1988, p. 1). Field-workers inscribe social discourse. They write it down, turning a passing event into something that now exists in its inscriptions (Geertz, 1973, p. 19). What is written down is itself interpretive, for the researcher interprets while writing, attempting in the process to rescue the " 'said' I of such discourse from its perishing occasions and fix it in perusable terms" (Geertz, 1973, p. 20). The intent is to create the conditions that will allow the reader, through the writer, to converse with (and observe) those who have been studied.

Building on what has been described and inscribed, interpretation creates the conditions for authentic, or deep, emotional understanding. Authentic understanding is created when readers are able to live their way into an experience that has been described and interpreted. Return to Rosaldo's (1989) Ilongot headhunters. Early in his research, Rosaldo explained the headhunting ritual with exchange theory. He presented his theory to an older Ilongot man named Insan:

> What did he think, I asked, of the idea that headhunting resulted from the way that one death (the beheaded victim's) canceled another (the next of kin). He looked puzzled, so I went on to say that a victim of a beheading was exchanged for the death of one's own kin. . . . Insan reflected a moment, and replied that he imagined somebody could think such a thing . . . but that he and other Ilongots did not think any such thing. (pp. 3-4)

Fifteen months after his wife Michelle's tragic death in the field, Rosaldo returned to his headhunting materials. There, attempting to deal with his own rage, he found the meaning of the Ilongot ritual, and the rage that headhunting addressed. He states, "Either you understand it or you don't" (pp. 1-2). Unless you have had the experience, you cannot understand it.

Interpretation is done, of course, by an interpreter, or storyteller. There are two types of interpreters: people who have actually experienced what has been described, and those who are often ethnographers, or field-workers, so-called well-informed experts. These two types (local and scientific) of interpreters often give different meanings to the same set of thickly described/inscribed experiences. Local interpreters use experience-near concepts—words and meanings that actually operate in the worlds studied (Geertz, 1983, p. 57). These individuals seek emic, or contextual, situated understandings. Scientific interpreters frequently use experience-distant terms—words whose meanings lie in the observer's theory (Geertz, 1983, p. 57). They produce etic, or abstract, noncontextualized interpretations. Geertz (1973) clarifies the goal in this situation:

> [We] set down the meaning particular social actions have for the actors whose actions they are . . . stating as explicitly as we can manage, what the knowledge thus attained demonstrates about the society in which it is found. . . . Our double task is to uncover the conceptual structures that inform our subject's acts, the "said" of social discourse, and to construct a

system of analysis . . . [which reveals] what is generic to those structures. (p. 27)

Thick descriptions and inscriptions create thick interpretations.[7] Thick interpretations interpret thick descriptions, in terms of the local theories that are structuring people's experiences.

In nearly all situations, individuals are able to articulate interpretive stories, or working theories, about their conduct and their experiences. These theories-as-stories are contained in the oral and cultural texts of the group and are based on local knowledge—that is, what works for them (Geertz, 1983). These pragmatic theories give meaning to problematic experiences. The interpreter attempts to uncover these theories, showing how they work in the lives of the individuals studied.

The Text, Its Authority, and Style

A text and an author's authority can always be challenged. This is so for three reasons. First, stories can always be told (inscribed) in different ways, and the Others who are spoken for may offer different tellings of their story. Second, all texts are biased productions. Many reflect patriarchal, male, interpretive biases (Collins, 1990, pp. 203-206). Third, the interpretive criteria that an author employs may be questioned, and the logic of the text that is assembled may be called into doubt. I will briefly discuss each of these points.

Different Tellings

In a recent article, W. A. Marianne Boelen (1992) criticizes William Foote Whyte's classic study *Street Corner Society* (1943) on several grounds. She notes that Whyte did not know Italian, was not an insider to the group studied, did not understand the importance of the family in Italian group life, and, as a consequence, seriously misrepresented many of the facts in "Cornerville" society. Whyte (1992) has disputed Boelen's charges, but they linger, especially in light of Doc's (Whyte's key informant) estrangement from Whyte. But unnoticed in the Whyte-Boelen exchange is the fact that no permanent telling of a story can be given. There are only always different versions of different, not the same, stories, even when the same site is studied.[8]

Writing Styles

There are several styles of qualitative writing, several different ways of describing, inscribing, and interpreting reality. Each style creates the conditions for its own criticism. Some version of the realist tale, or style, however, predominates. The realist tale attempts to make the subject's world transparent, to bring it alive, to make it visible (Clough, 1992, p. 132). There are three prevailing realist styles: mainstream, interpretive, and descriptive.

Mainstream realist writing presents thick and thin descriptions of the worlds studied, giving accounts of events, persons, and experiences. These texts assume the author can give an objective accounting, or portrayal, of the realities of a group or an individual. Such texts often utilize experience-distance concepts, such as kinship structure, to explain a group's way of life. Mainstream realism leads to the production of analytic, interpretive texts that are often single voiced.

Interpretive realism describes those texts where authors insert their personal interpretations into the life situations of the individuals studied. Clifford Geertz's (1973) study of the Balinese (which uses thick description) frequently privileges Geertz's interpretations. For example, he states: "In the cockfight, man and beast, good and evil, ego and ideology . . . fuse in a bloody drama of hatred, cruelty, violence and death" (p. 442). Here experience and its meanings are filtered through the researcher's, not the subject's, eyes.

In descriptive realism the writer attempts to stay out of the way and to allow the world being described to speak for itself. Of course, this is impossible, for all writing is interpretive. However, the impulse is to tell a multivoiced story (see, for example, Bruner & Gorfain, 1991; Ulmer, 1989). The excerpt from the Carver story quoted above is an example of this form of storytelling.[9]

Bias

Viewing the world through the male voice and gaze, too many writers equate masculinity with objectivity and femininity with subjectivity. In general, as Reinharz (1992) observes, "quantitative research defines itself as hard, firm, real . . . and strong . . . [and] defines qualitative research as soft, mushy, fuzzy, and weak" (p. 295). (This point is explored extensively by Richardson in Chapter 12, this volume, and by Fine, Chapter 4, and

Olesen, Chapter 9, in Volume 1 of this series.) But all texts are biased, reflecting the play of class, gender, race, ethnicity, and culture, suggesting that so-called objective interpretations are impossible.

The Logic of the Text

Any social text as a story can be analyzed in terms of its treatment of five paired terms:

1. the real world of lived experience and its representation in the text;
2. the text itself and the author, including the author's voice (first person, third person);
3. lived experience and its representation in the text (transcriptions from interviews and so on); and
4. subjects and their intentional meanings
5. the reader and the text (see Van Maanen, 1988, p. 6).

In telling a story, the author attempts to weave a text that re-creates for the reader the real world that was studied. Subjects, including their actions, experiences, words, intentions, and meanings, are then anchored inside this world as the author presents experience-near, experience-distant, local, and scientific theories of it. Readers take hold of this text and read their way into it, perhaps making it one of the stories they will tell about themselves. They develop their own naturalistic generalizations and impressions, based on the tacit knowledge and emotional feelings the text creates for them (see Stake, 1983, p. 282; see also Chapter 4, Volume 1, this series).

As a narrative production, interpretive writing is like fiction. It is created out of the facts of experience (things that did occur, might have occurred, or could occur). The story that is told often turns the researcher into a masculinized hero who confronts and makes sense of the subject's life situation. This situation is frequently conceptualized as a struggle that locates the subject's experiences within the primordial contexts of work, family, kinship, and marriage. This struggle is given meaning by the writer of the text, who becomes the only person authorized to represent the subject's story. The story that is finally told becomes the researcher's accomplishment, his or her self-fashioned narration of the subject's story (Clough, 1992, p. 17).

◆ An Analysis of Interpretive Practices

To summarize: The art of interpretation produces understandings that are shaped by genre, narrative, stylistic, personal, cultural, and paradigmatic conventions. I turn next to a review of the major paradigms and perspectives that now structure qualitative research writing practices: positivist and postpositivist, constructivist, critical (Marxist, emancipatory), and poststructuralist—including ethnic, feminist, and cultural studies—models. I select an exemplar from each tradition.[10] As Yvonna Lincoln and I argue in Chapter 1 of this volume, qualitative research is now in its "fifth moment," writing its way out of writing culture.

Grounded Theory as an Interpretive Style (Postpositivism)

The grounded theory perspective reflects a naturalistic approach to ethnography and interpretation, stressing naturalistic observations, open-ended interviewing, the sensitizing use of concepts, and a grounded (inductive) approach to theorizing, which can be both formal and substantive. Strauss and Corbin (1990; see also Chapter 7, Volume 2, this series) outline the criteria for judging a grounded theory study. They preface their discussion thus: "The usual canons of 'good science' should be retained, but require redefinition in order to fit the realities of qualitative research" (p. 250). These usual canons of good science are significance, theory-observation compatibility, generalizability, consistency, reproducibility, precision, and verification. Strauss and Corbin argue, for example, that if a similar set of conditions exists, and if the same theoretical perspective and the same rules for data gathering and analysis are followed, two researchers should be able to reproduce the same theoretical explanations of a given phenomenon.

Investigators should be able to provide information on the sample (including theoretical variations), core categories, key events and incidents, hypotheses, and negative cases that emerged and were pursued during the research process. The empirical grounding of a study (its grounded theory) should be judged by the range, density, linkages between, and systematic relatedness of its theoretical concepts, as well as by the theory's specificity and generality. Strauss and Corbin (1990) urge that these criteria be followed so that readers can "judge the credibility of [the] theory" (p. 258).

The grounded theory perspective is the most widely used qualitative interpretive framework in the social sciences today.[11] Its appeals are broad, for it provides a set of clearly defined steps any researcher can follow (see also Prus, 1991). Its dangers and criticisms, which arise when it is not fully understood, are multiple. There may be a flood of concepts unattached to the empirical world, and the analyst may get lost in coding and category schemes. Just exactly what a theory is, is also not clear (see Woods, 1992, p. 391). Some suggest that because the facts of a theory are always theory laden, a theory can only ever discover and hence ground itself (Lincoln & Guba, 1985, p. 207). The overemphasis on theory has also been criticized, including the use of previous theory as a guide to research and the attempts to make previous theory more dense (but see Gerson, 1991, p. 285). This preoccupation with prior theory can stand in the way of the researcher's attempts to hear and listen to the interpretive theories that operate in the situations studied. The perspective's affinities with positivism have also been criticized (Roman, 1992, p. 571). There is also a textual style that frequently subordinates lived experience and its interpretations to the grounded theorist's reading of the situation.

At the same time, grounded theory answers to a need to attach the qualitative research project to the "good science" model. Yet the perspective (see Strauss & Corbin, Chapter 7, Volume 2, this series) continues to fit itself to feminist and other poststructural, postmodern interpretive styles (Star, 1991).

Constructivism as an Interpretive Style

The constructivist program of Lincoln, Guba, and others represents a break with the postpositivist tradition, while retaining (at one level) a commitment to the grounded theory approach of Strauss and associates.[12] A good constructionist interpretation (text) is based on purposive (theoretical) sampling, a grounded theory, inductive data analysis, and idiographic (contextual) interpretations. The foundation for interpretation rests on triangulated empirical materials that are trustworthy. Trustworthiness consists of four components: credibility, transferability, dependability, and confirmability (these are the constructionist equivalents of internal and external validity, reliability, and objectivity; Lincoln & Guba, 1985, p. 300).[13]

Trustworthy materials are subjected to the constant comparative method of analysis that grounded theory deploys, that is, comparing incidents applicable to categories, integrating categories and their properties, delimiting and writing the theory. These materials are then developed into a case report that is again subjected to a comprehensive member check and an external audit. This done, the study is ready for public release (Lincoln & Guba, 1985, p. 381).

These constructivist interpretive strategies address many of the perceived problems in grounded theory, including the theory- and value-laden nature of facts, ambiguities in incidence, and category analysis. The paradigm, while disavowing the ontology, epistemology, and methodologies of postpositivism (Guba, 1990a, p. 27), sustains, at one level, Strauss and Corbin's commitment to the canons of good science. Hence the enormous commitment to methods and procedures that will increase a text's credibility, transferability, dependability, and confirmability.

Feminists, liberation theologists, Freirian critical theorists, and neo-Marxists may criticize the paradigm for not being ideological enough (Lincoln, 1990, p. 83). However, it is moving in these directions, as the authors seek a language and a set of practices that more fully celebrate and implement the moral, ethical, and political dimensions of social research (Lincoln, 1990, p. 86). Still, some would contend that it (like grounded theory) has yet to engage fully the new sensibilities flowing from the poststructural and postmodern perspectives.

Critical Theory as an Interpretive Style

There are multiple critical theory and participatory action frameworks (Guba, 1990a, p. 25; see also the works in this series by Kincheloe & McLaren, Chapter 8, and Fiske, Chapter 11, Volume 1; and Reason, Chapter 10, Volume 2). All share a critical realist ontology, a subjectivist epistemology, and a dialogic, transformative, ethnographic methodology (Guba, 1990a, p. 25). This often produces a criticism of traditional, naturalistic ethnographies (Roman, 1992, p. 558).

There are two distinct traditions within the cultural studies, critical theory model. One school, following Paulo Freire (1982, p. 30), regards concrete reality, dialectically conceived, as the starting point for analysis that examines how people live their facts of life into existence. The other school reads social texts (popular literature, cinema, popular music) as empirical materials that articulate complex arguments about race, class, and gender in contemporary life. Some scholars merge the ethnographic and textual approaches (see Fiske, Chapter 11, Volume 1, this series), examining how cultural interpretations are acted on and given meaning in concrete local cultural communities. Such work moves back and forth between concrete ethnographic texts and the content, semiotic, and narrative analysis of systems of discourse—for example, a particular television show or a film (see Manning & Cullum-Swan, Chapter 9, this volume).

Critical inquiry is theory driven by neo-Marxist and cultural studies models of the raced, classed, and gendered structures of contemporary societies (Carspecken & Apple, 1992, pp. 541-542). An emancipatory principle drives such research, which is committed to engaging oppressed groups in collective, democratic theorizing about "what is common and different in their experiences of oppression and privilege" (Roman, 1992, p. 557). A constant focus is given to the material and cultural practices that create structures of oppression.

A critical text is judged by its ability to reveal reflexively these structures of oppression as they operate in the worlds of lived experience. A critical text thus creates a space for multiple voices to speak; those who are oppressed are asked to articulate their definitions of their situations. For some, critical theory must be testable, falsifiable, dialogic, and collaborative (Carspecken & Apple, 1992, pp. 547-548). Others reject the more positivist features of this formulation (Roman, 1992, p. 558). Dorothy Smith (1992, p. 96), for example, evaluates a text by its ability to reveal the invisible structures of oppression in women's worlds.

Thus a good critical, emancipatory text is one that is multivocal, collaborative, naturalistically grounded in the worlds of lived experience, and organized by a critical, interpretive theory. Such formulations have been criticized for their tendency to impose their voices and values on the groups studied (Quantz, 1992, p. 471), for not being reflexive enough, and for being too theoretical (top-down theory), too preoccupied with theory verification (Roman, 1992, p. 571), and not sufficiently aware of postmodern sensibilities concerning the text and its social construction (Clough, 1992, p. 137).

These approaches, with their action criteria, politicize qualitative research. They foreground praxis, yet leave unclear the methodological side of the interpretive process that is so central to the grounded theory and constructionist approaches.

Poststructural Interpretive Styles

I will discuss three poststructural interpretive styles, those connected to the standpoint and cultural studies perspectives (Clough, 1992; Denzin, 1989; Lather, 1991, 1993; Smith, 1992; see also Olesen, Chapter 9, Volume 1, this series), those articulated by women of color (Collins, 1990; hooks, 1990), and my own approach, interpretive interactionism. Each of these perspectives is intimately connected to the critical and emancipatory styles of interpretation.

Style 1: Women of Color

Collins (1990, pp. 206-219) offers four criteria of interpretation, which are contrasted to the positivist approaches to research. Derived from an Afrocentric standpoint, her criteria focus on the primacy of concrete lived experience, the use of dialogue in assessing knowledge claims, the ethic of caring, and the ethic of personal accountability.

Experience as a criterion of meaning directs attention to black sisterhood, to the stories, narratives and Bible principles embodied in black church and community life. Concrete black feminine wisdom is contrasted to knowledge without wisdom: "A heap see, but a few know" (Collins, 1990, p. 208). Wisdom is experiential, cultural, and shared in the black feminine community. Dialogue, bell hooks argues, is humanizing speech. Black feminists assess knowledge claims through discourse, storytelling, connected dialogue in a group context. This emphasis on dialogue is directly translated into the black feminist text. Zora Neale Hurston, for example, located herself inside the folktales she collected, and carried on extensive dialogues with them, thus creating a multivocal text (Collins, 1990, p. 214).

Dialogue extends to the ethic of caring, which suggests that "personal expressiveness, emotions and empathy are central to the knowledge validation process" (Collins, 1990, p. 215). This ethic values individual uniqueness and the expression of emotionality in the text, and seeks writers who can create emotional texts that others can enter into. The ethic of personal accountability makes individuals accountable for their values and the political consequences of their actions.

These four criteria embody a "self-defined Black women's standpoint using an Afrocentric epistemology" (Collins, 1990, p. 219). They call into question much of what now passes for truth in methodological discourse.

They articulate criteria that stand in vivid contrast to those criteria contained in the grounded theory, constructionist, critical, and emancipatory traditions.

Style 2: Poststructural Feminist Interpretive Styles

Fonow and Cook (1991, pp. 2-13) suggest that four interpretive themes structure feminist research: an emphasis on researcher and textual reflexivity; an action and praxis orientation; an attention to the affective, emotional components of research; and concrete grounding in immediate situations. Lather (1991) extends this discussion. Her argument is threefold. First, feminist research challenges narrative realism, and the traditional naturalistic ethnography, because there is now an "uncertainty about what constitutes an adequate depiction of reality" (p. 91). As noted above, Lather argues that the age of description has ended. We are, as we have always been, in the moment of inscription, wherein writers create their own situated versions of the worlds studied. Accordingly, the social text becomes a stage, or a site where power and knowledge are presented. This means, third, we must explore alternative ways of presenting and authorizing our texts.

Lather (1993) then turns to a discussion of five new forms of validity, different ways of authorizing a text. These new forms are called reflexive, ironic, neopragmatic, rhizomatic, and situated validity. Each enacts a multivoiced, reflexive, open-ended, emotionally based text that is action, or praxis, based. For Lather and others in this tradition, theory is interpretation. There is no break between empirical activity (gathering empirical materials, reading social texts) and theorizing. Theory as interpretation is always anchored in the texts that it analyzes and reads. Conceptualizing theory-as-interpretation or theory-as-criticism means that the writer employs a style that immediately connects a theoretical term to its referent. For example, ideology is given in a popular culture text, or desire is present in a Madonna pose. Rosaldo (1989) provides an example; here the text merges with its subject matter—criticism and interpretation are not separated:

My anger at recent films that portray imperialism with nostalgia informs this chapter. Consider the enthusiastic reception of *Heat and Dust, A Passage to India, Out of Africa,* and *The Gods Must Be Crazy.* The white colonial societies portrayed in these films appear decorous and orderly, as

334

if constructed in accord with the norms of classic ethnography. . . . Evidently a mood of nostalgia makes racial domination appear innocent and pure. (p. 68)

Style 3: Interpretive Interactionism

I turn now to a brief exposition of another interpretive style, what I have elsewhere termed *interpretive interactionism* (Denzin, 1989). Interpretive research begins and ends with the biography and the self of the researcher. The events and troubles that are written about are ones the writer has already experienced and witnessed firsthand. The task is to produce "richly detailed" inscriptions and accounts of such experiences.

The focus of the research is on those life experiences (epiphanies) that radically alter and shape the meanings persons give to themselves and their life projects. In epiphanies, personal character is manifested and made apparent. By recording these experiences in detail, and by listening to the stories people tell about them, the researcher is able to illuminate the moments of crisis that occur in a person's life. Having had such experiences, the individual is often never quite the same again. (Examples of epiphanies include religious conversions, divorces, incidents of family violence, rape, incest, murder, and loss of a job.)

Sartre's (1963, pp. 85-166) progressive-regressive method of analysis organizes the interpretive process. The investigator situates a subject, or class of subjects, within a given historical moment. Progressively, the method looks forward to the conclusion of a set of acts or experiences undertaken by the subject. Regressively, the method works back in time to the historical, gender, class, race, cultural, biographical, and emotional conditions that moved the subject forward into the experience that is being studied.

Interpretive materials are evaluated by their ability to illuminate phenomena as lived experience. Such materials should be based on thickly contextualized materials that are historical, relational, and processual. The core of these materials will be the personal experience stories subjects tell one another. These stories should be connected to larger institutional, group, and cultural contexts, including written texts and other systems of discourse (cinema, music, folklore). The understandings that are put forth should engulf all that has been learned about the phenomenon. The moral biases that organize the research should be made evident to the reader. The competing models of truth and interpretation (rationality and emotionality) that operate in the subject's situations should be revealed. The stories that are presented to readers should be given in the language, feelings, emotions, and actions of those studied.[14]

Criticisms of Poststructuralism

Poststructural, postmodern, feminist texts have been criticized because of their interpretive criteria. Critics complain that there is no way to evaluate such work because traditional, external standards of evaluation (internal and external validity, reliability, objectivity) are not followed. This means, the argument goes, that there is no way to evaluate a good or bad poststructural, feminist text. Others argue that the feminist and poststructural text imposes an interpretive framework on the world, and does not allow subjects to speak. These criticisms come, of course, from the positivist and postpositivist traditions.

These criticisms are rejected on several grounds. First, they are seen as not reflecting an understanding of the new postmodern sensibility, which doubts and challenges any attempt to legitimate a text in terms of positivist or postpositivist criteria. Such criteria represent attempts to bring legitimacy and authority to the scientific project. Science, in its traditional forms, is the problem. Knowledge produced under the guise of objective science is too often used for purposes of social control (Clough, 1992, p. 134). The criteria of evaluation that poststructuralists employ answer to a different set of problems and to a different project. They seek a morally informed social criticism, a sacred version of science that is humane, caring, holistic, and action based (see Reason, 1993; see also Lincoln & Denzin, Chapter 13, Volume 1, this series).

Poststructuralists celebrate uncertainty and attempt to construct texts that do not impose theoretical frameworks on the world. They seek to let the prose of the world speak for itself, while they remain mindful of all the difficulties involved in such a commitment. They, more than their postpositivist counterparts, are sensitive to voice and to multiple perspectives.

◆ Multiple Interpretive Communities

There are many ways to move from the field to the text, many ways to inscribe and describe experience. There are multiple interpretive commu-

TABLE 11.1 Two Interpretive Communities

Tender-Minded	Tough-Minded
Intuitive	Hard-nosed empiricists
Emotional	Rational, cognitive
Open-ended texts	Closed texts, systems
Interpretation as art	Interpretation as method
Personal biases	Neutrality
Experimental texts	Traditional texts
Antirealism	Realist texts
Antifoundational	Foundational
Criticism	Substantive theory
Science-as-power	Good science canons
Multivoiced texts	Single-voiced texts

nities that now circulate within the many terrains of qualitative research. These communities take different stances on the topics treated above, including the matters of writing, description, inscription, interpretation, understanding, representation, legitimation, textual desire, and the logic and politics of the text.

A simplistic approach to the many paradigm dialogues that are now occurring (Guba, 1990a) might use the old-fashioned distinctions between humanists and scientists, between the "tender-minded" and the "tough-minded," to borrow William James's (1908/1978, pp. 10-13) terms. Such distinctions are displayed in Table 11.1. But critical analysis soon makes this pretty picture messy. On the surface, critical, emancipatory, feminist, interactional, poststructural, and postmodern researchers belong to the tender-minded interpretive community. Following James, they are more intuitive, emotional, and open-ended in their interpretive work. Some are quite dogmatic about this. But many critical theorists write realist texts, are hard-nosed empiricists, work within closed theoretical systems, and follow the canons of good science.

In the same vein, positivists, postpositivists, grounded theorists, and constructivists appear to belong to the tough-minded interpretive community. They are hard-nosed empiricists, system builders, often pluralistic in their use of theory, and skeptical of nonsystematic theory and empirical work. But there are feminists who use grounded theory methods and produce traditional-looking texts, based on foundational criteria. There are tough-minded constructivists who are antirealist and antifoundational, and who regard interpretation as more art than method.

Clearly, simplistic classifications do not work. Any given qualitative researcher-as-*bricoleur* can be more than one thing at the same time, can be fitted into both the tender- and the tough-minded categories. It is clear that in the fifth (and sixth) moments of qualitative research, the concerns from each of James's two communities work alongside and inform one another. Accordingly, it can be argued that the following contradictory understandings operate in this broad field we have called qualitative research.

Interpretation is an art that cannot be formalized. Scholars are increasingly concerned with the logic of the text, especially the problems involved in presenting lived experience and the point of view of the Other. Many are preoccupied with the biases in the emotional stories they tell and are drawn to experimental forms of writing; some reject mainstream narrative realism. It is common for texts now to be grounded in antifoundational systems of discourse (local knowledge, local emotions). These texts tell emancipatory stories grounded in race, class, and gender. Personal experience is a major source of empirical material for many, as are cultural texts and materials gathered via the ethnographic method. More than a few researchers expose their writerly selves in first-person accounts, and many are attempting to produce reader-friendly, multivoiced texts that speak to the worlds of lived experience. It is becoming commonplace for qualitative researchers to be advocates of the moral communities they represent, while attempting to participate directly in social change.

At the same time, there are those who remain committed to mainstream realism. They write texts that adhere to complex sets of methodological principles connected to postpositivist foundational systems of meaning ("good science"). Their texts are grounded in concrete empirical materials (case studies) and are inductively interpreted through the methods of grounded theory or variations thereof. Existing theories, both substantive and formal, structure inquiry, which is organized in a rigorous, stepwise manner.

Finally, there are conflicting views and disagreements on the very topic of interpretation itself. The immediate, local, personal, emotional biases of many lead them to tell stories that work outward from the self to society. These writers are writing to make sense of their own lives. Others write to make sense of "another's" life. In the end it is a matter of storytelling and the stories we tell each other.

◆ Into the Future

Of course, persons who do interpretations feel uncomfortable doing predictions. But where the field of interpretation, the art and politics of telling stories, will be in 10 years should be addressed. If the past predicts the future, and if the decade of the 1980s and the first half of the 1990s are to be taken seriously, then interpretation is moving more and more deeply into the regions of the postmodern sensibility. A new postconstructivist paradigm may emerge. This framework may attach itself to a new and less foundational postpositivism and a more expansive critical theory framework built on modified grounded theory principles.

Epistemologies of color will proliferate, building on Afrocentric (Collins), Chicana (Rosaldo, Chabram-Daernersesian, Anzaldua), Native American, Asian (Trinh T. Minh-ha), Third World (Spivak), and other minority group perspectives. More elaborated epistemologies of gender (and class) will appear, including "queer theory" (Seidman, 1993), and feminisms of color. These interpretive communities will draw on their minority group experiences as the basis of the texts they write, and they will seek texts that speak to the logic and cultures of these communities.

These race-, ethnicity-, and gender-specific interpretive communities will fashion interpretive criteria out of their interactions with the postpositivist, constructivist, critical theory, and poststructural sensibilities. These criteria will be emic, existential, political, and emotional. They will push the personal to the forefront of the political, where the social text becomes the vehicle for the expression of politics.

This projected proliferation of interpretive communities does not mean that the field of qualitative research will splinter into warring factions, or into groups that cannot speak to one another. Underneath the complexities and contradictions that define this field rest three common commitments. The first reflects the belief that the world of human experience must be studied from the point of view of the historically and culturally situated individual. Second, qualitative researchers will persist in working outward from their own biographies to the worlds of experience that surround them. Third, scholars will continue to value and seek to produce works that speak clearly and powerfully about these worlds. To echo Raymond Carver (1989, p. 24), the real experimenters will always be those who Make it New, who find things out for themselves, and who want to carry this News from their world to ours.

And so the stories we tell one another will change and the criteria for reading stories will also change. And this is how it should be. The good stories are always told by those who have learned well the stories of the past, but who are unable to tell them any longer because those stories no longer speak to them, or to us.

◆ Notes

1. Here I deal with the constructivism of Guba and Lincoln, not the social constructionism of Gergen. Schwandt (Chapter 7, Volume 1, this series) compares and contrasts these two frameworks.

2. See the relevant chapters in this series that take up each of these traditions, including those in Volume 1 by Fine (Chapter 4), Guba and Lincoln (Chapter 6), Schwandt (Chapter 7), Kincheloe and McLaren (Chapter 8), Olesen (Chapter 9), Fiske (Chapter 11), and Marcus (Chapter 12); those in Volume 2 by Atkinson and Hammersley (Chapter 5), Holstein and Gubrium (Chapter 6), and Strauss and Corbin (Chapter 7); and those in this volume by Altheide and Johnson (Chapter 10) and Richardson (Chapter 12).

3. Rosaldo (1989) argues that anthropological doctrine presents this as a three-step process, involving preparation, knowledge, and sensibility, but cautions that "one should work to undermine the false comfort it can convey. At what point can people say that they have completed their learning or life experience?" (p. 8).

4. Mitch Allen and Yvonna Lincoln clarified these steps for me.

5. Yvonna Lincoln suggests that this may have been less the case in earlier historical moments, when realist tales were organized in terms of well-understood conventions.

6. I am deeply indebted to Meaghan Morris for her help in clarifying the meanings in this section.

7. Elsewhere I have offered a typology of descriptions and interpretations, including descriptions that are primarily micro, macro, biographical, situational, interactional-relational, incomplete, glossed, pure, and interpretive, and interpretations that are thin, thick, native, observer based, analytic, descriptive-contextual, and relational-interactive (Denzin, 1989, pp. 99, 111-120).

8. The Whyte-Boelen exchange is similar, in these respects, to earlier controversies in this area, including the famous Redfield-Sanchez and Mead-Freeman debates over who got it right—the original, classic study or the reinvestigation of the same site by a later researcher.

9. Mainstream, interpretive, and descriptive realist stories may be supplemented by more traditional and experimental formats, including confessional ("the problems I encountered doing my study") and impressionistic ("dramatic and vivid pictures from the field") tales of the field (Van Maanen, 1988), as well as personal memoirs of the field experience (Stoller & Olkes, 1987), narratives of the self (see Ellis & Bochner, 1992; Ellis & Flaherty, 1992; Ronai, 1992), fiction texts (Stewart, 1989), and ethnographic dramas and performance texts (McCall & Becker, 1990; Richardson & Lockridge, 1991; for a review, see Richardson, Chapter 12, this volume).

10. These, of course, are my interpretations of these interpretive styles. The reader should also consult the presentation of these paradigms by Guba and Lincoln in Chapter 6, Volume 1 of this series, as well as Chapter 1 in this volume.

11. The presence is greatest, perhaps, in education, the health sciences, and communication, but also in sociology, less so in anthropology. When one peels back the layers of discourse embedded in any of the numerous qualitative guides to interpretation and theory construction, the core features of the Strauss approach are present, even when Strauss and associates are not directly named.

12. It argues that the facts for any theory are always interpreted and value laden, that no theory can ever be fully tested (or grounded), and an interactive relationship always exists between the observer and the observed. A dialectical, dialogic hermeneutic posture organizes inquiry that is based on thick descriptions of action and subjective experience in natural situations.

13. Specific strategies and criteria are attached to each of these components. Credibility is increased through prolonged field engagement, persistent observation, triangulation, peer debriefing, negative case analysis, referential analysis (Eisner's term for cinematic methods that provide a record of social life), and member checks (talking to people in the field). Thick description provides for transferability, whereas dependability can be enhanced through the use of overlapping methods, stepwise replications, and inquiry (dependability) audits (the use of well-informed subjects) (Lincoln & Guba, 1985, p. 316). Confirmability builds on audit trails (a "residue of records stemming from inquiry"; p. 319) and involves the use of written field notes, memos, a field diary, process and personal notes, and a reflexive journal.

14. The five steps to interpretation (Denzin, 1989, p. 27) should be followed: deconstruction, capture, bracketing, construction, contextualization.

◆ References

Argyris, C., & Schön, D. A. (1974). *Theory in practice.* San Francisco: Jossey-Bass.

Bakhtin, M. M. (1986). *Speech genres and other essays.* Austin: University of Texas Press.

Barthes, R. (1975). *The pleasure of the text.* New York: Hill & Wang.

Becker, H. S. (1986). *Writing for social scientists: How to start and finish your thesis, book, or article.* Chicago: University of Chicago Press.

Boelen, W. A. M. (1992). *Street Corner Society*: Cornerville revisited. *Journal of Contemporary Ethnography, 21,* 11-51.

Brady, I. (Ed.). (1991). Introduction. In I. Brady (Ed.), *Anthropological poetics* (pp. 3-36). Savage, MD: Rowman & Littlefield.

Bruner, E. M., & Gorfain, P. (1991). Dialogic narration and the paradoxes of Masada. In I. Brady (Ed.), *Anthropological poetics* (pp. 177-206). Savage, MD: Rowman & Littlefield.

Carspecken, P. F., & Apple, M. (1992). Critical research: Theory, methodology, and practice. In M. D. LeCompte, W. L. Millroy, & J. Preissle (Eds.), *The handbook of qualitative research in education* (pp. 507-554). New York: Academic Press.

Carver, R. (1989). *Fires*. New York: Vantage.

Clough, P. T. (1992). *The end(s) of ethnography: From realism to social criticism*. Newbury Park, CA: Sage.

Collins, P. H. (1990). *Black feminist thought: Knowledge, consciousness and the politics of empowerment*. New York: Routledge.

Denzin, N. K. (1989). *Interpretive interactionism*. Newbury Park, CA: Sage.

Denzin, N. K. (1990). Harold and Agnes: A feminist narrative undoing. *Sociological Theory, 8*, 198-216.

Dilthey, W. L. (1976). *Selected writings*. Cambridge: Cambridge University Press. (Original work published 1900)

Ellis, C., & Flaherty, M. G. (Eds.). (1992). *Investigating subjectivity: Research on lived experience*. Newbury Park, CA: Sage.

Ellis, C., & Bochner, A. P. (1992). Telling and performing personal stories: The constraints of choice in abortion. In C. Ellis & M. G. Flaherty (Eds.), *Investigating subjectivity: Research on lived experience* (pp. 79-101). Newbury Park, CA: Sage.

Fish, S. (1980). *Is there a text in this class? The authority of interpretive communities*. Cambridge, MA: Harvard University Press.

Freire, P. (1982). *Pedagogy of the oppressed*. New York: Continuum.

Fonow, M. M., & Cook, J. A. (1991). Back to the future: A look at the second wave of feminist epistemology and methodology. In M. M. Fonow & J. A. Cook (Eds.), *Beyond methodology: Feminist scholarship as lived research* (pp. 1-15). Bloomington: Indiana University Press.

Geertz, C. (1973). *The interpretation of cultures: Selected essays*. New York: Basic Books.

Geertz, C. (1983). *Local knowledge: Further essays in interpretive anthropology*. New York: Basic Book.

Geertz, C. (1988). *Works and lives: The anthropologist as author*. Stanford, CA: Stanford University Press.

Gerson, E. M. (1991). Supplementing grounded theory. In D. R. Maines (Ed.), *Social organization and social process: Essays in honor of Anselm Strauss* (pp. 285-302). New York: Aldine de Gruyter.

Guba, E. G. (1990a). The alternative paradigm dialog. In E. G. Guba (Ed.), *The paradigm dialog* (pp. 17-30). Newbury Park, CA: Sage.

Guba, E. G. (1990b). Carrying on the dialog. In E. G. Guba (Ed.), *The paradigm dialog* (pp. 368-378). Newbury Park, CA: Sage.

Guba, E. G., & Lincoln, Y. S. (1989). *Fourth generation evaluation*. Newbury Park, CA: Sage.

Hammersley, M. (1992). *What's wrong with ethnography? Methodological explorations*. London: Routledge.

hooks, b. (1990). *Yearning: Race, gender, and cultural politics*. Boston: South End.

James, W. (1978). *Pragmatism and the meaning of truth*. Cambridge, MA: Harvard University Press. (Original work published 1908)

Krieger, S. (1991). *Social science and the self: Personal essays as an art form*. New Brunswick, NJ: Rutgers University Press.

Lather, P. (1991). *Getting smart: Feminist research and pedagogy with/in the postmodern*. New York: Routledge.

Lather, P. (1993). Fertile obsession: Validity after poststructuralism. *Sociological Quarterly, 35.*

Lincoln, Y. S. (1990). The making of a constructivist: A remembrance of transformations past. In E. G. Guba (Ed.), *The paradigm dialog* (pp. 67-87). Newbury Park, CA: Sage.

Lincoln, Y. S., & Guba, E. G. (1985). *Naturalistic inquiry.* Beverly Hills, CA: Sage.

Lévi-Strauss, C. (1966). *The savage mind* (2nd ed.). Chicago: University of Chicago Press.

McCall, M., & Becker, H. S. (1990). Performance science. *Social Problems, 32,* 117-132.

Plath, D. (1990). Fieldnotes, filed notes, and the conferring of note. In R. Sanjek (Ed.), *Fieldnotes: The makings of anthropology* (pp. 371-384). Albany: State University of New York Press.

Prus, R. C. (1991). *Road hustler* (exp. ed.). New York: Steranko.

Quantz, R. A. (1992). On critical ethnography (with some postmodern considerations). In M. D. LeCompte, W. L. Millroy, & J. Preissle (Eds.), *The handbook of qualitative research in education* (pp. 447-505). New York: Academic Press.

Reason, P. (1993). Sacred experience and sacred science. *Journal of Management Inquiry, 2,* 10-27.

Reinharz, S. (1992). *Feminist methods in social research.* New York: Oxford University Press.

Richardson, L. (1990). *Writing strategies.* Newbury Park, CA: Sage.

Richardson, L. (1991). Postmodern social theory: Representational practices. *Sociological Theory, 9,* 173-179.

Richardson, L. (1992). The consequences of poetic representation: Writing the other, rewriting the self. In C. Ellis & M. G. Flaherty (Eds.), *Investigating subjectivity: Research on lived experience* (pp. 125-137). Newbury Park, CA: Sage.

Richardson, L., & Lockridge, E. (1991). The sea monster: An ethnographic drama. *Symbolic Interaction, 14,* 335-340.

Ricoeur, P. (1985). *Time and narrative* (Vol. 2). Chicago: University of Chicago Press.

Roman, L. G. (1992). The political significance of other ways of narrating ethnography: A feminist materialist approach. In M. D. LeCompte, W. L. Millroy, & J. Preissle (Eds.), *The handbook of qualitative research in education* (pp. 555-594). New York: Academic Press.

Ronai, C. R. (1992). The reflexive self through narrative: A night in the life of an erotic dancer/researcher. In C. Ellis & M. G. Flaherty (Eds.), *Investigating subjectivity: Research on lived experience* (pp. 102-124). Newbury Park, CA: Sage.

Rosaldo, R. (1989). *Culture and truth: The remaking of social analysis.* Boston: Beacon.

Rose, D. (1990). *Living the ethnographic life.* Newbury Park, CA: Sage.

Ryle, G. (1968). *The thinking of thoughts* (University Lectures, No. 18). Saskatoon: University of Saskatchewan.

Sanjek, R. (1990). *Fieldnotes: The makings of anthropology.* Albany: State University of New York Press.

Sartre, J.-P. (1963). *Search for a method.* New York: Alfred A. Knopf.

Seidman, S. (1991). The end of sociological theory: The postmodern hope. *Sociological Theory, 9,* 131-146.

Seidman, S. (1993). *Embattled Eros: Sexual politics and ethics in contemporary America.* New York: Routledge.

Smith, D. (1992). Sociology from women's perspective: A reaffirmation. *Sociological Theory, 10,* 88-97.

Stake, R. (1983). The case study method in social inquiry. In G. Madaus, M. Scriven, & D. Stufflebeam (Eds.), *Evaluation models* (pp. 279-286). Boston: Kluwer-Nijhoff.

Star, S. L. (1991). The sociology of the invisible: The primacy of work in the writings of Anselm Strauss. In D. R. Maines (Ed.), *Social organization and social process: Essays in honor of Anselm Strauss* (pp. 265-284). New York: Aldine de Gruyter.

Stewart, J. (1989). *Drinkers, drummers and decent folk: Ethnographic narratives of Village Trinidad.* Albany: State University of New York Press.

Stoller, P., & Olkes, C. (1987). *In sorcery's shadow.* Chicago: University of Chicago Press.

Strauss, A. L., & Corbin, J. (1990). *Basics of qualitative research: Grounded theory procedures and techniques.* Newbury Park, CA: Sage.

Todorov, T. (1977). *The poetics of prose.* Ithaca, NY: Cornell University Press.

Ulmer, G. (1989). *Teletheory.* New York: Routledge.

Van Maanen, J. (1988). *Tales of the field: On writing ethnography.* Chicago: University of Chicago Press.

Whyte, W. F. (1943). *Street corner society: The social structure of an Italian slum.* Chicago: University of Chicago Press.

Whyte, W. F. (1992). In defense of *Street Corner Society. Journal of Contemporary Ethnography, 21,* 52-68.

Wolcott, H. F. (1990). *Writing up qualitative research.* Newbury Park, CA: Sage.

Woods, P. (1992). Symbolic interactionism: Theory and method. In M. D. LeCompte, W. L. Millroy, & J. Preissle (Eds.), *The handbook of qualitative research in education* (pp. 336-404). New York: Academic Press.

12

Writing

A Method of Inquiry

Laurel Richardson

> The writer's object is—or should be—to hold the reader's attention. . . . I want the reader to turn the page and keep on turning to the end.
>
> —Barbara Tuchman,
> *New York Times,* February 2, 1989

◆ In the spirit of affectionate irreverence toward qualitative research, I consider writing as a *method of inquiry,* a way of finding out about yourself and your topic. Although we usually think about writing as a mode of "telling" about the social world, writing is not just a mopping-up activity at the end of a research project. Writing is also a way of "knowing"—a method of discovery and analysis. By writing in different ways, we discover new aspects of our topic and our relationship to it. Form and content are inseparable.

I have composed this chapter into two *equally* important, but differently formatted, sections. I emphasize the *equally* because the first section, an essay, has rhetorical advantages over its later-born sibling. In the first

AUTHOR'S NOTE: I thank Ernest Lockridge for reading this chapter multiple times. I also thank Arthur Bochner, Norman Denzin, Carolyn Ellis, Michelle Fine, Yvonna Lincoln, Meaghan Morris, and John Van Maanen for their readings of earlier versions of this chapter and Barrie Thorne for her suggestions.

section, "Writing in Contexts," I position myself as a reader/writer of qualitative research. Then, I discuss (a) the historical roots of social scientific writing, including its dependence upon metaphor and prescribed formats, and (b) the postmodernist possibilities for qualitative writing, including experimental representation. In the second section, "Writing Practices," I offer a compendium of writing suggestions and exercises organized around topics in the text.

Necessarily, the chapter reflects my own process and preferences. I encourage researchers to explore their own processes and preferences through writing—and rewriting and rewriting. Writing from our Selves should strengthen the community of qualitative researchers and the individual voices within it, because we will be more fully present in our work, more honest, more engaged.

◆ Writing in Contexts

I have a confession to make. For 30 years, I have yawned my way through numerous supposedly exemplary qualitative studies. Countless numbers of texts have I abandoned half read, half scanned. I'll order a new book with great anticipation—the topic is one I'm interested in, the author is someone I want to read—only to find the text boring. Recently, I have been "coming out" to colleagues and students about my secret displeasure with much of qualitative writing, only to find a community of like-minded discontents. Undergraduates are disappointed that sociology is not more interesting; graduate students confess that they do not finish reading what has been assigned because it is boring; and colleagues express relief to be at long last discussing qualitative research's own dirty little secret: Our empire is (partially) unclothed.

Speaking of this, and in this way, risks identifying my thoughts with that dreadful genre, *putdownism*. But that is not the emotional core or intention of my remarks. Rather, I want to raise a serious problem. Although our topics often are riveting and our research carefully executed, our books are underread. Unlike quantitative work, which can carry its meaning in its tables and summaries, qualitative work depends upon people's reading it. Just as a piece of literature is not equivalent to its "plot summary," qualitative research is not contained in its abstracts. Qualitative research has to be read, not scanned; its meaning is in the reading.

Qualitative work could be reaching wide and diverse audiences, not just devotees of the topic or the author. It seems foolish at best, and narcissistic and wholly self-absorbed at worst, to spend months or years doing research that ends up not being read and not making a difference to anything but the author's career. Can something be done? That is the question that drives this chapter: How do we create texts that are vital? That are attended to? That make a difference? One way to create those texts is to turn our attention to writing as a method of inquiry.

I write because I want to find something out. I write in order to learn something that I didn't know before I wrote it. I was taught, however, as perhaps you were, too, not to write until I knew what I wanted to say, until my points were organized and outlined. No surprise, this static writing model coheres with mechanistic scientism and quantitative research. But, I will argue, the model is itself a sociohistorical invention that reifies the static social world imagined by our nineteenth-century foreparents. The model has serious problems: It ignores the role of writing as a dynamic, creative process; it undermines the confidence of beginning qualitative researchers because their experience of research is inconsistent with the writing model; and it contributes to the flotilla of qualitative writing that is simply not interesting to read because adherence to the model requires writers to silence their own voices and to view themselves as contaminants.

Qualitative researchers commonly speak of the importance of the individual researcher's skills and aptitudes. The researcher—rather than the survey, the questionnaire, or the census tape—is the "instrument." The more honed the researcher, the greater the possibility of "good" research. Students are trained to observe, listen, question, and participate. Yet they are trained to conceptualize writing as "writing up" the research, rather than as a method of discovery. Almost unthinkingly, qualitative research training validates the mechanistic model of writing, even though that model shuts down the creativity and sensibilities of the individual researcher.

One reason, then, that our texts are boring is that our sense of self is diminished as we are homogenized through professional socialization, through rewards and punishments. Homogenization occurs through the suppression of individual voices. We have been encouraged to take on the omniscient voice of science, the view from ev- erywhere. How do we put ourselves in our own texts, and with what consequences? How do we nurture our own individuality and at the same time lay claim to "knowing" something? These are both philosophically and practically difficult problems.

Postmodernist Context

We are fortunate, now, to be working in a postmodernist climate (see, e.g., Agger, 1990; Lehman, 1991; Lyotard, 1979). Postmodernism has affected all the disciplines and has gained ascendancy in the humanities, arts, philosophy, and the natural sciences. Disciplinary boundaries are regularly broken. Literary studies are about sociological questions; social scientists write fiction; sculptors do performance art; choreographers do sociology; and so on. (See, for literary criticism, Eagleton, 1983; Morris, 1988. For philosophy, see Hutcheon, 1988; Rorty, 1979; Nicholson, 1990. For physics, Gleick, 1984. For mathematics, Kline, 1980. For arts, Trinh, 1989. For communications, Carey, 1989. For social sciences, Clifford & Marcus, 1986; Clough, 1992; Denzin, 1986, 1991; Fiske & Schweder, 1986; Geertz, 1983; Marcus & Fischer, 1986; Richardson, 1991; Seidman & Wagner, 1991; Turner & Bruner, 1986. For education, Lather, 1991.)

The core of postmodernism is the *doubt* that any method or theory, discourse or genre, tradition or novelty, has a universal and general claim as the "right" or the privileged form of authoritative knowledge. Postmodernism *suspects* all truth claims of masking and serving particular interests in local, cultural, and political struggles. But postmodernism does not automatically reject conventional methods of knowing and telling as false or archaic. Rather, it opens those standard methods to inquiry and introduces new methods, which are also, then, subject to critique.

The postmodernist context of doubt distrusts all methods equally. No method has a privileged status. The superiority of "science" over "literature"—or, from another vantage point, "literature" over "science"—is challenged. But a postmodernist position does allow us to know "something" without claiming to know everything. Having a partial, local, historical knowledge is still knowing. In some ways, "knowing" is easier, however, because postmodernism recognizes the situational limitations of the knower. Qualitative writers are off the hook, so to speak. They don't have to try to play God, writing as disembodied omniscient narrators claiming universal, atemporal general knowledge; they can eschew the questionable metanarrative of scientific objectivity and still have plenty to say as situated speakers, subjectivities engaged in knowing/telling about the world as they perceive it.

A particular kind of postmodernist thinking that I have found especially helpful is *poststructuralism* (for an overview, see Weedon, 1987). Poststructuralism links language, subjectivity, social organization, and power. The centerpiece is language. Language does not "reflect" social reality, but produces meaning, creates social reality. Different languages and different discourses within a given language divide up the world and give it meaning in ways that are not reducible to one another. Language is how social organization and power are defined and contested and the place where our sense of selves, our *subjectivity,* is constructed. Understanding language as competing discourses, competing ways of giving meaning and of organizing the world, makes language a site of exploration, struggle.

Language is not the result of one's individuality; rather, language constructs the individual's subjectivity in ways that are historically and locally specific. What something means to individuals is dependent on the discourses available to them. For example, being hit by one's spouse is experienced differently if it is thought of within the discourse of "normal marriage," "husband's rights," or "wife battering." If a woman sees male violence as "normal" or a "husband's right," then she is unlikely to see it as "wife battering," an illegitimate use of power that should not be tolerated. Experience is thus open to contradictory interpretations governed by social interests rather than objective truth. The individual is both site and subject of discursive struggles for identity. Because the individual is subject to multiple and competing discourses in many realms, one's subjectivity is shifting and contradictory, not stable, fixed, rigid.

Poststructuralism thus points to the *continual cocreation of Self and social science*; they are known through each other. Knowing the Self and knowing "about" the subject are intertwined, partial, historical, local knowledges. Poststructuralism, then, permits—nay, invites—no, incites us to reflect upon our method and explore new ways of knowing.

Specifically, poststructuralism suggests two important things to qualitative writers: First, it directs us to understand ourselves reflexively as persons writing from particular positions at specific times; and second, it frees us from trying to write a single text in which everything is said to everyone. Nurturing our own voices releases the censorious hold of "science writing" on our consciousness, as well as the arrogance it fosters in our psyche. Writing is validated as a method of knowing.

Historical Contexts: Writing Conventions

Language, then, is a constitutive force, creating a particular view of reality and of the Self. Producing "things" always involves value—what to produce, what to name the productions, and what the relationship between the producers and the named things will be. Writing "things" is no exception. No textual staging is ever innocent (including this one). Styles of writing are neither fixed nor neutral but reflect the historically shifting domination of particular schools or paradigms.

Having some sense of the history of our writing practices helps us to demystify standard practices and loosen their hold on our psyches. Social scientific writing, like all other forms of writing, is a sociohistorical construction and, therefore, mutable.

Since the seventeenth century, the world of writing has been divided into two separate kinds: literary and scientific. Literature, from the seventeenth century onward, was associated with fiction, rhetoric, and subjectivity, whereas science was associated with fact, "plain language," and objectivity (Clifford, 1986, p. 5). Fiction was "false" because it invented reality, unlike science, which was "true," because it simply "reported" "objective" reality in a single, unambiguous voice.

During the eighteenth century, assaults upon literature intensified. John Locke cautioned adults to forgo figurative language lest the "conduit" between "things" and "thought" be obstructed. David Hume depicted poets as professional liars. Jeremy Bentham proposed that the ideal language would be one without words, only unambiguous symbols. Samuel Johnson's dictionary sought to fix "univocal meanings in perpetuity, much like the univocal meanings of standard arithmetic terms" (Levine, 1985, p. 4).

Into this linguistic world the Marquis de Condorcet introduced the term *social science*. He contended that "knowledge of the truth" would be "easy and error almost impossible" if one adopted precise language about moral and social issues (quoted in Levine, 1985, p. 6). By the nineteenth century, literature and science stood as two separate domains. Literature was aligned with "art" and "culture"; it contained the values of "taste, aesthetics, ethics, humanity, and morality" (Clifford, 1986, p. 6), and the rights to metaphoric and ambiguous language. Given to science was the belief that its words were objective, precise, unambiguous, noncontextual, nonmetaphoric.

But because literary writing was taking a second seat in importance, status, impact, and truth value to science, some literary writers attempted to make literature a part of science. By the late nineteenth century, "realism" dominated both science and fiction writing (Clough, 1992). Honoré de Balzac spearheaded the realism movement in literature. He viewed society as a "historical organism" with "social species" akin to "zoological species." Writers deserving of praise, he contended, must investigate "the reasons or causes" of "social effects"—the "first principles" upon which society is based (Balzac, 1842/1965, pp. 247-249). For Balzac, the novel was an "instrument of scientific inquiry" (Crawford, 1951, p. 7). Following Balzac's lead, Emile Zola argued for "naturalism" in literature. In his famous essay "The Novel as Social Science," he argued that the "return to nature, the naturalistic evolution which marks the century, drives little by little all the manifestation of human intelligence into the same scientific path." Literature is to be "governed by science" (Zola, 1880/1965, p. 271).

Throughout the twentieth century, crossovers—uneasy and easy, denied and acknowledged—have characterized the relationship between science and literary writing. Today, scholars in a host of disciplines are involved in tracing these relationships and in deconstructing scientific and literary writing (see Agger, 1989; Atkinson, 1990; Brodkey, 1987; Brown, 1977; Clough, 1992; Edmondson, 1984; Nelson, Megill, & McCloskey, 1987; Simons, 1990). Their deconstructive analyses concretely show how all disciplines have their own set of literary devices and rhetorical appeals, such as probability tables, archival records, and first-person accounts.

Each writing convention could be discussed at length, but I will discuss only two of them—metaphor and writing formats. I choose these because I believe they are good sites for experimenting with writing as a method of inquiry (see the section "Writing Practices," below). Thinking critically about social science's metaphors and writing formats helps break their brake on our pens and word processors.

Metaphor

A literary device, *metaphor,* is the backbone of social science writing. Like the spine, it bears weight, permits movement, is buried beneath the surface, and links parts together into a functional, coherent whole. As this metaphor about metaphor suggests, the essence of metaphor is the experiencing and understanding of one thing in terms of another. This is accomplished through comparison (e.g., "My love is like a green, green toad") or analogy (e.g., "the evening of life").

Social scientific writing uses metaphors at every "level." Social science depends upon a deep epistemic code regarding the way "that knowledge and understanding in general are figured" (Shapiro, 1985-1986, p. 198). Metaphors external to the particular piece of research prefigure the analysis with a "truth-value" code belonging to another domain (Jameson, 1981). For example, the use of *enlighten* to indicate imparting or gaining knowledge is a light-based metaphor, what Derrida (1982) refers to as the "heliocentric" view of knowledge, the passive receipt of rays. Immanent in these metaphors are philosophical and value commitments so entrenched and familiar that they can do their partisan work in the guise of neutrality, passing as literal.

Consider the following statements about theory (examples inspired by Lakoff & Johnson, 1980, p. 46):

- What is the *foundation* of your theory?
- Your theory needs *support.*
- Your position is *shaky.*
- Your argument is *falling apart.*
- Let's *construct* an argument.
- The *form* of your argument needs buttressing.
- Given your *framework,* no wonder your argument *fell apart.*

The italicized words express our customary, unconscious use of the metaphor, "Theory is a building." The metaphor, moreover, structures the actions we take in theorizing and what we believe constitutes theory. We try to build a theoretical structure, which we then experience as a structure, which has a form and a foundation, which we then experience as an edifice, sometimes quite grand, sometimes in need of shoring up, and sometimes in need of dismantling or, more recently, deconstructing.

Metaphors are everywhere. Consider *functionalism, role* theory, *game* theory, *dramaturgical analogy, organicism, social evolutionism,* the social *system, ecology, labeling* theory, *equilibrium, human capital,* the *power elite, resource mobilization,* ethnic *insurgency, developing* countries, *stratification,* and *significance* tests. Metaphors organize sociological work and affect the interpretations of the "facts"; indeed, facts are interpretable ("make sense") only in terms of their place within a metaphoric structure. The "sense making" is always value constituting—making sense in a particular way, privileging one ordering of the "facts" over others.

Writing Formats

In addition to the metaphoric basis of social scientific writing, there are prescribed writing formats: How we are expected to write affects what we can write about. The referencing system in the social sciences, for example, discourages the use of footnotes, a place for secondary arguments, novel conjectures, and related ideas. Knowledge is constituted as "focused," "problem" (hypothesis) centered, "linear," straightforward. Other thoughts are extraneous. Inductively accomplished research is to be reported deductively; the argument is to be abstracted in 150 words or less; and researchers are to identify explicitly with a theoretical label. Each of these conventions favors—creates and sustains—a particular vision of what constitutes sociological knowledge. The conventions hold tremendous material and symbolic power over social scientists. Using them increases the probability of one's work being accepted into "core" social science journals, but is not *prima facie* evidence of greater—or lesser—truth value or significance than social science writing using other conventions.

Additional social science writing conventions have shaped ethnographies. Needful of distinguishing their work from travelers' and missionaries' reports as well as from imaginative writing, ethnographers adopted an impersonal, third-person voice to explain an "observed phenomenon" and trumpet the authenticity of their representations. John Van Maanen (1988) identifies four conventions used in traditional ethnographies, or what he calls "realist tales." First, there is *experiential author(ity)*. The author as an "I" is mostly absent from the text, which talks about the people studied; the author exists only in the preface, establishing "I was there" and "I'm a researcher" credentials. Second, there is *documentary style,* with a plethora of concrete, particular details that presume to represent the typical activity, pattern, or culture member. Third, *the culture members' point of view* is claimed to be presented through their accounts, quotations, explanations, language, cultural clichés, and so on. And fourth, the author claims *interpretive omnipotence*. The ethnographer's "no-nonsense" interpretations of the culture are claimed as valid. Many of the classic books in the social sciences are realist tales. These include Kai Erikson's *Everything in Its Path* (1976), William Foote Whyte's *Street Corner Society* (1943), Elliot Liebow's *Tally's Corner* (1967), and Carol Stack's *All Our Kin* (1974).

Other genres of qualitative writing—such as texts based on life histories or in-depth interviews—have their own sets of traditional conventions (see Mischler, 1991; Richardson, 1990). In these traditional texts, the researcher proves his or her credentials in the introductory or methods section, and writes the body of the text as though the quotations and document snippets are naturally there, genuine evidence for the case being made, rather than selected, pruned, and spruced up for their textual appearance. Like ethnography, the assumption of *scientific authority* is rhetorically displayed in these qualitative texts. Examples of traditional "life-story" texts include Lillian Rubin's *Worlds of Pain* (1976), Sharon Kaufman's *The Ageless Self* (1986), and my own *The New Other Woman* (Richardson, 1985).

Experimental Writing

In the wake of feminist and postmodernist critiques of traditional qualitative writing practices, qualitative work has been appearing in new forms; genres are blurred, jumbled. I think of them as *experimental representations*. Because experiments are experimental, it is difficult to specify their conventions. One practice these experiments have in common, however, is the *violation of prescribed conventions*; they transgress the boundaries of social science writing genres.

Experimental representation is an emergent and transgressive phenomenon. Although some people are uncomfortable with it both as an idea and as a practice, I highly recommend experimental writing as a method of knowing. Because experimentation is taking place in (because of?) the postmodernist context, experimentation can be thought about within that frame. Working within the "ideology of doubt," experimental writers raise and display postmodernist issues. Chief among these are questions of how the author positions the Self as a knower and teller. For the experimental writer, these lead to the intertwined problems of subjectivity/authority/authorship/reflexivity, on the one hand, and representational form, on the other.

Postmodernism claims that writing is always partial, local, and situational, and that our Self is always present, no matter how much we try to suppress it—but only partially present, for in our writing we repress parts of ourselves, too. Working from that premise, we are freed to write material in a variety of ways: to tell and retell. There is no such thing as "getting it right," only "getting it" differently contoured and nuanced. When experimenting with form, ethnographers learn about the topic and about themselves what is unknowable, unimaginable, using prescribed writing formats. So, even if one chooses to write a final paper in a conventional form, experimenting with format is a practical and powerful way to expand one's interpretive skills and to make one's "old" materials "new."

We can deploy different forms for different audiences and different occasions. Some experimentation can be accomplished simply by writing the same piece of research for an academic audience, a trade book audience, and the popular press (see Richardson, 1990). The potential for alternative forms of representation, however, go way beyond those stagings.

Social scientists are now writing "narratives of the self" (e.g., Ellis, 1992, 1993; Geertz, 1988; Kondo, 1990; Krieger, 1991; Ronai, 1992; Steedman, 1986; I. K. Zola, 1983), fiction (see Frohock, 1992; Stewart, 1989; Wolf, 1992), poetry (e.g., Brady, 1991; Diamond, 1981; Patai, 1988; Prattis, 1985; Richardson, 1992a), drama (Ellis & Bochner, 1992; Paget, 1990; Richardson, 1993; Richardson & Lockridge, 1991), "performance science" (McCall & Becker, 1990), "polyvocal texts" (e.g., Butler & Rosenblum, 1991; Krieger, 1983; Schneider, 1991), "responsive readings" (see Richardson, 1992b), "aphorisms" (E. Rose, 1992), comedy and satire (e.g., Barley, 1986, 1988), visual presentations (e.g., Harper, 1987), mixed genres (e.g., Dorst, 1989; Fine, 1992; hooks, 1990; Lather, 1991; Linden, 1992; Pfohl, 1992; D. Rose, 1989; Stoller, 1989; Trinh, 1989; Ulmer, 1989; Walkerdine, 1990; Williams, 1991; Wolf, 1992), and more. It is beyond the scope of this chapter to outline or comment on each of these experimental forms. Instead, I will address a class of experimental genres that deploy literary devices to re-create lived experience and evoke emotional responses. I call these *evocative representations*. I resist providing the reader with snippets from these forms because snippets will not do them justice and because I hope readers will read and experiment for themselves. I do describe some texts, but I have no desire to valorize a new canon. Again, *process* rather than product is the purpose of this chapter.

Evocative experimental forms display interpretive frameworks that demand analysis of themselves as cultural products and as methods for rendering the sociological. Evocative representations are a striking way of seeing through and beyond sociological naturalisms. They are powerful tools in the "writing as analysis" tool chest. Casting sociology into evocative forms reveals the underlying labor of sociological production and its rhetoric, as well as its potential as a human endeavor, because evocative writing touches us where we live, in our bodies. Through it we can experience the self-reflexive and transformational process of self-creation. Trying out evocative forms, we relate differently to our material; we know it differently. We find ourselves attending to feelings, ambiguities, temporal sequences, blurred experiences, and so on; we struggle to find a textual place for ourselves and our doubts and uncertainties.

One form of evocative writing is the *narrative of the self*. This is a highly personalized, revealing text in which an author tells stories about his or her own lived experience. Using dramatic recall, strong metaphors, images, characters, unusual phrasings, puns, subtexts, and allusions, the writer constructs a sequence of events, a "plot," holding back on interpretation, asking the reader to "relive" the events emotionally with the writer. Narratives of the self do not read like traditional ethnography because they use the writing techniques of fiction. They are specific stories of particular events. Accuracy is not the issue; rather, narratives of the self seek to meet literary criteria of coherence, verisimilitude, and interest. Because narratives of the self are staged as imaginative renderings, they allow the field-worker to exaggerate, swagger, entertain, make a point without tedious documentation, relive the experience, and say what might be unsayable in other circumstances. Writing these frankly subjective narratives, ethnographers are somewhat relieved of the problems of speaking for the "Other," because they are the Other in their texts.

In *ethnographic fictional representations,* another evocative form, writers define their work as fiction, as products of the imagination. The writers are seeking a format in which to tell a "good story"; that story might be about the self, but more likely it is about the group or culture studied. In addition to the techniques used by self-narrators, ethnographic fiction writers draw upon other devices, such as flashback, flashforward, alternative points of view, deep characterization, tone shifts, synecdoche, dialogue, interior monologue, and, sometimes, even the omniscient narrator. The ethnographic setting encases the story, the cultural norms are seen through the characters, but the work is understood as fiction. Although writing up qualitative research as fiction frees the author from the constraints of science, competing with "real" fiction writers is chancy. And if the author wants the work to have an impact for social change, fiction may be a rhetorically poor way to stage the research. But it may just be a good way for the writer to see the material from different points of view.

A third evocative form is *poetic representation.* A poem, as Robert Frost articulates it, is "the shortest emotional distance between two points"—the speaker and the reader. Writing sociological interviews as poetry displays the role of the *prose trope* in constituting knowledge. When we read or hear poetry, we are continually nudged into recognizing that the text has been constructed. But all texts are constructed—prose ones, too; therefore, poetry helps problematize reliability, validity, and "truth."

When people talk, whether as conversants, storytellers, informants, or interviewees, their speech is closer to poetry than it is to sociological prose (Tedlock, 1983). Writing up interviews as poems honors the speaker's pauses, repetitions, alliterations, narrative strategies, rhythms, and so on. Poetry may actually better represent the speaker than the practice of quoting snippets in prose. Further, poetry's rhythms, silences, spaces, breath points, alliterations, meter, cadence, assonance, rhyme, and off-rhyme engage the listener's body, even when the mind resists and denies it. "Poetry is above all a concentration of the power of language which is the power of our ultimate relationship to everything in the universe. It is as if forces we can lay claim to in no other way become present to us in sensuous form" (DeShazer, 1986, p. 138). Settling words together in new configurations lets us hear, see, and feel the world in new dimensions. Poetry is thus a *practical* and *powerful* method for analyzing social worlds.

Ethnographic drama is a fourth evocative genre. Drama is a way of shaping an experience without losing the experience; it can blend realist, fictional, and poetic techniques; it can reconstruct the "sense" of an event from multiple "as-lived" perspectives; and it can give voice to what is unspoken, but present, such as "cancer," as portrayed in Paget's (1990) ethnographic drama, or abortion, as in Ellis and Bochner's (1992) drama. When the material to be displayed is intractable, unruly, multisited, and emotionally laden, drama is more likely to recapture the experience than is standard writing.

Constructing drama raises the postmodern debate about "oral" and "written" texts. Which comes first? Which one should be (is) privileged, and with what consequences? Why the bifurcation between "oral" and "written"? Originating in the lived experience, encoded as field notes, transformed into an ethnographic play, performed, tape-recorded, and then reedited for publication, the printed script might well be fancied the definitive or "valid" version, particularly by those who privilege the published over the "original" or the performance over the lived experience. What happens if we accept this validity claim? Dramatic construction provides multiple sites of invention and potential contestation for validity, the blurring of oral and written texts, rhetorical moves, ethical dilemmas, and authority/authorship. It doesn't just "talk about" these issues, it *is* these issues.

A last evocative form to consider is *mixed genres*. The scholar draws freely in his or her productions from literary, artistic, and scientific genres, often breaking the boundaries of each of those as well. In these productions, the scholar might have different "takes" on the same topic, what I think of as a postmodernist deconstruction of triangulation.

In traditionally staged research we valorize "triangulation" (for discussion of triangulation as method, see Denzin, 1978; for an example, see

357

Statham, Richardson, & Cook, 1991). In that process, a researcher deploys "different methods"—such as interviews, exploration of census data, and document checking—to "validate" findings. These methods, however, carry the *same domain* assumptions, including the assumption that there is a "fixed point" or "object" that can be triangulated. But in postmodernist mixed-genre texts, we do not triangulate; we *crystallize*. We recognize that there are far more than "three sides" from which to approach the world.

I propose that the central image for "validity" for postmodernist texts is not the triangle—a rigid, fixed, two-dimensional object. Rather, the central image is the crystal, which combines symmetry and substance with an infinite variety of shapes, substances, transmutations, multidimensionalities, and angles of approach. Crystals grow, change, alter, but are not amorphous.

Crystals are prisms that reflect externalities and refract within themselves, creating different colors, patterns, arrays, casting off in different directions. What we see depends upon our angle of repose. Not triangulation, crystallization. In postmodernist mixed-genre texts, we have moved from plane geometry to light theory, where light can be both waves and particles.

Crystallization, without losing structure, deconstructs the traditional idea of "validity" (we feel how there is no single truth, we see how texts validate themselves); and crystallization provides us with a deepened, complex, thoroughly partial, understanding of the topic. Paradoxically, we know more and doubt what we know.

We see this crystallization process in several recent books. Margery Wolf, in *A Thrice-Told Tale* (1992), takes the same event and tells it as fictional story, field notes, and a social scientific paper. John Stewart, in *Drinkers, Drummers and Decent Folk* (1989), writes poetry, fiction, ethnographic accounts, and field notes about Village Trinidad. Valerie Walkerdine's *Schoolgirl Fictions* (1990) develops/displays the theme that "masculinity and femininity are fictions which take on the status of fact" (p. xiii) by incorporating into the book journal entries, poems, essays, photographs of herself, drawings, cartoons, and annotated transcripts. Ruth Linden's *Making Stories, Making Selves: Feminist Reflections on the Holocaust* (1992) intertwines autobiography, academic writing, and survivors' stories in a Helen Hooven Santmyer Prize in Women's Studies book, which was her dissertation. Patti Lather's *Getting Smart: Feminist Research and Pedagogy with/in the Postmodern* (1991), a winner of the American Educational Studies Critics Choice book award, displays high theory and transcript, pedagogue and students. John Dorst's *The Written Suburb*

(1989) presents a geographic site as site, image, idea, discourse, and an assemblage of texts.

In some mixed-genre productions, the writer/artist roams freely around topics, breaking our sense of the externality of topics, developing our sense of how topic and self are twin constructs. With the artful self in display, the issues of constructedness and authorial responsibility are profiled. Susan Krieger's *Social Science and the Self: Personal Essays on an Art Form* (1991) is a superb example. The book is "design oriented," reflecting Krieger's attachment to Pueblo potters and Georgia O'Keefe, and, as she says, it "looks more like a pot or a painting than a hypothesis" (p. 120). Trinh T. Minh-ha's *Woman, Native, Other* (1989) breaks down writing conventions within each of the essays that constitute the book, mixing poetry, self-reflection, feminist criticism, photographs, and quotations that help readers experience postcoloniality. John Van Maanen's *Tales of the Field* (1988) analyzes examples of realist, confessional, and impressionist narratives. Stephen Pfohl's *Death at the Parasite Cafe* (1992) employs collage strategies and synchronic juxtapositions, blurring critical theory and militant art forms. Anthologies also reflect these mixed genres. Carolyn Ellis and Michael Flaherty's *Investigating Subjectivity: Research on Lived Experience* (1992) is one example, and the series, *Studies in Symbolic Interaction,* is another.

Whither and Whence?

The contemporary postmodernist context in which we work as qualitative researchers is a propitious one. It provides an opportunity for us to review, critique, and re-vision writing. Although we are freer to present our texts in a variety of forms to diverse audiences, we have different constraints arising from self-consciousness about claims to authorship, authority, truth, validity, and reliability. Self-reflexivity unmasks complex political/ideological agendas hidden in our writing. Truth claims are less easily validated now; desires to speak "for" others are suspect. The greater freedom to experiment with textual form, however, does not guarantee a better product. The opportunities for writing worthy texts—books and articles that are "good reads"—are multiple, exciting, and demanding. But the work is harder. The guarantees are fewer. There is a lot more for us to think about.

One thing for us to think about is whether writing experimentally for publication is a luxury open only to those who have academic sinecure.

Can/should only the already tenured write in experimental modes? Are the tenured doing a disservice to students by introducing them to alternative forms of writing? Will teaching them hereticisms "deskill" them? Alienate them from their discipline? These are heady ethical, pedagogical, and practical questions. I struggle with them in my teaching, writing, and collegial discussions. I have no definitive answers, but I do have some thoughts on the issues.

First, there are many different avenues open for the sociological writer (see Denzin, 1994; Richardson, 1990). There is no single way—much less "right" way—of staging a text. The same material can be written for different audiences—positivists, interactionists, postmodernists, feminists, humanities professors, cultural studies scholars, policy makers, and so on. That is why it is called *material.* Like wet clay, it is there for us to shape. What are our purposes? What are our goals? Who do we want to reach? What do we want to accomplish? If you are a graduate student, your likely purpose is the approval of your Ph.D. dissertation by your committee; if you are an untenured academic, your concern is probably the acceptance of an article by a mainline journal. Writing for those purposes is one way of knowing the material and one way of communicating with one kind of reader. Writing in standard ways does not prevent us from writing in other ways. We cannot write every way, for every purpose, at the same time. Most important, once we understand how to stage a dissertation or journal article rhetorically, we are more likely to get it accepted, get tenured, or the like. Even liberatory and radical messages can be published in conservative journals, if the writer follows the rules (Agger, 1990). Consequently, deconstructing traditional writing practices is a way of making writers more conscious of writing conventions, and, therefore, more competently able to meet them and to get their messages into mainstream social science.

Second, writing is a process of discovery. My purpose is not to turn us into poets, novelists, or dramatists—few of us will write well enough to succeed in those competitive fields. Most of us, like Poe, will be at best only almost poets. Rather, my intention is to encourage individuals to accept and nurture their own voices. The researcher's self-knowledge and knowledge of the topic develops through experimentation with point of view, tone, texture, sequencing, metaphor, and so on. The whole enterprise is demystified. Even the analysis paralysis that afflicts some readers of postmodernism is attenuated when writers view their work as process rather than as definitive representation.

Third, writing practices can improve traditional texts because writers relate more deeply and complexly to their materials. The writer understands the material in different ways. The deepened understanding of a Self deepens the text. The text will be less boring because the writer will be more consciously engaged in its production, more present to self and others.

Finally, contemporary experimental writing is a harbinger; qualitative research has been and will continue to be changed by and through it. High-grade journals—such as *The Sociological Quarterly, Symbolic Interaction, Journal of Contemporary Ethnography,* and *Qualitative Sociology*—already publish experimental pieces. The annual, *Studies in Symbolic Interaction,* showcases evocative writing. Presses such as Routledge, University of Chicago, University of Michigan, University of Indiana, University of Pennsylvania, Rutgers University Press, and Sage Publications regularly publish experimental work by both well-known and lesser-known authors. Traditional ethnographers write more reflexively and self-consciously (see Thorne, 1993). Even those opposed to postmodernism legitimate it through dialogue (Whyte, 1992). Throughout the social sciences, convention papers include transgressive presentations. Entire conferences are devoted to experimentation, such as the "Redesigning Ethnography" conference at the University of Colorado, which featured speakers from different disciplines. At least two well-respected interpretive programs—at the University of Illinois (under Norman Denzin) and at the University of South Florida (under Arthur Bochner and Carolyn Ellis)—are teaching about representational issues. All of these changes in academic practices are signs of *paradigm changes.*

In the 1950s, the sociology of science was a new, reflexively critical area. Today, the sociology of science undergirds theory, methods, and interdisciplinary "science studies." In the 1960s, "gender" emerged as a theoretical perspective. Today, gender studies is one of the largest (if not the largest) subfield in social sciences. In part, science studies and gender studies thrived because they identified normative assumptions of social science that falsely limited knowledge. They spoke "truly" to the everyday experiences of social scientists. The new areas hit us where we lived—in our work and in our bodies. They offered alternative perspectives for understanding the experienced world.

Today, the postmodernist critique is having the same impact on social sciences that science studies and gender have had, and for similar reasons.

Postmodernism identifies unspecified assumptions that hinder us in our search for understanding "truly," and it offers alternative practices that work. We feel its "truth"—its moral, intellectual, aesthetic, emotional, intuitive, embodied, playful pull. Each researcher is likely to respond to that pull differently, which should lead to writing that is more diverse, more author centered, less boring, and humbler. This is a time of transition, a propitious moment. Where this experimentation will eventually take us, I do not know, but I do know that we cannot go back to where we were.

◆ Writing Practices

> Writing, the creative effort, should come first—at least for some part of every day of your life. It is a wonderful blessing if you will use it. You will become happier, more enlightened, alive, impassioned, light hearted and generous to everybody else. Even your health will improve. Colds will disappear and all the other ailments of discouragement and boredom. (Ueland, 1938/1987)

In what follows, I suggest some ways of using writing as a method of knowing. I have chosen exercises that have been productive for me and my students because they demystify writing, nurture the researcher's voice, and serve the process of discovery. I wish I could guarantee them to bring good health as well! The practices are organized around topics discussed in the text.

Metaphor

Using old, wornout metaphors, although easy and comfortable, after a while invites stodginess and stiffness. The stiffer you get, the less flexible you are. You invite being ignored. In less metaphoric terms, if your writing is clichéd, you will not stretch your own imagination (ouch! hear the cliché! hear the cliché of me pointing out the cliché!) and you will bore people.

1. In standard social scientific writing, the metaphor for theory is that it is a "building" (structure, foundation, construction, deconstruction, framework, form, and so on). Consider a different metaphor for theory, such as "theory as a tapestry" or "theory as an illness." Write a paragraph about theory using your metaphor. (See above for examples of "theory as

building.") Do you "see" differently and "feel" differently about theorizing when you use an unusual metaphor?

2. Consider alternative sensory metaphors for "knowledge" other than the heliocentric one mentioned above. What happens when you rethink/ resense "knowledge" as situated in "voice"? In touch?

3. What metaphors do you use in your writing? Take a look at one of your papers and highlight your metaphors and images. What are you saying through metaphors that you did not realize you were saying? What are you reinscribing? Do you want to? Can you find different metaphors that change how you "see" ("feel"?) the material? Your relationship to it? Are your mixed metaphors pointing to confusion in yourself or to social science's glossing over of ideas?

4. Take a look at George Lakoff and Mark Johnson's *Metaphors We Live By* (1980). It is a wonderful book, a compendium of examples of metaphors in everyday life and how they affect our ways of perceiving, thinking, and acting. What everyday metaphors are shaping your knowing/writing? What alternative ones can you find?

Writing Formats

1. Choose a journal article that you think exemplifies the writing conventions of the mainstream of your discipline. Then write a two- to four-page analysis of that article. How is the argument staged? Who is the presumed audience? How does the paper inscribe ideology? How does the author claim "authority" over the material? Where is the author? Where are "you" in this paper? Who are the subjects and who are the objects of research here?

2. Choose a journal article that exemplifies excellence in qualitative research, and write a two- to four-page analysis of that article. How has the article built upon normative social science writing? How is authority claimed? Where is the author? Where are "you" in the article? Who are the subjects and who are the objects of research here?

3. Choose a paper you have written for a class or that you have published that you think is pretty good. How did you follow the norms of your discipline? Were you conscious of doing so? How did you stage your paper? What parts did your professor/reviewer laud? How did you depend upon those norms to carry your argument? Did you elide over some difficult areas through vagueness, jargon, calls to authorities, or other

rhetorical devices? What voices did you exclude in your writing? Who is the audience? Where are the subjects in the paper? Where are you? How do you feel about the paper now? About your process of constructing it?

Experimental Writing

An excellent way to open yourself up to experimental writing is to learn from creative writers. They have much to teach us about writing, and about ourselves. Even if you chose to write a fairly traditional text, the creative writing experience will enrich that text.

1. Join or start a writing group. This could be a writing support group, a creative writing group, a poetry group, a dissertation group, or another kind. (For dissertation and article writing, see Becker, 1986; Fox, 1985; Richardson, 1990; Wolcott, 1990.)

2. Work through a creative writing guidebook. Natalie Goldberg (1986, 1990), Rust Hills (1987), Brenda Ueland (1938/1987), and Deena Metzger (1993) all provide excellent guides.

3. Enroll in a creative writing workshop. This experience is valuable for both beginning and experienced researchers. Here is testimony from Barrie Thorne (personal communication, September 2, 1992), an experienced, compelling, and traditionally inclined ethnography writer: "Taking a weekly creative writing class from Deena Metzger has been an important part of this quest. She encourages connecting with the unconscious, reaching for unusual verbs and evocative concrete detail, and exploring the emotional side of writing."

4. Use "writing up" field notes as an opportunity to expand your writing vocabulary, habits of thought, and attentiveness to your senses, and as a bulwark against the censorious voice of science. Where better to develop your sense of self, your voice, than in the process of doing your research? Apply creative writing skills to your field notes. I turn again to Barrie Thorne's description and testimony, not only because it is instructive, but because she writes within mainstream ethnographic tradition:

Field notes . . . have a private and intimate character; one can innovate, make false starts, flare up with emotions without feeling an anonymous audience at one's shoulder. . . . As I write field notes, I push for full description, avoiding sociological jargon, staying close to what I saw, while letting my imagination roam around the event, searching for patterns and larger chains of significance (as they occur to me, I write these analytic hunches in capital letters in parentheses).

5. Some of us are more "choked" than Barrie Thorne in our field note writing, and we may need other devices to free our writing. For some it may mean rethinking what we have been taught about objectivity, science, and the ethnographic project. What works for me is to give different labels to different content. Building upon Glaser and Strauss's (1967) work, I use four categories, which you may find of value:

- *Observation notes* (ON): These are as concrete and detailed as I am able to make them. I want to think of them as fairly accurate renditions of what I see, hear, feel, taste, and so on.
- *Methodological notes* (MN): These are messages to myself regarding how to collect "data,"—who to talk to, what to wear, when to phone, and so on. I write a lot of these because I like methods, and I like to keep a process diary of my work.
- *Theoretical notes* (TN): These are hunches, hypotheses, poststructuralist connections, critiques of what I am doing/thinking/seeing. I like writing these because they open up my text—my field note text—to alternative interpretations and a critical epistemological stance. It is a way of keeping me from being hooked on my "take" on reality.
- *Personal notes* (PN): These are feelings statements about the research, the people I am talking to, myself doing the process, my doubts, my anxieties, my pleasures. I do no censoring here at all. I want all my feelings out on paper because I like them and because I know they are there anyway, affecting what/how I lay claim to knowing. Writing personal notes is a way for me to know myself better, a way of using writing as a method of inquiry into the self.

6. Keep a journal. In it, write about your feelings about your work. This not only frees up your writing, it becomes the "historical record" for writing a narrative of the self.

7. If you wish to experiment with evocative writing, a good place to begin is by transforming your field notes into drama. See what ethnographic rules you are using (such as fidelity to the speech of the participants, fidelity in the order of the speakers and events) and what literary ones you are invoking (such as limits on how long a speaker speaks, keeping the "plot" moving along, developing character through actions). Writing dramatic presentations accentuates ethical considerations. If you doubt that,

365

contrast writing up an ethnographic event as a "typical" event with writing it as a play, with you and your hosts cast in roles that will be performed before others. Who has ownership of spoken words? How is authorship attributed? What if people don't like how they are characterized? Are courtesy norms being violated? Experiment here with both oral and written versions of your drama.

8. Experiment with transforming an in-depth interview into a poetic representation. Try using only the words, rhythms, figures of speech, breath points, pauses, syntax, and diction of the speaker. Where do you figure in the poem? What do you know about the interviewee and about yourself that you did not know before you wrote the poem? What poetic devices have you sacrificed in the name of science?

9. Experiment with writing narratives of the self. Keep in mind Barbara Tuchman's warning: "The writer's object is—or should be—to hold the reader's attention. . . . I want the reader to turn the page and keep on turning to the end. This is accomplished only when the narrative moves steadily ahead, not when it comes to a weary standstill, overlaced with every item uncovered in the research" (in *New York Times,* February 2, 1989).

10. Consider a fieldwork setting. Consider the various subject positions you have or have had within it. For example, in a store you might be a salesclerk, customer, manager, feminist, capitalist, parent, child, and so on. Write about the setting (or an event in the setting) from several different subject positions. What do you "know" from the different positions? Next, let the different points of view dialogue with each other. What do you discover through these dialogues?

11. Consider a paper you have written (or your field notes). What has been left out? Who is not present in this text? Who has been repressed? Who has been marginalized? Rewrite the text from that point of view.

12. Write a story about the "self" from your point of view (such as something that happened in your family or in your seminar). Then, interview another participant (such as a family or seminar member) and have that person tell you his or her story of the event. See yourself as part of the other individual's story in the same way he or she is part of your story. How do you rewrite your story from the other person's point of view? (This is an exercise used by Carolyn Ellis.)

13. Collaborative writing is a way to see beyond one's own naturalisms of style and attitude. This is an exercise that I have used in my teaching,

but it would be appropriate for a writing group as well. Each member writes a story of his or her life. It could be a feminist story, success story, quest story, cultural story, professional socialization story, realist tale, confessional tale, or whatever. All persons' stories are photocopied for the group. The group is then broken into subgroups (I prefer groups of three), and each subgroup collaborates on writing a new story, the collective story of its members. The collaboration can take any form: drama, poetry, fiction, narrative of the selves, realism, whatever the subgroup chooses. The collaboration is shared with the entire group. All members then write about their feelings about the collaboration and what happened to their stories, their lives, in the process.

14. A variant on exercise 13 is for each member to tape-record his or her own story and for other members to create a written text out of the oral one (a technique used by Art Bochner). The "originator" of the story then comments upon the others' telling. This is a good way to break down oral and written codes.

I hope these exercises are helpful. I hope you find new ways to experiment. I hope we all do.

> Willing is doing something you know already—there is no new imaginative understanding in it. And presently your soul gets frightfully sterile and dry because you are so quick, snappy, and efficient about doing one thing after another that you have no time for your own ideas to come in and develop and gently shine. (Ueland, 1938/1987, p. 29)

Happy writing and rewriting!

◆ References

Agger, B. (1989). *Reading science: A literary, political and sociological analysis.* Dix Hills, NY: General Hall.

Agger, B. (1990). *The decline of discourse: Reading, writing and resistance in postmodern capitalism.* Bristol, PA: Falmer.

Atkinson, P. A. (1990). *The ethnographic imagination: Textual constructions of reality.* London: Routledge.

Balzac, H. de. (1965). Preface to *The human comedy,* from *At the sign of the cat and racket* (C. Bell, Trans., 1897; original work published 1842). In R. Ellman & C. Feidelson,

Jr. (Eds.), *The modern tradition: Backgrounds of modern literature* (pp. 246-254). New York: Oxford University Press.

Barley, N. (1986). *Ceremony: An anthropologist's misadventures in the African bush*. New York: Henry Holt.

Barley, N. (1988). *Not a pleasant sport*. New York: Henry Holt.

Becker, H. S. (1986). *Writing for social scientists: How to finish your thesis, book, or article*. Chicago: University of Chicago Press.

Brady, I. (Ed.). (1991). *Anthropological poetics*. Savage, MD: Rowman & Littlefield.

Brodkey, L. (1987). *Academic writing as social practice*. Philadelphia: Temple University Press.

Brown, R. H. (1977). *A poetic for sociology*. Cambridge: Cambridge University Press.

Butler, S., & Rosenblum, B. (1991). *Cancer in two voices*. San Francisco: Spinsters.

Carey, J. W. (1989). *Communication as culture: Essays on media and society*. Cambridge: Cambridge University Press.

Clifford, J. (1986). Introduction: Partial truths. In J. Clifford & G. E. Marcus (Eds.), *Writing culture: The poetics and politics of ethnography* (pp. 1-26). Berkeley: University of California Press.

Clifford, J., & Marcus, G. E. (Eds.). (1986). *Writing culture: The poetics and politics of ethnography*. Berkeley: University of California Press.

Clough, P. T. (1992). *The end(s) of ethnography: From realism to social criticism*. Newbury Park, CA: Sage.

Crawford, M. A. (1951). Introduction. In H. de Balzac, *Old Goriot*. New York: Penguin.

Denzin, N. K. (1978). *The research act*. New York: McGraw-Hill.

Denzin, N. K. (1986). A postmodern social theory. *Sociological Theory, 4,* 194-204.

Denzin, N. K. (1991). *Images of postmodern society*. Newbury Park, CA: Sage.

Denzin, N. K. (1994). Evaluating qualitative research in the poststructural moment: The lessons James Joyce teaches us. *Qualitative Studies in Education, 7,* 295-308.

Derrida, J. (1982). *The margins of philosophy* (A. Bass, Trans.). Chicago: University of Chicago Press.

DeShazer, M. K. (1986). *Inspiring women: Reimagining the muse*. New York: Pergamon.

Diamond, S. (1981). *Totems*. Barrytown, NY: Open Book.

Dorst, J. D. (1989). *The written suburb: An American site, an ethnographic dilemma*. Philadelphia: University of Pennsylvania Press.

Eagleton, T. (1983). *Literary theory: An introduction*. Minneapolis: University of Minnesota Press.

Edmondson, R. (1984). *Rhetoric in sociology*. London: Macmillan.

Ellis, C. (forthcoming). *Final negotiations*. Philadelphia: Temple University Press.

Ellis, C. (1993). Telling a story of sudden death. *Sociological Quarterly, 34,* 711-730.

Ellis, C., & Bochner, A. P. (1992). Telling and performing personal stories: The constraints of choice in abortion. In C. Ellis & M. G. Flaherty (Eds.), *Investigating subjectivity: Research on lived experience* (pp. 79-101). Newbury Park, CA: Sage.

Erikson, K. T. (1976). *Everything in its path: Destruction of the community in the Buffalo Creek flood*. New York: Simon & Schuster.

Fine, M. (1992). *Disruptive voices: The possibility of feminist research*. Ann Arbor: University of Michigan Press.

Fiske, D. W., & Schweder, R. A. (Eds.). (1986). *Metatheory in social science: Pluralisms and subjectivities.* Chicago: University of Chicago Press.

Fox, M. F. (Ed.). (1985). *Scholarly writing and publishing: Issues, problems, and solutions.* Boulder, CO: Westview.

Frohock, F. (1992). *Healing powers.* Chicago: University of Chicago Press.

Geertz, C. (1983). *Local knowledge: Further essays in interpretive anthropology.* New York: Basic Books.

Geertz, C. (1988). *Works and lives: The anthropologist as author.* Stanford, CA: Stanford University Press.

Glaser, B. G., & Strauss, A. L. (1967). *The discovery of grounded theory: Strategies for qualitative research.* Chicago: Aldine.

Gleick, J. (1984, June 10). Solving the mathematical riddle of chaos. *New York Times Magazine,* pp. 30-32.

Goldberg, N. (1986). *Writing down the bones: Freeing the writer within.* Boston: Shambala.

Goldberg, N. (1990). *Wild mind: Living the writer's life.* New York: Bantam.

Harper, D. (1987). *Working knowledge: Skill and community in a small shop.* Chicago: University of Chicago Press.

Hills, R. (1987). *Writing in general and the short story in particular.* Boston: Houghton Mifflin.

hooks, b. (1990). *Yearning: Race, gender, and cultural politics.* Boston: South End.

Hutcheon, L. (1988). *A poetics of postmodernism: History, theory and fiction.* New York: Routledge.

Jameson, F. (1981). *The political unconscious.* Ithaca, NY: Cornell University Press.

Kaufman, S. (1986). *The ageless self: Sources of meaning in later life.* Madison: University of Wisconsin Press.

Kline, M. (1980). *Mathematics: The loss of certainty.* New York: Oxford University Press.

Kondo, D. (1990). *Crafting selves.* Chicago: University of Chicago Press.

Krieger, S. (1983). *The mirror dance: Identity in a women's community.* Philadelphia: Temple University Press.

Krieger, S. (1991). *Social science and the self: Personal essays on an art form.* New Brunswick, NJ: Rutgers University Press.

Lakoff, G., & Johnson, M. (1980). *Metaphors we live by.* Chicago: University of Chicago Press.

Lather, P. (1991). *Getting smart: Feminist research and pedagogy with/in the postmodern.* New York: Routledge.

Lehman, D. (1991). *Signs of the times: Deconstruction and the fall of Paul de Man.* New York: Poseidon.

Levine, D. N. (1985). *The flight from ambiguity: Essays in social and cultural theory.* Chicago: University of Chicago Press.

Liebow, E. (1967). *Tally's corner: A study of Negro street corner men.* Boston: Little, Brown.

Linden, R. R. (1992). *Making stories, making selves: Feminist reflections on the Holocaust.* Columbus: Ohio State University.

Lyotard, J.-F. (1979). *The postmodern condition: A report on knowledge* (G. Bennington & G. Masumi, Trans.). Minneapolis: University of Minnesota Press.

Marcus, G. E., & Fischer, M. J. M. (1986). *Anthropology as cultural critique: An experimental moment in the human sciences.* Chicago: University of Chicago Press.

McCall, M., & Becker, H. S. (1990). Performance science. *Social Problems, 32*, 117-132.

Metzger, D. (1993). *Writing for your life: A guide and companion to the inner worlds.* New York: Harper-Collins.

Mischler, E. G. (1991). *Research interviewing: Context and narrative.* Cambridge, MA: Harvard University Press.

Morris, M. (1988). *The pirate's fiancee: Feminism, reading, and postmodernism.* New York: Verso.

Nelson, J. S., Megill, A., & McCloskey, D. N. (Eds.). (1987). *The rhetoric of the human sciences: Language and argument in scholarship and human affairs.* Madison: University of Wisconsin Press.

Nicholson, L. J. (Ed.). (1990). *Feminism/postmodernism.* New York: Routledge.

Paget, M. (1990). Performing the text. *Journal of Contemporary Ethnography, 19,* 136-155.

Patai, D. (1988). Constructing a self: A Brazilian life story. *Feminist Studies, 14,* 142-163.

Pfohl, S. J. (1992). *Death at the Parasite Cafe: Social science (fictions) and the postmodern.* New York: St. Martin's.

Prattis, I. (Ed.). (1985). *Reflections: The anthropological muse.* Washington, DC: American Anthropological Association.

Richardson, L. (1985). *The new other woman: Contemporary single women in affairs with married men.* New York: Free Press.

Richardson, L. (1990). *Writing strategies: Reaching diverse audiences.* Newbury Park, CA: Sage.

Richardson, L. (1991). Postmodern social theory: Representational practices. *Sociological Theory, 9,* 173-180.

Richardson, L. (1992a). The consequences of poetic representation: Writing the other, rewriting the self. In C. Ellis & M. G. Flaherty (Eds.), *Investigating subjectivity: Research on lived experience* (pp. 125-140). Newbury Park, CA: Sage.

Richardson, L. (1992b). Resisting resistance narratives: A representation for communication. *Studies in Symbolic Interaction, 13,* 77-83.

Richardson, L. (1993). The case of the skipped line: Poetics, dramatics and transgressive validity. *Sociological Quarterly, 34,* 695-710.

Richardson, L., & Lockridge, E. (1991). The sea monster: An "ethnographic drama." *Symbolic Interaction, 14,* 335-340.

Ronai, C. R. (1992). The reflexive self through narrative: A night in the life of an erotic dancer/researcher. In C. Ellis & M. G. Flaherty (Eds.), *Investigating subjectivity: Research on lived experience* (pp. 102-124). Newbury Park, CA: Sage.

Rorty, R. (1979). *Philosophy and the mirror of man.* Princeton, NJ: Princeton University Press.

Rose, D. (1989). *Patterns of American culture: Ethnography and estrangement.* Philadelphia: University of Pennsylvania Press.

Rose, E. (1992). *The werald.* Boulder, CO: Waiting Room.

Rubin, L. B. (1976). *Worlds of pain: Life in the working-class family.* New York: Basic Books.

Schneider, J. (1991). Troubles with textual authority in sociology. *Symbolic Interaction, 14,* 295-320.

Seidman, S., & Wagner, D. (Eds.). (1991). *Postmodernism and social theory.* New York: Basil Blackwell.

Shapiro, M. (1985-1986). Metaphor in the philosophy of the social sciences. *Cultural Critique, 2,* 191-214.

Simons, H. W. (1990). *Rhetoric in the human sciences.* London: Sage.

Stack, C. B. (1974). *All our kin: Strategies for survival in a black community.* New York: Harper & Row.

Statham, A., Richardson, L., & Cook, J. A. (1991). *Gender and university teaching: A negotiated difference.* Albany: State University of New York Press.

Steedman, K. (1986). *Landscape for a good woman: A story of two lives.* New Brunswick, NJ: Rutgers University Press.

Stewart, J. (1989). *Drinkers, drummers and decent folk: Ethnographic narratives of Village Trinidad.* Albany: State University of New York.

Stoller, P. (1989). *Taste of ethnographic things: The senses in anthropology.* Philadelphia: University of Pennsylvania Press.

Tedlock, D. (1983). *The spoken word and the work of interpretation.* Philadelphia: University of Pennsylvania Press.

Thorne, B. (1993). *Gender play.* New Brunswick, NJ: Rutgers University Press.

Trinh T. M.-H. (1989). *Woman, native, other: Writing postcoloniality and feminism.* Bloomington: Indiana University Press.

Turner, V., & Bruner, E. M. (Eds.). (1986). *The anthropology of experience.* Champagne-Urbana: University of Illinois Press.

Ueland, B. (1987). *If you want to write: A book about art, independence and spirit.* Saint Paul, MN: Graywolf. (Original work published 1938)

Ulmer, G. (1989). *Teletheory: Grammatology in the age of video.* New York: Routledge.

Van Maanen, J. (1988). *Tales of the field: On writing ethnography.* Chicago: University of Chicago Press.

Walkerdine, V. (1990). *Schoolgirl fictions.* London: Verso.

Weedon, C. (1987). *Feminist practice and poststructuralist theory.* New York: Basil Blackwell.

Whyte, W. F. (1943). *Street corner society: The social structure of an Italian slum.* Chicago: University of Chicago Press.

Whyte, W. F. (1992). In defense of *Street corner society. Journal of Contemporary Ethnography, 21,* 52-68.

Williams, P. J. (1991). *The alchemy of race and rights: Diary of a law professor.* Cambridge, MA: Harvard University Press.

Wolf, M. (1992). *A thrice-told tale: Feminism, postmodernism, and ethnographic responsibility.* Stanford, CA: Stanford University Press.

Wolcott, H. F. (1990). *Writing up qualitative research.* Newbury Park, CA: Sage.

Zola, E. (1965). The novel as social science. In R. Ellman & C. Feidelson, Jr. (Eds.), *The modern tradition: Backgrounds of modern literature* (pp. 270-289). New York: Oxford University Press. (Original work published 1880)

Zola, I. K. (1983). *Missing pieces: A chronicle of living with a disability.* Philadelphia: Temple University Press.

13

Qualitative Program Evaluation

Practice and Promise

Jennifer C. Greene

Sylvia Winslow, chair of a state legislative committee on health, is concerned about the effectiveness of the state's prenatal care services. Recent reports from varied sources—most dramatically in the media—have underscored the difficulties that rural women especially have in finding prenatal care and the tragedies that result from inadequate care. Sylvia asks the staff of her health committee for a comprehensive update on the state's prenatal care program, with special focus on issues of access and quality.

Albert Peters enrolls his son in a new program at the local high school that claims to be offering a different vision of secondary education. Critical elements of this vision for Albert and his son include heterogeneous grouping, a curriculum infused with multicultural ideas and values, and a strong mentoring system in which faculty guide each youth's program and progress. Albert genuinely believes that a program, such as this one might be, in which all kids are respected and assumed to have unique and valuable gifts is the only way his son will make it through high school. It is October already, and Albert wants some information on the nature and quality of this educational experience for his son. Albert calls the high school principal to request such information.

AUTHOR'S NOTE: My sincere thanks to the reviewers and the editors for their constructive contributions to this chapter.

Chapter 1, the U.S. federal government's long-term compensatory education program, is up for reauthorization in two years. In anticipation of the probable debate, the chair of the Senate Education and Labor Committee asks the U.S. General Accounting Office to provide a summary assessment of Chapter 1 success over the past five years.

Evan Gonzalez, the human resource director at IVM, a major electronics corporation, is alarmed at the increasing number of employees utilizing the company's counseling and psychological services. Evan's concern is both for the employees—What is going on in the company or in specific communities to invoke such a demand for mental health services?—and for the company, as these services are extremely costly. Evan raises his questions at the next management meeting.

Sam Brown has been advocating for the homeless in his county for five years now, and he is weary. He needs some kind of catalyst to mobilize his constituents and to energize concerned supporters toward concrete action by the county board. If he could have current information on the numbers of homeless in the county, on their personal tragedies, and on the social costs of homelessness, well, that might just do the trick.

◆ Contexts of Program Evaluation

The above are examples of some of the many scenarios of social program evaluation. They vary in the nature of the social issues involved, in the perspectives taken on the issues, in the geographic scope of services to be reviewed, in the kinds of information sought, and in the stated purposes for which the information will be used. Underlying these differences, however, are some fundamental commonalities that demarcate evaluation contexts, and that thereby distinguish program evaluation as a unique form of social inquiry.

Perhaps most distinctive about program evaluation is its political inherency (Patton, 1987), the "recognition that politics and science are both integral aspects of evaluation" (Cronbach & Associates, 1980, p. 35), and that "the evaluator has political influence even when he does not aspire to it" (Cronbach & Associates, 1980, p. 3). Evaluations are conducted on social programs—most important, on social programs in the public domain.[1] Social programs are manifest responses to priority individual and community needs and are themselves "the creatures of political decisions.

They [are] proposed, defined, debated, enacted, and funded through political processes, and in implementation they remain subject to [political] pressures—both supportive and hostile" (Weiss, 1987, p. 47). So program evaluation is integrally intertwined with political decision making about societal priorities, resource allocation, and power. "By its very nature [evaluation] makes implicit political statements about such issues as the problematic nature of some programs and the unchallengeability of others" (Weiss, 1987, p. 48).

Moreover, the work of social program evaluators is framed by the concerns and interests of selected members of the setting being evaluated. Evaluation questions about the significance of program goals or about the quality and effectiveness of program strategies reflect not inquirer autonomy or theoretical predictions, but rather a politicized process of priority setting. In all evaluation contexts there are multiple, often competing, potential audiences—groups and individuals who have vested interests in the program being evaluated, called *stakeholders* in evaluation jargon. These range from policy makers and funders like Sylvia Winslow and the U.S. Congress, to program administrators and staff like Evan Gonzalez of IVM, to intended beneficiaries like parent Albert Peters and homeless advocate Sam Brown, and to the citizenry at large. And so, unlike most other social scientists, who assume an audience of peers/scholars, evaluators must negotiate whose questions will be addressed and whose interests will be served by their work.

Evaluation results then enter the political arena of social program and policy decision making not as decontextualized, abstract, or theoretical knowledge claims, but rather as practical knowledge claims, as empirically justified value judgments about the merit or worth of the program evaluated. Evaluators describe and infer about practical matters, about the significance of concrete program experiences for various stakeholders. But evaluators do more than describe and infer. At root, evaluation is about valuing (Scriven, 1967) and judging (Stake, 1967). Hence evaluators also infuse directly into the political strands of social policy making the standards or criteria used for rendering judgments. Like the selection of evaluation questions and audiences, determining the standards against which a program will be judged is a contested task. Increasingly, particularly in qualitative evaluations, these valuing standards are identified and offered pluralistically, as multiple sets. Program effectiveness, for example, has many hues, depending on one's vantage point in both space and time. Administrators might well understand effectiveness as efficiency, beneficiaries as significant relief from life's daily struggles, and funders as the long-term realization of tax dollars saved.

◆ Evaluation Methodologies

Yet neither these diverse criteria for program effectiveness nor different stakeholders' widely divergent evaluation questions can be equally well addressed by the same evaluation methodology. In this respect, it is the fundamental political nature of program evaluation contexts, intertwined with the predispositions and beliefs of the evaluator, that shape the contours of evaluation methodologies and guide the selection of a specific evaluation approach for a given context. Different evaluation methodologies are expressly oriented around the information needs of different audiences—from the macro program- and cost-effectiveness questions of policy makers to the micro questions of meaning for individual participants. These varied audience orientations further represent, explicitly or implicitly, the promotion of different values and political stances. Evaluation methodologies hence constitute coordinated frameworks of philosophical assumptions (about the world, human nature, knowledge, ethics), integrated with ideological views about the role and purpose of social inquiry in social policy and program decision making, with accompanying value stances regarding the desired ends of programs and of inquiry, and finally—last as well as least—with complementary methods preferences. Again, it is because evaluation is politically contextualized that constitutive differences in evaluation methodologies extend well beyond alternative methods and also beyond alternative philosophies of science (see Guba, 1990) to incorporate alternative ideologies (Scriven, 1983) and alternative philosophies of ethics, democracy, and justice (House, 1980).

Table 13.1 offers a descriptive categorization of four major genres of evaluation methodologies. The first, which represents the historically dominant tradition in program evaluation, is oriented around the macro policy issues of program effectiveness and cost efficiency. Sylvia Winslow's questions about the quality of her state's prenatal health care services and the U.S. Senate's questions about Chapter 1 success illustrate the broad program effectiveness issues this evaluation genre is designed to address. In this genre primary emphasis is placed on program effectiveness as outcomes and, concomitantly, on the social value of accountability. Early postpositivist evaluation was typified by large-scale studies of Great Society

TABLE 13.1 Major Approaches to Program Evaluation

Philosophical Framework	Ideological Framework/ Key Values Promoted	Key Audiences	Preferred Methods	Typical Evaluation Questions
Postpositivism	Systems theory/efficiency, accountability, theoretical causal knowledge	High-level policy and decision makers	Quantitative: experiments and quasi-experiments, systems analysis, causal modeling, cost-benefit analysis	Are desired outcomes attained and attributable to the program? Is this program the most efficient alternative?
Pragmatism	Management/ practicality, quality control, utility	Mid-level program managers, administrators, and other decision makers	Eclectic, mixed: structured and unstructured surveys, questionnaires, interviews, observations	Which parts of the program work well and which need improvement? How effective is the program with respect to the organization's goals? With respect to beneficiaries' needs?
Interpretivism	Pluralism/ understanding, diversity, solidarity	Program directors, staff, and beneficiaries	Qualitative: case studies, interviews, observations, document review	How is the program experienced by various stakeholders?
Critical, normative science	Emancipation/ empowerment, social change	Program beneficiaries, their communities, other "powerless" groups	Participatory: stakeholder participation in varied structured and unstructured, quantitative and qualitative designs and methods; historical analysis, social criticism	In what ways are the premises, goals, or activities of the program serving to maintain power and resources inequities in the society?

programs, such as the Head Start evaluation (Cicirelli & Associates, 1969) and, later, the New Jersey Negative Income Tax Experiment (Rossi & Lyall, 1978). These studies demonstrated well the failure of experimental logic to meet the demands of evaluation settings. Even so, with "old certainties unthroned, but not abolished" (Cook, 1985, p. 37) and new efforts to reclaim the primacy of science, and hence of scientists, in social programming—as best represented by theory-driven evaluation (Chen & Rossi, 1983)—post-positivist evaluators retain a strong position amidst theorists and methodologists and a still-dominant position among evaluation practitioners and, perhaps most notably, evaluation audiences. *How can this be an evaluation if it doesn't have a control group?* remains a familiar lament from the field.

The second genre of evaluation methodologies arose largely in response to the failure of experimental science to provide timely and useful information for program decision making. Characteristic of these methodologies are their orientation to decision making and hence to management, their primary emphasis on producing useful information, their practical and pragmatic value base, and their eclectic methodological stance. Evaluators in this genre pragmatically select their methods to match the practical problem at hand, rather than as dictated by some abstract set of philosophical tenets (Howe, 1988; Patton, 1988). For example, in order to decide what action if any to take in the face of IVM employees' increasing use of psychological services, Evan Gonzalez and other IVM managers are likely to need a variety of qualitative, quantitative, and perhaps even historical information related to the experiences and contexts of the workplace. Decision- and utilization-oriented evaluators focus on providing support for efficient and effective program management. As an unwavering champion of practical, utilization-focused evaluation, Michael Patton's (1990) approach to qualitative evaluation clearly falls within this genre.

Yet it is in the third cluster that more traditionally qualitative approaches to evaluation have found their home. Part of the interpretive turn in social science, these approaches share a common grounding in a basically interpretive philosophy of science (Smith, 1989; Soltis, 1990), a value orientation that characteristically promotes pluralism in evaluation contexts, and a case study methodological orientation with an accompanying reliance on qualitative methods. Part of the responsive tradition in program evaluation, these approaches seek to enhance contextualized program understanding for stakeholders closest to the program (like Albert Peters and his son), and thereby promote values of pluralism as well as forge direct channels to program improvement. Robert Stake's (1975) and Egon Guba and Yvonna Lincoln's (1981) responsive approaches to evaluation, and, though not as good a fit, Elliot Eisner's (1976) connoisseurship evaluation are major exemplars of qualitative evaluation approaches in this genre.

Finally, the fourth cluster represents the more recent *normative turn* in social science. The feminist, neo-Marxist, critical, and other theorists in this genre promote "openly ideological" forms of inquiry that seek to illuminate the historical, structural, and value bases of social phenomena and, in doing so, to catalyze political and social change toward greater justice, equity, and democracy. A normative evaluation stance well matches homeless advocate Sam Brown's need for information that would help catalyze action toward greater justice for homeless people. Although many proponents of a normative approach to evaluation are long on rhetoric and short on guidelines for the field, some work on the practice of normative evaluation is being done (Greene, 1991; McTaggart, 1990; Sirotnik & Oakes, 1990). For the present discussion, the democratic evaluation approach championed by British and Australian practitioners (MacDonald, 1976) is an important exemplar. As well, Guba and Lincoln's (1989) more recent development of fourth-generation evaluation bears examination as it promotes an activist ideology while maintaining a grounding in an essentially interpretivist philosophy.

Explicit recognition of the ideological contours of program evaluation did not always exist. Rather, both inside and outside the field, a methods orientation has predominated. One continuing legacy of this orientation is the naming of different evaluation approaches by their primary methods, no more common than in the label of "qualitative evaluation" for any approach that utilizes primarily qualitative methods. Yet, as just argued, what importantly distinguishes one evaluation methodology from another is not methods, but rather whose questions are addressed and which values are promoted. Among the major extant evaluation approaches that rely on qualitative methods, there is only some consensus on these political and value dimensions. Patton, Stake, MacDonald, and Guba and Lincoln represent distinct, even competing, positions on these dimensions. Qualitative research traditions show similar variability (Atkinson, Delamont, & Hammersley, 1988; Jacob, 1987).

In my discussion in this chapter I will emphasize distinctions among significant evaluation approaches that incorporate qualitative methods. And that's progress! Not long ago, interpretivist philosophies and qualitative methods were just gaining a toehold in the evaluation community, amidst considerable, often acrimonious, debate. In the next section, I offer a brief historical perspective on the ascendance and acceptance of qualitative methods in program evaluation methodologies. This is followed by an elaboration of the philosophical bases of qualitative evaluations, and then an examination of qualitative evaluations in practice. I conclude the chapter by noting the continuing challenges for program evaluators and providing a summary assessment regarding the future promise of qualitative evaluations. I will argue that because of their inherent paradigmatic relativity, many qualitative evaluation approaches can effectively respond to or be shaped to fit diverse and emergent inquiry forms and functions. Yet, absent a coherent value orientation or vision (such as the social activism that frames fourth-generation evaluation), qualitative evaluations cannot move beyond responsiveness to become proactive players in the social policy-making arena.

◆ From Whence Came Qualitative Evaluations

> In the mid-1960s, evaluators were urged to use one preferred set of methodological principles and procedures—those of the experimental model—to assess the extent to which programs had attained their goals. In keeping with the tenets of experimental science, evaluators of this era adopted stances of objectivity and believed that the results of their work would anchor social planning and policy making in a politically neutral and scientific rationality. (Greene & McClintock, 1991, p. 13)

This portrait of the early days of contemporary program evaluation is distinctive for its narrow vision and naive arrogance. What has happened in the last quarter century to so dramatically transform the theory and, to a lesser but still substantial degree, the practice of social program evaluation? Developments in two aspects of evaluation methodology stand out as major forces for change: (a) evaluation's contextual, political aspect, and (b) evaluation's philosophical, methodological aspect (Greene & McClintock, 1991). The intertwined process of reciprocal change and influence in these two aspects tells much of the story of contemporary evaluation's evolution.[2]

Taking Off the White Lab Coat

The failures of experimental program evaluations to contribute to the enthusiasm and innovation of the Great Society era are legendary. They include recognition of the lack of fit between the requirements of the experimental model and the exigencies of social program contexts. For example, there were serious questions raised about the ethics of denying a purportedly beneficial program to some people in order to fulfill the randomization requirement of experimental design. Moreover, as prescribed by the experimental model, early program evaluators distanced themselves from the political dimensions of their work, intentionally seeking the objective stance of "politically neutral and scientific rationality." Carol Weiss (1970, 1972, 1977) most influentially critiqued this distanced stance, arguing that it substantially underlay the marginal potency of evaluations of this era. Weiss maintained that social policy and program decision making were not rational processes to which data-based enterprises such as program evaluation could contribute the definitive piece of information. Rather, "the politics of program survival and the politics of higher policymaking accord evaluative evidence relatively minor weight in the decisional calculus" (Weiss, 1987, p. 62). In short, neither distanced objectivity nor neutral rationality was going to earn program evaluators a seat at the decision-making table.

There were other influential disjunctures between the framework of experimental science and the contexts of program evaluation. As early as 1963, Lee Cronbach questioned the dominant focus of evaluative efforts on the stated goals and objectives of social programs, arguing that evaluation could more usefully contribute to program improvement through a focus on program planning and implementation. Over the years, Cronbach has continued to argue for a pragmatic, contextually useful role for program evaluation (see, e.g., Cronbach, 1982; Cronbach & Associates, 1980), in contrast to a scientist or theory-oriented role. As a highly respected and influential theorist, Cronbach provided arguments that were important in easing the later entry and acceptance of qualitative evaluation approaches. Cronbach's views are tellingly and engagingly represented in his now-famous debate with Donald Campbell over the relative importance in evaluation studies of external validity and contextual meaningfulness (championed by Cronbach) versus internal validity and causal claims (promoted by Campbell) (for a summary of this debate, see Mark, 1986).

Michael Scriven (1967) has also challenged the goal orientation of experimental evaluation, arguing not against a focus on program outcomes or effects, but rather against an exemption of stated program goals and objectives from evaluative scrutiny. Social programs, that is, should be evaluated according to the merit and worth of their actual effects, independent of their intended effects. Adopting this explicitly value-oriented framework for evaluation, Scriven argues, renders existing social policy and program goals themselves contestable. *In what ways does this program effectively meet an important need among the designated beneficiaries?* is a Scrivenesque evaluation question, later popularized, in theory though far less in practice, in his goal-free approach to program evaluation (Scriven, 1973).

Additionally, Ernest House (1976, 1977, 1980) has contributed a distinctive and important voice to the argument that the white-coated experimental scientist is not an appropriate role model for program evaluators. House's views blend several different strands of logic and argumentation, including the fundamental grounding of evaluative work in political considerations of social and distributive justice, and developments in the philosophy of science (outlined in the next section). House (1980) argues that experimental science as a model for program evaluation fails because "it focuses on the truth aspect of validity to the exclusion of the credibility and normative aspects" (p. 251). Yet, by essence of his or her social function, "the evaluator is engaged with the world. His [or her] work directly affects who gets what" (pp. 254-255). Further, as an inherently political activity, evaluation "is intimately implicated in the distribution of basic goods in society . . . [So] evaluation should not only be true; it should also be just" (p. 121).

Challenging (Especially Cartesian) Foundations

A significant force for change in the form and function of program evaluation, then, were contextual challenges to the meaningfulness of experimental logic for evaluation—challenges that arose largely from within the evaluation community. Interwoven with these challenges were major fractures in the philosophical justification for experimental inquiry that permeated the evaluation community from the outside domains of the philosophy of science. In particular, the Cartesian foundationalism of positivistic science—and the concomitant premiums placed on objectivity, the proper methods, detached neutrality, and grand theory—were dethroned. Many philosophers of science came to agree that there is no place or time outside the observer from which he or she can objectively view and judge the validity of knowledge claims. Rather, all observations are imbued with the historical, theoretical, and value predispositions of the observer. Hence knowledge claims are not separable from, but rather interlocked with values; are not universal, but rather time and place bound; are not certain, but rather probabilistic and contestable (see Bernstein, 1983, for an outstanding example of these philosophical projects).

Endeavoring to be participants and not just bystanders in this Kuhnian challenge to *normal science,* program evaluators read philosophy, educated themselves about long-standing philosophical issues such as the fact/value distinction, and argued with each other at conferences and in other public forums about the intrinsic sensibility of varied philosophical developments and about their relevance to the essentially practical work of evaluation. It was in this context that interpretivist philosophies and qualitative methods entered evaluative discourse. Evaluation methodologies rooted in interpretivist philosophies and incorporating qualitative methods were developed as alternatives to a rejected positivist philosophy and experimentalist methodology (Guba & Lincoln, 1981; House, 1980; Parlett & Hamilton, 1976; Stake, 1975, 1978). In fact, within the evaluation and some other applied social science communities, much of this discourse was familiarly named the *quantitative-qualitative paradigm debate.* Although qualitative evaluations were initially contested on both practical and methodological grounds, the debate eventually evolved to a detente (Cook & Reichardt, 1979; Smith & Heshusius, 1986), signaling the important acceptance of these alternative evaluation methodologies, at least among many evaluation theorists and methodologists.[3] Coming both from long-standing inquiry traditions such as ethnography, symbolic interactionism, and phenomenology and from the more recent critiques of established social science, the arguments favoring the legitimacy and potential usefulness of qualitative approaches to applied social inquiry quite simply overwhelmed, or in some cases co-opted (Gage 1989), the opposition.

Accepting Diversity in Approaches to Evaluation

It was actually the combined force of the political-contextual and the methodological-philosophical arguments that catalyzed the development and later acceptance of a diverse range of alternative approaches to program evaluation, including practical, decision-oriented approaches and approaches framed around qualitative methodologies. This diversity is now being extended, with increasing calls to recenter social program evaluation around normative concerns (Schwandt, 1989; Sirotnik, 1990), as addressed in ensuing sections of this chapter.

The current accepted legitimacy of diverse evaluation approaches is well illustrated by the *Standards for Evaluation of Educational Programs, Projects, and Materials,* originally developed in 1981 by the Joint Committee on Standards for Educational Evaluation, representing 12 professional associations, and in the process of being updated. Reflecting the importance of contextual sensitivity and methodological diversity in the evaluation field, the 30 standards developed are clustered within four critical attributes of program evaluation: utility, feasibility, propriety, and accuracy. Moreover, the standards "do not exclusively endorse any one approach to evaluation. Instead, the Joint Committee has written standards that encourage the sound use of a variety of evaluation methods. . . . Usually, it is desireable to employ multiple methods, qualitative as well as quantitative" (Stufflebeam, 1991, p. 257). In other words, "merit lies not in form of inquiry, but in relevance of information" (Cronbach & Associates, 1980, p. 7). Although praised for their openness to alternative methods, the standards have also been criticized for their decision-oriented bias, for their reliance to some degree on the conceptual vocabulary of conventional science, and hence for their only partial embracement of alternative evaluation methodologies (e.g., Linn, 1981).

With these historical notes as important context, the next two sections of this chapter more closely examine qualitative approaches to evaluation, first in their philosophical form and then in their practical form.

◆ The Logic of Justification for Qualitative Evaluations

Just as there is no one form of qualitative evaluation practice, there is no single philosophical logic of justification universally embraced by qualitative evaluators. Yet, there is a dominant set of philosophical tenets and stances guiding qualitative evaluation fieldwork, one with both a historical legacy and a strong contemporary presence in other domains of applied social science. This philosophical inquiry framework—variously called qualitative, ethnographic, and naturalistic—is most aptly called interpretivist (Smith, 1989). This label directly connotes one of its central premises, namely, that "in the world of human experience, there is only interpretation" (Denzin, 1989, p. 8). The dominance of an interpretivist logic of justification for qualitative evaluations can be traced primarily to the highly influential work of Yvonna Lincoln and Egon Guba (1985; Guba & Lincoln, 1981, 1989). These authors have been leading advocates of alternative paradigm inquiry, particularly within the evaluation field. Consistently grounded in detailed explications of philosophical debates and developments, their work has been influential in making the philosophical premises of inquiry both visible and accessible to many in the evaluation community. Although Guba and Lincoln's own philosophical thinking and naming have evolved over the years, core elements of their philosophical worldview have remained essentially the same. Drawing on their work and that of others, notably John Smith (1989), I will now provide an overview of the interpretivist paradigm, as generally understood and utilized by qualitative program evaluators.

The Interpretivist Paradigm in Evaluation

At root, interpretivism is about *contextualized meaning*. Interpretivist logic rejects the primacy of scientific realism, in either its traditional or more contemporary forms (House, 1991), along with its accompanying correspondence theory of truth. Rather, in interpretivism, social reality is viewed as significantly socially constructed, "based on a constant process of interpretation and reinterpretation of the intentional, meaningful behavior of people—including researchers" (Smith, 1989, p. 85), and "truth is ultimately a matter of socially and historically conditioned agreement" (p. 73). "'Reality' resides neither with an objective external world nor with the subjective mind of the knower, but within dynamic transactions between the two" (Barone, 1992b, p. 31). Social inquiry therefore is mind dependent; inquiry descriptions and interpretations are themselves constructions and (re)interpretations; and there can be no separation of the investigator from the investigated (Smith, 1989, chap. 4). Interpretivist inquiry is unabashedly and unapologetically subjectivist. It is also dialectic, for the process of meaning construction transforms the constructors.

Moreover, what is important to know, what constitutes an appropriate and legitimate focus for social inquiry, is the phenomenological meaningfulness of lived experience—people's interpretations and sense makings of their experiences in a given context. As Smith (1989) notes, this process is inevitably hermeneutical because "investigators, like everyone else, are part of the circle of interpretation" (p. 136). So understanding meaning as the goal of interpretivist inquiry "is not a matter of manipulation and control, particularly via method, but rather it is a question of openness and dialogue" (p. 137).

Meanings thus understood, or knowledge claims in interpretivist inquiry, take the form of working hypotheses or contextualized, temporary knowledge. Interpretivist knowledge claims are contestable precisely because they are contextualized and multiplistic, and also because they represent an intertwinement of facts and values. There are "no facts without values, and different values can actually lead to different facts" (Smith, 1989, p. 111). In this respect, interpretivism is value laden while it is simultaneously value relative or equally malleable by inquirers with quite different value stances (Greene, 1990, 1992). That is, interpretivist practice intentionally reveals the value dimensions of lived experience (because there are no facts without values), but the dimensionality revealed is importantly connected to, even constitutive of, the value orientations and stances of the inquirer (because different values can lead to different facts). Interpretivism as a philosophical logic of justification for inquiry acknowledges, even celebrates, the permeation of values throughout the inquiry process and results, but does not advocate or prescribe any one particular set of values for social inquiry. These are thus brought by the inquirer and, in this way, the values promoted by interpretivist inquiry practice are inherently varied and diverse.

Methodologically, interpretivism is most consonant with natural settings, with the human inquirer as the primary gatherer and interpreter of meaning, with qualitative methods, with emergent and expansionist inquiry designs, and with hermeneutic understanding, in contrast to interventionist prediction and control, as the overall goal of inquiry (Guba & Lincoln, 1989; Lincoln, 1990).

Yet, perhaps more significantly, the interpretive logic of justification represents a decentering of inquiry theory and practice from questions of method (Greene, 1992). In the field of program evaluation, which has long been characterized as, if not faulted for being, method driven, this is a substantial change. Like other interpretive inquirers, interpretivist evaluators reject the conventional stance that proper methods can insulate against bias and thereby ensure objectivity and truth. Yet, unlike some of their more radical peers, who disclaim the existence of any privileged methods that will enhance the acceptability of an inquirer's interpretations (Smith, 1989, p. 160), most interpretivist evaluators seek some procedural guidelines and support for their work. In particular, interpretivist evaluators seek to authenticate their interpretations as empirically based representations of program experiences and meanings, rather than as biased inquirer opinion. Time-honored procedures such as triangulation and negative case analysis (Denzin, 1978) and newer procedures such as member checks, peer debriefers, and audits (Lincoln & Guba, 1985) are all utilized by interpretivist evaluators to enhance the credibility of their inferences. Evaluators sense particular pressure to invoke such procedures because the contexts of program evaluation continue to demand assurances of methodological quality and data integrity in evaluative work. This work can make no contributions to social policy and program decision making unless it is perceived as credible and trustworthy.

So, although methods may not occupy center stage in interpretive evaluation approaches, questions of procedure in these approaches remain. And these questions are problematic because "to argue that certain procedures are required would simply pose a contradiction—the attempt to provide a methodological foundation for knowledge based on nonfoundational assumptions" (Smith, 1989, p. 159). On the one hand, interpretivist evaluators need methodological quality assurances for their audiences. On the other hand, the very idea of prescriptions for quality or any other methodological concern is philosophically inconsistent with the basic tenets of interpretivism. In response to this dilemma, interpretivist evaluators have generally accepted Smith's (1989, 1990) recasting of methodological concerns as choices, procedural guidelines as heuristics, and quality criteria as ever-evolving, open-ended lists.

Paradigms and Practice

Of course, not all qualitative evaluators find Smith's perspective sensible. Patton (1990), for example, offers a highly interpretivist frame for his qualitative evaluation approach in the form of "strategic themes," and simultaneously—without a single pang of philosophical conscience—promotes conventional measurement validity and reliability as key quality dimensions of qualitative data (p. 461). This is because Patton (1988, 1990) eschews the idea that inquiry paradigms frame or delimit methodological choices:

> Rather than believing that one must choose to align with one paradigm or another, I advocate a paradigm of choices. A paradigm of choices rejects methodological orthodoxy in favor of *methodological appropriateness* as the primary criterion for judging methodological quality. The issue then becomes . . . whether one has made sensible methods decisions given the purpose of the inquiry, the questions being investigated, and the resources available. (Patton, 1990, pp. 38-39)

For Patton, the selection, design, and implementation of evaluation methods should be flexibly based on practical need and situational responsiveness, rather than on the consonance of a set of methods with any particular philosophical paradigm. And so, "objectivist" and "subjectivist" methods can be used together unproblematically. This *practical pragmatic* stand is strongly supported by other applied social inquirers (e.g., Bryman, 1988; Firestone, 1990; Pitman & Maxwell, 1992), as well as by arguments from a position of *philosophical pragmatism* (e.g., Howe, 1988).

Although clearly supporting multiplistic mixes of qualitative and quantitative methods at the methodological level, Guba and Lincoln strongly contest the mixing of inquiry approaches at the paradigm level. They argue, for example, that one cannot simultaneously adhere to the objectivist detachment of conventional science and the subjectivist involvement of interpretivism. There are others who agree that paradigms are irreconcilable, yet still seek not accommodation but dialectically enhanced inquiry benefits through a pluralistic acceptance of multiple ways of knowing. To illustrate, Salomon (1991) maintains that social issues are vastly complex and thus require both an "analytic" and a "systemic" approach to inquiry, used in a complementary fashion across studies toward more complete understanding. This essential tension between philosophical paradigms and practice is likely to remain contested. It matters to evaluators because it has important effects on how we envision and do our work, as elaborated in the next section.

◆ The Practice of Qualitative Evaluations

There are several critical dimensions of qualitative evaluation practice. Most qualitative evaluators (a) use case studies to frame their work and hence emphasize context, but not generalizability, as an essential element of meaning; (b) rely heavily but not exclusively on qualitative methods for meaning construction; (c) acknowledge if not celebrate the influential presence of their own selves in the inquiry process; and (d) seek in their work primarily to augment practical program understanding. The ensuing discussion will elaborate these dimensions, as well as connect them to prominent qualitative evaluation theories. In this way, salient features of each theory are highlighted, allocating more comprehensive portrayals of the theories to the works referenced.

Cases and Contexts

Some years ago, Robert Stake (1978) began encouraging evaluators to direct their energies toward the practical program concerns of stakeholders in the immediate context, rather than toward the more abstract questions of remote decision makers. Stake argued that by responsively focusing on the priority issues of practitioners within a given program or bounded case, evaluators can construct rich experiential understandings of that case. Such understandings, in turn, not only provide powerful information for program improvement, but also constitute a basis for *naturalistic generalizations,* which are grounded in the vicarious experience and tacit knowledge of the case reader. "Naturalistic generalizations develop within a person as a product of experience. They derive from the tacit knowledge of how things are . . . they seldom take the form of predictions but lead regularly to expectations. They guide action, in fact they are inseparable from action" (Stake, 1983, p. 282). Eisner (1991) makes a similar argument regarding the thematics of evaluative connoisseurship. Thematics represent the concrete universals of the case evaluated, the lessons learned, the moral of the story, and, as such, are of likely interest to others outside the case evaluated.

However, developing generalizable knowledge—even in such nonpropositional forms—is not the primary justification for embracing a case study framework for qualitative evaluations. Quite the contrary—the case for case studies in qualitative evaluations rests on a confluence of their responsive political-value stance and their underlying interpretivist assumptions. *Responsive* evaluation, first championed by Stake (1975; see also Stake, 1991), seeks expressly to uncover and then address the concerns of program stakeholders in the setting being evaluated toward the improvement of practice in that setting. From this responsive perspective, program improvement is more likely if local rather than remote concerns are addressed in the evaluation and if local rather than remote values are explicated and used to make program judgments. Although not all qualitative evaluators maintain an exclusive focus on program practitioners, most remain within evaluation's responsive tradition. In large part, this is because this tradition is philosophically buttressed by interpretivism's view of knowledge as contextualized meaning. As an essential part of meaning, context must be described and its contributions understood.

Qualitative evaluations thus characteristically take the form of case studies, with respectful attention to context, and rarely, if ever, resemble surveys, quasi-experiments, or other inquiry formats. Deciding just what constitutes a case, however, usually requires considered judgment, involving a balancing of desired results with available resources. Rarely do evaluation resources enable an in-depth assessment of all possible cases in a program setting. In an educational program evaluation, for example, considering the whole school district as a case is unlikely to be as feasible or as useful as considering schools, or grade levels within schools, or social groups within neighborhoods as possible cases. The latter are more likely to offer differentiated understandings of such key evaluation foci as peer group norms and influences.

A Preference for Qualitative Methods

All qualitative approaches to program evaluation are distinguished by their preference for qualitative methods, including open-ended interviews, on-site observation, participant observation, and document review. For many theorists and practitioners, these methods offer the greatest consonance with the interpretivist perspective that frames and guides their work. Qualitative methods rely on the interactional, adaptive, and judgmental abilities of the human inquirer; the interpretivist challenge of understanding and interpreting meaning demands no less.

Methods choices in evaluation studies are not only influenced by philosophical assumptions and frameworks. As important, or even more important, methods choices must match the information needs of the identified evaluation audiences. For this reason, surveys, client record analysis, and other quantitative methods are commonly incorporated into interpretivist evaluations. Representing an extreme position on this matter, the influential evaluation theorist Michael Patton (1990) advocates qualitative methods when they represent the best match to the intended evaluation user's information needs, rather than because they are consonant with interpretivism. That is, Patton contends that methods choices should devolve not primarily from some abstract philosophical paradigm, but rather substantially from the concrete information needs of identified evaluation users. When these information needs comprise multiple perspectives, contextualized meanings, or the experience of program participation, for example, then qualitative methods should be employed. This aphilosophical stance on the justification for methods choices sets Patton somewhat apart from most other qualitative evaluation theorists, including Stake, Guba and Lincoln, and Eisner.

The Acknowledged Self in Inquiry

Perception of the world is perception influenced by skill, point of view, focus, language, and framework. The eye, after all, is not only a part of the brain, it is a part of tradition. . . . [So what] we know is a function of a *transaction* between the qualities of the world we cannot know in their pure, nonmediated form, and the frames of reference, personal skills, and individual histories we bring to them. . . . [Knowledge or] experience thus conceived is a form of human achievement; it is not simply had, it is made. (Eisner, 1992, pp. 11-13)

Evaluators are subjective partners with stakeholders in the literal creation of evaluation data. (Guba & Lincoln, 1989, p. 110)

Although Eisner and Guba and Lincoln differ in significant aspects of their theories, they share the premise that human knowledge is literally constructed during inquiry and hence is inevitably entwined with the perceptual frames, histories, and values of the inquirer. Qualitative evaluation à la Eisner or Guba and Lincoln is unabashedly subjective, unapologetically imbued with the individual perspectives and frames of the inquirer. No apologies are offered here, for two main reasons. First, along with many others in and outside of interpretivism, these theorists maintain that objectivity—understood as distanced detachment and neutrality intended to guard against bias and thereby to ensure the attainment of truth—is not possible and therefore should be rejected as a regulative ideal for social inquiry. Second, from an interpretivist perspective, it is precisely the individual qualities of the human inquirer that are valued as indispensable to meaning construction. In fact, Eisner's evaluation theory directly calls upon the substantive expertise of the individual connoisseur or expert. With a conjoint grounding in the arts, this theory highlights the enlightened eye and the seasoned judgment of the inquirer, along with his or her expertise in representation or in making public what has been seen. Eisner's evaluation connoisseur is an expert in the program to be assessed. Relying heavily on qualitative methods, the connoisseur collects information and then uses his or her expert frames and insights to integrate, interpret, and judge.

Thus the self of the qualitative evaluator is acknowledged to be present in the inquiry, a presence that permeates all methodological decisions and penetrates the very fabric of meaning constructed. Yet, just how much influence is acceptable and just how such influence can be monitored or detected, as needed, are issues of little consensus within the qualitative evaluation community. Eisner would contend, for example, that as the connoisseur, the qualitative evaluator carries authority that is supreme, and his or her influence in all aspects of the inquiry is expressly valued. In contrast with his view of the evaluator as a technical consultant, Patton would allocate more substantive authority to evaluation users. And he would rely on the proper application of qualitative methods to minimize the evaluator's presence in the program experiences and meanings investigated and understood. Given their vision of the evaluator as a negotiator, Guba and Lincoln would take a middle position, arguing that the meanings created and the interpretation and use of those meanings are responsibilities shared among the evaluator and program stakeholders. This range of views on the desired presence of self in qualitative evaluation is reflected in varied views on its primary purpose, as discussed next.

The Envisioned Inquiry in Society

Some vision of purpose is, at root, what guides all evaluation practice. In the responsive tradition in evaluation, inquirers have sought to augment local program understanding with the hope of moving toward program improvement. And the primary audiences for responsive evaluation have been program practitioners and participants. This vision of evaluation as the generation of local contextualized insights, as the reflective sharing of new program perspectives, as the telling of diverse program stories, is highly congruent with an interpretivist philosophy and a qualitative methodology. For example, participant observation is ideally suited for constructing the emic meaning of program participation for varied participants in that particular context.

For some within the evaluation community, however, understanding emic meaning and relating diverse program stories is not enough. Rather, as social inquirers in the public domain, we are morally and ethically compelled to assume greater responsibility for and a more active role in the social policy arena. Because our work can affect who gets what (House, 1980), we must be actively engaged with the consequences of our work. Yet, because of its inherent value relativity, interpretivism—while permitting alternative visions of evaluation purpose—does not in and of itself provide sufficient guidance or warrant for any particular alternative vision.

Such guidance and warrant must come from somewhere outside the interpretivist logic of justification.

One important, long-standing exemplar of such politically engaged evaluation is the democratic evaluation tradition promoted by MacDonald (1976), Simons (1987), McTaggart (1990), and others. This evaluation model most centrally seeks to balance the public's right to know with the individual's right to privacy and to be discrete. The balance is sought via prescribed procedures for accessing, reviewing, negotiating, and releasing evaluation data. The concept of democratic evaluation is derived from the tradition of liberal democracy, and is thus politically and morally acceptable to existing power holders in democratic societies. At the same time, democratic evaluation seeks within its own boundaries to forge power-equalizing interactions and to establish a flow of information that is independent of hierarchical interests. Hence, in a democratic evaluation context, all relevant perspectives can be represented, information can be fairly and equitably exchanged, and open deliberation can be encouraged (Simons, 1987).

Guba and Lincoln's (1989) more recent fourth-generation evaluation approach represents a purposeful blending of an essentially interpretivist philosophy with an outside warrant for social action into what they call a *constructivist* framework for evaluation. Moving beyond the telling of stories, constructivism requires that evaluation catalyze social action. Yet, in consonance with interpretivism, the specific contours and facets of that action are not prescribed but rather emerge from the setting. In this way, constructivism differs from the more prescriptive empowerment, equity, and social justice agendas of critical, feminist, and other normative inquiry approaches. With this infusion of an outside warrant, fourth-generation evaluation seeks not so much program understanding as social change-oriented action, and the fourth-generation evaluator's role is not so much one of describer and consultant as one of negotiator and social change catalyst. More significantly, Guba and Lincoln's fourth-generation departures from the responsive tradition in evaluation well illustrate the critical vulnerabilities of qualitative evaluation today. These vulnerabilities are primarily in the areas of purpose and audience, in the envisioned role of inquiry in society. Interpretivism envisions no particular role, although an increasing clamor of contemporary voices is insisting otherwise. A sampling of these voices and what they portend for qualitative evaluation in the years ahead conclude this chapter.

◆ Continuing Challenges

> Given the inescapable incursion of values into human activity, Freire's . . .
> dictum that there can be no neutral education is extended to practices of
> social inquiry. The inescapable political content of theories and methodolo-
> gies becomes increasingly apparent. (Lather, 1992, p. 4)

> Social justice is among the most important values we should hope to secure
> in evaluation studies. . . . Public evaluation should be an institution for
> democratizing public decision making. . . . As a social practice, evaluation
> entails an inescapable ethic of public responsibility . . . [serving] the inter-
> ests of the larger society and of various groups within society, particularly
> those most affected by the program under review. (House, 1990, pp. 23-24)

Of pivotal significance to the dizzying pluralism of social inquiry in the
present era is the recognition that values permeate all observations, and
hence all methods that are used to gather the observations, and hence all
methodologies that frame and guide implementation of the methods. A
critical question of the era is, thus, What values or whose? And in the public
contexts of social program evaluation, the question becomes, What societal
values or what visions of community constitute warranted frames for
evaluation methodology?

Ernest House offers a vision rooted in conceptions of social justice (see
also Sirotnik, 1990). Thomas Schwandt (1989, 1991) argues for a morally
engaged evaluation practice that "aims at achieving insight and awareness
into what it means to live a human life" (1991, p. 70). Schwandt's ideas
incorporate recent challenges to the liberalist political tradition and concomitant arguments to replace our failed representative democracy with a
genuinely participatory one (Barber, 1984) or with a communitarian ethic
rooted in human interdependence and solidarity (Sullivan, 1986). An
additional emancipatory vision for applied social inquiry is broadly represented by critical social scientists (e.g., Fay, 1987) and, more tellingly, by
practicing participatory evaluators (Brunner & Guzman, 1989; Whitmore,
1990). In this vision, evaluation is viewed primarily as a process for
promoting empowerment and requisite structural change. All of these
visions offer an explicit political agenda for program evaluation, thereby
not only recognizing the presence of values in inquiry, but specifically
promoting one particular normative frame.

Of key relevance to the present discussion are questions of the intersection between this "inescapable" normative turn in social inquiry and qualitative approaches to program evaluation. In response, I would argue that qualitative approaches are highly compatible with and hence have much to offer more openly ideological approaches to program evaluation at the level of method or technique. Qualitative methods, for example, can effectively give voice to the normally silenced and can poignantly illuminate what is typically masked. Qualitative methods and approaches are already being employed in such ideologically oriented inquiry frameworks as critical ethnography (Anderson, 1989), narrative inquiry (Barone, 1992a; Bruner, 1986), and feminist social science (Lather, 1992). To illustrate, Fine (Chapter 4, Volume 1, this series), notes, "More interestingly, qualitative researchers have begun to interrupt Othering by forcing subjugated voices in context to the front of our texts and by exploiting privileged voices to scrutinize the technologies of Othering." And Lather (1992) states:

> Feminist methodologies and epistemologies, [Harding] suggests, require new feminist uses of these familiar research methods . . . [of] listening to informants, observing behavior, [and] examining historical records. . . . Studying women from the perspective of their own experiences so that they/we can better understand our situations in the world is research designed for women instead of simply research *about* women. (p. 6)

At the broader level of methodology or paradigm, however, the interpretivist framework does not provide sufficient warrant or guidance for any given normative agenda. Interpretivism justifies values in inquiry, but does not justify any particular ones. As participants in the social policy arena, program evaluators are increasingly being called upon to get involved, to be a part of the action, to become public scientists. With their acknowledgment of values, qualitative approaches can help evaluators illuminate alternative paths or courses of action. Such approaches can be molded to fit varied and emerging inquiry shapes, from technical reports to dramatic dialogue. And they can adaptively respond to varied and evolving inquiry functions, including shifting social action agendas. For these reasons, qualitative approaches are likely to continue to be a significant and useful alternative in the methodological repertoire of program evaluators. Yet, also for these reasons, qualitative evaluations as a genre are destined to remain within evaluation's responsive tradition—beautifully responsive but, in being so, unable to assume a more proactive role in the social policy sphere. And so, because the evaluator as public scientist must be proactive, must him- or herself become an active and accountable player in the policy arena, qualitative evaluations will not be enough.

◆ Notes

1. Evaluations are also conducted on objects (product evaluation) and on people (personnel evaluation), as well as on programs that few would consider social (e.g., executive professional development via outdoor experiences). Although Scriven (1991) and others would argue that the logic of evaluation is the same across different forms and objects of evaluation, I believe they constitute radically different tasks requiring qualitatively and politically different responses. This chapter, therefore, is restricted to social program evaluation, predominantly in the public domain.

2. Most major evaluation texts also have chapters on evaluation's history. See, for example, Guba and Lincoln (1981, 1989); Madaus, Scriven, and Stufflebeam (1983); Patton (1986); Rossi and Freeman (1985); and Shadish, Cook, and Leviton (1991).

3. That this debate runs deep and long is attested to by the recent sequence of Presidential Addresses by the 1990 and 1991 presidents of the American Evaluation Association, an exchange of quantitative and qualitative views that rekindled emotional layers of this debate (Lincoln, 1991; Sechrest, 1992). Moreover, as noted previously, important sectors of the evaluation community, including many practitioners and audiences, missed the qualitative-quantitative debate entirely. Admittedly, this debate can certainly be viewed as a rarefied intellectual exchange of no relevance to daily life. Nonetheless, there remains a gap between evaluation theory and practice, with much of the latter based on discarded epistemologies and paradigms. This gap remains troublesome to evaluators concerned about both defensible theory and meaningful practice.

◆ References

Anderson, G. L. (1989). Critical ethnography in education: Origins, current status, and new directions. *Review of Educational Research, 59,* 249-270.

Atkinson, P., Delamont, S., & Hammersley, M. (1988). Qualitative research traditions: A British response to Jacob. *Review of Educational Research, 58,* 231-250.

Barber, B. (1984). *Strong democracy: Participatory politics for a new age.* Berkeley: University of California Press.

Barone, T. E. (1992a). Beyond theory and method: A case of critical storytelling. *Theory Into Practice, 31*(2), 142-146.

Barone, T. E. (1992b). On the demise of subjectivity in educational inquiry. *Curriculum Inquiry, 22,* 25-38.

Bernstein, R. J. (1983). *Beyond objectivism and relativism.* Philadelphia: University of Pennsylvania Press.

Bruner, J. (1986). *Actual minds, possible worlds.* Cambridge, MA: Harvard University Press.

Brunner, I., & Guzman, A. (1989). Participatory evaluation: A tool to assess projects and empower people. In R. F. Conner & M. Hendricks (Eds.), *International innovations in evaluation methodology* (pp. 9-18). San Francisco: Jossey-Bass.

Bryman, A. (1988). *Quantity and quality in social research.* London: Unwin Hyman.

Chen, H., & Rossi, P. H. (1983). Evaluating with sense: The theory-driven approach. *Evaluation Review, 7,* 283-302.

Cicirelli, V. G., & Associates. (1969). *The impact of Head Start: An evaluation of the effects of Head Start on children's cognitive and affective development* (Report to the Office of Economic Opportunity). Athens, OH: Ohio University/Westinghouse Learning Corporation.

Cook, T. D. (1985). Postpositivist critical multiplism. In L. Shotland & M. M. Mark (Eds.), *Social science and social policy* (pp. 21-62). Beverly Hills, CA: Sage.

Cook, T. D., & Reichardt, C. S. (Eds.). (1979). *Qualitative and quantitative methods in evaluation research.* Beverly Hills, CA: Sage.

Cronbach, L. J. (1963). Course improvement through evaluation. *Teachers College Record, 64,* 672-683.

Cronbach, L. J. (1982). *Designing evaluations of educational and social programs.* San Francisco: Jossey-Bass.

Cronbach, L. J., & Associates. (1980). *Toward reform of program evaluation.* San Francisco: Jossey-Bass.

Denzin, N. K. (1978). *The research act: An introduction to sociological methods.* New York: McGraw-Hill.

Denzin, N. K. (1989). *Interpretive interactionism.* Newbury Park, CA: Sage.

Eisner, E. W. (1976). Educational connoisseurship and criticism: Their forms and functions in educational evaluation. *Journal of Aesthetic Education, 10,* 135-150.

Eisner, E. W. (1991). Taking a second look: Educational connoisseurship revisited. In M. W. McLaughlin & D. C. Phillips (Eds.), *Evaluation and education: At quarter century* (pp. 169-187). Chicago: University of Chicago Press.

Eisner, E. W. (1992). Objectivity in educational research. *Curriculum Inquiry, 22,* 9-15.

Fay, B. (1987). *Critical social science.* Ithaca, NY: Cornell University Press.

Firestone, W. A. (1990). Accommodation: Toward a paradigm-praxis dialectic. In E. G. Guba (Ed.), *The paradigm dialog* (pp. 105-124). Newbury Park, CA: Sage.

Gage, N. L. (1989). The paradigm wars and their aftermath: A "historical" sketch of research on teaching since 1989. *Educational Researcher, 18*(7), 4-10.

Greene, J. C. (1990). Three views on the nature and role of knowledge in social science. In E. G. Guba (Ed.), *The paradigm dialog* (pp. 227-245). Newbury Park, CA: Sage.

Greene, J. C. (1991). *Responding to evaluation's moral challenge.* Paper presented at the annual meeting of the American Educational Research Association, Chicago.

Greene, J. C. (1992). The practitioner's perspective. *Curriculum Inquiry, 22*(1), 39-45.

Greene, J. C., & McClintock, C. (1991). The evolution of evaluation methodology. *Theory Into Practice, 30*(1), 13-21.

Guba, E. G. (Ed.). (1990). *The paradigm dialog.* Newbury Park, CA: Sage.

Guba, E. G., & Lincoln, Y. S. (1981). *Effective evaluation.* San Francisco: Jossey-Bass.

Guba, E. G., & Lincoln, Y. S. (1989). *Fourth generation evaluation.* Newbury Park, CA: Sage.

House, E. R. (1976). Justice in evaluation. In G. V Glass (Ed.), *Evaluation studies review annual* (Vol. 1). Beverly Hills, CA: Sage.

House, E. R. (1977). *The logic of evaluative argument.* Los Angeles: University of California, Center for the Study of Evaluation.

House, E. R. (1980). *Evaluating with validity.* Beverly Hills, CA: Sage.

House, E. R. (1990). Methodology and justice. In K. A. Sirotnik (Ed.), *Evaluation and social justice* (pp. 23-36). San Francisco: Jossey-Bass.

House, E. R. (1991). Realism in research. *Educational Researcher, 20*(6), 2-9.

Howe, K. R. (1988). Against the quantitative-qualitative incompatibility thesis or dogmas die hard. *Educational Researcher, 17*(8), 10-16.

Jacob, E. (1987). Qualitative research traditions: A review. *Review of Educational Research, 57,* 1-50.

Joint Committee on Standards for Educational Evaluation. (1981). *Standards for evaluations of educational programs, projects, and materials.* New York: McGraw-Hill.

Lather, P. (1992). Critical frames in educational research: Feminist and poststructural perspectives. *Theory Into Practice, 31*(2), 1-13.

Lincoln, Y. S. (1990). The making of a constructivist: A remembrance of transformations past. In E. G. Guba (Ed.), *The paradigm dialog* (pp. 67-87). Newbury Park, CA: Sage.

Lincoln, Y. S. (1991). The arts and sciences of program evaluation (AEA 1991 Presidential Address). *Evaluation Practice, 12*(1), 1-7.

Lincoln, Y. S., & Guba, E. G. (1985). *Naturalistic inquiry.* Beverly Hills, CA: Sage.

Linn, M. (1981). Standards for evaluating out-of-school learning. *Evaluation News, 2*(2), 171-176.

MacDonald, B. (1976). Evaluation and the control of education. In D. A. Tawney (Ed.), *Curriculum evaluation today: Trends and implications.* London: Falmer.

Madaus, G. F., Scriven, M., & Stufflebeam, D. L. (Eds.). (1983). *Evaluation models: Viewpoints on educational and human services evaluation.* Boston: Kluwer-Nijhoff.

Mark, M. M. (1986). Validity typologies and the logic and practice of quasi-experimentation. In W. M. K. Trochim (Ed.), *Advances in quasi-experimental design and analysis.* San Francisco: Jossey-Bass.

McTaggart, R. (1990, April). *Dilemmas in democratic evaluation: Politics and validation.* Paper presented at the annual meeting of the American Educational Research Association, Boston.

Parlett, M., & Hamilton, D. (1976). Evaluation as illumination: A new approach to the study of innovative programs. In G. V Glass (Ed.), *Evaluation studies review annual* (Vol. 1). Beverly Hills, CA: Sage.

Patton, M. Q. (1986). *Utilization-focused evaluation* (2nd ed.). Beverly Hills, CA: Sage.

Patton, M. Q. (1987). Evaluation's political inherency: Practical implications for design and use. In D. J. Palumbo (Ed.), *The politics of program evaluation* (pp. 100-145). Newbury Park, CA: Sage.

Patton, M. Q. (1988). Paradigms and pragmatism. In D. M. Fetterman (Ed.), *Qualitative approaches to evaluation in education: The silent scientific revolution* (pp. 116-137). New York: Praeger.

Patton, M. Q. (1990). *Qualitative evaluation and research methods* (2nd ed.). Newbury Park, CA: Sage.

Pitman, M. A., & Maxwell, J. A. (1992). Qualitative approaches to evaluation: Models and methods. In M. D. LeCompte, W. L. Millroy, & J. Preissle (Eds.), *The handbook of qualitative research in education* (pp. 729-770). New York: Academic Press.

Rossi, P. H., & Freeman, H. E. (1985). *Evaluation: A systematic approach* (3rd ed.). Beverly Hills, CA: Sage.

Rossi, P. H., & Lyall, K. C. (1978). An overview of the NIT experiment. In T. D. Cook, M. L. DelRosario, K. M. Hernigan, M. M. Mark, & W. M. K. Trochim (Eds.), *Evaluation studies review annual* (Vol. 3, pp. 412-428). Beverly Hills, CA: Sage.

Salomon, G. (1991). Transcending the qualitative-quantitative debate: The analytic and systemic approaches to educational research. *Educational Researcher, 20*(6), 10-18.

Schwandt, T. A. (1989). Recapturing moral discourse in evaluation. *Educational Researcher, 18*(8), 11-16, 34.

Schwandt, T. A. (1991). Evaluation as moral critique. In C. L. Larson & H. Preskill (Eds.), *Organizations in transition: Opportunities and challenges for evaluation* (pp. 63-72). San Francisco: Jossey-Bass.

Scriven, M. (1967). The methodology of evaluation. *AERA Monograph Series in Curriculum Evaluation, 1,* 39-83.

Scriven, M. (1973). Goal-free evaluation. In E. R. House (Ed.), *School evaluation: The politics and process* (pp. 319-328). Berkeley, CA: McCutchan.

Scriven, M. (1983). Evaluation ideologies. In G. F. Madaus, M. Scriven, & D. L. Stufflebeam (Eds.), *Evaluation models: Viewpoints on educational and human services evaluation* (pp. 229-260). Boston: Kluwer-Nijhoff.

Scriven, M. (1991). Beyond formative and summative evaluation. In M. W. McLaughlin & D. C. Phillips (Eds.), *Evaluation and education: At quarter century* (pp. 19-64). Chicago: University of Chicago Press.

Sechrest, L. (1992). Roots: Back to our first generations (AEA 1991 Presidential Address). *Evaluation Practice, 13*(1), 1-7.

Shadish, W. R., Cook, T. D., & Leviton, L. C. (1991). *Foundations of program evaluation: Theories of practice.* Newbury Park, CA: Sage.

Simons, H. (1987). *Getting to know schools in a democracy: The politics and process of evaluation.* London: Falmer.

Sirotnik, K. A. (Ed.). (1990). *Evaluation and social justice.* San Francisco: Jossey-Bass.

Sirotnik, K. A., & Oakes, J. (1990). Evaluation as critical inquiry: School improvement as a case in point. In K. A. Sirotnik (Ed.), *Evaluation and social justice* (pp. 37-53). San Francisco: Jossey-Bass.

Smith, J. K. (1989). *The nature of social and educational inquiry: Empiricism versus interpretation.* Norwood, NJ: Ablex.

Smith, J. K. (1990). Alternative research paradigms and the problem of criteria. In E. G. Guba (Ed.), *The paradigm dialog* (pp. 167-187). Newbury Park, CA: Sage.

Smith, J. K., & Heshusius, L. (1986). Closing down the conversation: The end of the quantitative-qualitative debate. *Educational Researcher, 15*(1), 4-12.

Soltis, J. F. (1990, April). *The hermeneutics/interpretive tradition and its virtues.* Paper presented at the annual meeting of the American Educational Research Association, Boston.

Stake, R. E. (1967). The countenance of educational evaluation. *Teachers College Record, 68,* 523-540.

Stake, R. E. (1975). *Evaluating the arts in education: A responsive approach.* Columbus, OH: Merrill.

Stake, R. E. (1978). The case study method in social inquiry. *Educational Researcher, 7*(2), 5-8.

Stake, R. E. (1983). The case study method in social inquiry. In G. F. Madaus, M. Scriven, & D. L. Stufflebeam (Eds.), *Evaluation models: Viewpoints on educational and human services evaluation* (pp. 279-286). Boston: Kluwer-Nijhoff.

Stake, R. E. (1991). Retrospective on "The countenance of educational evaluation." In M. W. McLaughlin & D. C. Phillips (Eds.), *Evaluation and education: At quarter century* (pp. 67-88). Chicago: University of Chicago Press.

Stufflebeam, D. L. (1991). Professional standards and ethics for evaluators. In M. W. McLaughlin & D. C. Phillips (Eds.), *Evaluation and education: At quarter century* (pp. 249-282). Chicago: University of Chicago Press.

Sullivan, W. M. (1986). *Reconstructing public philosophy.* Berkeley: University of California Press.

Weiss, C. H. (1970). The politicization of evaluation research. *Journal of Social Issues, 26,* 57-68.

Weiss, C. H. (Ed.). (1972). *Evaluating action programs: Readings in social action and education.* Boston: Allyn & Bacon.

Weiss, C. H. (Ed.). (1977). *Using social research in public policy making.* Lexington, MA: Lexington.

Weiss, C. H. (1987). Where politics and evaluation research meet. In D. J. Palumbo (Ed.), *The politics of program evaluation* (pp. 47-70). Newbury Park, CA: Sage.

Whitmore, E. (1990). *Focusing on the process in evaluation: It's the "how" that counts.* Paper presented at the annual meeting of the American Evaluation Association, Washington, DC.

14

Influencing the
Policy Process With
Qualitative Research

Ray C. Rist

◆ More than 20 years ago, James Coleman wrote, "There is no body
of methods; no comprehensive methodology for the study of the
impact of public policy as an aid to future policy." This now-famous quote
still rings true. Indeed, one can argue that in the intervening decades, the
tendency in policy research and analysis has become ever more centrifugal,
spinning off more methodologies and variations on methodologies, more
conceptual frameworks, and more disarray among those who call themselves policy analysts or see themselves working in the area of policy
studies. A number of critics of the current scene of policy studies and the
attendant applications of so many different methodologies have argued
that any improvements in the techniques of policy research have not led
to greater clarity about what to think or what to do. More charitably, it
could be said that the multiplicity of approaches to policy research should
be welcomed, as they bring different skills and strengths to what are
admittedly difficult and complex issues.

AUTHOR'S NOTE: The views expressed here are those of the author, and no endorsement by the
U.S. General Accounting Office is intended or should be inferred.

400

Regardless of whether one supports or challenges the contention that policy research has had a centrifugal impact on the knowledge base relevant to policy making, the bottom line remains much the same: What policy researchers tend to consider as improvements in their craft have not significantly enhanced the role of research in policy making. Instead, the proliferation of persons, institutes, and centers conducting policy-related work has led to more variation in the manner by which problems are defined, more divergence in the ways in which studies are designed and conducted, and more disagreement and controversy over the ways in which data are analyzed and findings reported. The policy maker now confronts a veritable glut of differing (if not conflicting) research information.

A sobering but provocative counterintuitive logic is at work here: Increased personnel, greater allocation of resources, and growing sophistication of methods have not had the anticipated or demonstrated effect of greater clarity and understanding of the policy issues before the country. Rather, current efforts have led to a more complex, complicated, and partial view of the issues and their solutions. Further, as Smith (1991) would argue, this tendency to greater complexity has left both the policy makers and the citizens less able to understand the issues and to see how their actions might affect the present condition.

Whereas one may grant that early analyses, for example, in the areas of education or social welfare, were frequently simplistic and not especially sophisticated in either the design or application of policy methods, the inverse does not, in and of itself, work to the advantage of the policy maker. Stated differently, to receive a report resplendent with "state-of-the-art" methodologies and complex analyses that tease out every nuance and shade of meaning on an issue may provide just as little guidance for effective decision making as did the former circumstances. The present fixation on the technical adequacy of policy research without a commensurate concern for its utilization is to relegate that work to quick obscurity (Chelimsky, 1982).

If this admittedly brief description of the current state of policy research approximates the reality, then a fundamental question arises: Is the presumption correct that research cannot be conducted that is relevant to the policy process? It is my view that the presumption is not correct. Research can contribute to informed decision making, but the manner in which this is done needs to be reformulated. We are well past the time when it is possible to argue that good research will, because it is good, influence the policy process. That kind of linear relation of research to action simply is not a viable way in which to think about how knowledge can inform decision making. The relation is both more subtle and more tenuous. Still, there is a relation. It is my intent in this chapter to address how some of the linkages of knowledge and action are formed, particularly for the kinds of knowledge generated through qualitative research.[1]

◆ The Nature of Policy Decision Making

Policy making is multidimensional and multifaceted. Research is but one (and often minor at that) among the number of frequently contradictory and competing sources that seek to influence what is an ongoing and constantly evolving process. The emphasis here on policy making being a *process* is deliberate. It is a process that evolves through cycles, with each cycle more or less bounded, more or less constrained by time, funds, political support, and other events. It is also a process that circles back on itself, iterates the same decision issue time and again, and often does not come to closure. Choosing not to decide is a frequent outcome.

Such a description of the policy process suggests the need for a modification, if not a fundamental reframing, of the traditional understanding of policy making. In this latter, more traditional approach, decision making in the policy arena is understood as a discrete event, undertaken by a defined set of actors working in "real time" and moving to their decision on the basis of an analysis of their alternatives. Weiss (1982) has nicely summarized this notion of "decision making as an event":

> Both the popular and the academic literature picture decision making as an event; a group of authorized decision makers assemble at particular times and places, review a problem (or opportunity), consider a number of alternative courses of action with more or less explicit calculation of the advantages and disadvantages of each option, weigh the alternatives against their goals or preferences, and then select an alternative that seems well suited for achieving their purposes. The result is a decision. (p. 23)

She also nicely demolishes this view when she writes:

> Given the fragmentation of authority across multiple bureaus, departments, and legislative committees, and the disjointed stages by which actions coalesce into decisions, the traditional model of decision making is a highly stylized rendition of reality. Identification of any clear-cut group of decision

402

makers can be difficult. (Sometimes a middle-level bureaucrat has taken the key action, although he or she may be unaware that his or her action was going to be—or was—decisive.) The goals of policy are often equally diffuse, except in terms of "taking care of" some undesirable situation. Which opinions are considered, and what set of advantages or disadvantages are assessed, may be impossible to tell in the interactive, multiparticipant, diffuse process of formulating policy. The complexity of governmental decision making often defies neat compartmentalization. (p. 26)

Of particular relevance here is that the focus on decision making as an ongoing set of adjustments, or midcourse corrections, eliminates the bind of having to pinpoint the event—that is, the exact time, place, and manner—in which research has been influential on policy. Parenthetically, because the specifics can seldom be supplied, the notion that research *should* have an impact on decision making seems to have become more and more an article of faith. That researchers have so persistently misunderstood decision making, and yet have constantly sought to be of influence, is a situation deserving of considerably more analysis than it receives. So long as researchers presume that research findings must be brought to bear upon a single event, a discrete act of decision making, they will be missing those circumstances and processes where, in fact, research can be useful. However, the reorientation away from "event decision making" and to "process decision making" necessitates looking at research as serving an "enlightenment function" in contrast to an "engineering function" (see Janowitz, 1971; Patton, 1990; Weiss, 1988).

Viewing policy research as serving an enlightenment function suggests that policy researchers work with policy makers and their staffs over time to create a contextual understanding about an issue, build linkages that will exist over time, and strive constantly to educate about new developments and research findings in the area. This is in contrast to the engineering perspective, where it is presumed that sufficient data can be brought to bear to determine the direction and intensity of the intended policy initiative, much as one can develop the specifications for the building of a bridge. If the policy direction is sufficiently explicit, then the necessary information relevant to the development of the policy can be collected, so this view would contend, and the policy actions can be deliberate, directed, and successful.

These comments should not be taken as a diatribe against research or an argument that knowledge counts for naught. Quite the contrary. Systematic knowledge generated by research is an important and necessary component in the decision-making process. Further, it is fair to note that there is seldom enough research-based information available in the policy arena. William Ruckelshaus once noted that although he was the administrator of the Environmental Protection Agency, he made many decisions when there was less than 10% of the necessary research information available to him and his staff. The relevance and usefulness of policy research will not become apparent, however, unless there is a reconsideration of what is understood by decision making in the policy process. A redefinition is needed of the context in which to look for a linkage between knowledge and action. Unpacking the nature of the policy cycle is the strategy employed here to address this redefinition of policy decision making.

◆ The Policy Cycle and Qualitative Research

There are two levels of decision making in the policy arena. The first involves the establishment of the broad parameters of government action, such as providing national health insurance, establishing a national energy policy, restructuring the national immigration laws, or reexamining the criteria for determining the safety and soundness of the country's financial institutions. At this level and in these instances, policy research input is likely to be quite small, if not nil. The setting of these national priorities is a political event, a coming together of a critical mass of politicians, special interest groups, and persons in the media who are able among them to generate the attention and focus necessary for the items to reach the national agenda.

"Iron triangles" built by the informal linking of supporters in each of these three arenas are not created by the presence or absence of policy research. One or another research study might be quoted in support of the contention that the issue deserves national attention, but it is incidental to the more basic task of first working to place the issue on the national agenda. If one wishes to influence any of the players during this phase of the policy process, it is much more likely to be done through personal contact, by organizations taking positions, or through the creation of sufficient static in the policy system (for example, lining up special interest groups in opposition to a proposal, even as there are groups in favor). This works to the benefit of the opposition in that media coverage will have to be seen to be "balanced" and coverage of the opposition can create the impression that there is not the strong unified support for a position that otherwise would seem to be the case.

Once the issue is on the agenda of key actors or organizations within the policy establishment, there are possibilities for the introduction and utilization of policy research. It is here at this second level of policy making—the level where there are concerns about translating policy intentions into policy and programmatic realities—that I will focus in this chapter.

The framework in which the contributions of policy research in general and qualitative research in particular can best be understood is that of the policy cycle, a concept that has been addressed for more than a decade (see, e.g., Chelimsky, 1985; Guba, 1984; Nakamura & Smallwood, 1980; Rist, 1989, 1990, 1993). I will develop my discussion of the policy cycle here according to its three phases—policy formulation, policy implementation, and policy accountability. Each of these three phases has its own order and logic, its own information requirements, and its own policy actors. Further, there is only some degree of overlap among the three phases, suggesting that they do merit individual analysis and understanding.

The opportunities for qualitative research within the policy cycle are thus defined and differentiated by the information requirements at each phase. The questions asked at each phase are distinct, and the information generated in response to these same questions is used to different ends. It is to a detailed examination of these three phases of the policy cycle and the manner in which qualitative research can inform each phase that I now turn.

◆ Policy Formulation

Nakamura and Smallwood (1980) define a policy as follows: "A policy can be thought of as a set of instructions from policy makers to policy implementers that spell out both goals and the means for achieving those goals" (p. 31). How is it that these instructions are crafted, by whom, and with what relevant policy information and analysis? The answers can provide important insights into the process of policy formulation. Nakamura and Smallwood offer a relevant departure point with their description of the actors involved in policy formulation:

405

In general, the principal actors in policy formulation are the "legitimate" or formal policy makers: people who occupy positions in the governmental arena that entitle them to authoritatively assign priorities and commit resources. These people include elected officials, legislators, and high-level administrative appointees, each of whom must follow prescribed paths to make policy. . . . Since these formal policy makers represent diverse constituencies—electoral, administrative, and bureaucratic—the policy making process offers many points of access through which interest groups and others from arenas outside government can exercise influence. Thus policy making usually involves a diverse set of authoritative, or formal, policy makers, who operate within the governmental arena, plus a diverse set of special interest and other constituency groups from outside arenas, who press their demands on these formal leaders. (pp. 31-32)

As the formulation process begins, there are a number of pressing questions. Answering each question necessitates the compiling of whatever information is currently available plus the development of additional information when the gaps are too great in what is currently known. The information needs can generally be clustered around three broad sets of questions. Each of these clusters is highly relevant to policy formulation; in each there are important opportunities for the presentation and utilization of qualitative research.

The first set of information needs revolves around an understanding of the policy issue at hand. What are the contours of this issue? Is the problem or condition one that is larger now than before, about the same, or smaller? Is anything known about whether the nature of the condition has changed? Do the same target populations, areas, or institutions experience this condition now as earlier? How well can the condition be defined? How well can the condition be measured? What are the different interpretations and understandings about the condition, its causes and its effects? The issue here, stated differently, is one of the ability of policy makers to define clearly and understand the problem or condition that they are facing and for which they are expected to develop a response.

Charles Lindblom (1968) has nicely captured some of the conceptual complexity facing policy makers as they try to cope with the definition of a policy problem or condition:

Policy makers are not faced with a given problem. Instead they have to identify and formulate their problem. Rioting breaks out in dozens of

American cities. What is the problem? Maintaining law and order? Racial discrimination? Incipient revolution? Black power? Low income? Lawlessness at the fringe of an otherwise relatively peaceful reform movement? Urban disorganization? Alienation? (p. 13)

The second cluster of questions focuses on what has taken place previously in response to this condition or problem. What programs or projects have previously been initiated? How long did they last? How successful were they? What level of funding was required? How many staff members were required? How receptive were the populations or institutions to these initiatives? Did they request help or did they resist the interventions? Did the previous efforts address the same condition or problem as currently exists, or was it different? If it was different, how so? If it was the same, why are yet additional efforts necessary? Are the same interest groups involved? What may explain any changes in the present interest group coalition?

The third cluster of questions relevant to the policy formulation stage of the cycle focuses on what is known of the previous efforts and their impacts that would help one choose among present-day options. Considering trade-offs among various levels of effort in comparison to different levels of cost is but one among several kinds of data relevant to considering the policy options. There may also be data on the time frames necessary before one could hope to see impacts. Trade-offs between the length of the developmental stage of the program and the eventual impacts are relevant, particularly if there are considerable pressures for short-term solutions. The tendency to go to "weak thrust, weak effect" strategies is well understood in these circumstances. Alternatively, if previous efforts did necessitate a considerable period of time for measurable outcomes to appear, how did the policy makers in those circumstances hold on to the public support and keep the coalitions intact long enough for the results to emerge?

Qualitative research is highly relevant to the information needs at this stage in the policy cycle. Studies on the social construction of problems, on the differing interpretations of social conditions, on the building and sustaining of coalitions for change, on previous program initiatives and their impacts, on community and organizational receptivity to programs, on organizational stability and cohesion during the formulation stage, and on the changing nature of social conditions are all germane to the questions posed here.

There is an additional contribution that qualitative work can make at this stage of the policy process, and it is that of studying the intended and unintended consequences of the various policy instruments or tools that might be selected as the means to implement the policy (Salamon, 1989). There is a present need within the policy community to ascertain what tools work best in which circumstances and for which target populations. Very little systematic work has been done in this area—which frequently leaves policy makers essentially to guess as to the trade-offs between the choice of one tool and another.

Information of the kind provided by qualitative research can be of significant help in making decisions, for example, about whether to provide direct services in health, housing, and education or provide vouchers to recipients, whether to provide direct cash subsidies or tax credits to employers who will hire unemployed youth, and whether to increase funding for information campaigns or to increase taxes as strategies to discourage smoking. These are but three examples where different policy tools are available and where choices will have to be made among them.

Key among the activities in the policy formulation stage is the selection of the most appropriate policy strategy to achieve the desired objective. Central to the design of this strategy is the selection of one or more tools available to the government as the means to carry out its intentions. Qualitative studies of how different tools are understood and responded to by target populations is of immense importance at this stage of the policy process.

Unfortunately, although the demand for analysis of this type is great, the supply is extremely limited. The qualitative study of policy tools is an area that is yet to be even modestly explored within the research community.

Although qualitative research can be relevant at this stage, it is also the case that its applications are problematic. The basic reason is that seldom is there enough time to both commission and complete new qualitative research within the existing window of opportunity during policy formulation. Thus the applications have to rely on existing qualitative research—and that may or may not exist. Here is one key means by which good, well-crafted qualitative work on topical social issues can find its way into the policy arena. As policy makers start on the formulation effort, their need to draw quickly on existing work puts a premium on those research studies that have worked through matters of problem definition, the social construction of problems, community studies, retrospective assessments of prior initiatives, and so on.

The problematic nature of the applications of qualitative research at this stage is further reinforced by the fact that seldom are research funds available for studies that address the kinds of questions noted above in the three clusters. If the problem or condition is not seen to be above the horizon and thus on the policy screen, there is little incentive for a policy maker or program manager to use scarce funds for what would appear to be nonpragmatic, "theoretical" studies. And by the time the condition has sufficiently changed or become highly visible as a social issue for the policy community, qualitative work is hard-pressed to be sufficiently time sensitive and responsive. The window for policy formulation is frequently very small and open only a short time. The information that can be passed through has to be ready and in a form that enhances quick understanding.

The above constraints on the use of qualitative research at this stage of the policy cycle should not be taken as negative judgments on either the utility or the relevance of such information. Rather, it is only realistic to acknowledge that having the relevant qualitative research available when it is needed for policy formulation is not always possible. As noted earlier, this is an area where there are potentially significant uses for qualitative studies. But the uses are likely to come because of scholars and researchers who have taken on an area of study for their own interest and to inform basic understandings in the research community, rather than presuming before they begin that they would influence the formulation process. It is only the infrequent instance where there is sufficient time during the formulation stage for new qualitative work to be conducted.

It should be stressed here that the restrictions on the use of qualitative work during the formulation phase of the policy cycle come much more from the nature of the policy process than from the nature of qualitative work. The realities of the legislative calendar, the short lives of most senior political appointees in any one position, the mad scramble among competing special interest groups for their proposals to be addressed and acted upon, and the lack of concentration by the media on any issue for very long all inhibit the development of research agendas that address the underlying issues. This is ironic because it is clear that the country will face well into the foreseeable future the issues of health care allocation and quality, immigration controls and border security, educational retraining of dislocated workers, and youth unemployment, to name but four areas that have heretofore persistently stayed near or at the top of the national policy agenda. Basic, in-depth qualitative work in these and other key areas could inform the policy formulation process for years to come. But the pressures and structural incentives in the policy system all go in the other direction. To wit: Develop short-term proposals with quick impacts to show responsiveness and accommodate all the vested interests in the iron triangle.

In sum, with respect to this first phase of the policy cycle, qualitative research can be highly influential. This is particularly so with respect to problem definition, understanding of prior initiatives, community and organizational receptivity to particular programmatic approaches, and the kinds of impacts (both anticipated and unanticipated) that might emerge from different intervention strategies. This information would be invaluable to policy makers. But, as noted, the use of the material can be hindered by such factors as whether or not the information exists, is known to the policy community, and is available in a form that makes it quickly accessible. Overcoming these obstacles does not guarantee the use of qualitative research in the formulation process, but one can be strongly assured that if these obstacles are present, the likelihood of the use of qualitative material drastically diminishes.

◆ Policy Implementation

The second phase of the policy cycle is that of policy implementation. It is in this stage that the policy initiatives and goals established during policy formulation are to be transformed into programs, procedures, and regulations. The knowledge base that policy makers need to be effective in this phase necessitates the collection and analysis of different information from that found in policy formulation. With the transformation of policies into programs, the concern moves to the operational activities of the policy tool and the allocation of resources. The concern becomes one of how to use the available resources in the most efficient and effective manner in order to have the most robust impact on the program or condition at hand. As Pressman and Wildavsky (1984) have written in this regard:

> Policies imply theories. Whether stated explicitly or not, policies point to a chain of causation between initial conditions and future consequences. If X, then Y. Policies become programs when, by authoritative action, the initial conditions are created. X now exists. Programs make the theories operational by forging the first link in the causal chain connecting actions to objectives. Given X, we act to obtain Y. Implementation, then, is the

ability to forge subsequent links in the causal chain so as to obtain the
desired results. (p. xxii)

The research literature on policy and program implementation indicates
that that is a particularly difficult task to accomplish (see, e.g., Hargrove,
1985; Pressman & Wildavsky, 1984; Yin, 1985). Again, quoting Pressman
and Wildavsky:

Our normal expectations should be that new programs will fail to get off
the ground and that, at best, they will take considerable time to get started.
The cards in this world are stacked against things happening, as so much
effort is required to make them work. The remarkable thing is that new
programs work at all. (p. 109)

It is in this context of struggling to find ways of making programs work that
the data and analyses from qualitative research can come into play. The
information needs from qualitative research at this stage of the policy cycle
cluster into several areas. First, there is a pressing need for information on
the implementation process per se. Qualitative researchers, through case
studies, program monitoring, and process evaluations, can inform program
managers responsible for the implementation of the policy initiative.

Qualitative work can focus on such questions as the degree to which the
program is reaching the intended target audience, the similarities and
contrasts in implementation strategies across sites, the aspects of the
program that are or are not operational, whether the services slated to be
delivered are in fact the ones delivered, and the operational burdens placed
on the institution or organization responsible for implementation (i.e., Is
there the institutional capacity to respond effectively to the new policy
initiative?). The focus is on the day-to-day realities of bringing a new
program or policy into existence. This "ground-level" view of implementation is best done through qualitative research. The study of the rollout
of an implementation effort is an area where qualitative work is at a clear
advantage over other data collection strategies.

A second cluster of research questions amenable to qualitative work in
the implementation arena focuses on the problem or condition that prompted
the policy or program response in the first place. No problem or condition
stands still, simply because the policy community has decided to take action
on what was known at the time the decision was made. Problems and
conditions change—both before and after a policy response is decided

upon. Thus the challenge for qualitative researchers is to continue to track the condition, even as the implementation effort swings into action. Qualitative work can provide ongoing monitoring of the situation— whether the condition has improved, worsened, remained static; whether the same target population is involved as earlier; whether the condition has spread or contracted; and whether the aims of the program still match the assumptions and previous understandings of the condition. Qualitative work can provide an important reality check for program managers as to whether the program is or is not appropriate to the current condition. Qualitative work that monitors the condition in real time can play a key role in the continuous efforts of program managers to match their services or interventions to the present circumstances.

The third cluster of necessary policy questions during this implementa- tion phase of the policy cycle focuses on the efforts made by the organiza- tion or institution to respond to the initiative. Here, for example, qualita- tive data would be relevant for learning how the organizational response to the condition or problem has been conceptualized. Are the social constructions of the problem that were accepted at the policy formulation stage by federal policy makers accepted during implementation by the program managers and staff months later and perhaps thousands of miles away? What has been the transformation of the understandings that have taken place when the policy or program is actually being implemented? Do the policy makers and the program implementation folks accept the same understandings as to the intent of the policy—let alone the same under- standings of the problem that the policy is suppose to address?

Another aspect of this need for qualitative data concerns the organiza- tional response. Here questions would be asked that address the expertise and qualifications of those responsible for the implementation effort, the interest shown by management and staff, the controls in place regarding the allocation of resources, the organizational structure and whether it adequately reflects the demands on the organization to respond to this initiative, what means exist in the organization for deciding among com- peting demands, the strategies the organization uses to clarify misunder- standings or ambiguities in how it defines its role in implementation, and, finally, what kinds of interactive information or feedback loops are in place to assist managers in their ongoing efforts to move the program toward the stated objectives of the policy. It is information of precisely this type on the implementation process that Robert Behn (1988) notes is so critical to managers as they struggle to "grope along" and move toward organizational goals.

◆ Policy Accountability

The third stage in the policy cycle comes when the policy or program is sufficiently mature that one can address questions of accountability, impacts, or outcomes. Here again, the information needs are different from those in the two previous stages of the policy cycle. The contributions of qualitative research can be pivotal in assessing the consequences of the policy and program initiative. Just as the questions change from one part of the policy cycle to another, so too does the focus of the qualitative research necessary to answer these same questions.

First there is the matter of what the program or policy did or did not accomplish: Were the objectives for the program met? Qualitative research can specifically help in this regard by addressing, for example, whether the community and police were actively working together in a neighborhood "crime watch" program, whether the appropriate target audience of homeless persons in another program received the health services they were promised, and whether in a third program youth were given the type and quantity of on-the-job training that resulted in successful placements in permanent positions.

When a program reaches the stage that it is appropriate to discuss and assess impacts, qualitative research provides a window on the program that is simply not available in any other way. Qualitative research allows for the study of both anticipated and unanticipated outcomes, changes in understandings and perceptions as a result of the efforts of the program or policy, the direction and intensity of any social change that results from the program, and the strengths and weaknesses of the administrative/organizational structure that was used to operationalize the program. Policy makers have no equally grounded means of learning about program impacts and outcomes as they do with qualitative research findings.

These grounded means of knowing also carry over into what one might traditionally think of as quantitative assessments of policy. Qualitative work can provide to program managers and policy makers information on how confident they can or should be in the measures being used to determine program influence. Although the intent may be that of a highly

413

reliable and replicable instrument that allows for sophisticated quantification, it is the qualitative work that can address the issue of validity.

The issues of reliability and validity are well-known in the research literature and need not be reviewed here. Suffice it to say that policy makers and program managers have been misled more than once by investing a great deal of time and effort on their instrumentation without equal emphasis on answering the question of whether their measures were the appropriate ones to the problem or condition at hand. Studies of school desegregation and busing or health care in nursing homes are but two areas where a heavy emphasis on quantifying outcomes and processes have left key aspects of the condition undocumented and thus unattended to by those who should have been paying attention.

There is an additional aspect of this first cluster of information needs that merits special attention vis-à-vis qualitative research. This has to do with whether the original objectives and goals of the policy stayed in place through implementation. One message has come back to policy makers time and again: Do not take for granted that what was intended to be established or put in place through a policy initiative will be what one finds after the implementation process is complete. Programs and policies make countless midcourse corrections, tacking constantly, making changes in funding levels, staff stability, target population movements, political support, community acceptance, and the like.

It is through the longitudinal perspective of qualitative work that such issues can be directly addressed. Blitzkrieg assessments of programs are simply unable to pick up the backstage issues and conflicts that will inevitably be present and that may directly influence the direction and success of the program (Rist, 1980). To ignore staff turnover in a program that is highly staff-intensive in the provision of services, for instance, is to miss what may be the key ingredient in any study of implementation. But recognizing that it may be an issue in the first place is one of the ways in which qualitative work distinguishes itself from other research strategies.

The second cluster of information needs that emerge when a program is being assessed for impacts and outcomes is that of addressing whether and what changes may have occurred in the problem or condition. Central to any study of outcomes is the determination of whether in fact the condition itself has changed or not and what relevance the program or policy did or did not have to the present circumstances.

Although it is rudimentary to say so, it is worth stating explicitly that problems can change or not, totally independently of any policy or program initiative. Conceptually what we have is a situation in which impacts could or could not have occurred, and the consequence would be change or no change in a program or condition.

For example, a positive outcome of a policy could be no worsening of a condition, that is, no change in the original status that first prompted the policy response. Developing local intervention programs that stalled any growth in the number of child abuse cases could be considered a positive outcome. The key question is, of course, whether the evidence of no growth can be attributed to the intervention program or some other factor that was affecting the community independent of the intervention program itself, such as broad media coverage of a particularly savage beating of a child and, in the aftermath, considerable additional media coverage of how parents can cope with their urges to injure their children.

Qualitative work in this instance could focus on such impacts as the outreach efforts of the program to attract parents who had previously abused their children; efforts to reach parents who are seeking help to build better skills in working with their children; patterns and trends in child abuse as discussed by schoolteachers, day-care providers, and others who have ongoing and consistent contact with children; and whether and how parents are now coping with the stresses that might cause them to abuse their children.

The above discussion also generates an additional area in which qualitative work can assist at this stage of the policy cycle. It is the close-in and intensive familiarity with the problem or condition that comes from conducting qualitative work that would allow the researcher to make judgments on whether the situation is of a magnitude and nature that further action is necessary. If the study indicates that the problem or condition is diminishing in severity and prevalence, then further funding of a programmatic response may not be necessary. As a contrary example, the data from qualitative work may suggest that the condition has changed directions—that is, moved to a new target population—and a refocusing of the program is necessary if it is to be responsive.

Social conditions do not remain static, and the realization that the characteristics of a condition can change necessitates periodic reexamination of the original policy intent (policy formulation). Qualitative researchers can position themselves so that they can closely monitor the ongoing characteristics of a condition. With this firsthand and close-in information, they are well suited to suggest any necessary changes to both the policy formulation and implementation strategies for subsequent intervention efforts.

The third information need at this stage of the policy cycle where qualitative work can be of direct use comes with the focus on accountability. Here qualitative work can address concerns of management supervision, leadership of the organization with clear goals in mind, the attention to processes and procedures that would strengthen the capacity of the organization to implement the policy initiative effectively, the use of data-based decision making, and the degree of alignment or congruence between the leadership and the staff. All of these issues speak directly to the capacity of an organization to mobilize itself to provide effective service to its customers. If the organization is not positioned to do so, then there are clear issues of accountability that rest with the leadership.

Qualitative researchers who come to know an organization thoroughly and from the inside will be in a unique position from which to address the treatment and training of staff, reasons for attrition and low morale, the service-oriented philosophy (or lack of it) among the staff and leadership, the beliefs of the staff in the viability and worthiness of the program to address the problem, the quality and quantity of information used within the program for decision making, and the like. These are true qualitative dimensions of organizational life. It is essential that these be studied if judgments are to be made on the efficiency and effectiveness of any particular programmatic strategy. These judgments become central to subsequent decisions on the potential selection of a policy tool that would require a similar program intervention.

There are clear concerns of management accountability that must be discussed and assessed whenever programs are to be funded anew or redirected. Some of these concerns deal directly with impacts on the problem or condition, whereas others focus on the internal order and logic of the organization itself. Stated differently, it is important during the accountability phase to determine the degree to which any changes in the condition or problem can be directly attributed to the program and whether the program optimized or suboptimized the impact it had. Likewise, it is important to ascertain whether the presence (or absence) of any documented impacts is the result of the coherence of the policy formulation or the nature of program implementation. Finding that instance where coherent and robust policy initiatives are operationalized within a well-managed organization necessitates the complex assessment of what impacts can be attributed to the policy and what to its successful implementation. Qualitative research has a perspective on how to undertake this kind of assessment that other research approaches do not and for which the other approaches would have to rely heavily on proxy measures.

◆ Policy Tools

The analysis thus far has focused on the nature of the policy cycle and how each phase of the cycle has different information requirements for policy makers and program managers. The effort has been to document how qualitative research can play an active and positive role in answering the information needs at each of these phases and for both the policy makers and the program managers. In this section, the attention shifts to a focus on what are termed *policy tools.*

Such an emphasis is important because a deeper understanding of the tools available to government and how each can be more or less effectively used to achieve policy objectives can clearly inform all three stages of the policy cycle. Key to the efforts in policy formulation is the selection of an appropriate tool—be it a grant, a subsidy, a tax credit, a loan, a new regulation, the creation of a government-sponsored enterprise, or the provision of direct services, to name but 7 of the more than 30 tools currently used by government.

The selection of one tool rather than another is a policy choice for which few guiding data are available. Further, research to help policy makers in this regard is extremely sparse. Policy makers decide either based on past experience with a tool ("We used tax credits before, let's use tax credits again") or because they have a clear proclivity for or against a particular tool (conservatives would resist direct government services and seek instead a tool that locates the activity in the private sector, e.g., grants for the construction of public housing or the privatization of all concessions in national parks). It is safe to assert that neither qualitative nor quantitative researchers have shown much interest in this area. Beyond the works of Linder (1988), Linder and Peters (1984, 1989), May (1981), and Salamon (1981, 1989), there is not much research, either theoretical or empirical, to be cited.

What follows is an effort to identify four areas where qualitative work could be highly valuable to discussions regarding policy tools. For each of these areas, there is at present a nearly complete research void. It should be stressed that the short discussion to follow is not meant to be a definitive statement on how qualitative work can address the information needs of policy makers as they choose among tools, nor is it the definitive research agenda on the strengths and weaknesses of different tools.

It needs to be restated that few researchers of any persuasion have moved into this difficult but highly policy-relevant area. The reasons for this hesitancy are outside the bounds of this discussion, but it is clear that the policy analysis and research communities have, with few exceptions, steered wide of this port of inquiry. Building primarily on the works of Linder, Peters, and Salamon, what follows is offered as a modest agenda for those qualitative researchers who are interested in exploring new and untested ways of involving qualitative work within the policy arena. A more elaborate and detailed research agenda in this area is still well over the horizon.

As noted, four areas amenable to qualitative study will be briefly discussed. These are resource intensiveness, targeting, institutional constraints, and political risks. The tentativeness of this proposal has to be stressed yet again. There may well be multiple other ways in which to frame the qualitative study of policy tools. What follows here is predicated on the previous discussion regarding the policy cycle. The framework for the qualitative study of policy tools is essentially a matrix analysis, whereby each of these four areas can be studied in each of the three phases of the policy cycle. All 12 combinations will not be individually addressed here; rather, the focus will be on the four broad areas that can help to clarify the trade-offs among tools.

Resource intensiveness refers to the constellation of concerns involving the complexity of the operations, the relative costliness of different options, and the degree of administrative burden that different tools place on organizations. Tools vary widely in their complexity, their demands on organizations for technical expertise to administer and manage, their direct and indirect costs by sector, and the degree to which they are direct or indirect in their intent. And just to complicate matters more, the mix of these concerns for any given tool will shift as one moves from one phase of the policy cycle to another. Keeping the financial costs low and federal involvement to a minimum, for example, may be high priorities in Washington during the policy formulation stage, but these will also have the consequences during the policy implementation stage of serving few of the eligible target population, adding complexity through mandated state administration, and reducing direct impacts. Managing toxic waste clean-ups is but one example that is somewhat parallel to this brief scenario.

For qualitative researchers, the challenges here are multiple, not the least because they would necessitate more direct attention to organizational analysis. But there is also the clear opportunity to ask questions within organizations and to assess organizational capacity in ways that have not traditionally been done. Administrative burden has not been a topic of much (if any) qualitative research, but it is a very real consideration in the policy arena. Learning more of how to conceptualize this concern, how it is understood at various levels of government and within the private sector, and how different tools vary in this regard would be of considerable interest to policy makers in departments as well as those responsible for regulator and administrative oversight in organizations such as the Office of Management and Budget in the White House.

At present, a concept such as administrative burden is ill defined and subject to widely varying interpretations. In the absence of any systematic research, one person's definition and experience with "administrative burden" is as good as any other person's—and maybe better if he or she has more institutional or organizational influence. Additional examples concerning such concepts as "operational complexity" and "institutional capacity" are readily apparent.

Targeting refers to the capacity of the policy tool to be aimed at particular populations, problems, or institutions for whom the tool is primarily intended. A tool that, for example, seeks to help homeless persons who are mentally ill and also veterans would be highly targeted. Such a tool would be differentiated from a tool that is either diffuse or low in target specificity, for example, a tax credit for the interest earned in individual retirement accounts.

There are several key aspects of the targeting issue for a policy tool that qualitative researchers could address. First, there is the matter of the precision of the targeting. Qualitative researchers, in reference to the example just given, could help policy makers work through the strategies and definitional problems inherent in determining who is or is not homeless, who has or has not been diagnosed as mentally ill, and how to screen homeless veterans for service when documentation, service records, and so on are all likely to be lost or when persons simply cannot remember their own names.

A second aspect of targeting in selecting a policy tool is that of the amenability of the tool to adjustment and fine tuning. If the characteristics of the target population start to change, can the tool be adjusted to respond to this change? Flexibility in some instances would be highly desirable, whereas in others it may be irrelevant. For example, it would be beneficial to choose a policy instrument that responds to fluctuations and variations in the refugee populations coming into the United States, whereas it would be unnecessary in the instance of an entitlement program for which age is the only criterion for access to services.

Qualitative studies of different populations targeted by tools and the need (or lack thereof) of specificity in the targeting would be highly useful in policy formulation. There is also the opportunity in this area to explore whether those who have been targeted by a program believe this to be the case. Establishing community mental health centers could have some in the target population coming because of the "community health" emphasis, others coming for the "mental health" emphasis, and still others not showing up at all because they are not certain whose community is being referred or because they would never want anyone in their own neighborhood to know they have mental health problems. Linking services to target populations in the absence of such qualitative information suggests immediately the vulnerability and precariousness of presuming to establish service centers without the detailed knowledge of the populations for whom the effort is intended.

The example of community mental health centers leads to a third consideration in the targeting area—that of adaptability across uses. Can community mental health centers also serve other needs of the designated population, for example, nutrition and education, as well as serve as centers for entirely other target populations who are in the same residential vicinity? Can they serve as centers for the elderly, for latchkey children, for infant nutrition programs, and so on? The issue is one of flexibility and acceptance as well as neutrality in the perceptions of the other target groups. There may be groups who would not want to come to a mental health center, but who would be quite pleased to meet in a church or at a school. Gaining insight on these matters is clearly important as decisions are made on the location and mix of community services to be offered at any one location. Qualitative studies on these issues can inform policy makers and program managers in ways that will clearly affect the success or failure of different strategies.

Institutional capacity refers to the ability of the institution to deliver on the tasks that have been delegated to it. When a policy option clearly relies on a single institution to achieve certain objectives—for example, using the public schools as the vehicle to teach English to non-English-speaking children—there has to be some degree of certainty that the institution has the capacity to do so. Countless experiences with different policy initiatives have shown time and again that some institutions simply did not have, at the time, the capacity to do what was expected of them.

Further, there can be constraints placed on the institution that make it difficult if not impossible for the objective to be achieved. In addition to the more readily anticipated constraints of funding, staff availability, quality of facilities, and low political support, there are also constraints associated with the degree of intrusiveness the institution can exercise as well as the level of coerciveness allowed. The hesitancy of policy makers to allow intrusive efforts by the Internal Revenue Service to collect unpaid taxes has a clear impact on the ability of the organization to do so. The same can be said with respect to the IRS on the matter of coerciveness. Policy makers have simply decided to keep some organizations more constrained than others in carrying out their functions, for fear of abuse. Policy tools that have to rely on voluntary compliance or are framed to have an indirect effect face constraints different from those where these do not apply.

Qualitative research into the domain of institutional constraints and how it is that these constraints play out in the relation of the organization to the fulfillment of its mission is not, to my knowledge, now being done. It may be argued that it is not necessary, as the constraint dimension for any policy tool is too removed from research influence. That is, any constraints on an organization are more philosophical and ideological than operational. Yet the issue of institutional capacity and what does or does not hinder the ability of the organization to achieve its stated objectives is important to understand explicitly. If policy makers establish the parameters around an organization to the degree that it can never clearly achieve its goal (e.g., the IRS and unpaid back taxes), then there is a built-in level of failure that ought not be ignored and for which the institution should not be held accountable.

Political risk is the fourth dimension of the study of policy tools where qualitative research can directly contribute. Here the issues cluster around concerns of unanticipated risk, chances of failure, and timing. The selection of a policy tool is made with some outcome in mind—either direct or indirect. Yet there is always the possibility of unanticipated outcomes— again either direct or indirect. The selection of a tool necessarily has to take into account the risk of unknown outcomes and how these might affect the success of the policy.

Qualitative research, by the nature of its being longitudinal, done in naturalistic settings, and focused on the constructions of meaning developed by participants, is in a unique position from which to assess the possibility of tools having the impacts intended by policy makers. Low risk of unknown outcomes—for example, in increasing the security at U.S. federal courthouses—eliminates some level of uncertainty from the decision that does not happen when the risk of unknown outcomes is quite high, such as moving to year-round school schedules or as was learned when the movement to deinstitutionalize the mentally ill resulted in tens of thousands of mentally ill persons being left on their own with no means of support or treatment.

One other aspect of the political risk factor that qualitative research can address is the sustainability of the policy initiative. Close-in studies of the operational life of a policy initiative can gain a perspective on the commitment of those involved, their belief in the worthiness of the effort, the amount of political support they are or are not engendering, and the receptivity of the target population to the effort. If all these indicators are decidedly negative, then the sustainability of the initiative is surely low.

It is difficult to achieve success in policy efforts in the best of circumstances; it is that much harder when all the indicators point in the opposite direction. Qualitative research should have a distinct window from which to judge matters of political risk. Understanding of the participants, willingness to assume the causal linkage posited in the policy itself, and the degree of risk of unknown outcomes all influence the likelihood that any policy tool will achieve its intended results.

◆ Concluding Observations

In reviewing this assessment of the contributions of qualitative work to the policy process, it is apparent that the contributions are more in the realm of the potential than the actual. There is no broad-based and sustained tradition within contemporary social science of focusing qualitative work specifically on policy issues, especially given the real time constraints that the policy process necessitates. Yet it is also clear that the opportunities are multiple for such contributions to be made. The issue is chiefly one of how to link those in the research and academic communities who are knowledgeable in conducting qualitative research studies to those in the policy arena who can commission such work and who will make use of the findings. The analysis of different strategies for building these linkages would require a separate paper; suffice it to say here that much hard thinking and numerous exploratory efforts will be required for the potential to become the actual. The issues of institutional cultures, academic reward systems, publication requirements, funding sources, and methodological limitations are but five among many that will have to be addressed if the linkages are to be built. And even beyond the resolution of (or at least the careful thinking about) these issues is the fundamental question of whether there is the will to bring qualitative work directly into the policy arena. Much of what has been written here will remain speculative unless and until there is some consensus among the practitioners of qualitative research that making this transition is worthwhile. The policy community is, I believe, ready for and would be receptive to anything those in the qualitative research community could offer, should they choose to make the effort to do so.

◆ Note

1. I want to stress early on that in this chapter I will not seek to develop distinctions among various conventionally used terms for qualitative research. Thus, in the pages that follow, terms such as *qualitative work, qualitative research,* and *qualitative methods* will all be used to denote the same frame of reference. I most frequently use the term that appears in the title of this handbook, *qualitative research.* I leave it to other authors in this volume to develop those distinctions as appropriate. I would also note, in defense of not trying to specify in much detail just exactly what the meaning is behind the use of any one of these terms, that early reviewers of this chapter suggested at least four other terms I might use in lieu of those I have. These terms included *naturalistic, constructionist, interpretive,* and *ethnographies.* I am sure that the delineation of distinctions has an important place in this book; it is just not my intent to do so here.

I also want to note early on that I am not going to try to differentiate among various qualitative data collection strategies, or means of analysis, as to their particular spheres of potential influence. Thus in this chapter I will not try to indicate what policy relevance or influence one might expect from case studies (and there are multiple variations in this single area alone) in contrast, for example, to multimethod studies. My intent is to place qualitative work broadly within the policy arena, not to develop a prescriptive set of categories about which methods or modes of analysis are likely to lead to what types of influence.

◆ References

Behn, R. D. (1988). Managing by groping along. *Journal of Policy Analysis and Management,* 7(4).

Chelimsky, E. (1982). Making evaluations relevant to congressional needs. *GAO Review,* 17(1).

Chelimsky, E. (1985). Old patterns and new directions in program evaluation. In E. Chelimsky (Ed.), *Program evaluation: Patterns and directions*. Washington, DC: American Society For Public Administration.

Guba, E. G. (1984). The effect of definitions of policy on the nature and outcomes of policy analysis. *Educational Leadership, 42*(2).

Hargrove, E. (1985). *The missing link: The study of the implementation of social policy.* Washington, DC: Urban Institute Press.

Janowitz, M. (1971). *Sociological methods and social policy.* New York: General Learning Press.

Lindblom, C. E. (1968). *The policy making process.* Englewood Cliffs, NJ: Prentice Hall.

Linder, S. H. (1988). Managing support for social research and development: Research goals, risk, and policy instruments. *Journal of Policy Analysis and Management, 7*(4).

Linder, S. H., & Peters, B. G. (1984). From social theory to policy design. *Journal of Public Policy, 4*(3).

Linder, S. H., & Peters, B. G. (1989). Instruments of government: Perceptions and contexts. *Journal of Public Policy, 9*(1).

May, P. J. (1981). Hints for crafting alternative policies. *Policy Analysis, 7*(2).

Nakamura, R. T., & Smallwood, F. (1980). *The politics of policy implementation.* New York: St. Martin's.

Patton, M. Q. (1990). *Qualitative evaluation and research methods* (2nd ed.). Newbury Park, CA: Sage.

Pressman, J. L., & Wildavsky, A. (1984). *Implementation* (3rd ed.). Berkeley: University of California Press.

Rist, R. C. (1980). Blitzkrieg ethnography: On the transformation of a method into a movement. *Educational Researcher, 9*(2).

Rist, R. C. (1989). Management accountability: The signals sent by auditing and evaluation. *Journal of Public Policy, 9*(3).

Rist, R. C. (Ed.). (1990). *Program evaluation and the management of government: Patterns and prospects across eight nations.* New Brunswick, NJ: Transaction.

Rist, R. C. (1993). Program evaluation in the United States General Accounting Office: Reflections on question formulation and utilization. In R. Conner et al. (Eds.), *Advancing public policy evaluation: Learning from international experiences.* Amsterdam: Elsevier.

Salamon, L. M. (1981). Rethinking public management: Third-party government and the changing forms of government action. *Public Policy, 29*(3).

Salamon, L. M. (1989). *Beyond privatization: The tools of government action.* Washington, DC: Urban Institute Press.

Smith, J. A. (1991). *The idea brokers: Think tanks and the rise of the new policy elite.* New York: Free Press.

Weiss, C. H. (1982). Policy research in the context of diffuse decision making. In R. C. Rist (Ed.), *Policy studies review annual.* Beverly Hills, CA: Sage.

Weiss, C. H. (1988). Evaluations for decisions: Is anybody there? Does anybody care? *Evaluation Practice, 9*(1).

Yin, R. K. (1985). Studying the implementation of public programs. In W. Williams (Ed.), *Studying implementation.* Chatham, NJ: Chatham House.

Suggested Readings

◆ Chapter 1

Behar, R. (1996). *The vulnerable observer: Anthropology that breaks your heart*. Boston: Beacon.

Behar, R., & Gordon, D. A. (Eds.). (1996). *Women writing culture*. Berkeley: University of California Press.

Olson, G. A., & and Olson, E. (Eds.). (1995). *Women writing culture* (foreword by Donna Haraway; afterword by Henry A. Giroux). Albany: State University of New York Press.

◆ Chapter 2

Babbie, E. (1992). *The practice of social research*. Belmont, CA: Wadsworth.

Dickens, D., & Fontana, A. (Eds.). (1994). *Postmodernism and social inquiry*. New York: Guilford.

Frey, J., & Oishi, S. M. (1995). *How to conduct interviews by telephone and in person*. Thousand Oaks, CA: Sage.

Gluck, S. B., & Patai, D. (Eds.). (1991). *Women's words: The feminist practice of oral history*. London: Routledge.

Kvale, S. (1996). *Interviews: An introduction to qualitative research*. Thousand Oaks, CA: Sage.

Mason, K. (1996). *Qualitative researching*. Thousand Oaks, CA: Sage.

Morgan, D. (1988). *Focus groups as qualitative research*. Newbury Park, CA: Sage.

Payne, S. L. (1951). *The art of asking questions*. Princeton, NJ: Princeton University Press.

Reinharz, S. (1992). *Feminist methods in social research*. New York: Oxford University Press.

Spradley, J. P. (1979). *The ethnographic interview*. New York: Holt, Rinehart & Winston.

◆ Chapter 3

Adler, P. A., & Adler, P. (1987). *Membership roles in field research*. Newbury Park, CA: Sage.

Cahill, S. (1990). Childhood and public life: Reaffirming biographical divisions. *Social Problems, 37*, 390-402.

Douglas, J. D. (1976). *Investigative social research*. Beverly Hills, CA: Sage.

Ellis, C. (1991). Sociological introspection and emotional experience. *Symbolic Interaction, 14*, 23-50.

Hayano, D. (1979). Auto-ethnography: Paradigms, problems, and prospects. *Human Organization, 38*, 99-104.

Heritage, J. (1984). *Garfinkel and ethnomethodology*. Cambridge: Polity.

Johnson, J. (1975). *Doing field research*. New York: Free Press.

Lofland, L. (1973). *A world of strangers*. New York: Basic Books.

Lofland, L. (1994). Observations and observers in conflict: Field research in the public realm. In S. Cahill & L. Lofland (Eds.), *The community of the streets*. Greenwich, CT: JAI.

Nash, J. (1981). Relations in frozen places: Observations on winter public order. *Qualitative Sociology, 4*, 99-124.

Riemer, J. (1977). Varieties of opportunistic research. *Urban Life, 5*, 467-477.

◆ Chapter 4

Ashcroft, B., Griffiths, G., & Tiffin, H. (Eds.). (1995). *The post-colonial studies reader*. New York: Routledge.

◆ Chapter 5

Chow, R. (1995). *Primitive passions: Visuality, sexuality, ethnography and contemporary Chinese cinema*. New York: Columbia University Press.

Hall, S. (1981). The whites of their eyes: Racist ideologies and the media. In G. Bridges & R. Brunt (Eds.), *Silver linings* (pp. 36-37). London: Laurence & Wishart.

Hall, S. (1989). Cultural identity and cinematic representation. *Framework, 36*, 68-81.

Trinh T. M.-H. (1991). *When the moon waxes red: Representation, gender, and cultural politics*. New York: Routledge.

◆ Chapter 6

Anzaldúa, G. (1987). *Borderlands/la frontera: The new mestiza*. San Francisco: Aunt Lute.

Bateson, M. C. (1989). *Composing a life*. New York: Atlantic Monthly Press.

Bateson, M. C. (1995). *Peripheral visions*. New York: Harper-Collins.

Bruner, J. (1996). *The culture of education*. Cambridge, MA: Harvard University Press.

Clandinin, D. J., & Connelly, F. M. (1995). *Teachers' professional knowledge landscapes*. New York: Teachers College Press.

Freeman, M. (1993). *Rewriting the self: History, memory, narrative.* London: Routledge.

Geertz, C. (1995). *After the fact: Two countries, four decades, one anthropologist.* Cambridge, MA: Harvard University Press.

Hoffman, E. (1989). *Lost in translation: A life in a new language.* Middlesex, UK: Penguin.

Lopate, P. (1994). *The art of the personal essay.* New York: Doubleday.

Lutwig, A. (1997). *How do we know who we are? A biography of the self.* Oxford: Oxford University Press.

Mallon, T. (1984). *A book of one's own: People and their diaries.* Middlesex, UK: Penguin.

Marmon-Silko, L. (1997). *Yellow woman and a beauty of the spirit.* New York: Simon & Schuster.

Paley, V. G. (1992). *You can't say you can't play.* Cambridge, MA: Harvard University Press.

Paley, V. G. (1995). *Kwanzaa and me: A teacher's story.* Cambridge, MA: Harvard University Press.

Schafer, R. (1992). *Retelling a life: Narration and dialogue in psychoanalysis.* New York: Basic Books.

◆ Chapter 7

Alasuutari, P. (1995). *Researching culture: Qualitative method and cultural studies.* London: Sage. (See especially Part III, "Unriddling.")

Coles, R. (1997). *Doing documentary work.* Oxford: Oxford University Press. (See especially Chapter 4, "A range of documentary inquiry.")

de Certeau, M. (1984). *The practice of everyday life.* Berkeley: University of California Press.

Glaser, B. (1992). *Emergence versus forcing: Basics of grounded theory analysis.* Mill Valley, CA: Sociology Press. (See especially Chapter 8, "Techniques for enhancing theoretical sensitivity.")

King, G., Keohane, R., & Verba, S. (1994). *Designing social inquiry: Scientific inference in qualitative research.* Princeton, NJ: Princeton University Press. (See especially Section 2, "Descriptive Inference.")

Nielson, J. M. (1990). *Feminist research methods.* Boulder, CO: Westview. (See especially Chapter 3.)

Perakyla, A. (1997). Reliability and validity in research based on transcripts. In D. Silverman (Ed.), *Qualitative research: Theory, method, and practice* (pp. 201-220). Thousand Oaks, CA: Sage.

Ragin, C. (1992). Introduction to qualitative comparative analysis. In T. Janoski & A. Hicks (Eds.), *The comparative political economy of the welfare state* (pp. 299-319). New York: Cambridge University Press.

Steinberg, M. (1997). Fence-sitting for a better view: Finding a middle ground between materialism and the linguistic turn in the epistemology of history. *Qualitative Inquiry, 3,* 26-52.

Weitzman, E., & Miles, M. (1995). *Computer programs for qualitative data analysis: A software sourcebook.* Thousand Oaks, CA: Sage.

Wells, A., Hirshberg, D., Lipton, M., & Oakes, J. (1995). Bounding the case within its context: A constructivist approach to studying detracking reform. *Educational Researcher, 24*(5), 18-24.

◆ Chapter 8

NOTE: All software discussed in Chapter 8 has of course progressed to new revisions since the original publication of the *Handbook*; indeed, the most recent publications are already out of date. Internet discussion groups and Web sites now reliably provide latest information and sharing of user experience. The central academic Web site on qualitative computing is run by the CAQDAS Project, Department of Sociology, University of Surrey, Guilford GU2 5XH, UK (telephone +44 [0] 1483 259455; fax +44 [0] 1483 306290; from the CAQDAS WWW page, http://www.soc.surrey.ac.uk/caqdas/). Researchers can access software demonstration versions and learn of recent publications and software developments.

Burgess, R. W. (Ed.). (1995). *Computing and qualitative analysis.* London: JAI.

Coffey, A., Holbrook, B., & Atkinson, P. (1996). Qualitative data analysis: Technologies and representations. *Sociological Research On-Line, 1*(1). (http://www.socresonline.org.uk/socresonline/1/1/4.html)

Dartnall, T. (Ed.). (1994). *Artificial intelligence and creativity: An interdisciplinary approach.* Dordrecht, Netherlands: Kluwer.

Fisher, M. (1997). *Qualitative computing: Using software for qualitative data analysis.* Aldershot, UK: Ashgate.

Kelle, U. (Ed.). (1995). *Computer-aided qualitative data analysis: Theory, methods and practice.* London: Sage.

Lee, R. (Ed.). (1995). *Information technology for the social scientist.* London: UCL Press.

Papazoglou, M. P., & Zeleznikow, J. (Eds.). (1992). *The next generation of information systems: From data to knowledge.* Berlin: Springer-Verlag.

Richards, L. (1997). Computers and qualitative analysis. In *The international encyclopedia of education* (2nd ed.). Oxford: Elsevier Science.

Richards, L. (1997). User's mistake as developer's challenge. *Qualitative Health Research, 7,* 406-416.

Weaver, A., & Atkinson, P. (1994). *Microcomputing and qualitative data analysis.* Aldershot, UK: Avebury.

◆ Chapter 9

Brown, R. H., & Clignet, R. (1991). A semiotics of the American self: Personal identity in the abstract society. *American Journal of Semiotics, 8*(4), 17-39.

Culler, J. (1981). *The pursuit of signs: Semiotics, literature, deconstruction.* Ithaca, NY: Cornell University Press.

Culler, J. (1988). *Framing the sign: Criticism and its institutions.* Norman: University of Oklahoma Press.

Cullum-Swan, B., & Manning, P. K. (1998). *Imaginative ethnography.* Boulder, CO: Westview.

Cullum-Swan, B., & Manning, P. K. (in press). Narrative discourses. *Cultural Studies.*

Danesi, M. (1994). *Cool: The signs and meanings of adolescence.* Toronto: University of Toronto Press.

Defending ways of knowing; expanding forms of presentation: Response to Michael Schwalbe's The responsibilities of sociological poets [Symposium]. *Qualitative Sociology, 19,* 517-541.

Denzin, N. K. (1997). *Interpretive ethnography: Ethnographic practices for the 21st century.* Thousand Oaks, CA: Sage.

Ellis, C., & Bochner, A. P. (Eds.). (1997). *Composing ethnography: Alternative forms of qualitative writing.* Walnut Creek, CA: AltaMira.

Hertz, R. (Ed.). (1997). *Reflexivity and voice.* Thousand Oaks, CA: Sage.

Hertz, R., & Glassner, B. (Eds.). (1998). *Qualitative sociology as everyday life.* Thousand Oaks, CA: Sage.

Lather, P. (1993). Fertile obsession: Validity after poststructuralism. *Sociological Quarterly, 34,* 673-693.

Lewis, D. J., & Smith, R. L. (1980). *American sociology and pragmatism.* Chicago: University of Chicago Press.

Richardson, L. (1997). *Fields of play: Constructing an academic life.* New Brunswick, NJ: Rutgers University Press.

Ritzer, G. (1996). *The McDonaldization of society: An investigation into the changing character of contemporary life.* Thousand Oaks, CA: Pine Forge.

Rochberg-Halton, E. (1986). *Meaning and modernity.* Chicago: University of Chicago Press.

Snow, R., & Morrill, C. (1995). Review of *Handbook of qualitative research*: A revolutionary handbook or a handbook for revolution? *Journal of Contemporary Ethnography, 24,* 341-349. (See also Norman Denzin's reply to this review, Transforming qualitative methods: Is it a revolution? [pp. 349-358], and Snow & Morrill's further response, Ironies, puzzles, and contradictions in Denzin and Lincoln's vision for qualitative research [pp. 359-362].)

◆ Chapter 10

Altheide, D. L. (1995). Horsing around with literary loops, or why postmodernism is fun. *Symbolic Interaction, 18,* 519-526.

Altheide, D. L. (1996). *Qualitative media analysis.* Thousand Oaks, CA: Sage.

Altheide, D. L., & Johnson, J. M. (1997). Ethnography and justice. In G. Miller & R. Dingwall (Eds.), *Context and method in qualitative research* (pp. 172-183). Thousand Oaks, CA: Sage.

Charmaz, K., & Mitchell, R. G. (1996). The myth of silent authorship: Self, substance, and style in ethnographic writing. *Symbolic Interaction, 19,* 285-302.

Couch, C. J. (1995). Oh, what webs those phantoms spin. *Symbolic Interaction, 18,* 229-245.

Ellis, C., & Bochner, A. P. (Eds.). (1996). Taking ethnography into the twenty-first century [Special issue]. *Journal of Contemporary Ethnography, 25*(1).

Emerson, R. M., Fretz, R. I., & Shaw, L. L. (1995). *Writing ethnographic field notes.* Chicago: University of Chicago Press.

Fuller, S. (1993). *Philosophy, rhetoric, and the end of knowledge.* Madison: University of Wisconsin Press.

Gubrium, J. F., & Holstein, J. A. (1997). *The new language of qualitative methods.* New York: Oxford University Press.

Weick, K. E. (1995). *Sensemaking in organizations.* Thousand Oaks, CA: Sage.

Wilbur, K. (1996). *A brief history of everything.* Boston: Shambhala.

◆ Chapter 11

Denzin, N. K. (1997). *Interpretive ethnography: Ethnographic practices for the 21st century.* Thousand Oaks, CA: Sage.

Krieger, S. (1996). *The family silver.* Berkeley: University of California Press.

Paget, M. A. (1993). *A complex sorrow: Reflections on cancer and an abbreviated life* (M. L. DeVault, Ed.). Philadelphia: Temple University Press.

Stack, C. (1996). *Call to home: African Americans reclaim the rural South.* New York: Basic Books.

Wolcott, H. F. (1993). *The art of fieldwork.* Walnut Creek, CA: AltaMira.

◆ Chapter 12

Brady, I. (Ed.). (1991). *Anthropological poetics.* Savage, MD: Rowman & Littlefield.

Clifford, J., & Marcus, G. E. (Eds.). (1986). *Writing culture: The poetics and politics of ethnography.* Berkeley: University of California Press.

Denzin, N. K. (1997). *Interpretive ethnography: Ethnographic practices for the 21st century.* Thousand Oaks, CA: Sage.

Ellis, C., & Bochner, A. P. (Eds.). (1997). *Composing ethnography: Alternative forms of qualitative writing.* Walnut Creek, CA: AltaMira.

Kondo, D. K. (1990). *Crafting selves: Power, gender, and discourses of identity in a Japanese workplace.* Chicago: University of Chicago Press.

Krieger, S. (1991). *Social science and the self: Personal essays on an art form.* New Brunswick, NJ: Rutgers University Press.

Lather, P., & Smithies, C. (1997). *Troubling the angels: Women living with HIV/AIDS.* Boulder, CO: Westview.

Lawrence-Lightfoot, S. (1994). *I've known rivers: Lives of loss and liberation.* Reading, MA: Addison-Wesley.

Richardson, L. (1990). *Writing strategies: Reaching diverse audiences.* Newbury Park, CA: Sage.

Richardson, L. (1997). *Fields of play: Constructing an academic life.* New Brunswick, NJ: Rutgers University Press.

Van Maanen, J. (1988). *Tales of the field: On writing ethnography.* Chicago: University of Chicago Press.

Van Maanen, J. (Ed.). (1995). *Representation in ethnography.* Thousand Oaks, CA: Sage.

◆ Chapter 13

Adelman, C. (1996). Anything goes: Evaluation and relativism. *Evaluation, 2,* 291-305.

Chelimsky, E., & Shadish, W. R. (Eds.). (1997). *Evaluation for the 21st century: A handbook.* Thousand Oaks, CA: Sage.

Fetterman, D. M. (Ed.). (1988). *Qualitative approaches to evaluation in education: The silent scientific revolution.* New York: Praeger.

Greene, J. C. (1996). Qualitative evaluation and scientific citizenship: Reflections and refractions. *Evaluation, 2,* 277-289.

Heshusius, L. (1994). Freeing ourselves from objectivity: Managing subjectivity or turning toward a participatory mode of consciousness. *Educational Researcher, 23*(3), 15-22.

House, E. R. (1993). *Professional evaluation: Social impact and political consequences.* Newbury Park, CA: Sage.

Lincoln, Y. S. (1995). Emerging quality in qualitative and interpretive inquiry. *Qualitative Inquiry, 1,* 275-289.

Schwandt, T. A. (1997). Evaluation as practical hermeneutics. *Evaluation, 3,* 1-14.

Schwandt, T. A. (1997). *Qualitative inquiry: A dictionary of terms.* Thousand Oaks, CA: Sage.

Schwandt, T. A. (1997). Reading the "problem of evaluation" in social inquiry. *Qualitative Inquiry, 3,* 4-25.

Stake, R. E. (1995). *The art of case study research.* Thousand Oaks, CA: Sage.

Name Index

Subject Index

About the Authors

Patricia A. Adler (Ph.D., University of California, San Diego) is Associate Professor of Sociology at the University of Colorado. She has written and taught in the areas of deviance, drugs and society, social theory, and the sociology of children. A second edition of her book *Wheeling and Dealing* was released in 1993. She is coeditor, with Peter Adler, of *Constructions of Deviance,* now in its second edition (1997). She is also author, with Peter Adler, of *Backboards and Blackboards* (1991), a study of college athletes, and *Membership Roles in Field Research* (1987), a volume in the Sage Publications series Qualitative Research Methods. Her most recent book, also with Peter Adler, is *Peer Power* (1998), a study of preadolescent children. With Peter Adler, she served as coeditor of *Journal of Contemporary Ethnography* from 1986 to 1994 and was co-founding editor of *Sociological Studies of Child Development* (now *Sociological Studies of Children*). Currently, she and Peter Adler are studying the culture of resort workers.

Peter Adler (Ph.D., University of California, San Diego) is Professor of Sociology at the University of Denver, where he served as Department Chair from 1987 to 1993. His research interests include social psychology, qualitative methods, and the sociology of sport and leisure. His recent publications include articles in *Sociological Inquiry, Qualitative Sociology, Journal of Marriage and the Family, Social Psychology Quarterly,* and

Sociological Quarterly. In 1996-1997, he served as Chair of the American Sociological Association section on the Sociology of Children. He is coeditor, with Patricia A. Adler, of *Constructions of Deviance,* now in its second edition (1997). He is also author, with Patricia Adler, of *Backboards and Blackboards* (1991), a study of college athletes, and *Membership Roles in Field Research* (1987), a volume in the Sage Publications series Qualitative Research Methods. His most recent book, also with Patricia Adler, is *Peer Power* (1998), a study of preadolescent children. With Patricia Adler, he served as coeditor of *Journal of Contemporary Ethnography* from 1986 to 1994 and was co-founding editor of *Sociological Studies of Child Development* (now *Sociological Studies of Children*). Currently, he and Patricia Adler are studying the culture of resort workers.

David L. Altheide (Ph.D., University of California, San Diego) is a Regents' Professor in the School of Justice Studies at Arizona State University. His research interests in mass media, social control, and qualitative research methods are recorded in several books, including *Creating Reality: How TV News Distorts Events* (1976) and *Media Power* (1985). He is the 1986 Winner of the Charles Horton Cooley Award of the Society for the Study of Symbolic Interaction. He is also coauthor, with John M. Johnson, of *Bureaucratic Propaganda* and, with Robert P. Snow, *Media Worlds in the Postjournalism Era* (1991). Two of his recent books are *An Ecology of Communication: Cultural Formats of Control* (1995) and *Qualitative Media Analysis* (1996).

D. Jean Clandinin is Associate Professor and Director of the Centre for Research for Teacher Education and Development at the University of Alberta, Edmonton, Canada. She is a former teacher, counselor, and school psychologist and has worked in educational research in teaching and teacher education for the past 15 years. She is author or coauthor of several books, including *Teachers as Curriculum Planners: Narratives of Experience* (with F. Michael Connelly; 1988) and *Learning to Teach: Teaching to Learn. Stories of Collaboration in Teacher Education* (with Pat Hogan, Annie Davies, and Barbara Kennard; 1993). She is currently working on two new books with F. Michael Connelly titled *Narrative and Education* and *Teachers' Professional Knowledge Landscapes.* She is the 1993 winner of the American Educational Research Association Raymond B. Cattell Early Career Award.

F. Michael Connelly studied at the University of Alberta, Columbia University, and the University of Chicago. He is Professor and Director, Joint Centre for Teacher Development, Ontario Institute for Studies in Education, and the Faculty of Education, University of Toronto. He previously taught secondary school in Alberta and has held teaching positions at the Universities of Alberta, Illinois, and Chicago. He coordinated the Canadian component of the Second International Science Study, serves as editor of *Curriculum Inquiry,* and is a former member of the board of directors of the John Dewey Society for Study of Education and Culture. He is codirector, with D. Jean Clandinin, of a long-term study of teachers' personal practical knowledge and teachers' professional knowledge landscapes. He has published numerous articles and chapters in contributed volumes and is coauthor, with D. Jean Clandinin, of *Teachers as Curriculum Planners: Narratives of Experience* (1988). He was the recipient of the 1987 Outstanding Canadian Curriculum Scholar Award of the Canadian Society for the Study of Education and of the 1991 Canadian Education Association/Whitworth Award for Educational Research.

Betsy Cullum-Swan (M.A., 1987; Ph.D., 1994) is an Instructor in the Department of Sociology and the Department of Pediatrics and Human Development at Michigan State University and in the Department of Sociology at Oakland University in Rochester, Michigan. She has published several chapters in books, and her reviews and articles have appeared in such journals as *Semiotica* and *Symbolic Interaction.* Her research interests are in the areas of social psychology (sex and gender roles) and medical semiotics. She has been the recipient of the Excellence in Teaching Award of Michigan State University. She is currently researching, using semiotic discourse analysis, the meanings and consequences of invasive trauma.

Norman K. Denzin is Distinguished Professor of Communications, College of Communications scholar, and Professor of Sociology and Humanities at the University of Illinois, Urbana-Champaign. He is the author of numerous books, including *The Cinematic Society, Images of Postmodern Society, The Research Act, Interpretive Interactionism, Hollywood Shot by Shot, Symbolic Interactionism and Cultural Studies, The Recovering Alcoholic,* and *The Alcoholic Self,* which won the Cooley Award from the Society for the Study of Symbolic Interaction in 1988. He is editor of *Studies in Symbolic Interaction: A Research Annual, Cultural Studies,* and *Sociological Quarterly.* He is coeditor of the *Handbook of Qualitative Research* and of *Qualitative Inquiry*. In 1997, he won the George Herbert Mead Award from the Society for the Study of Symbolic Interaction. This award recognizes lifetime contributions to the study of human behavior.

Andrea Fontana is Professor of Sociology at the University of Nevada, Las Vegas. He received his Ph.D. from the University of California, San Diego, in 1976. He has published articles on aging, leisure, theory, and postmodernism. He is the author of *The Last Frontier,* coauthor of *Social Problems* and *Sociologies of Everyday Life,* and coeditor of *The Existential Self in Society* and *Postmodernism and Social Inquiry*.

James H. Frey is Professor of Sociology and Director of the Center for Survey Research at the University of Nevada, Las Vegas. He is the author of *Survey Research by Telephone* and *An Organizational Analysis of University-Environment Relations* in addition to several papers on survey methods, sport sociology, work in the leisure industry, and deviance. He is coauthor of *The Group Interview* and *Government and Sport: The Public Policy Issues*.

Jennifer C. Greene is an Associate Professor in the field of human service studies at Cornell University. As an applied methodologist, she works primarily within a graduate-level program in human service program evaluation and planning. Her responsibilities include both teaching and research in the broad domain of applied social inquiry methodology. She has also been a practicing evaluator for 15 years. Her research interests focus on the social-political dimensions of applied social inquiry, specifically on enhancing the potential of social research to contribute to democratic principles and practices. Methodologically, these interests encompass qualitative, participatory, action-oriented, and mixed-methods approaches to social inquiry.

Douglas Harper is Professor and Chair of the Department of Sociology, Duquesne University, in Pittsburgh, Pennsylvania. He has published ethnographies with a visual bent and is founding editor of *Visual Sociology,* the journal of the International Visual Sociology Association.

Ian Hodder is Professor of Archaeology at the University of Cambridge; a Fellow of Darwin College, Cambridge; and a Fellow of the British Academy. He obtained his B.A. in archaeology in the University of London in

1971 and his Ph.D. in the University of Cambridge in 1975, the latter on the topic of spatial analysis in archaeology. From 1974 to 1977 he was a Lecturer in the Department of Archaeology, University of Leeds, before returning to Cambridge. He has also been a Visiting Professor at the University of Amsterdam and Paris 1/Sorbonne, the State University of New York, Binghamton, and the University of Minnesota, and a Fellow at the Center for Advanced Studies in the Behavioral Sciences, Stanford. His books include *Spatial Analysis in Archaeology* (with C. Orton; 1976), *Symbols in Action* (1982), *The Present Past* (1982), *Reading the Past* (1986), *The Domestication of Europe* (1990), and *Theory and Practice in Archaeology* (1992).

A. Michael Huberman, an educational psychologist, is Visiting Professor at the Harvard University Graduate School of Education and Senior Research Associate at the New England Laboratory for School Improvement. Previously, for some 20 years, he was Professor of Education at the University of Geneva in Switzerland. His objective in coming to the United States has been to harmonize work in the field with teaching and research in a university setting. His main fields of interest are teachers' life cycles, program implementation, and qualitative methodologies. His most recent books are *The Lives of Teachers* (1993), a translation from the French, and *Qualitative Data Analysis* (second edition, 1994), coauthored with Matthew Miles.

John M. Johnson (Ph.D., University of California, San Diego) is a Professor in the School of Justice Studies at Arizona State University. He has published numerous books and articles on field research, including his pathbreaking *Doing Field Research* (1975) and *Existential Sociology* (1977), coedited with Jack Douglas. He is a former President of the Society for the Study of Symbolic Interaction and serves as editor of the journal *Symbolic Interaction.* His current research interests include the sociology of emotions, domestic violence, and deviance.

Yvonna S. Lincoln is Professor of Higher Education and Head of the Department of Educational Administration at Texas A&M University. She has an Ed.D. from Indiana University and previously taught at the University of Kansas and Vanderbilt University. She is a specialist in higher education research, organizational analysis, program evaluation, and alternative paradigm research. Her work has been published in such well-received books as *Fourth Generation Evaluation, Naturalistic Inquiry, Effective Evaluation* (all coauthored with Egon Guba), and *Organizational Theory and Inquiry,* as well as in a host of papers and conference presentations. She has been honored with awards for her research from the American Evaluation Association, Division J (Postsecondary and Higher Education) of the American Educational Research Association, and the Association for Institutional Research. She has served as President of the American Evaluation Association and as Vice President of Division J of the American Educational Research Association, and has been keynote speaker at more than a dozen conferences.

Peter K. Manning (Ph.D., Duke University, 1966) is Professor of Sociology and Criminal Justice at Michigan State University. He has been a Visiting Professor at the State University of New York, Albany, MIT, and the University of London, Goldsmiths' College, and was a Fellow at the U.S. Justice Department and of Balliol and Wolfson Colleges, Oxford. During 1983-1986, he held a senior research position in the Centre of Socio-Legal Studies, Oxford. He is the author of many articles, chapters, and books, including *Police Work* (1977), *Narcs' Game* (1980), *Symbolic Communication* (1990), and *Organizational Communication* (1992). He is listed in *Who's Who in the World* and *Who's Who in America,* and has been awarded the Beto Lectureship at Sam Houston State University, a Special Recognition Award from the Society for Symbolic Interaction, and in 1993, the Bruce Smith Sr. Award of the Academy of Criminal Justice Sciences for "outstanding contributions to criminal justice."

Matthew B. Miles was a social psychologist and Senior Research Associate at the Center for Policy Research, New York. Before that he was Professor of Psychology and Education at Teachers College, where he started working in 1953. He had long-term interest in planned educational change, leading studies of leadership and intensive group training, school organizational renewal, educational innovation, program implementation, design of new schools, and the work of "change agents." Recent books he coauthored include *Assisting Change in Education* (1990), *Improving the Urban High School: What Works and Why* (1990), *How Schools Improve: International Report* (1992), *Qualitative Data Analysis* (second edition, 1994), and *Computer Programs for Qualitative Data Analysis* (1994). His later research focused on cognitive mapping of school restructuring, and on advances in qualitative data analysis.

Lyn Richards is Director of Research Services at Qualitative Solutions and Research, Melbourne, and Adjunct Professor at the University of Western Sydney. Formerly, she was Associate Professor in Sociology at La Trobe University, where she taught qualitative methods at the graduate and undergraduate levels as well as family and women's studies. She has an honors degree in politics from the University of Adelaide and an M.A. in sociology from La Trobe University. Her works as a family sociologist have been addressed to both popular and academic audiences, with a strong motivation always to make the funded research relevant to the people studied. Her fourth book, *Intermission,* with Carmel Seibold and Nicole Davis, was published in 1997. In this and her three previous books—*Having Families, Mothers and Working Mothers* (with Jan Harper), and *Nobody's Home*—she uses qualitative methods to explore issues of traditional family ideology and women's support networks and health. Through these research projects, she developed and tested ways of handling and analyzing very unstructured data, leading to the development, with Tom Richards, of the 10-year NUD•IST research project on ways of handling Nonnumerical Unstructured Data by Indexing, Searching, and Theorizing. The software that resulted from this research is now in its fourth version, and she is a widely published writer in the growing field of qualitative computing and a primary author of the software's documentation. She has taught qualitative computing to more than 2,000 researchers in 12 countries.

Thomas J. Richards is Managing Director and Chief Scientist of Qualitative Solutions and Research Pty Ltd, and formerly Reader and Associate Professor in Computer Science at La Trobe University, Melbourne, Australia. He did his undergraduate work at Victoria University of Wellington and his D.Phil. at University College, Oxford, and has since held posts at the University of Auckland and La Trobe University. He is a Fellow of the Royal Astronomical Society, London. He comes to computer science from a research and teaching background in mathematical logic, philosophy and methodology of science, and formal theory of languages and knowledge. His current areas of research and teaching are artificial intelligence and software science. He has a long history of international publications in these fields, including two books on mathematical logic. His current research, with his wife, Lyn Richards, is on the application of software science, artificial intelligence, and logical theory to the analysis of unstructured qualitative data.

Laurel Richardson is Professor Emerita of Sociology, Professor of Cultural Studies (College of Education), and Graduate Professor of Women's Studies at the Ohio State University. She has written extensively on qualitative research methods, ethics, and issues of representation and is the author of seven books, including *Writing Strategies: Reaching Diverse Audiences* (1990). Her most recent book is *Fields of Play: Constructing an Academic Life* (1997). Currently, she is interested in the relationships between conceptual and personal constructions of space/place, narratives of the self, and knowledge practices.

Ray C. Rist is the Evaluation Adviser to the Economic Development Institute of the World Bank. His most recent previous position (1993-1997) was that of Director of the Center for Policy Studies Program at the George Washington University. Prior to that (1981-1993), he held a number of senior positions at the U.S. General Accounting Office in Washington, D.C. He served as Associate Director of the National Institute of Education from 1974 through 1976, and has also held a number of academic appointments, including at Cornell University, George Washington University, and, most recently, as the first holder of the Leon Sachs Chair in Public Policy at the Johns Hopkins University. He has authored or edited 18 books and has published more than 100 articles. He has also lectured in more than 30 countries and has served as the Senior Fulbright Fellow at the Max Planck Institute in Berlin, Germany.